ARBITRATION CLAUSES AND THIRD PARTIES

LLOYD'S ARBITRATION LAW LIBRARY

Arbitration Practice and Procedure
Interlocutory and Hearing Problems
Third Edition
Mark Cato, Julian Critchlow and Robert Merkin

Rules of Evidence in International Arbitration
An Annotated Guide
Nathan D. O'Malley

Injunctive Relief and International Arbitration
Hakeem Seriki

Singapore Arbitration Legislation
Annotated
Second Edition
Robert Merkin and Johanna Hjalmarsson

The Practice of International Commercial Arbitration
A Handbook for Hong Kong Arbitrators
Anselmo Reyes

Transnational Construction Arbitration
Key Themes in the Resolution of Construction Disputes
Edited by Renato Nazzini

Rules of Evidence in International Arbitration
An Annotated Guide
Second Edition
Nathan D. O'Malley

Merkin and Flannery on the Arbitration Act 1996
Sixth Edition
Robert Merkin and Louis Flannery

International Investment Dispute Awards
Facilitating Enforcement
Esra Yildiz Üstün

Arbitration Clauses and Third Parties
Aslı Arda

For more information about this series, please visit:
www.routledge.com/Lloyds-Arbitration-Law-Library/book-series/LALL

ARBITRATION CLAUSES AND THIRD PARTIES

ASLI ARDA

informa law
from Routledge

First published 2024
by Informa Law from Routledge
4 Park Square, Milton Park, Abingdon, Oxon OX14 4RN

and by Informa Law from Routledge
605 Third Avenue, New York, NY 10158

Informa Law from Routledge is an imprint of the Taylor & Francis Group, an informa business

British Library Cataloguing-in-Publication Data
A catalogue record for this book is available from the British Library

ISBN: 978-1-032-21500-6 (hbk)
ISBN: 978-1-032-21501-3 (pbk)
ISBN: 978-1-003-26867-3 (ebk)

DOI: 10.4324/9781003268673

Typeset in Times New Roman
by Apex CoVantage, LLC

To my grandfather Refik Özdinç, whom I miss dearly

CONTENTS

CASES

Australia

Canada

Hong Kong

EU

Netherlands

Philippines

Singapore

UK

CASES

PREFACE

With arbitration profoundly being a consensual method of dispute resolution, the evaluation of its possible correlation with third parties has always been interesting. From the perspective of contract law, the concept of incorporation of arbitration clauses from other contracts or documents, as well as some situations under which the third parties may be bound by arbitration clauses, constitutes circumstances where arbitration clauses are possibly correlated with third parties and they are brought to the scope of arbitration clauses. The contractual method of incorporation is widely used in shipping, reinsurance, and construction chain contracts and the relevant areas of law usually affect each other concerning the implementation of incorporation. However, the sometimes 'blindfolded' application of principles pertaining to a certain branch of law in a different one may create inconsistent and possibly unreasonable legal outcomes. To put it differently, the water sometimes gets muddied where the question is one of incorporation. Accordingly, the book investigates the peculiarities of shipping, reinsurance, and construction contracts in English law concerning the way incorporation in these works possibly affects each other. This part also includes a chapter on Singapore law, which evaluates how the incorporation of arbitration clauses works in this particular jurisdiction. It is specifically chosen because, until its independence, Singapore had been subject to the substantial influence of English law. Singapore now follows somewhat of a different pathway concerning how the incorporation of arbitration clauses functions, and Singaporean courts tend to interpret the consent regarding the incorporation of arbitration clauses very broadly. The book further explores some situations other than incorporation under which third parties are affected by arbitration. These do not constitute examples of incorporation, but they have a close analogy with it since similar outcomes are usually produced.

It would be impossible to complete this book without the invaluable support and guidance of Robert Merkin KC throughout the years. I was lucky enough to conduct research as his PhD student in the past and it has always been a true joy to work with him since day one. I would like to thank him for all his brilliant comments and his time and patience concerning the manuscript. I am enormously grateful to him for making this book possible.

I would also like to thank Dr Tim Dodsworth, Dr Nathan Tamblyn, Dr Meixian Song, Sylvie Cécile Cavaleri, Dr Kyriaki Noussia, Ayşe Kurtoğlu, Maxim Usynin, and Ekin Deniz İlhan for their excellent comments and their support on individual chapters of the book. Their comments were painstaking and helped me a lot to reshape some of the chapters to develop a much more elucidatory context. I am truly grateful to each one of them for their support. I would also like to thank each of my wonderful colleagues in CEPRI of the

University of Copenhagen, Faculty of Law, for creating such a great working environment and for their continuous support.

I would also like to thank Routledge editor Guy Loft and editorial assistant Amelia Bashford for their assistance throughout the process.

Finally, I would like to thank my parents, Berna and Tayfun, for always being there for me and supporting me unconditionally in whatever I do. Their love made this book possible.

Aslı Arda
Copenhagen, November 2022

PART I

MUDDYING THE WATER

Incorporation of Arbitration Clauses in Shipping, Reinsurance, and Construction Chain Contracts

This is the only book written so far that is concerned with the legal concept of incorporation of arbitration clauses on such a large scale. The book compares different branches of law – namely, shipping, reinsurance, and construction, in which the legal notion of incorporation is often implemented. It evaluates how differences and peculiarities of the said branches affect the outcome of the incorporation of arbitration clauses and, thus, why a 'one size fits all' approach should essentially be avoided. The book provides an in-depth legal analysis of the incorporation of arbitration clauses, the legal position of the third parties concerning arbitration agreements, and the relevant case law. It further provides a unique comparative analysis of English law and Singapore law pertaining to the incorporation of arbitration clauses. It further provides some tangible outcomes concerning the assessment of the proper incorporation of arbitration clauses and the circumstances under which arbitration clauses bind third parties. The provided outcomes go back to the core principles of contract law and re-evaluate and, eventually, re-emphasize their applicability concerning the position of third parties and arbitration agreements.

DOI: 10.4324/9781003268673-1

CHAPTER 1

The Foundations of Incorporation and Arbitration Clauses

1. Incorporation and Arbitration

The concept of incorporation of terms into a contract is vital as it provides an undeniably handy shortcut for the parties involved in commercial transactions. It provides convenience as it removes the need to spend more time and money than is necessary. Thus, the concept, in general, is highly appealing to traders. As a result, a lot of commercial contracts are being entered into by the incorporation of terms, which are contained in a separate document that the parties are referring to. The implementation of the concept is commonly seen in the form of the incorporation of standard terms and conditions of one of the parties and of provisions of specific trading communities.[1] Evidently, this convenience minimizes the need for time and money to be spent on negotiations. In other words, incorporation facilitates the emergence of a new contractual framework made on the standard terms of one of the parties, terms set out by trade associations, or even the previous dealings of the parties, without the need for drafting a contractual document from scratch.

Incorporation may be regarded as a twofold concept: It first deals with the identification of the provision to be incorporated and, then, the adequate method of incorporating it. The notion of incorporation may stem from various sources, such as the standard terms and conditions of a party, terms and conditions of trade associations, former contracts between parties, ordinary course of dealing, the custom of trade, or other contracts.[2] Subsequent to such a specification, the method of incorporating the specified provision would be the next assessment to be made.

The component to be incorporated may be the standard terms and conditions of a party involved. Concerning the incorporation of such, the essential requirement is usually to bring all relevant terms and conditions to the attention of the other party. Comprehensively drafted standard terms and conditions inevitably contain a dispute resolution clause. Incorporation may also stem from the standard terms set out by trade associations. Such associations usually aim to establish a degree of harmonization and commercial foreseeability and thus provide some comprehensive set of provisions that widely cover legal issues that may arise in commercial transactions. These often include dispute resolution clauses too. Furthermore, the provisions of some formerly concluded contracts between the relevant parties or the

1 Domenico Di Pietro, Incorporation of Arbitration Clauses by Reference, 2004, *Journal of International Arbitration*, 21(5), 439–452, 439.

2 Andrea Lista, *International Commercial Sales: The Sale of Goods on Shipment Terms*, Informa Law from Routledge, 2017, 43.

DOI: 10.4324/9781003268673-2

terms of completely remote contracts may also possibly be subject to incorporation. It is true that there is an array of different types of dispute resolution clauses that provide a variety of dispute resolution mechanisms for the resolution of existing or future disputes. However, because arbitration clauses have their legal peculiarities and arbitration agreements are frequently incorporated in commercial contracts, the incorporation of this specific dispute resolution method requires specific examination.

There are two fundamental elements of the incorporation of arbitration clauses as a legal concept. The first is the actual legal notion of 'incorporation,' and the second is the arbitration clause itself. Very often, incorporation is from previous dealings between the parties themselves or from a former contract that concluded between different parties. Frequently, a reference is made to a contract that one of the contracting parties entered into with a third party. Concerning such contractual interaction, one of the most interesting parts to look at is the incorporation of a contract between A and B into a contract between B and C (or possibly even C and D). Incorporation from one contract to another has the specific problem that at least one of the parties is different and the contracts are different, giving rise to possible inconsistency and the need for manipulation of the words to be incorporated. Since the parties are different, it may be the case that at least one party is unaware of the actual meaning of a term or intention behind adding such a term to the original contract. They may even possibly be oblivious concerning the existence of such a term. A common example of this is a subcontract incorporating the provisions of the main contract by reference, and such a practice is routinely employed in drafting chain contracts, particularly in the contexts of shipping, reinsurance, and construction.

Constituting the second element of the concept, arbitration clauses are frequently contained in commercial contracts. Their incorporation has essentially something to do with the right to seek and obtain a remedy through formal institutions of justice. It is a human right to have access to one's home courts. An arbitration clause removes that possibility by ousting the jurisdiction of the court to intervene both during the arbitration and at the enforcement stage unless something has gone very wrong in the arbitration. The idea of incorporating an arbitration clause from one contract to another is, therefore, potentially problematic in that the courts have to ensure that there is a true agreement manifesting party autonomy to take the dispute away from the courts and into arbitration.

Accordingly, this chapter is concerned with two keystone elements of the incorporation of arbitration clauses as a legal concept. Initially, the meaning and methods of incorporation as a legal tool are evaluated to provide a comprehensive analysis concerning its implementation. After that, in light of the legal peculiarities of arbitration agreements, the specific concept of the incorporation of arbitration clauses is examined because the characteristic features of arbitration agreements are likely to affect the assessment pertaining to incorporation. Thus, the distinctive features of arbitration clauses are considered to understand the possible exclusive requirements to be sought in dealing with the incorporation of such clauses. Moreover, the form of arbitration clauses and their incorporation are also evaluated from a legislative perspective. Finally, all the provided aspects of the incorporation of arbitration clauses as a legal concept are analyzed together. Considering the deductions that are made as a result of this analysis, the current standpoint on the matter is discussed. Hence, in brief, the structure of this chapter is as follows. First, methods of incorporation are evaluated. Second, the specific incorporation of arbitration clauses, considering their characteristics, is discussed. Third, the relevant legal framework is explored. Fourth, an analysis of the incorporation of arbitration clauses and the current standpoint on the matter is provided. The format of this chapter being revealed, the methods of incorporation are looked at below to visualize the implementation of incorporation as a legal tool.

1.1. Methods of Incorporation

A provision may be incorporated into a contract mainly by three methods:[3] by giving notice of the provision that is wished to be incorporated; through a reference to a term that is contained in a distinct document, or by virtue of the relevant clause turning into a familiar provision due to its consistent appearance in the course of transactions between the same parties.[4] In terms of incorporation by notice and reference, if reasonable steps are taken to bring the term or terms to be incorporated to the notice of the party (its sufficiency to be assessed through both contractual and factual analyses)[5] before or at the time of contracting,[6] incorporation would usually be effective. As to the third method, incorporation may be sufficiently implemented through 'the ordinary/consistent course of dealing'[7] or due to the custom of the trade. The essential features of such an ordinary dealing are consistency and regularity. Furthermore, parties may also be in the same trade or industry. In that case, incorporation may be effective based on the common understanding of the parties that is derived from the practice of the trade.[8] The mentioned methods of incorporation are explored in the following sections.

---

3 Ewan McKendrick, *Contract Law, Text, Cases and Materials*, Oxford University Press, 2016, 7th Edn., 315; Lista (n 2) 44; Janet O'Sullivan and Jonathan Hillard, *The Law of Contract*, Oxford University Press, 1998, 7th Edn., 176.

4 Ibid. Besides, incorporation of a term by signature may be given as the most straightforward and simple method of incorporation. This plainly means that the party to a contractual relationship is bound by their signature. As a result of the general rule adopted in English law, the party signing the document is bound by the terms of it, regardless of whether they have read the terms contained in the relevant document. The justification of this principle is to promote certainty and protect the interests of the third parties. *L'Estrange v F. Graucob Ltd* [1934] 2 KB 394 would be useful to mention here as it sets this general principle and highlights the significance of freedom of contract. The plaintiff agrees to buy a slot machine for cigarettes and signs a sale agreement, which includes the following clause in small print: 'This agreement contains all the terms and conditions under which I agree to purchase the machine specified above and any express or implied condition, statement or warranty, statutory or otherwise not stated herein or hereby excluded.' It was contended by the plaintiff that they were induced by misrepresentation to sign the contract without knowing its terms. However, the Court of Appeal found no sign of alleged misrepresentation. The plaintiff had signed the document headed 'Sale Agreement.' The intention of purchase was not denied by the plaintiff, and the signed document by the plaintiff included an exclusion clause. It was held by the Court of Appeal that the plaintiff may not be heard to say that they are not bound by the terms of the document because they had not read them. *L'Estrange* sets forth the rule that the signing party will be bound by the terms of the contract that they have signed irrespective of the fact that they possibly had not read the contents of it. As indicated, such presumption provides benefits for the promotion of commercial certainty as it protects the interests of third parties, who may rely on to their detriment upon the validity of the signature.

5 *Interfoto Picture Library Ltd v Stiletto Visual Programmes Ltd* [1987] EWCA Civ 6. For an excellent analysis of incorporation in maritime law and other contexts, see Melis Özdel, Incorporation of Charterparty Arbitration Clauses into Bills of Lading: Peculiar to Maritime Law?, in Malcom Clarke (ed.) *Maritime Law Evolving*, Bloomsbury, 2013, 181–195.

6 *Thornton v Shoe Lane Parking Ltd* [1971] 2 QB 163. As a general principle, any clause which has not reasonably been brought to the notice of the other party before or at the time of contacting will not be incorporated into the contract if the contract does not contain a signature.

7 Elizabeth MacDonald, Incorporation of Contract Terms by a 'Consistent Course of Dealing,' March 1, 1998, *Legal Studies*, 8(1), 48–60. Also see *Habas Sinai v Sometal SAL* [2010] EWHC 29 (Comm).

8 McKendrick (n 3) 337. Also see *British Crene Hire Corporation v Ipswich Plant Hire Ltd* [1975] QB 303.

1.1.1. Incorporation by Notice

Incorporation of a provision, which is included in a different document, is usually only successful if the attempt to incorporate meets the relevant criteria of enabling incorporation by notice. The party who wishes to incorporate terms contained in a distinct document must satisfy some requirements for the effective incorporation of such terms. The burden of both bringing the terms to the attention of the other party and proving doing this would be on the party who wishes to incorporate the provisions of a remote document into the contract in hand. The timing, comprehensiveness, and reasonableness of the notice of a term that is purported to be incorporated constitute the elementary elements of this type of incorporation.

The notice pertaining to the existence of the term and the intention to make such a term a part of the contract[9] must be given before the contract is concluded or at the time the contract is being concluded. In this sense, the term referred to should have been intended to have a contractual effect.[10] A term contained in a document which does not possess contractual characteristics (e.g. a receipt) may not be effective to incorporate the terms into the contract.[11]

Olley v Marlborough Court Ltd[12] is one of the fundamental cases on the incorporation of terms because it elucidates the general approach of the courts concerning the timing of contract formation and incorporation. The notice in relation to the exclusion of liability of a hotel in respect of stolen personal belongings of customers held not to be satisfying by the Court of Appeal given such notice was located in the bedroom of the hotel customer and not at the hotel reception or at another place that the attention of the customer could be drawn to it at or before the time of the formation of the contract. The notice was, therefore, too late to be effective and to exclude the liability of the hotel.[13]

The comprehensiveness of the notice and the reasonableness of the steps taken to bring the terms to the attention of the other party constitute other important issues to be assessed. Firstly, the comprehensiveness – in other words, the extent of the notice – depends upon the characteristics and complexity of the terms to be incorporated. Evidently, for the incorporation of a straightforward (and reasonable) term, a simple notice of the term may be considered sufficient. However, if the term is onerous[14] or unusual, the party who is

---

9 There must be an intention to make the term to be incorporated an actual part of the contract. In other words, the document that contains the terms to be incorporated should have contractual effect. In this sense, a receipt will not be effective to incorporate the terms into the contract as a receipt would not be evaluated as a contractual document. See *Chapelton v Barry UDC* [1940] 1 KB 532.

10 McKendrick (n 3) 325.

11 *Chapelton v Barry UDC* [1940] 1 KB 532. A given ticket held not to be a contractual document and, therefore, held not to be effective to give the hirer of the deckchair the notice of terms.

12 [1949] 1 KB 532.

13 Similarly in *Thornton v Shoe Lane Parking* [1971] 2 QB 163 an exemption notice was located inside the car park and not at the entrance of it or any other place that the notice of the customer could be drawn to it. Notice (and, hence, the exclusion) was too late to be incorporated. See also Lord Denning's comments on the same case: 'The customer pays his money and gets a ticket. He cannot refuse it. He cannot gets his money back . . . The contract was concluded at that time . . . The terms of the offer are contained in the notice placed on or near the machine stating what is offered for the money. The customer is bound by those terms as long as they are sufficiently brought to his notice before-hand, but not otherwise. He is not bound by the terms printed on the ticket if they are different from the notice, because the tickets comes too late. The contract has already been made' ([1971] 2 QB 163, 169).

14 For the examination of 'onerous terms,' see O'Sullivan and Hillard (n 3) 181.

willing to make such a term a part of the contract must be able to indicate that clear and reasonable efforts were made by them to bring the relevant term to the attention of the other party. This requirement may be evaluated as the reflection of the principle of fair and open dealing. In essence, it is a balance mechanism of freedom of contract, which gives discretion to parties to negotiate and set their own rules while restricting it by means of stipulating fair play, 'coming clean putting one's cards face upwards on the table.'[15] In this sense, palpably, drawing the parties' attention specifically to the onerous or unusual terms, such as a high price to be paid if the goods are returned later than the agreed date or to a particular term which involves the abrogation of a right given,[16] is crucial to effectively make such a term part of the contract. Furthermore, the pursuit of English law to develop 'piecemeal solutions to demonstrated problems of unfairness'[17] seem to be in line with the usual test of the courts of whether greater efforts are put forward to draw the attention of the other party to the terms which are unusual or onerous. Secondly, such an examination must be an objective one.[18] This means that the responsibility of taking reasonable steps to bring the terms to the other party's attention is on the party who would like to make such terms a part of the contract.[19] To put it differently, it may possibly be irrelevant whether the other party has spotted, read, or understood the provisions in question.[20]

1.1.2. Incorporation by Consistent Course of Dealing

There are also some other fashions in which incorporation may take place. For instance, a term may be incorporated as a possibly expected result of the course of dealing of the parties. It may also be commercially foreseeable for a term to be incorporated due to the regular practices of custom of the trade or by reason of parties to the transaction being in the same trade or industry.

If the parties have had former dealings, it may possibly be successfully argued that their former terms are incorporated into their current contract[21] regardless of whether these terms are expressly referred to.[22] That is to say, this may take place based on the course of dealing between the parties. If the legal requirements to establish an ordinary/consistent course of dealing are met, the terms of previous contractual dealings may possibly be incorporated

---

15 Bingham LJ in *Interfoto Picture Library Ltd v Stiletto Visual Programmes Ltd* [1987] EWCA Civ 6.

16 *AEG (U.K.) Ltd v Logic Resource Ltd* [1996] CLC 265. The position in *Interfoto Picture Library Ltd v Stiletto Visual Programmes Ltd* was endorsed by the Court of Appeal. See Lista (n 2) 45.

17 Bingham LJ in *Interfoto Picture Library Ltd v Stiletto Visual Programmes Ltd* [1987] EWCA Civ 6.

18 O'Sullivan and Hillard (n 3) 177.

19 *Thompson v London Midland & Southern Railway Co* [1930] 1 KB 41. An exclusion clause contained on a certain page of the timetable is held to be reliable by the company regardless of unawareness of such a clause by the other party. The ticket contained the words 'issued subject to the conditions and regulations in the company's timetables and notices and other bills.' However, today, a different approach would perhaps be adopted due to the prohibition of 'very wide' exclusion clauses under the Unfair Contract Terms Act 1977 and the Consumer Rights Act 2015. Nevertheless, the principle of objectivity remains relevant.

20 O'Sullivan and Hillard (n 3) 177.

21 MacDonald (n 7) 48. *McCutcheon v David MacBrayne Ltd* [1964] 1 WLR 430; *Transmotors Ltd v Robertson, Buckley & Co Ltd* [1970] 1 Lloyd's Rep 232; *Hollier v Rambler Motors* [1972] 2 QB 71; *British Crane Hire v Ipswich Plant Hire* [1975] QB 303; *Walek v Chapman* [1980] 2 Lloyd's Rep 279; *Lamport & Holt Lines Ltd v Caubro & Scrutton Ltd* [1981] 2 Lloyd's Rep 659; *Chevron International Oil Co Ltd v A/S Sea Team* [1983] 2 Lloyd's Rep 356; *Habas Sinai ve Tibbi Gazlar Isthisal Endustri A.S. v Sometal S.A.L.* [2010] EWHC 29 (Comm); *Transformers & Rectifiers Ltd v Needs Ltd* [2015] EWHC 269 (TCC), [2015] BLR 336.

22 O'Sullivan and Hillard (n 3) 178.

into a current contract between the same parties.[23] Predominantly two requirements must be fulfilled for transactions to create a 'consistent course of dealing' in the legal sense. The dealing should both be consistent and regular. If the course of conduct is inconsistent, 'there would be no reason why it should still produce an invariable contractual result.'[24] Indeed, if the characteristics of the dealings between the parties do not show undeniable similarities, then it may not be possible to successfully argue that a future dealing to be subject to the governance of a provision from a former dealing, which was fundamentally different in nature.

Furthermore, the course of conduct should have some sort of regularity.[25] Undoubtedly, repetition constitutes one of the elementary requirements for the establishment of a consistent course of dealing. It would be unreasonable to consider individual dealings as parts of a bigger picture if these do not have a regular and tangible pattern. Although what the concept of regularity entirely entails in a contractual context may be considered elusive to a certain extent, from a simplistic perspective, this requirement doubtlessly necessitates that certain terms have appeared at a sufficient frequency to illustrate parties had intended to conduct business on such a basis.[26]

Additionally, parties to the contract may be in the same trade or industry. For instance, both parties may be in the crane hiring business, so both may have standard terms and conditions based on the same trade association form, as this was the case in *British Crane Hire v Ipswich Plant Hire*.[27] It is clarified in this particular case that one of the key elements in deciding whether incorporation by the consistent course of dealing has been established is whether both parties are businesspersons.[28] This is because, it is harder to argue that the incorporation had occurred due to the course of dealing if one of the parties to the transaction has the 'consumer' status since 'the knowledge of business practice, which can be imputed to a businessman would be more than for a consumer.'[29] English courts usually turn to general contract law principles in assessing whether contracting parties intended to incorporate implied terms. An implied choice must be inferred with certainty[30] and should only be made if the parties' conduct is more consistent with the intention 'to contract' than with an intention to 'not to contract.'[31] In light of this general test, the comprehensiveness of the word 'consistency' in testing whether there is an established course of dealing may be considered an arguable one. However, this may possibly override the necessity of such a test because, in this case, the issue to be assessed would be whether the past dealings of

23 McKendrick (n 3) 336.

24 Lord Pearce in *McCutcheon v David MacBrayne Ltd* [1964] 1 WLR 125, 138. However, Lord Reid in the same case argued that the definition of consistency should be subject to a more general test and examined comprehensively as the question merely should be whether the past dealings between the parties were such that each party was 'reasonably entitled to conclude, from the attitude of the other . . . that conditions were intended . . . to be a part of the contract.' [1964] 1 WLR 125 at [128].

25 *Hollier v Rambler Motors* [1972] 2 QB 71.

26 O'Sullivan and Hillard (n 3) 178.

27 [1975] QB 303.

28 MacDonald (n 7) 53. *Hollier v Rambler Motors* [1972] 2 QB 71; *British Crane Hire v Ipswich Plant Hire* [1975] QB 303.

29 MacDonald (n 7) 54.

30 Zheng Sophia Tang, *Jurisdiction and Arbitration Agreements in International Commercial Law*, Routledge, 2014, 1st Edn., 35.

31 For a couple of illustrations of the matter, see Bingham LJ in *The Aramis* [1989] 1 Lloyd's Rep 213, 224 and Stocker LJ in *Blackpool and Fylde Aero Club v Blackpool Borough Council* [1990] EWCA Civ 13.

the parties were such that each party was 'reasonably entitled to conclude, from the attitude of the other . . . that conditions were intended . . . to be part of the contract.'[32] The issue of incorporation by a consistent course of dealing is analyzed in more detail in the following chapters. The particular focus is given to *Habas Sinai v Sometal*[33] as it provides a detailed taxonomy of contracts that very much facilitate the proper assessment of the incorporation of terms in a multi-layered contractual structure.

1.1.3. Incorporation by Reference

Parties may seek to incorporate a provision which is contained in a separate or distinct document into their current contract, with a contractually binding effect. This usually necessitates parties to reflect on their intention to do this so and to properly identify the provisions to be incorporated. Incorporation by reference is a matter of contractual construction.[34] If parties are referring to their standard terms, the test pertaining to the assessment of their relevant intention and the identification of provisions to be incorporated is usually a lenient one. However, when the reference is made to the terms of an entirely different agreement, difficult disputes that arise are commonly followed by a more complex test.[35] The disputes generally stem from the higher number of permutations that contracting parties may generate. Incorporation by reference facilitates the incorporation from a contract between A and B into a contract between B and C (or possibly even C and D). The remoteness and multitude of the parties raise the possibility of facing inconsistent outcomes and the need for contractual manipulation. When the incorporation of arbitration clauses is added to the equation, the situation gets even more convoluted due to peculiarities pertaining to arbitration agreements and their incorporation. Accordingly, the next part evaluates why arbitration clauses are presumed different than the rest of the provisions of the contract and whether they need some sort of special treatment, particularly in the context of incorporation.

1.2. Nature of Arbitration Clauses and How It Affects Their Incorporation

The concept of incorporation in commercial contracts is significant as it provides an irrefutably handy shortcut. Incorporation provides convenience as it enables parties to spend less money and time than is truly necessary. In this sense, it is usually preferred by the parties to refer to their standard contract terms or to the terms of a different contract to make such terms a part of the newly formed contract without the need for further negotiation.[36]

---

32 Lord Reid in *McCutcheon v David McBrayne* [1964] 1 WLR 125, 128.

33 [2010] EWHC 29 (Comm).

34 See *Excess Insurance Co Ltd v Mander* [1997] 2 Lloyd's Rep 119 (Comm); *AIG Europe SA v QBE International Insurance Ltd* [2002] Lloyd's Rep IR 22; *Axa Re v Ace Global Markets Ltd* [2006] EWHC 216 (Comm); [2006] Lloyd's Rep IR 683.

35 Clare Ambrose, Karen Maxwell, and Michael Collett, *London Maritime Arbitration*, Informa Law from Routledge, 2018, 4th Edn., 52, 4.35.

36 However, see 'battle of forms.' A battle of forms arises when two businesspersons are negotiating the terms of a contract and each party wants to contract based on their own terms. The paradigm battle of forms occurs when A offers to buy goods from B on its (A's) standard terms and B purports to accept the offer on the basis of its own standard terms. In this situation, the battle is often won by the party who 'fired the last shot' that is, the last party to put forward terms and conditions that were not explicitly rejected by the recipient. See *Butler Machine Tool Co*

Incorporation of standard terms is the most simplistic method of incorporation as it is confined to some identified rules that are familiar. However, the reference for the purposes of incorporation may also be made to a distinct contract or document. The fundamental purpose of incorporation is to illustrate the clear intention to merge remote provisions 'into one or more contracts in the making so that they become the same.'[37] Accordingly, the once remote term that is incorporated obtains contractual enforceability under this new contract as it merges into it. The existence of arbitration clauses in such an equation has the potential to seriously complicate things.

Arbitration clauses contained in a set of standard rules are generally incorporated along with the rest of the contractual terms without the need for a specific reference to them and further fuss.[38] The goal in such a case is usually the successful incorporation of these standard terms as a whole by reference.[39] Thus, the arbitration clause constituting one of the standard terms is not sought. Because the intention to incorporate the arbitration clause among others is usually clear or easily ascertainable, this type of incorporation is usually unproblematic. Accordingly, the arbitration clause in this scenario is treated the same as the rest of the terms of the contract being incorporated.

On the other hand, it is usually treated differently when contained in a distinct contract. An arbitration clause is generally subject to some different and stricter criteria in assessing its incorporation from remote contracts and documents.[40] *Aughton Ltd v MF Kent Services*[41] provides some reasons that stricter criteria apply in such a context: Arbitration potentially ousts the jurisdiction of the courts, and because they need to be in writing, they must be subject to a more formalistic test.[42] The question of whether these arguments are truly legitimate is discussed in different parts throughout the chapters.

This part considers two fundamental issues. It first investigates the right to access a court and the potential impediment to the jurisdiction of the courts by the incorporation of an arbitration agreement. The magnitude of this issue stems from the fact that access to a court is a human right. Referring a dispute to arbitration would amount to the waiver of such a right.[43] Hence, addressing the criteria for the incorporation of arbitration clauses

---

Ltd v Excell-O-Corpn (England) Ltd [1979] 1 WLR 401; *Tekdata Interconnections Ltd v Amphenol Ltd* [2009] EWCA Civ 1209; *Ghsp Inc v Ab Electronic Ltd* [2010] EWHC 1828 (Comm).

37 Arjya B. Majumdar, Incorporation by Reference in Maritime Arbitration, 2013, *Transportation Law Journal*, 40, 91–112, 98.

38 Incorporation of Standard Terms, *Merkin on Arbitration Law*, Incorporation of Standard Terms, 1991, Vol. 1, Ch. 5, para 5.20; Langley J in *Sea Trade Maritime Corp v Hellenic Mutual War Risks Association, The Athena (No 2)* [2006] EWHC 2530 (Comm) at [66]: 'I can see little or no reason for a rule which incorporates some but not all of the terms of a reference document, provided at least that, as a matter of construction, the incorporated terms can readily apply to relevant contract without violence to the principles on which the contracts are to be construed.'

39 The incorporation of an arbitration clause that is included in the standard terms of the defendant was considered in *Willcock v Pickfords Removals Ltd* [1979] 1 Lloyd's Rep 224.

40 Masood Ahmed, Arbitration Clauses: Fairness, Justice and Commercial Certainty, 2010, *Arbitration International*, 26(3), 412, LCIA.

41 [1991] 57 BLR 1.

42 Also, the separability of arbitration agreements, as they can be treated as distinct contracts from the main one they are contained in, is provided as one of the reasons justifying the adoption of a stricter approach incorporating an arbitration clause from a different contract: [1991] 57 BLR 1, 30. The issue of separability is considered in more detail under '2.3.3.4.3. Separability of Arbitration Agreements' under Chapter 2 'Incorporation of Charterparty Arbitration Clauses into Bills of Lading.'

43 Unless something goes very wrong with the arbitration, the court will have no right to intervene in the process. The role of the court in arbitration is discussed under '1.3.3. Stay of Legal Proceedings.'

constitutes a significant issue as such a legal notion may potentially create the effect of a party's right to go to a court to be abolished without them being aware of such a possibility.

It then considers the concepts of party autonomy and intention as these constitute the backbone of any arbitration agreement. The intention of the parties plays a significant role when it comes to the admissibility of arbitration agreements, especially when the arbitration agreement is incorporated from a distinct contract. The intention regarding such incorporation – and thus the intention for the dispute not to be subject to the jurisdiction of the court – must be clearly distinguished to achieve the incorporation of the distinct arbitration clause. With the concepts of the impediment of the jurisdiction of the courts and the intention of the parties to impede this so potentially being interrelated, these issues are evaluated together in the following sections.

1.2.1. The Right to Access to a Court and the Impediment of the Jurisdiction of the Courts

One of the complications that may arise from incorporating a contractual clause which refers to a dispute to arbitration is the possibility of the infringement of one's human right that is to be heard by the court.[44] It is regulated under the European Convention of Human Rights that 'in the determination of his civil rights and obligations . . . everyone is entitled to a fair and public hearing within a reasonable time by an independent impartial tribunal established by law.'[45] It would be considered unjustifiable and inadmissible to refer a dispute to an alternative resolution model, where the parties have not revealed any willingness to adopt such an alternative.[46] In the case where parties exercising their right to refer their disputes to arbitration – waiving their right to access to a court – it must be ensured that no unfair constraints are imposed. In this regard, obliging unwilling parties to refer their disputes to any alternative dispute resolution model would be a clear violation of the right to access a court as such an implementation would create a legally unacceptable

---

44 The term 'access to a court' may be understood as 'access to justice' or 'judicial protection.' The general acceptance of the concept may be said to be evinced from the human rights instruments adopted since the establishment of the United Nations; Article 6(1) of the European Convention on Human Rights and Fundamental Freedoms, 1950 (CETS No 005) provides that '[i]n the determination of his civil rights and obligations or of any criminal charge against him, everyone is entitled to a fair and public hearing within a reasonable time by an independent and impartial tribunal established by law.' Furthermore, Article 25, regulating 'the Right to Judicial Protection' of the American Convention on Human Rights 1978, states, 'Everyone has the right to simple and prompt recourse, or any other effective recourse, to a competent court or tribunal for protection against acts that violate his fundamental rights recognized by the constitution or laws of the state concerned or by this Convention, even though such violation may have been committed by persons acting in the course of their official duties.' Moreover, Article 7(1) of the African Charter on Human and Peoples' Rights 1981 ([1982] 21 ILM 58) indicates, 'Every individual shall have the right to have his cause heard. This comprises: a) The right to an appeal to competent national organs against acts of violating his fundamental rights as recognized and guaranteed by conventions, laws, regulations and customs in force; b) The right to be presumed innocent until proved guilty by a competent court or tribunal; c) The right to defense, including the right to be defended by counsel of his choice; d) The right to be tried within a reasonable time by an impartial court or tribunal.' Also see Francesca Francioni, *Access to Justice as a Human Right*, Oxford Scholarship Online, March 2012, Print Publication, 2007, 3–4.

45 Article 6 of the European Convention on Human Rights 1950, 'Right to a fair trial.'

46 *AIG Europe SA v QBE International Insurance Ltd* [2002] Lloyd's Rep IR 22. The case includes an arbitral procedure clause stating that in case of a dispute between the insured and the insurers, the parties will apply to the Tribunal de Commerce in Paris for an arbitrator to be appointed. The arbitrator will be proposing an agreement, which is acceptable for both parties.

impediment to such a right.[47] Essentially, the foundation of the principle lies under the objective that nobody is to be bereft of their right to a fair trial by being compelled to refer their dispute to an alternative dispute resolution mechanism that they are not willing to resort to. Nevertheless, parties being asked to negotiate with one another as a procedural step may not truly be perceived as a deprivation of the right to be heard by a court.[48] Parties may be asked to comply with such procedural requirements, and if they do not, they may possibly be fined pursuant to pre-action protocols.[49] If the parties are unable to agree after such a procedural step is taken, this would not be assessed as depriving them of a 'fair and public hearing within a reasonable time.'[50]

The issue possibly gets complex in dealing with an arbitration agreement[51] as such restricts the accessibility of the courts since it reveals a voluntary surrender of the right to be heard by the court and precludes further legal action.[52] It is 'judicially confirmed'[53] by the European Court of Human Rights that the voluntary submission of the disputes to arbitration creates the presumption that the parties have waived their right to access to a court. One of the most crucial examinations to be made concerning the validity of such waiver is the legal capability of it to satisfy a standard level of fairness, which exists at a basic due process. There are control mechanisms, such as the stay of proceedings, to ensure a dispute is referred to arbitration fairly and legitimately. Therefore, one of the fundamental concerns in implementing arbitration agreements is usually whether the renunciation of the right to go to a court is indeed voluntary.[54]

Arbitration has an expansive potential of promoting the true wishes of the parties pertaining to the settlement of the dispute in question. It advances self-determination and autonomy while empowering parties to control the outcome.[55] Contemporary disputes come with the inherent requirement of modern solutions. Further, arbitration provides creative and tailor-made resolutions that meet the needs and realities of the dispute in question. Arbitration, in this regard, may be perceived as a more favourable method of dispute resolution by the parties to a dispute, who need such resolutions. It provides more wide-ranging non-fiscal remedies,[56] unlike the ones granted by the courts abiding by some

47 *Deweer v Belgium* [1980] 2 European Human Rights Reports 439, para 49. Also see *Halsey v Milton Keynes General NHS Trust* [2004] EWCA (Civ) 576 at 9. The argument heard by the court was regarding whether it had power to order parties to submit their disputes to mediation against their will.

48 However, this issue can be regarded as arguable whether referring parties to mediation prior to a hearing would infringe Article 6 of the European Convention of Human Rights 1950. See Hazel Genn, Paul Fenn, and Marc Mason, *Twisting Arms: Court Referred and Court Linked Mediation Under Judicial Pressure*, Ministry of Justice Research Series 1/07, Ministry of Justice, May 2007.

49 It should be noted that in England and Wales, the High Court can impose cost penalties where parties fail to consider mediation prior to trial if they are directed to do so on the grounds that 'litigation should be last resort.' Pre-action protocols available at www.justice.gov.uk/courts/procedure-rules/civil/protocol.

50 Henry Brown and Arthur Marriott, *ADR: Principles and Practice*, Sweet & Maxwell, 2011, 3rd Edn., 95–96, 5–089.

51 See Kyriaki Noussia, *Confidentiality in International Commercial Arbitration: A Comparative Analysis of the Position Under English, US, German and French Law*, Springer, 2010, 48–49.

52 Francioni (n 44) 40.

53 *Suovaniemi v Finland* Application No. 31737/96, Decision of February 23, 1999.

54 Francioni (n 44) 40.

55 Dominique Allen, Against Settlement? Owen Fiss, ADR and Australian Discrimination Law, 2009, *International Journal of Discrimination and the Law*, 10, 195.

56 Michael Moffitt, Three Things to Be Against (Settlement not Included), 2009, *Fordham Law Review*, 3, 1203–1245, 1212.

strict limits and tariffs. Arbitration may be considered a 'privatized justice system.'[57] In this respect, it is not reasonable to expect such a 'private' system to bear the same characteristics or procedures as its public 'counterpart.' By its nature, arbitration is private and, therefore, lacks transparency, unlike court proceedings. Nonetheless, the opacity it provides enables parties to possibly fix and preserve their relationship. Moreover, due to being private, the decisions given in arbitration are scarcely open to the public, unlike court judgements. Hence, it also enables parties to protect the private aspects of their dealings and trade if they wish so.

Alternatives to due process are usually more flexible and they advance self-determination and autonomy.[58] An effort to institutionalize the method more than it is needed would potentially induce it is getting 'increasingly formal and complex.'[59] One of the fundamental elements granting arbitration its favourable status is the flexibility of the concept that party autonomy facilitates.[60]

1.2.2. The Intention of the Parties and Party Autonomy

Parties are free to determine the resolution mechanism applicable to their dispute.[61] Notwithstanding, concerning the nature and the application of arbitration agreements, such autonomy has a broad interference in international commercial arbitration. Parties to disputes with international characters also have the autonomy to choose the applicable resolution method or how the process is conducted. It is crucial that arbitration proceedings are thoroughly coherent with the aspirations of the parties.[62]

The concepts of autonomy and empowerment of parties constitute the cornerstones of arbitration. The empowerment and flexibility of the parties to choose the applicable method for the resolution of their dispute constitute an essential distinction between court proceedings and arbitration. As the parties to a dispute gain more control over the substantial parts of its resolution, the strictness of the relevant regulation and the formality of the rules to be applied may be softened to reflect the true intention and autonomy of the parties to the arbitration.[63]

---

57 Francesca Francioni, Access to Justice, Denial of Justice and International Investment Law, in Pierre-Marie Dupuy, Ernst-Ulrich Petersmann and Francesca Francioni (eds.) *Human Rights in International Investment Law and Arbitration*, Oxford University Press, 2010, 63 at 70.

58 Isabelle R. Gunning, Diversity Issues in Mediation: Controlling Negative Cultural Myths, 1995, *Journal of Dispute Resolution*, 55.

59 Lisa E. Bernstein, Understanding the Limits of Court-Connected ADR: A Critique of Federal Court-Annexed Arbitration Programs, 1993, *University of Pennsylvania Law Review*, 141, 2242.

60 The fundamental characteristics of the alternative dispute resolution methods may be given as 'consent, participation, empowerment, dignity, respect, empathy and emotional catharsis, privacy, efficiency, quality solutions, equity, access and yes, even justice.' Carrie Menkel-Meadow, Whose Dispute Is It Anyway?: A Philosophical and Democratic Defense of Settlement (In Some Cases), 1995, *Georgetown Law Journal*, 83, 2663–2696, 2669–2670.

61 For the views of the Court of Appeal concerning freedom of parties: *Granville Oil & Chemicals Ltd v Davis Turner* [2003] 2 Lloyd's Rep 356.

62 C. Chatterjee, The Reality of Party Autonomy Rule in International Arbitration, 2003, *Journal of International Arbitration*, 20(6), 539–560, 540. However, party autonomy is not unlimited as the mandatory rules of law of place or public policy rules of law applicable to substance may have restrictions.

63 Felix Steffek, Hannes Unberath, Hazel Genn, Reinhard Greger, and Carrie Menkel-Meadow (eds.), Guide for Regulating Dispute Resolution (GRDR): Principles and Comments, in *Regulating Dispute Resolution: ADR and Access to Justice at the Crossroads*, Hart Publishing, 2013, 217.

Being a fundamental principle of arbitration, the concept of party autonomy had been subject to many attempts of getting defined. For instance, it was considered to be 'the guiding principle in determining the procedure to be followed in international commercial arbitration. It is a principle that has been endorsed not only in national laws but by international arbitral institutions and organizations.'[64] It has also been outlined in Article 19(1) of the United Nations Commission on International Trade Law Model Law on International Commercial Arbitration (Model Law) 1985 that the parties are free to agree on the procedure to be followed by the arbitral tribunal in conducting proceedings.[65] Furthermore, the Arbitration Act 1996 indicates that 'the parties should be free to agree how their disputes are resolved, subject only to such safeguards as are necessary for the public interest.'[66] Moreover, similar to Article 19(1) of the UNCLOS Model Law, the Arbitration Act 1996 also states that all procedural and evidential matters are to be decided by the tribunal but are subject to the right of the parties to agree on any matter.[67]

It should be noted that arbitration agreements may not bind third parties. Nevertheless, pursuant to the Contracts (Rights of Third Parties) Act 1999, they may give a third party the right to execute a substantive term of the contract provided the right to do so is conferred to them. To put it differently, this piece of legislation is particularly 'designed to give a third party to a contract the right to enforce a substantive term of the contract if a benefit is conferred on that party.'[68] This clearly means that if a right to a third party is conferred within an arbitration agreement, that party would be able to exercise such a conferred right. Indeed, the arbitration agreement may confer a benefit or a right to a third party. Though, in terms of being binding, an arbitration agreement does not bind a third party. In other words, only a benefit or a right, which the exercise of it is optional, may be conferred to a third party and not a directly binding responsibility,[69] or a disadvantage may be imposed. For instance, since an arbitration agreement would only bind the parties to it, the arbitral tribunal would not have the power to compel the attendance of the third parties as witnesses or the capability to order such attendance.[70]

The intention of the parties to refer their disputes to arbitration is directly interrelated with the impediment of the court's jurisdiction. Nonetheless, this essentially should not be regarded as a concern where the intention of the parties to arbitrate is clear. There are some statutory devices to be used to assess whether it is indeed the intention of the parties to arbitrate (arbitration agreement to be in writing) and, also, redress mechanisms to be

---

64 Alan Redfern, *Law and Practice of International Commercial Arbitration*, Oxford University Press, 2004, 4th Edn., 315.

65 Article 19(1) of the UNCITRAL Model Law 1985 states, 'Subject to the provisions of this Law, the parties are free to agree on the procedure to be followed by the arbitral tribunal in conducting the proceedings.'

66 Section 1(b) of the Arbitration Act 1996.

67 Section 34(1) of the Arbitration Act 1996. Also, for the restrictions on the party autonomy in international commercial arbitration, see Michale Pryles, Limits to Party Autonomy in Arbitral Procedure, 2007, *Journal of International Arbitration*, 24(3), 327–339, Kluwer Law International (especially on time limits); Andrew Tweeddale and Keren Tweeddale, *Arbitration of Commercial Disputes*, Oxford University Press, 2007, 256.

68 Robert Merkin and Louis Flannery, *Arbitration Act 1996*, Informa Law from Routledge, 2020, 9.2.2.

69 Sunday A. Fagbemi, The Doctrine of Party Autonomy in International Commercial Arbitration: Myth or Reality?, 2015, *AFE Babalola University, Journal of Sustainable Development Law and Policy*, 6(1), 222–246, 242.

70 Şeyda Dursun, A Critical Examination of the Role of Party Autonomy in International Commercial Arbitration and an Assessment of Its Role and Extent, 2012, *Yalova Üniversitesi Hukuk Fakültesi Dergisi*, 161–188, 171.

implemented where it is clear that parties intend to take the dispute to arbitration, but it is somehow brought to court (stay of proceedings).[71]

1.3. Benefits of Arbitration and the Legislative Aspects of the Incorporation of Arbitration Clauses

Alternative methods of dispute resolution[72] have become more and more favoured every day as these methods have been getting increasingly institutionalized and accessible.[73] Arbitration, being one of these alternatives, is a private form of adjudication outside the court system. Arbitration may be seen as beneficial in the regard that it 'gets the ball rolling.' Even if the agreed provisions of the arbitration agreement are generic, parties may still depend on these rather than waiting for long court proceedings that follow strict and detailed procedural rules.[74] The existence of an agreement regarding dispute resolution, which is to a certain level agreeable by the parties,[75] provides something constructive towards reaching a tangible resolution. Correspondingly, parties may prefer the quicker initiation of the resolution process rather than the conflict remaining unresolved for relatively longer in the court.

Arbitration in the UK is a process regulated by legislation, which allows parties to choose the arbitral tribunal by means of applying the rules of an institution or privately. Consequently, this neutral tribunal makes a binding decision. Section 15(1) of the Arbitration Act 1996 indicates that parties are free to choose the number of arbitrators to form the arbitral tribunal and 'for all practical purposes (i.e. 99% of all known commercial arbitrations), the choice is between one or three.'[76]

The arbitration process is similar to litigation in some ways.[77] However, the parties referring their conflict to arbitration may agree to choose the arbitrator and the procedure of arbitration may be tailored to meet the specific needs of the parties and characteristics

---

71 Section 9 of the Arbitration Act 1996 regulates the stay of legal proceedings. The section merely re-enacts Section 4 of the Arbitration Act 1950 and Section 1 of the Arbitration Act 1975 with some alterations.

72 It can also be referred to as a 'appropriate' or 'proportionate' dispute resolution. 'This is because the means and costs of resolving disputes should be proportionate to the importance and nature of the issue at stake. Serious and important disputes should call for more rigorous dispute resolution procedures than trivial and unimportant disputes.' See Mark Elliott and Robert Thomas, Tribunal Justice and Proportionate Dispute Resolution, July 2012, *Cambridge Law Journal*, 71(2), 297–324, 299; Michael Adler, Tribunal Reform: Proportionate Dispute Resolution and the Pursuit of Administrative Justice, 2006, *Modern Law Review*, 69, 958.

73 Lorna McGregor, Alternative Dispute Resolution and Human Rights: Developing a Rights-Based Approach Through the ECHR, 2015, *The European Journal of International Law*, 26(3), published by Oxford University Press on behalf of EJIL Ltd, 1.

74 Brown and Marriott (n 50) 30.

75 Parties may choose freely to refer some of their disputes to arbitration while preferring some other potential ones that might emerge in the future to be heard by a court. This is also reflected in the Arbitration Act 1996 Section 82(1) under which, a dispute is simply defined as 'any differences.' In other words, showing regard to the possibility of the emergence of future disputes, the Arbitration Act 1996 does not set a quantitative limit for the number of disputes that can be referred to arbitration. Settling some of their disputes in a way that is compatible with the wishes of the parties would undoubtedly be preferable than not settling any of them.

76 Merkin and Flannery (n 68) 15.1: Furthermore, 'in investment treaty arbitrations, the invariable trend is for three arbitrators, and for some larger international boundary or territorial disputes, five arbitrators is common.'

77 A formal and coercive method of dispute resolution. See Ian Richard Scott, The Courts and Alternative Dispute Resolution, in Julio C. Betancourt and Jason A. Crook (eds.) *ADR, Arbitration and Mediation, a Collection of Essays*, AuthorHouse, September 2014, 64–83; McGregor (n 73) 1.

of the dispute in question. Furthermore, arbitration provides a suitable private environment for the repairment of damaged relationships and for the preservation of those that are at stake of becoming damaged.[78] Litigation usually does not provide such benefits due to having public proceedings, which are also frequently longer. Arbitration also increases the chances of the parties to protect their reputations and trade secrets.[79]

1.3.1. Legislation Pertaining to the Incorporation of Arbitration Clauses

Courts procure their jurisdiction from legislation and from the rules enshrined in statutory provisions.[80] On the other hand, the process and authority of arbitration majorly depend on the arbitration agreement. Nonetheless, the arbitration process may also be derived from mandatory procedural requirements. Even though the statutory provision for arbitration in the UK is fundamentally regulated under the Arbitration Act 1996, there are some other examples of arbitration based directly or indirectly on other statutory provisions.[81]

The question of whether an arbitration clause is incorporated into a contract is generally contemplated as a matter of contract construction.[82] Where the arbitration clause is contained within the standard terms of one of the parties, intention regarding its incorporation usually does not cause any problems. However, difficulties may arise where the validity of the incorporation from an entirely different agreement by reference is being assessed, and the issue may be much more complex to resolve. It should be noted that such difficulties do not arise due to arbitration clauses being onerous or unreasonable.[83] On the contrary, arbitration clauses are often accepted as ordinary clauses indicating the ordinary method of dispute resolution. Their existence is considered typical, especially where the contracting parties are conducting commercial dealings. The reason that their incorporation is usually subject to some specific criteria to meet is that these clauses require special notice to be drawn to them.[84] Accordingly, the manifestation of party autonomy constitutes a fundamental necessity. Where parties seek to incorporate the terms of a third party's contract – as this often happens in shipping, reinsurance, and construction contexts – difficulties may arise due to the multitude of parties involved in the often complex and multi-layered contractual structure these consist of. To put it differently, the remoteness of third parties involved in the contractual structure usually blurs the manifestation of the party autonomy that is tried to be obtained.

---

78 Brown and Marriott (n 50) 36.

79 Bernstein (n 59) 2239.

80 Brown and Marriott (n 50) 595. Furthermore, the courts, as a common law doctrine, may have inherent jurisdiction. The doctrine suggests a superior court has jurisdiction to hear any matter comes before it unless such authority is restricted by statue.

81 For instance, statutory arbitration might arise under various laws, such as the Schedule 12(1)(3) of the Water Industry Act 1991 and Section 13 of the Telecommunications Act 1984. However, for the sake of consistency, solely the Arbitration Act 1996 and its provisions regarding the incorporation of arbitration clauses are considered in this chapter.

82 *Excess Insurance Co Ltd v Mander* [1997] 2 Lloyd's Rep 119 (Comm), 123; *AIG Europe SA v QBE International Insurance Ltd* [2002] Lloyd's Rep IR 22; *Axa Re v Ace Global Markets Ltd* [2006] EWCH 216 (Comm); [2006] Lloyd's Rep IR 683.

83 Ambrose, Maxwell, and Collett (n 35) 53, 4.36.

84 *Stretford v Football Association Limited* [2006] EWHC 479 (Ch); [2007] EWCA Civ 238; [2007] 2 Lloyd's Rep 31, 34.

The Arbitration Act 1996, trying to find a common ground for the incorporation of arbitration clauses, regulates the matter in a general sense by means of giving room for flexibility for the construction of arbitration agreements.

Section 6(2) of the Arbitration Act 1996 particularly deals with the incorporation of arbitration agreements by reference and provides that 'the reference in an agreement to a written form of arbitration clause or to a document containing an arbitration clause constitutes an arbitration agreement if the reference is such as to make that clause part of the agreement.' Being in line with the Model Law,[85] Section 6(2) regulates that a reference to an arbitration clause or to a document containing an arbitration clause creates the result of incorporation.[86] Accordingly, legislation specifically regulates the legal concept of incorporation of an arbitration clause by reference provided legal requirements are met. Section 6(2) preconditions agreement to be in writing and an intention to integrate that agreement into the existing one to be manifested. Nevertheless, it does not pursue strict formalities. This reflects the non-interventionist character of the Act concerning the incorporation of arbitration agreements, as the Act avoids imposing strict restrictions on how this is implemented and assessed. These matters are regulated in a fairly general way.

Two issues arise with respect to the interpretation of the indicated provision of the Act. First, the wording and, second, the comprehensiveness of the provision create ambiguity. Initially, 'if the reference is such as to make that clause part of the agreement' may also be read as the made reference to be 'proper' to facilitate incorporation. While accepting that such a method is perfectly convenient for the parties to implement, Section 6(2) does not really answer the question of when a reference, in fact, amounts to sufficient incorporation.[87] In other words, it may be argued that the provision is seeking pertinence and incorporation by reference to be 'proper'[88] while not clarifying what 'proper' means in this context. As to recapitulate, the provision itself contains ambiguous wording follows as 'if the reference is such as to make that clause part of the agreement,' which anyway may be evaluated as 'such reference to be done properly toward a sufficient incorporation.' The provision also does not provide any reference points for 'actually how' such a reference amounts to incorporation. It is suggested in *Trygg Hansa Insurance Co Ltd v Equitas* that, on the grounds that the wording of the Model Law is permissive to incorporation by general words, Section 6(2) of the Arbitration Act 1996 is to be interpreted in the same sense and

85 UNCITRAL Model Law on International Commercial Arbitration 1985, 2006 Option II of the Art 7(6): 'The reference in a contract to any document containing an arbitration clause constitutes an arbitration agreement in writing, provided that the reference is such as to make that clause part of the contract.' It should be noted that the wording of this provision can be considered as almost identical to the last sentence of the 1985 version of Art 7(2), under which a reference to a document containing an arbitration clause 'constitutes an arbitration agreement provided that the contract is in writing and the reference is such as to make that clause part of the agreement.'

86 Section 6(2) of the Arbitration Act 1996. *AIG Europa (UK) Ltd v The Ethniki* [2000] Lloyd's Rep IR 343 at [37] was concerned with the incorporation of jurisdiction clauses but still Evans LJ referred to arbitration clauses and states that 'there was a time when the objection to incorporation was expressed on semantic grounds (the arbitration clause was or was not, a "term, condition or exception," etc.) but this was overtaken by the closer analysis of the nature of an arbitration agreement which appeared in *Bremer Vulkan v South India Shipping Co.* [1981] A.C. 909.' See also *Secretary of State for Foreign and Commonwealth Affairs v Percy Thomas* [1998] 65 Con LR 11; *Axa Re v Ace Global Markets Ltd* [2006] Lloyd's Rep IR 683; *Sea Trade Maritime Corporation v Hellenic Mutual War Risks Association (Bermuda) Ltd* [2006] 2530 (Comm); *Heifer International Inc v Christansen* [2007] EWHC 3015 (TCC).

87 Merkin and Flannery (n 68) 6.1.5.

88 Properly constructed so that it can fully function 'to make' that clause part of the agreement.

should be brought in line.[89] However, due to the fact that the required level of specificity is left unclear, the issue of whether the employment of general words of incorporation would suffice to incorporate also remains unaddressed in light of the Arbitration Act 1996. Accordingly, the general requirement of English law pertaining to the incorporation of arbitration clauses is incorporating words to be expressed or equivalently put forward.[90]

Secondly, Section 6(2) deliberately leaves the question open whether an arbitration clause contained in standard terms or in a separate contract can effectively be incorporated by reference solely to that document, or whether it is required to refer specifically to the arbitration clause itself.[91] In other words, this particular provision is not very clear concerning the assessment of how far the incorporation should stretch. Prior to the Act, this matter was also open to debate,[92] and it is evident that it still is. Incorporation of arbitration clauses especially being problematic in the contexts of shipping, reinsurance, and construction, the next chapters analyze the different approaches to the matter from the aspects of the indicated branches of law and address the possibility of providing piecemeal solutions.

Regardless of its shortcomings, the Arbitration Act 1996 creates an evidently vital foundation facilitating the analysis of the concept of incorporation of arbitration clauses. Hence, for the purposes of understanding the stance of the Arbitration Act 1996 concerning the issue of incorporation, the meaning of the relevant provision should initially be analyzed. When we evaluate the wording of Section 6(2) of the Act, the initial problematic part strikes us as being the lack of clarification of what is actually considered 'being in writing.' Furthermore, this 'ambiguity' was also provided as a reason for not allowing the incorporation of arbitration clauses by virtue of employing general words in *Aughton Ltd v MF Kent Services* (1991) 57 BLR 1, prior to the Arbitration Act 1996. Consequently, the next part examines the 'being in writing' requirement in English law from the aspect of incorporation of arbitration clauses.

1.3.2. Arbitration Agreement Is Made in Writing

An arbitration agreement is an agreement to refer present or future disputes to arbitration disregarding whether they are contractual or not,[93] and 'dispute' is defined to include any difference.[94] An arbitration agreement constitutes 'the primary source of arbitration and the strongest evidence of party autonomy.'[95] An agreement that is conferring the right to submit an issue to arbitration only to one party alone is still a valid one, even though it does not bestow the same to the counterparty of the contractual relationship.[96]

---

89 [1998] 2 Lloyd's Rep 439.

90 Incorporation of Standard Terms (n 38) 5.23.

91 Ambrose, Maxwell, and Collett (n 35) 53, 4.38.

92 See *Aughton Ltd v MF Kent Services* [1991] 57 BLR 1, a construction case.

93 Section 6(1) of the Arbitration Act 1996.

94 Section 82(1) of the Arbitration Act 1996. Even though a difference and a dispute might be interpreted as similar concepts in general, drawing a distinction between this two would rarely cause a difficulty in the commercial context. See Merkin and Flannery (n 68) 6.1.2. In *Lombard North Central PLC & Anr v GATX Corp* [2012] EWHC 1067 at [20] the distinction between two was considered as a 'semantic' one by Andrew Smith J.

95 Elizabeth Shackelford, Party Autonomy and Regional Harmonization of Rules in International Commercial Arbitration, 2006, *University of Pittsburgh Law Review*, 67, 897, 900.

96 Fox LJ in *Pittalis v Sherefettin* [1986] Q.B. 868: 'There is a fully bilateral agreement which constitutes a contract to refer. The fact that the option is exercisable by one of the parties only seems to me to be irrelevant.

The agreement itself does not need to meet any specific form requirements.[97] This suggestion, as here it stands, does not mean that there are no formal requirements at all. It merely signalizes that there are minimal formal requirements for the construction of arbitration agreements and this level of formality provides some elbow room for flexibility. A properly constructed arbitration clause forms an arbitration agreement, even in a summary form.[98] For instance, 'arbitration to be settled in London,'[99] 'arbitration . . . in London,'[100] 'arbitration, if any, by ICC rules in London,'[101] or 'suitable arbitration clause,'[102] in a clear and well-formed arbitration clause, sufficiently establishes an arbitration agreement.

For an arbitration agreement to be potentially subject to the governance of Section 6(2) concerning incorporation, it initially needs to meet the legal requirement of being an actual agreement. Thus, before anything else, an agreement should be capable of being defined as an arbitration agreement under the Arbitration Act 1996. Otherwise, it would not be possible to discuss whether incorporation took place. The Arbitration Act 1996 applies to arbitration agreements in writing, and also to any other agreement between the parties that refer their disputes to arbitration, providing such an agreement 'being in writing' for the purposes of the act.

The requirement that the arbitration agreement be in writing in English law hinges upon Article 7 of the Model Law[103] and the pursuance of the Departmental Advisory Committee

---

The arrangement suits both parties . . . the landlord is protected, if there is no arbitration, by his own assessment of the rent as stated in his notice: and the tenant is protected, if he is dissatisfied with the landlord's assessment of the rent, by his right to refer the matter to arbitration. Both sides have, therefore, accepted the arrangement and there is no lack of mutuality.'

97 However, this issue should not be understood as there are no formality requirements at all when it comes to the formation of an arbitration agreement. Section 5 of the Arbitration Act 1996 regulates the provision that 'agreements to be in writing.' However, in terms of being 'in writing,' there are other issues to be concerned about, and there are different requirements regarding that in different national and international laws. 'Does not need to meet any specific requirements,' as it stands here, merely indicates the lack of formality requirement and width of flexibility when it comes to constructing an arbitration agreement.

98 See Merkin and Flannery (n 68) 6.1.5.

99 *Tritonia Shipping Inc. v South Nelson Products Corpn.* [1966] 1 Lloyd's Rep 114 looks at the meaning of 'arbitration to be settled in London' in considering whether there was an actual contractual submission to arbitration. See also *Naviera Amazonica Peruara v Compania Internacional de Seguros de Feru* [1988] 1 Lloyd's Rep 116. The Court of Appeal was concerned with the determination of the seat of arbitration pertaining to a policy containing an arbitration clause providing the arbitration to take place in Peru subject to English procedural law.

100 *Transamerican Ocean Contractors Inc v Transchemical Rotterdam B.V.* [1978] 1 Lloyd's Rep 238.

101 *Mangistaumunaigaz Oil Production Association v United World Trade Inc.* [1995] 1 Lloyd's Rep 617.

102 *Hobbs Padgett & Co. (Reinsurance) Ltd v Kirkland Ltd* [1969] 2 Lloyd's Rep 547.

103 UNCITRAL Model Law on International Commercial Arbitration 1985, Art 7 'Definition and Form of Arbitration Agreement': (1) '"Arbitration agreement" is an agreement by the parties to submit to arbitration all or certain disputes which have arisen or which may arise between them in respect of a defined legal relationship, whether contractual or not. An arbitration agreement may be in the form of an arbitration clause in a contract or in the form of a separate agreement. (2) The arbitration agreement shall be in writing. (3) An arbitration agreement is in writing if its content is recorded in any form, whether or not the arbitration agreement or contract has been concluded orally, by conduct, or by other means. (4) The requirement that an arbitration agreement be in writing is met by an electronic communication if the information contained therein is accessible so as to be useable for subsequent reference; "electronic communication" means any communication that the parties make by means of data messages; "data message" means information generated, sent, received or stored by electronic, magnetic, optical or similar means, including, but not limited to, electronic data interchange (EDI), electronic mail, telegram, telex or telecopy. (5) Furthermore, an arbitration agreement is in writing if it is contained in an exchange of statements of claim and defence in which the existence of an agreement is alleged by one party and not denied by the other. (6) The reference in a contract to any document containing an arbitration clause

(DAC)[104] to ensure that the right to recourse to the courts not to be lost unless such waiver is clearly provided in a written format. The right to access to a court is perceived 'too important a right to be lost by oral agreement.'[105] It may be argued that DAC was pursuing to create some sort of safety net before allowing the waiver of the right to go to a court directly.[106]

1.3.2.1. Decoding Section 5: Being in Writing and What It Entails

As indicated, the Arbitration Act 1996 only applies if the arbitration agreement meets the legal requirement of being in writing.[107] However, an arbitration agreement to be in writing has a broad definition concerning the description provided in the Arbitration Act 1996. The description does not indicate that there should be a certain document involving the words 'arbitration agreement.' In other words, the Act provides flexibility in terms of the required formality to conclude an arbitration agreement. There would be a valid arbitration agreement in writing if (1) the agreement is made in writing (regardless of it being signed or not by the parties), (2) the agreement is made by an exchange of communications in writing, or (3) the agreement is evidenced in writing or by the exchange of written submissions.[108] It should be noted that arbitration agreements differ from the rest of the agreements in English law in the sense that law customarily allows the construction of the contracts in writing, orally, or by conduct. On the other hand, the Arbitration Act 1996, specifically requiring an arbitration agreement 'to be in writing,' precludes oral agreements and conducts from producing formal arbitration agreements. To put it differently, an oral agreement to arbitrate would be valid as a matter of English law but would not be subject to the provisions of the Arbitration Act 1996.[109] The significant position of arbitration agreements may perhaps be apprehended considering such fundamental discrepancy they create within English law.

The first category of Section 5(2) of the Arbitration Act 1996 indicates written agreements to be accepted as arbitration agreements, regardless of being signed.[110] The second

---

constitutes an arbitration agreement in writing, provided that the reference is such as to make that clause part of the contract.' It should be noted that there are two versions of Art 7 in the 2006 version of the Model Law with adopted amendments. There is a long version, Option I, and there is a short version, Option II. Most countries have adopted the Option I of Art 7. See www.uncitral.org.

104 Hereinafter DAC & DAC Report, chaired by Lord Justice Saville, February 1996 Report on Arbitration Bill.

105 See Merkin and Flannery (n 68) 5.2. In theory, it would be possible to have an oral arbitration agreement. However, it would almost be impossible for such arbitration agreement to be enforced or even come into existence. See Incorporation of Standard Terms (n 38) 6.1.5. Also, such arbitration agreements are not enforceable under the New York Convention on the Recognition and Enforcement of Foreign Arbitral Awards (New York Arbitration Convention) 1958. NY Convention Art II (2) provides, 'The term "agreement in writing" shall include an arbitral clause in a contract or an arbitration agreement, signed by the parties or contained in an exchange of letters or telegrams.'

106 An arbitration provision to be accepted as validly incorporated only by means of an express reference to it within the wording of the incorporation was the position before the Arbitration Act 1996. See *Thomas & Portsea Steamship* [1912] A.C.1; *The Nerano* [1994] 2 Lloyd's Rep 50.

107 Section 5(1) of the Arbitration Act 1996.

108 Section 5(2)(f) the Arbitration Act 1996. See Incorporation of Standard Terms (n 38) 3.14.

109 Section 81(1)(b) of the Arbitration Act 1996.

110 Section 5(2)(a) of the Arbitration Act 1996. The Model Law also has no requirement of signature at all. The 1985 version of the Article 7(2) only allowed the signed agreements but doing so, contained a vague definition of 'being signed.' The definition was rectified in 2006. Problems may arise if an award which is based

category establishes that the written exchange of communications produce an arbitration agreement.[111] The third one includes the agreements that are evidenced in writing[112] and both unsigned contracts and the contracts signed by solely one party.[113] These provisions of the Arbitration Act 1996 should be read in compliance with Section 5(6),[114] stating that 'references in this part to anything being written or in writing include it is being recorded by any means.'[115] Section 5(5) also regulates the situation where written submissions are exchanged and states that 'an exchange of written submissions in arbitral or legal proceedings in which the existence of an agreement otherwise than in writing is alleged by one party against another party and not denied by the other party in his response constitutes as between those parties an agreement in writing to the effect alleged.' In other words, the lack of denial of the contended existence of an arbitration agreement may possibly indicate its presence is accepted.

The Arbitration Act 1996 necessitates an arbitration agreement to be in writing. Therefore, the question 'what constitutes writing' is a fundamental one to be posed to determine whether an arbitration agreement exists. As pointed out, it is a precondition for the agreement to first fall into the scope of a confined contractual territory to eventually be able to assess whether the implementation of its incorporation is legally possible. To ascertain if an agreement is eligible for incorporation in that regard, initially, there must be an actual agreement. Agreement to 'be in writing' constitutes the fundamental requirement for such an agreement to come into existence. Therefore, the meaning of this is evaluated below in light of the Arbitration Act 1996 and English law.

1.3.2.1.1. Agreement to Be Made in Writing

In order to construct a valid arbitration agreement that falls into the scope of the Arbitration Act 1996, the agreement must be in writing.[116] However, this does not directly create the result that an arbitration agreement that is not in writing is ineffective.[117] The relevant provisions of the Arbitration Act 1996, when read together, indicate that the Act has flexibility in terms of the necessary requirements for the construction of arbitration

on an unsigned arbitration agreement is sought to be enforced in another jurisdiction under New York Convention on the Recognition and Enforcement of Foreign Arbitral Awards (New York Arbitration Convention) 1958. As to overcome such possible problem, all parties signing the terms of reference, pursuant to Article 18 of the ICC Rules, would be undeniably valuable.

111 Section 5(2)(b) of the Arbitration Act 1996.

112 *National Boat Shows Ltd v Tameside Marine*, July 2001, unreported; the acceptance of an offer in a prospectus by submission of an application form was held to involve an agreement to be bound by the terms of the prospectus and therefore to constitute an agreement in writing.

113 Section 5(2)(c) of the Arbitration Act 1996.

114 Merkin and Flannery (n 68) 5.3.

115 Section 5(6) of the Arbitration Act 1996.

116 Any other agreement between the parties such as an agreement excluding a non-mandatory provision of the Arbitration Act 1996 would only be effective for the purposes of the Arbitration Act 1996, Part I, if it is in writing. However, it should be noted that, the one exception to this is an agreement to terminate the arbitration agreement. It was considered by the DAC that it would be impractical to put a requirement as such to terminate an arbitration, indicating that 'parties may well simply walk away from proceedings.' See DAC Report, February 1996, at para 40. See also Tweeddale and Tweeddale (n 67) 506, 16.34.

117 Section 81(1)(b) of the Arbitration Act 1996 provides that 'nothing in this Part shall be construed as excluding the operation of any rule of law consistent with the provisons of this Part, any rule of law as to . . . (b) the effect of an oral arbitration agreement.'

agreements.[118] With regard to the wording and interpretation of the related provisions of the Act, it may be contended that an agreement which is made partially oral and partially written falls into the scope of the Arbitration Act 1996. This is because the Act mainly seeks the arbitration agreement to be at least evidenced in writing, and it promotes flexibility to enable different types of agreements to be effective if intended for them to do so and not to stumble just because of a strict requirement that they may not be able to fulfil due to being in a 'different' type. For instance, where salvage contracts[119] are agreed orally by reference to institutional standard clauses that include an arbitration clause,[120] the strict 'being in writing or signed' requirement would be hard to justify as 'the exigencies of the disaster may eliminate the possibility to sign the necessary documents.'[121] The fundamental reason for validating arbitration agreements that are concluded partially orally and partially written is provided in the DAC Report dated February 1996 as the desire for giving effect to different types of agreements. The importance of doing this so is highlighted as 'seen in salvage contracts covering frequent and important occasions.'[122] In accordance with the commentary of the DAC, it is enacted that, when parties agree otherwise than in writing by reference to terms, which are in writing, they make an agreement in writing.[123] To put this differently, an orally concluded agreement to incorporate does not itself constitute an obstacle to the incorporation of an arbitration clause, unless the explicit intention to incorporate such a clause is otherwise demonstrated.[124] It should be noted that, outside of the context of salvage contracts, the application of Section 5(3) of the Arbitration Act 1996 would not be likely and the said provision would apply where such an oral agreement is confined to the incorporation of arbitration clauses only. On the other hand, parties may agree orally on the standard terms and conditions, which are in writing and include an arbitration agreement in principle.[125]

The meaning of an 'arbitration agreement to be in writing' and its effect on incorporation were considered in *Bony v Kacou and Others*.[126] The case arose as a part of the claimant, Wilfried Bony, a premiership footballer, to recover £8 million of alleged secret commissions received by his former agents (the first and the third defendants, A1

118 Reading Section 5(2)(c) of the Arbitration Act 1996, 'the agreement evidenced in writing,' Section 5(2)(a), considering a partially orally made arbitration agreement, 'agreement . . . made in writing,' and Section 5(3), 'where parties agree otherwise than in writing by reference to terms which are in writing, they make an agreement in writing,' the wording of the provisions illustrates the generous approach adopted by the Act that a partly written partly oral agreement falls within the scope of the act as it would at least be evidenced in writing.

119 Ship salvage agreements were also mentioned with regard to incorporation of arbitration clauses by reference when a non-written agreement is involved in *Bony v Kacou and Others* [2017] EWHC 2146 (Ch) para [34]: 'A non-written agreement that incorporates by reference written terms that consist of or include an arbitration clause constitutes an arbitration agreement in writing – see Section 5(3). Thus, for example, it is not unusual for a ship salvage agreement to be made orally by reference to Lloyd's Open Form. Where such an agreement is made, the agreement includes an arbitration agreement in the terms set out in the form.'

120 For instance, by reference to Lloyd's Standard Form of salvage agreement.

121 David St John Sutton, Judith Gill, and Matthew Gearing, *Russel on Arbitration*, Thomson, Sweet & Maxwell, 2007, 23rd Edn., 51, 2–041. Also, for example, for an appeal from an arbitration award from Lloyd's salvage, see *The Owners of the Motor Vessel Tojo Maru v NV Bureau Wijsmuller (The Tojo Maru)* [1972] AC 242.

122 DAC Report 1996, para 36.

123 Section 5(3) of the Arbitration Act 1996.

124 Incorporation of Standard Terms (n 38) 3.11.

125 Sutton, Gill, and Gearing (n 121) 51, 2–041.

126 [2017] EWHC 2146 (Ch).

and A3), and their corporate vehicles (the second and fourth defendants, A2 and A4). The claimant transferred from the Dutch club Vitesse to Swansea City in July 2013 for £12 million. He joined Manchester City in 2015 for £28 million but then he rejoined Swansea City in August 2017 for an undisclosed fee. The alleged secret commission of £8 million was secured from Swansea City by his agents on his initial transfer to the said football club. The claimant was represented by four different entities and only two of these agents were authorized, A1 and A3. The other entities, A2 and A4, were the corporate vehicles of the authorized agents. Furthermore, the A1 contract did not include an arbitration clause. The contract between the claimant and A3 pertaining to the relationship between the claimant and Swansea City was oral rather and not in writing, except for a former written agreement which was in force between 2013 and 2015 containing the following:

> This written agreement contained an express dispute resolution provision to the following effect: 'the settlement of disputes between the Player's Agent and Client, club or another player's agent of whom all are registered with the same national association (national disputes) is the responsibility of the respective national association . . . Any other complaint which is not subject to the preceding Paragraph thereof shall have to be transferred to the FIFA Players' Status Committee.' The Football Association Rules (FA Rules) themselves included arbitration provisions. Rule K provided that 'any dispute or difference between any two or more Participants . . . shall be referred to and finally resolved by arbitration under these Rules.' The definition of the word 'Participant' is provided in the FA Rules, meaning 'an authorised agent . . . club . . . licenced agent, player and all such persons who are time to time participating in any activity sanctioned either directly or indirectly by the Association.'

The agents unsuccessfully applied to stay the court proceedings on the basis that the FA Rules, which included an arbitration clause, applied to disputes between 'members of the football family.' Football, being a highly regulated sport and the Fédération Internationale de Football Association (FIFA), required all disputes to be referred to arbitration, the agents argued that Rule K of the FA Rules was applicable.

The stay was refused. With regard to A1, it was held that there was no arbitration agreement in or incorporated into the agency agreement. Regarding A3, it was held that there was a valid written agreement from February 2013 to February 2015, but the arbitration clause was of no assistance as the provision of the agreement regarding dispute resolution involved the requirement of both parties to be registered with the same national association: The claimant was registered with the English Football Association, and A3 was registered with the Football Association of Czech Republic. Regarding the alleged incorporation of Rule K of the FA Rules, it was held that Section 5 of the Arbitration Act 1996 required an agreement to be in writing, and it could not be right that anyone involved in football to be bound by the FA Rules by default, irrespective of the existence of a written agreement incorporating an arbitration agreement. The existence of an implied contract that incorporated the FA Rules (in particular, Rule K) constituted the main aspect of the appeal process. It was emphasized by the court that the obligation to grant a stay would only arise if there is a valid arbitration agreement compatible with Section 5 of the Arbitration Act 1996 and also if the requirement under Section 5(3) is satisfied: If the parties orally agreed to incorporate a written arbitration clause. The court mainly focused on assessing whether the parties had expressly or impliedly agreed to incorporate FA Rules – and, in particular, Rule K (dispute resolution and arbitration) – into their agency agreements. Concerning whether contracts existed,[127] it was indicated that there were no contracts at all between the claimant and A2 or A4. There were also no contracts between the FA and A1, A2, and A4. There were only express contracts between the claimant and A1 and between the claimant and A3, but there was no sign that those contracts incorporated the FA Rules. Therefore, it was concluded that it would be inappropriate for the stay to be granted. Fundamentally, the dispute was concerning whether the parties had expressly or impliedly agreed to incorporate Rule K into the agency agreements. There was no express or implied reference to FA Rules, which includes an arbitration clause. None of the agreements, both written and oral, included a valid arbitration clause. Hence, the incorporation of the arbitration clause was not allowed.

The *Bony v Kacou* may be regarded as notable as it lays down the connection between Section 5 and Section 9 of the Arbitration Act 1996, which are concerned with the arbitration agreement being in writing and stay of proceedings, respectively. Doing so, the case clarifies the effects of the said sections on the incorporation of arbitration agreements. Stay of proceedings, if granted inappropriately, would constitute a significant violation of one's right to go to court. For a stay to be granted, the fundamental element to be sought would be the existence of an arbitration agreement. Moving back to the source, for an arbitration agreement to be accepted as 'existing' as to fall in the scope of the Arbitration Act 1996, it has to fulfil the requirement of 'being in writing' in the way that the law stipulates.[128] For the stay to be granted, there must be an arbitration agreement that satisfies the requirements of Section 5 and the definitional requirements for the construction of an arbitration agreement that are provided within Section 6 of the Arbitration Act 1996. Therefore, for a stay to be granted due to the existence of an arbitration agreement, such an agreement must meet the legal requirements that are laid down in Section 5 of the Act.[129]

1.3.2.1.2. Agreement Is Made by an Exchange of Communications in Writing

When there is an arbitration agreement that falls under the first category (an agreement that is made in writing), then a problem regarding the assessment of its existence or validity rarely arises. This is because the relevant parties only concern with a single written document that visibly includes the agreement to refer their dispute to arbitration. The assessment of the consented method of dispute resolution would, in that case, be quite straightforward. However, when the presumed agreement to refer a dispute to arbitration is said to be made by an exchange of written communications, it evidently would be relatively harder to assess the mutual consent to refer a dispute to arbitration than ascertaining such consent as manifested in a single document in a written form indicating an arbitration agreement.

The requirement for an arbitration agreement to be in writing is set forth in the Model Law. While Article 7(2) requires the agreement to be in writing, the definition of the writing requirement is provided in Article 7(4) as

---

127 *Clarke v The Earl of Dunraven and Mount-Earl, The Satanita* [1897] AC 59; was relied upon by the defandants. It was held in this case that each individual participant in a tacht race who had entered into a contract with the organisers had also entered into an implied contract with each other under which they agreed to abide by the rules of the race. However it was held by HHJ Pelling QC that *The Satanita* was in no assist of defendants in the *Bony v Kacou and Others*, as only some of the parties had contracts with each other, and there was no party actually had a contract with the rest of the parties that the case concerned with.

128 [2017] EWHC 2146 (Ch) para [15].

129 [2017] EWHC 2146 (Ch) para [34].

> an electronic communication if the information contained therein is accessible so as to be usable for subsequent reference; 'electronic communication' means any communication that the parties make by means of data messages; 'data message' means information generated, sent, received or stored by electronic, magnetic, optical or similar means, including but not limited to, electronic data interchange, electronic email, telegram, telex or telecopy.[130]

For the purposes of Section 5(2)(b) of the Arbitration Act 1996, where parties make an agreement in exchange of letters or emails, they would actually be making an agreement in writing. The problems mainly arise, when the arbitration agreement that is said to exist is constructed by virtue of exchanged emails attaching drafts of agreements in MS Word format due to the significance of properly assessing party consent to arbitrate and because sometimes it is not that easy to ascertain the *consensus ad idem* from the overall context of the correspondence.[131] Problems frequently arise regarding the formation and validity of arbitration agreements. However, when the relevant agreement is contained in an exchange of documents, courts essentially seek to ascertain *consensus ad idem*. The written evidence of an existing *consensus ad idem* is usually the major requirement for the arbitration agreement that is contained in exchanged documents to be accepted as incorporated.

It should also be noted that what the word 'exchange' entails also has some unclarity concerning its scope and between which parties this may take place.[132] Furthermore, the DAC Report does not clarify this issue. However, paragraph 34 of the Report indicates that the reason for generalizing the 'being in writing' requirement was to widen the scope for a finding of an arbitration agreement under the widest possible terms without the specific need of spelling any of them out.[133] Accordingly, this may also depend on the determination of the court of *consensus ad idem*.

1.3.2.1.3. Agreement Is Evidenced in Writing

Section 5(2)(c) of the Arbitration Act 1996 states that 'there is an agreement in writing . . . if the agreement is evidenced in writing.' This may be regarded as the last exit before the highway that the Arbitration Act 1996 provides. The provision enables agreements that are essentially not drafted as arbitration agreements in writing to eventually constitute valid arbitration agreements, provided they are evidenced in writing.[134] The law simply requires an agreement in writing, which is tangible in that regard. Section 5(4) states that 'an agreement is evidenced in writing if an agreement made otherwise than in writing is recorded by one of the parties, or by a third party, with the authority of the parties to the agreement.' Furthermore, Article 7(2) of the Model Law indicates that there will be an actual agreement in writing if the content of it is recorded in any form, regardless of the arbitration agreement has been concluded orally, by conduct, or by other means. Thus, it would be reasonable to suggest that the Arbitration Act 1996 and Model Law are back-to-

130 The Model Law has been amended in 2006. In its original form it was provided that an agreement would be under the scope of the said law if 'it is contained . . . in an exchange of letters, telex, telegrams or other means of telecommunications which provide a record of the agreement.'

131 Merkin and Flannery (n 68) 6.1.5.

132 For instance, see *Jiangxi Provincial Metal and Minerals Import and Export Corp v Sulanser Co Ltd* [1996] ADRLJ 249 (a Hong Kong case).

133 Incorporation of Standard Terms (n 38) 3.12.

134 Ibid 3.13.

back concerning their requirements pertaining to contracts to be evidenced in writing. It should be noted that, for this provision to be effective there should have been existing oral or written negotiations, and they should satisfyingly add up as 'forming a single arbitration agreement.'[135] Furthermore, the recording of the written evidence may have been done by one of the parties[136] or by a third party.[137]

This category encompasses both signed and unsigned contracts, as well as contracts that are signed by solely one party.[138] An agreement to be evidenced in writing to form an arbitration agreement is clearly a safety net that enables the formation of a valid arbitration agreement 'that is found in the sketchiest of documents.'[139]

What the provisions of the Arbitration Act 1996 actually provide from the aspect of the 'being in writing' requirement should be considered carefully because such an assessment plays a deterministic role in evaluating whether an arbitration agreement is effective. Nevertheless, considering the broad options that the law provides to 'effectuate' the validity of an arbitration agreement, the writing requirement may be regarded to be merely protective in nature. Section 5(3) of the Arbitration Act 1996 even validates 'unwritten arbitration agreements as long as they adopt written arbitration terms, provided, that the existence of such an agreement can be proved.'[140] With the theoretical aspect of admissibility of an oral arbitration agreement being undeniable, the likelihood of one ever coming into existence and then being enforced is 'close to zero.'[141] On the other hand, the irrefutably slim chance of such an agreement coming into existence anyway proves that the Arbitration Act 1996 allows the admissibility of the said method for the purposes of the formation of an arbitration agreement. Accordingly, the Arbitration Act 1996 enables the valid formation of arbitration agreements under different circumstances, where the intention to arbitrate is manifested in a way meeting the bare minimum required by the law for the arbitration agreement to come into existence. Consequently, its incorporation by reference would potentially be possible.

1.3.3. Stay of Legal Proceedings

Arbitration in the UK is predominantly regulated under the Arbitration Act 1996, which includes a limited number of exceptions that may result in giving discretion to the court to intervene in the process.[142] For instance, the court may intervene if a party involved in the arbitration process challenges the award of the tribunal regarding its substantial

---

135 Robert Merkin and Johanna Hjalmarsson, *Singapore Arbitration Legislation*, 2016, Annotated, 2nd Edn., 17. See, *Midgulf International Ltd v Groupe Chimique Tunisien* [2010] EWCA Civ 66.

136 *Toyota Tsusho Sugar Trading Ltd v Prolat Srl* [2014] EWHC 3649 (Comm); [2015] 1 Lloyd's Rep 344.

137 *Maccaba v Lichtenstein* [2006] EWHC 1901 QB, concerns with recording of the agreement by the arbitrator.

138 Merkin and Flannery (n 68) 5.3.

139 Ibid. Also see *Petredec Ltd v Takumaru Kaiun Co (The Sargasso)* [1994] 1 Lloyd's Rep 162, *Fahem Co v Mareb Yemen Insurance Co* [1997] 2 Lloyd's Rep 738, *West of England Ship Owners Mutual Protection and Indemnity Association (Luxembourg) v Hellenic Industrial Development Bank SA* [1999] 1 Lloyd's Rep 93, *Barrier Ltd v Redhall Marine Ltd* [2016] EWHC 381 QB.

140 Merkin and Flannery (n 68) 5.4.

141 Ibid 6.1.5. (they are also not enforceable under the New York Arbitration Convention 1958).

142 English law confers upon a party dissatisfied with the conduct of the arbitration proceedings or the ultimate award various rights of challenge. The three grounds are (1) want of jurisdiction on the part of the arbitrators, (2) procedural unfairness in the conduct of the proceedings or some defect in the award, and (3) error of law in the award. See Incorporation of Standard Terms (n 38) Vol. 2, Ch. 20 'Challenging the Proceedings and the Award.'

jurisdiction,[143] if there is an alleged serious irregularity with the given award[144] or if a party involved in the arbitration proceedings goes to the appeal of the award given by the tribunal.[145] These are the exceptional circumstances that may lead to the intervention of the court in the arbitration process.

Nonetheless, it is also technically possible for a party to go to court despite the existence of a valid arbitration agreement. This often takes place when a decision pertaining to the validity of the incorporation of an arbitration agreement is to be given. Such a submission to the court may be considered to cause a clash of rights to go to a court and go to an arbitrator. It further creates the result that parties to the dispute to also be involved in a subsequent dispute concerning the resolution method applicable.

Section 9(1) of the Arbitration Act 1996 confers upon a party to an arbitration agreement, who is being sued in a court, the right to apply for a stay of court proceedings, even if there are other co-defendants, and who are not parties to such an arbitration agreement.[146] A party may apply to the court as soon as a dispute arises. In that case, the court does not decline to accept jurisdiction just simply on the grounds of the existence of an arbitration clause. This is because the reason behind a party directly going to the court might be that the party not accepting the validity of an existing arbitration agreement, or maybe the party is being disposed to breach such an agreement.[147] The invalidity of an arbitration agreement as the reason for commencing court proceedings may straightforwardly be justified since the existence of a valid arbitration agreement constitutes the fundamental element of any arbitral proceeding. In other words, if the party is unsatisfied with the validity of an arbitration agreement, then the party may commence court proceedings. In such a case, the court proceedings start and continue until the application of the other party for a stay is granted by the court. The party who wishes to be heard at the court opposes the application to stay. The stay does not mean that the court action necessarily commenced before the arbitral proceedings. The court proceedings may start after the arbitral proceedings have been begun, and these two might also continue to exist in parallel with each other.[148] These proceedings (arbitral and court) do not constitute by default obstacles for one another. Arbitration proceedings do not affect court proceedings unless one of the parties applies for a stay to be granted.

The party who wishes to activate the arbitration process and avoid court proceedings may apply for a stay if court proceedings commenced in breach of an existing arbitration agreement. This party against whom the legal proceedings are brought in respect of a matter which, under the agreement, is to be referred to arbitration, may apply to the

---

143 Section 67(1) of the Arbitration Act 1996.

144 Section 68(1) of the Arbitration Act 1996.

145 Section 69(1) of the Arbitration Act 1996.

146 Merkin and Flannery (n 68) 9.2. See *Wealands v CLC Contractors Ltd* [1999] 2 Lloyd's Rep 739.

147 Sutton, Gill, and Gearing (n 121) 349. It may also be possible that one of the parties to wait until an unfavourable award is received and then commence court proceedings in an inappropriate jurisdiction to attack the award; *C v D* [2007] EWHC 1541; 2 Lloyd's Rep 367; affd. [2008] 1 Lloyd's Rep 239. Also see *Noble v Gerling* [2007] 1 CLC 85. It was found in this case that the behaviour of the London reinsurer Gerling, in attempting to nullify the result of an arbitration by bringing a suit in another jurisdiction, was vexatious, oppressive and abusive of the process, and/or unconscionable. It was held that 'a collateral attack on a binding judgment or award of a properly constituted tribunal is capable of being oppressive conduct, at least as much as if the same proceedings had been commenced before the judgment or award had been given.'

148 Sutton, Gill, and Gearing (n 121) 349.

court in which the proceedings have been brought, to stay the proceedings so far as they concern that matter.[149] If there is a valid arbitration clause[150] in the contract that is provided by the party[151] who wishes the proceedings to stay, then the arbitration process would be effectuated, the court would decline to deal with the issues and require the parties to refer the matter to arbitration as they have agreed upon.[152] If the stay is granted, then the other party would be facing two options to proceed: They may wish to contend their existing claim to arbitration, or they might prefer not to pursue their claim at all as once the stay is granted, then there would be no other option of having it dealt with by the court.[153]

An arbitration clause may come in various forms.[154] However, regardless of its form, the principal requirement for the effectiveness of an arbitration clause is the manifestation of party autonomy concerning the referral of disputes to arbitration. Courts stay their proceedings[155] unless satisfied that the arbitration agreement from which the application to stay stems is null and void, inoperative, or incapable of being performed.[156] In other words, putting aside the exceptions,[157] which may give the court discretion to intervene in the arbitration process,[158] the assessment pertaining to possible invalidity, inoperability, and incapability of being performed constitutes the only inspection mechanism that the court possesses over the process of arbitration. On the other hand, the contents of Section 9 of the Arbitration Act 1996 may not be regarded as comprehensive as the section merely regulates the circumstances under which the court shall grant a stay. The section does not provide any further suggestions or guidelines regarding how exactly the matter is to be referred to arbitration after the stay is granted.[159]

149 Section 9(1) of the Arbitration Act 1996. Other parties to the proceedings should be given notice of such an application of stay of legal proceedings.

150 Stay was refused on the grounds that there was no arbitration clause in or incorporated into the agency agreement and a general assumption that anyone involved in football to be directly bound by the FA Rules regardless of the existence of a written agreement incorporating an arbitration was not justifiable in; *Bony v Kacou and Others* [2017] EWHC 2146 (Ch).

151 Therefore, the breach of an arbitration agreement would be the issue.

152 Brown and Marriott (n 50) 598.

153 Sutton, Gill, and Gearing (n 121) 349.

154 A specific arbitrator might have been identified by name or reference. If any system of law or institutional or *ad hoc* arbitration is to apply, that should be pointed out. If this is not done, the provisions of the Arbitration Act 1996 apply where parties involved are subject to English law and procedure. In international contracts, it is crucial to provide for a venue. See Brown and Marriott (n 50) 598, 26–013.

155 Under Arbitration Act 1950, a stay was discretionary, and the court could partly or even fully enter summary judgement on the grounds that there was no real defence and, therefore, no actual dispute. See *Halki Shipping Corporation v Sopex Oils Ltd.* [1998] 1 Lloyd's Rep 465; *Wealands v CLC Contractors Ltd* [1999] 2 Lloyd's Rep 739.

156 Section 9(4) of the Arbitration Act 1996.

157 For instance, one exceptional circumstance is the situation in which there is simply no agreement to which the arbitration clause can relate. *Soleimany v Soleimany* [1998] 2 WLR 811 (illegality).

158 Section 67, Section 68, and Section 69 of the Arbitration Act 1996 – and also Section 70 if we add the supplementary provisions on challenge or appeal.

159 In this sense, Section 9 of the Arbitration Act 1996 reflects Article (8) of the Model Law. However, Article (8) of the Model Law may be regarded as a relatively comprehensive and positive provision as it requires the matter to be referred to arbitration by the court on staying its proceedings. There is also similar wording in the New York Convention on the Recognition and Enforcement of Foreign Arbitral Awards 1958. This similarity was noticed and pointed out by Lord Mustill in *Channel Tunnel Group Ltd v Balfour Beatty Construction Ltd.* [1993] AC 334, 354–355. Article 11(3) of the New York Convention provides the requirement of 'the court to refer the parties to arbitration unless it finds that the said agreement is null and void, inoperative, or incapable of being performed.' Also see Merkin and Flannery (n 68) 9.

The impediment of the court's jurisdiction due to the stay of legal proceedings is a significant concept pertaining to arbitration agreements as they prevent a party involved in the dispute from being heard by a court. Accordingly, the incorporation of arbitration clauses from distinct contracts or documents may be considered to have equal importance as it may possibly lead to the emergence of the same outcome. In a single-contract scenario, it is generally more or less clear for everyone involved that a present or future dispute is to be referred to arbitration. In other words, the parties in this context would be more or less aware of the renunciation of their right to go to a court to be directly effective in case a dispute arises. Nonetheless, even in such a scenario, there may be disputes over the validity of an arbitration agreement. Having said that, it would be easier to comprehend the potential complexity that may arise when the incorporation of an arbitration clause from a remote document is the case. Under those circumstances, a fundamental concern would be to assess the limit of the extent of holding a third party bound by an arbitration clause that is included in a contract to which they are not a party. It is indeed crucial to determine the circumstances under which courts would approve the incorporation of an arbitration agreement while holding an 'outsider' party bound by it and would decide their right to go to a court is abolished. In other words, it is important to evaluate the circumstances under which third parties may be involved in arbitration due to the court being persuaded that their inclusion would not cause any unfairness.

A stay shall be granted if court proceedings were initiated in breach of a valid arbitration agreement. If these proceedings have been commenced pertaining to a dispute, which is claimed to be falling under the scope of an allegedly existing, valid and binding arbitration agreement, then the defendant may seek to stay proceedings pursuant to Section 9 of the Arbitration Act 1996 by giving an application notice.[160] A copy of the application notice pursuing a stay must be served on any party to the legal proceedings, regardless of whether they are within the jurisdiction or not.[161]

If a dispute arises concerning the existence of an arbitration agreement, the court will have four different options to choose from if arbitrators have the power to determine their own jurisdiction.[162] First, the court may decide on the basis of written evidence and conclude that there is a valid and enforceable arbitration agreement and that the dispute in question falls within its scope. Second, the court may grant a stay to leave the settlement of the dispute concerning existence or validity to the arbitral tribunal. Third, the court may order an issue to be tried under Civil Procedure Rules 1998 as to the existence, scope, or validity of the arbitration clause. Where there is a dispute concerning the conclusion of an arbitration agreement or the extent of its scope involving the subject matter of the court proceedings, the court may decide that question or give directions to enable it to be decided and order the proceedings to stay pending its decision.[163] Fourth, the court may decide that there is no arbitration agreement or that the subject matter before it does not fall within the scope of an existing arbitration agreement and dismiss the application to stay.

160 Rule 62.3(2) of the Civil Procedure Rules.

161 Rule 62.8(2) of the Civil Procedure Rules.

162 The classification to determine the options that the court may have if there is a dispute concerning the existence of an agreement that is referring the disputes to arbitration is provided in *Birse Construction Ltd v St Davids Ltd* [1999] BLR 194. This classification was also adopted in *Fiona Trust v Privalov Ors* [2007] 2 Lloyd's Rep 267.

163 Rule 62.8(3) of the Civil Procedure Rules.

The courts essentially investigate whether there is a valid arbitration agreement before they decide to grant a stay and they must be persuaded that the existence of an arbitration agreement is precluding the jurisdiction of the court. This means that courts do not accept a dispute before them to be referred to arbitration instead unless convinced the actual wish of the parties is to refer it so. Therefore, the main assessment of the courts is predominantly whether party autonomy concerning the referral of disputes to arbitration is appropriately manifested in the form of a valid and binding agreement.

Indeed, there are some special features of arbitration agreements. These may potentially interrupt and even preclude the jurisdiction of the courts. Concerning the incorporation of such profoundly effective agreements, courts have been inclined to seek the manifestation of clear and express indications to do so. Hence, it is a well-settled principle of English law that, for the purposes of incorporation of arbitration agreements, a clear and express reference to do so is required. Nevertheless, some issues inevitably arise. For instance, does such a strict requirement really reflect the realities of the commercial market that widely implements the incorporation of arbitration clauses as a shortcut? Furthermore, are there really any true justifications for these clauses to be treated in a different way than the rest of the contract terms? Further considering the ambiguity of Section 6(2) of the Arbitration Act 1996, one may rightfully argue that the creators of this particular legislation had the underlying intention to leave the matter to the discretion of the courts. By means of drawing very vague borders, the legislation leaves the matter to the individual evaluation of the courts on each specific case.

1.4. An Update on the Relevant Case Law – Cockett Marine Oil v ING Bank *[2019]*

Cockett Marine Oil DMCC v ING Bank NV & Anor,[164] which was decided by the High Court back in 2019, illustrates the effectualness of some concepts that have been examined in this chapter.

In *Cockett Marine*, two arbitration awards were challenged pursuant to Section 67 of the Arbitration Act 1996 on the grounds that the arbitral tribunal had no jurisdiction. The modest claims were for amounts due in connection with the supply of bunkers. With regard to (1) the vessel *Ziemia Cieszynska*, Cockett Marine (Dubai) purchased bunkers from OW Bunker Malta, who in turn purchased the bunkers from Eko Marine Fuels, and (2) with regard to the vessel *Manifesto*, Cockett Marine (Asia) purchased bunkers from OW Bunker Middle East, who in turn purchased the bunkers from GS Caltex. The tribunal held that it had jurisdiction because the terms of the contract between the parties included a London arbitration clause. The claimants contended that the terms of the contract did not include such a clause and so the tribunal did not have jurisdiction. The defendants sought to uphold the decision of the tribunal and contended on the grounds that the contract included a London arbitration clause. In respect of the supply of bunkers to the *Ziemia Cieszynska*, the question was whether, when the contract was concluded, OW Bunker Group's standard terms and conditions, which included the London arbitration clause, constituted a part of the contract either because they were incorporated by reference or they were incorporated by reason of a course of dealing between OW Bunker Malta and Cockett Marine (Dubai).

164 [2019] EWHC 1533 (Comm) (June 17, 2019) (*Cockett Marine*).

1.4.1. Method of Incorporation – Drawing the Attention or Ordinary Course of Dealing?

One of the essential issues to assess before the court was regarding the method of incorporation. There was the possibility of incorporation to have taken place due to sufficient steps being taken to bring the clause in question to the attention of the counterparty. Another probability was the ordinary course of dealing between the parties to create a similar result.

In 2013, OW Bunker Group (OWBG) altered their terms and conditions. Prior to alteration, their terms and conditions provided for Danish law and Danish arbitration. Their '2013 Terms and Conditions' provides for English law and London arbitration. OWBG employed an independent company, Concep, for the purpose of effectively communicating with their customers rather than handling the communication themselves.

There was no evidence from Concep as to the steps they took to inform customers about the alteration of the terms and conditions. However, OWBG was able to access Concep's web page and by using a password, access information about the 'campaign' regarding the alteration of terms and conditions. This particular method of access was the method provided by Concep to its customers to provide them with the opportunity to assess the success of the 'campaign.' This method was used by the IT manager of OWBG, who had not contacted Concep but was familiar with the type of technology. The IT manager was able to access a copy of the pro forma email, which was sent to the customers of OWBG and it stated, 'please find attached OWBG terms and conditions of sale for marine bunkers edition 2013 being valid from . . . OW Bunker Group – Terms and Conditions.pdf.'

The information available from Concep revealed that the letter was sent to a total of 6,985 recipients and the technology that Concep provided facilitated to detect which recipients viewed and clicked on the attachment. The information from Concep also indicated that the pro forma letter was sent to the email addresses of both Cockett Marine companies that are involved in the relevant proceedings (Cockett Dubai and Cockett Asia). The 'campaign history' recorded that Cockett Dubai email address viewed the '2013 Terms and Conditions' 22 times and that the link was clicked on twice. The 'campaign history' for the Cockett Asia email address recorded that the letter had been viewed six times. Cockett Marine adduced evidence from the two traders involved in this case that the IT department of Cockett Marine had not found a copy of the email in question. However, there was, in fact, evidence from Concep web page that the email was viewed by one of the traders of Cockett Marine and they indicated that they might have read the subject of the email but not the terms and conditions themselves as this was the role of another department.

Furthermore, the High Court considered whether the OWBG '2013 Terms and Conditions' could have been incorporated by way of course of dealing. Between September 2013 and October 2014, there were nine sales of bunkers by OW Bunkers Malta and Cockett Dubai. In each transaction there was a formal nomination by Cockett Dubai, which set out the sale and requested a copy of 'your terms and conditions,' and also a sales order confirmation (SOC) from OW Bunkers Malta which stated that the order was subject to OWBG's terms and conditions 'which are known to you and remain in your position' but in case they were not, a hyperlink was provided. The hyperlink was evidenced to take the user to the '2013 Terms and Conditions' that provides for English law and London arbitration, which could be found on the OWBG website.

Teare J was satisfied on the balance of probabilities that OWBG's '2013 Terms and Conditions' was brought sufficiently to the attention of two Cockett Marine companies that were involved in the proceedings. This was because, first, the unchallenged evidence of the IT manager of OWBG, who has long experience in many aspects of the bunker business having worked for OWBG for over 35 years, is that normally the seller's terms and conditions apply to bunker supply contracts. Second, the trader acting for Cockett Dubai accepted in the arbitration that it may be usual for the seller's terms to apply at each stage of the contractual chain. Third, Cockett Marine's standard form of nomination asked for a copy of the seller's latest terms and conditions. Fourth, considering the steps taken by OWBG in 2013 to inform their customers regarding their '2013 Terms and Conditions,' they would now presume to be doing business on the basis of these particular terms and conditions. Cockett Dubai were already aware of the '2013 Terms and Conditions,' but if they were not, they would be in the position to access them by clicking on the hyperlink provided. The learned judge referring to a former decision of his indicated 'in this day and age when standard terms are frequently to be found on websites I consider that reference to the website is a sufficient incorporation of the warehousing terms to be found on the website.'[165] He, therefore, concluded that the contract for the supply of bunkers was on OWBG's '2013 Terms and Conditions' follows that the arbitral tribunal had jurisdiction.

The learned judge decided that the '2013 Terms and Conditions' of OWBG was incorporated by means of taking sufficient steps to draw the attention of Cockett Marine to these provisions. On the other hand, another issue that the court had to investigate was whether the incorporation of these terms and conditions was also possible due to the ordinary course of dealing. Examining this possibility, the learned judge decided that he would also have held that the '2013 Terms and Conditions' was incorporated by the course of dealing that took place between the parties since September 2013. Therefore, Teare J reaffirmed himself concerning the aptness of incorporating warehousing terms by referring to the website they are contained at.

What 'each party says and does is such as to lead a reasonable person in their position to believe that those terms were governing their legal relations'[166] has been one of the fundamental tests to be applied in determining incorporation by a course of dealing in *Balmoral Group Ltd v Borealis by Clarke J.*[167] Furthermore, the sequence and continuity of events would constitute one of the fundamental elements of the concept of the course of dealing.[168]

With regard to both vessels, *Ziemia Cieszynska* and *Manifesto*, Cockett Marine communicated a desire to purchase bunkers. OWBG replied with a monetary proposal for the supply, and Cockett Marine accepted the proposal. Cockett Marine then issued its nominations and also requested a copy of the OWBG's terms and conditions. In their reply, OWBG acknowledged the relevant nominations of the Cockett Marine and indicated that the delivery be subject to OWBG's '2013 Terms and Conditions.' It was argued by Cockett Marine that a legally binding contract was formed in both cases when the quotation of the OWBG was accepted. Therefore, with the reference of OWBG to their '2013 Terms and Conditions' being made after the formation of the contract, they were not incorporated into the relevant contracts. This was dismissed by the court. One of the reasons for dismissal was

165 Teare J in *Impala Warehousing and Logistics v Wanxiang Resources* [2015] EWHC 25 (Comm) at [16]; Teare J in *Cockett Marine Oil DMCC v ING Bank NV & Anor* [2019] EWHC 1533 (Comm) at [23].

166 Christopher Clarke J in *Balmoral Group Ltd v Borealis* [2006] 2 Lloyd's Rep 629 at [348].

167 Ibid.

168 Ibid [356].

that when Cockett Marine confirmed their order, they included additional terms and most importantly demanded a copy of OWBG terms and conditions. This strongly suggested that Cockett Marine did not think a binding agreement had already been reached.[169] The further communication of Cockett Marine was considered by the court as a counter-offer.[170] By means of sharing its '2013 Terms and Conditions,' OWBG identified the conduct which would amount to acceptance of the offer as receiving the bunkers and Cockett Marine, by accepting the bunkers with the lack of objection, accepted the OWBG '2013 Terms and Conditions.' It was emphasized by Teare J that it was crucial to look at the entire course of negotiations to decide whether an apparently unqualified acceptance did in fact conclude an agreement.[171]

What was clear in *Cockett Marine* is that there were 9 trades between Cockett Dubai and OW Bunker Malta during the period of September 2013 and October 2014. Accordingly, the nature of the relevant commercial transactions was considered frequent. In each case, OW Bunker Malta provided that the sale and delivery were subject to OW Bunker's terms and conditions, which are known to Cockett Dubai, but in case they were not, a hyperlink was provided each time. It was indicated by Teare J that 'a reasonable person viewing those trades . . . would have concluded that those terms were to govern the parties' relationship.'[172] It was held clear that all nine trades were completed without a single objection especially pertaining to the applicability of the '2013 Terms and Conditions,' and this was indicating the acceptance of those terms.

1.4.2. An Aftermath of *Cockett Marine Oil v ING Bank*

The 2019 judgement of the High Court in *Cockett Marine* may be considered an important and fairly recent example of English case law pertaining to the incorporation of arbitration clauses as of August 2022. The court in this case was concerned with matters such as sufficient notification, incorporation by a course of dealing, and the objectively ascertainable knowledge and intention of the parties to a commercial contract. Hence, in that regard, the case captures the essence of this particular chapter and the legal point of incorporation.

Fundamentally, this was an unsuccessful appeal from two arbitration awards on the grounds that the tribunal had no jurisdiction. The main argument was that the relevant contracts did not incorporate the terms and conditions of an involved entity, which provided for London arbitration. The court examined the methods of notification that are adopted by the entity, which was wishing to incorporate its terms and conditions into the contract in question.

As indicated before, the burden of both bringing the terms to the other party's attention and proving to have done so would be on the party who wishes to incorporate their terms and conditions into the contract. OWBG in *Cockett Marine* may be argued to be providing us with an illustration of how to lighten such a burden. OWBG, making alterations to its terms and conditions, would like to notify all of its customers and take the efficient, professional, and commercially speaking 'sound' steps to do so. For the purposes of efficiently informing their customers OWBG employs a company, which would fulfil this

169 Teare J in *Cockett Marine Oil DMCC v ING Bank NV & Anor* [2019] EWHC 1533 (Comm) at [21].
170 [2019] EWHC 1533 (Comm) at [22].
171 Teare J in *Cockett Marine Oil DMCC v ING Bank NV & Anor* [2019] EWHC 1533 (Comm) at [21].
172 [2019] EWHC 1533 (Comm) at para [32].

task in a more professional manner. The system that this company provides OWBG with the information revealing whether the email, which contains the altered terms and conditions has been viewed, clicked on, or bounced back by each and every customer. Providing such information, this system may be considered a quite reliable one. Also, the employment of the system provider is a reasonable step that is taken to properly inform the customers. Concerning the timing of it, it is clear that the notice should be given before the contract is concluded or at the time the contract is being concluded. *Cockett Marine* provides us with clear answers both regarding the timing of the reasonable steps to be taken to inform the other party (OWBG to employ Concep) and also the indication of the intention to incorporate terms and conditions during the phase of offer and acceptance. Going back to basics, the judgement is indeed a significant one as it elucidates some aspects concerning the implementation of incorporation as a legal concept.

Furthermore, the court in *Cockett Marine* also investigates the applicability of incorporation by a course of dealing. It may perhaps be noted that the court did not have such a task in this particular case in view of the fact that incorporation had been sufficiently made by means of properly notifying the counterparty. The issue of whether there was the incorporation by course of dealing was an alternative one. Nevertheless, being an alternative, this possibility was also held subject to investigation.

There were nine trades between the parties involved between 2013 and 2014, and in each case, OWBG provided the sale and delivery of the bunkers to be subject to their terms and conditions. Furthermore, at each time, Cockett Marine was provided with a hyperlink directing the user to the '2013 Terms and Conditions' of OWBG. A reasonable person examining the ways in which these transactions are conducted would have no hesitation in making the deduction that these were governed by the '2013 Terms and Conditions.'

Furthermore, Cockett Marine had never objected to the application of the aforementioned set of rules. On each separate occasion, the OWBG sales order confirmation provided for these particular terms and conditions to be applicable, and Cockett Marine always accepted the delivery of bunkers without objection.

As indicated, for the establishment of an ordinary course of dealing, there should be both consistency and regularity concerning the way in which dealing is conducted. In *Cockett Marine*, the nine dealings between the parties show undeniable similarities as they are all concerned with the supply of bunkers to ships. Furthermore, the regularity of these dealings also fulfils the requirement regarding the incorporation by a consistent course of dealing. The judgement not providing a clear time frame regarding these nine separate occasions, this being the number of commercial transactions that have been completed in a period of 13 months, indeed seems quite frequent.

Last but not least, this case very well illustrates the objectively ascertainable knowledge of the parties. The professional company that OWBG employed provided the court with the 'objectively ascertainable knowledge' of Cockett Marine. This, indeed, is a very precious element of any court case and evidently, not that easy to ascertain in every case. This issue also reflects the very significant position of technology in the modern commercial age. What we witness here is a company trading with another on a regular basis. Also, from a company structure point of view, there are two separate branches of Cockett Marine involved in the transactions. To put it differently, two branches of Cockett Marine were informed regarding the alterations made concerning the applicable set of rules individually, and hence, Cockett Marine as an entity was informed at least twice. The information system that Concep provides for OWBG reveals whether the emails regarding the alteration of terms and conditions have been read and clicked on and also reveals how many times these actions took place. This was not good news for Cockett Marine as the records revealed that the Cockett Dubai email address viewed the terms and conditions 22 times and they had been clicked on twice, and the Cockett Asia email address recorded that they had been viewed six times. Reaching two-digit numbers of views of the email, the argument that the company was not aware of the alterations that were made concerning the terms and conditions applicable to their commercial conduct was indeed not very convincing. Accordingly, the court was of the view that the incorporation of the terms and conditions contained in the document that was viewed over 20 times was successful and accordingly, the London arbitration clause constituting a part of these provisions has also been incorporated.

1.5. Concluding Remarks

The notable lack of clarity of the requirements in order to achieve the incorporation of arbitration clauses highlights the need for the conspicuous supplement that the case law provides. To be able to efficiently examine whether the arbitration agreement is incorporated, the relevant case law should be elaborated, and also, the facts of each case should be taken into account. Essentially, English case law indicates that an imprecise reference to a contract is considered an inadequate attempt to incorporate the arbitration clause of it into the referring contract.

In this regard, the case law mostly suggests that if the incorporation of an arbitration agreement is intended, then a specific reference to such an agreement needs to be provided. However, cases should be individually analyzed by taking the facts of each of them into consideration. To be able to analyze the relevant cases, a distinction in contractual structure is necessary to be made. This is because the relevant provisions of the Arbitration Act 1996 do not provide clear-cut instructions to be followed by the parties to be assured that the incorporation of an arbitration agreement is successfully achieved. Nonetheless, it is evident that Section 6(2) of the Arbitration Act 1996 provides flexibility in allowing the incorporation of arbitration agreements by reference. However, when we get to the point of ascertaining the necessities to ensure that such incorporation is indeed successful, the Act fails to provide a clear answer. At this point, case law comes to the rescue.

The relevant English case law predominantly adopts an opposing view to the 'by-default incorporation' of an arbitration clause by reference. It is generally accepted that, even if a contract is incorporating the terms of another one, the incorporation of the arbitration clause would be subject to different criteria that necessitate a specific reference to be made to it. The justification for this timid adoption is provided as the lack of capability of some general words to reflect the intention of the parties to become subject to arbitration.[173] When it comes to the incorporation of arbitration clauses, the law is not straightforward since each case should be analyzed, taking its own individual facts and nature into account. The case law provides an irrefutably applicative method and categorizes contracts under

173 Di Pietro (n 1) 451.

two divisions – single-contract scenarios and two-contract scenarios[174] – which also draws a road map for the assessment of the incorporation of arbitration clauses.

The single-contract scenario fundamentally includes two contracting parties. However, this does not necessarily mean that the arbitration clause to be incorporated is not contained in a remote document that the parties are referring to. For instance, the document that is being referred to may be the standard terms and conditions of one of the parties to the contractual relationship. Whatsoever, this category solely involves two contracting parties, and hence, the links that the contractual relationship establishes under this category would be quite close and straightforward. The second situation involves multiple parties and contracts: A contract between A and B and a different contract between B and C, and B seeking to incorporate by reference into its contract with A the arbitration agreement contained in the agreement with C (or even between C and D). The most common examples of the second category are seen in shipping, reinsurance, and construction chain contracts as these inherently include subcontracts and multiple parties. However, for the time being, the most comprehensive division of contracts attempting to clarify the taxonomy of contracts was provided not in a shipping, insurance, or construction case but in a case that involved a sale dispute. It was indicated by Clarke J in *Habas Sinai v Sometal*,[175] in which there are four fundamental divisions that legal contracts may fall into the scope.[176] The relevant categorization indeed provides a road map for the evaluation of incorporation. The categories were created to shed light on the nature of contracts, especially when they are multi-layered. Hence, the relevant categorization may be adopted as a fundamental guideline examining the incorporation of contractual provisions. On that account, after the true contractual configuration of the relevant contract is identified, the incorporation of the arbitration clause would also be subject to the specific contract law test that certain configuration necessitates.

The reason that the 'scenarios theory' and, hence, the structural divisions of contractual configurations may fall under have only been briefly mentioned so far is to create a substantial understanding of the notion of incorporation of arbitration clauses. These divisions are analyzed in more detail in Chapter 2, 'Incorporation of Charterparty Arbitration Clauses into Bills of Lading.' It should be noted that the scenarios theory was created in *The Athena*[177] and was further elaborated in *Habas Sinai v Sometal.*[178] These cases were in fact concerned with insurance and sale disputes, respectively. In other words, the judgements did not pertain to shipping disputes. The reason these cases and, thus, the scenarios theory are discussed in the next chapter is that the adopted approaches in shipping law have mostly dominated other relevant areas of law that are concerned with chain contracts, such as reinsurance law and construction law, which are also inherently concerned with the concept of the incorporation of arbitration clauses. For many years, the relevant approaches adopted in the shipping context pertaining to the incorporation of arbitration clauses have set the sole

---

174 Ahmed (n 40).
175 [2010] EWHC 29.
176 Ibid [13].
177 This is established by Langley J in *Sea Trade Maritime Corporation v Hellenic Mutual War Risks Association (Bermuda) Ltd, The Athena (No 2)* [2006] EWHC 2530 (Comm) at [62]. See Merkin and Flannery (n 68) 6.2.1., 6.2.2.
178 [2010] EWHC 29.

guideline for the aforementioned branches of law. The strict approach regarding the notion of incorporation that is set out in the shipping context has been adopted in these branches of law in a blindfolded manner, regardless of each having different types of contractual structures and their own legal peculiarities. For instance, one of the fundamental reasons that is provided to be justifying the adoption of the strict approach in shipping contracts has always been their negotiable nature as a peculiarity. However, even though dealing with contracts that are not even remotely negotiable, the said branches of law followed the case law on shipping in time. However, the indicated recent cases, *The Athena*[179] and *Habas Sinai v Sometal*,[180] being non-shipping cases, possess the potential to change the perspective of the courts concerning the notion of incorporation of arbitration clauses. Shipping cases, for decades, created almost the sole guideline for reinsurance and construction cases that are concerned with the incorporation of arbitration clauses. The indicated cases here, being non-shipping cases (or neither being reinsurance nor construction cases) should not be underestimated considering the substantial impact they created on the matter. The contractual division – or, in other words, the 'scenarios theory' – as elaborated in *Habas Sinai v Sometal*, is providing a clear perspective to re-evaluate the contractual configurations in a way eluding the dominancy of the restricted rules of shipping.

Bibliography

Adler, Michael, Tribunal Reform: Proportionate Dispute Resolution and the Pursuit of Administrative Justice, 2006, *Modern Law Review*, 69, 958.

Ahmed, Masood, Arbitration Clauses: Fairness, Justice and Commercial Certainty, 2010, *Arbitration International*, 26(3).

Allen, Dominique, Against Settlement? Owen Fiss, ADR and Australian Discrimination Law, 2009, *International Journal of Discrimination and the Law*, 10.

Ambrose, Clare, Maxwell, Karen and Collett, Michael, *London Maritime Arbitration*, Informa Law from Routledge, 2018, 4th Edn.

Bernstein, Lisa E., Understanding the Limits of Court-Connected ADR: A Critique of Federal Court-Annexed Arbitration Programs, 1993, *University of Pennsylvania Law Review*, 141.

Brown, Henry and Marriott, Arthur, *ADR: Principles and Practice*, Sweet & Maxwell, 2011, 3rd Edn.

Chatterjee, Charles, The Reality of Party Autonomy Rule in International Arbitration, 2003, *Journal of International Arbitration*, 20(6), 539–560.

Di Pietro, Domenico, Incorporation of Arbitration Clauses by Reference, 2004, *Journal of International Arbitration*, 21(5), 439–452.

Dursun, Şeyda, A Critical Examination of the Role of Party Autonomy in International Commercial Arbitration and an Assessment of Its Role and Extent, 2012, *Yalova Üniversitesi Hukuk Fakültesi Dergisi*, 161–188.

Elliott, Mark and Thomas, Robert, Tribunal Justice and Proportionate Dispute Resolution, July 2012, *Cambridge Law Journal*, 71(2), 297–324.

Fagbemi, Sunday A., The Doctrine of Party Autonomy in International Commercial Arbitration: Myth or Reality?, 2015, *AFE Babalola University, Journal of Sustainable Development Law and Policy*, 6(1), 222–246.

179 [2006] EWHC 2530 (Comm).

180 [2010] 1 Lloyd's Rep 661.

Francioni, Francesca, *Access to Justice as a Human Right*, Oxford Scholarship Online, March 2012, Print Publication, 2007.

Francioni, Francesca, Acces to Justice, Denial of Justice and International Investment Law, in Dupuy, Pierre-Marie, Petersmann, Ernst-Ulrich and Francioni Francesca Francioni (eds.) *Human Rights in International Investment Law and Arbitration*, Oxford University Press, 2010.

Genn, Hazel, Fenn, Paul and Mason, Marc, *Twisting Arms: Court Referred and Court Linked Mediation Under Judicial Pressure*, Ministry of Justice Research Series 1/07, Ministry of Justice, May 2007.

Gunning, Isabelle R., Diversity Issues in Mediation: Controlling Negative Cultural Myths, 1995, *Journal of Dispute Resolution*, 1.

Incorporation of Standard Terms, *Merkin on Arbitration Law*, Incorporation of Standard Terms, 1991, Vol. 1, Ch. 5.

Lista, Andrea, *International Commercial Sales: The Sale of Goods on Shipment Terms*, Informa Law from Routledge, 2017.

MacDonald, Elizabeth, Incorporation of Contract Terms by a 'Consistent Course of Dealing,' March 1, 1998, *Legal Studies*, 8(1), 48–60.

Majumdar, Arjya B., Incorporation by Reference in Maritime Arbitration, 2013, *Transportation Law Journal*, 40, 91–112.

McGregor, Lorna, Alternative Dispute Resolution and Human Rights: Developing a Rights-Based Approach Through the ECHR, 2015, *The European Journal of International Law*, 26(3), published by Oxford University Press on Behalf of EJIL Ltd.

McKendrick, Ewan, *Contract Law, Text, Cases and Materials*, Oxford University Press, 2016, 7th Edn.

Menkel-Meadow, Carrie, Whose Dispute Is It Anyway?: A Philosophical and Democratic Defense of Settlement (In Some Cases), 1995, *Georgetown Law Journal*, 83, 2663–2696.

Merkin, Robert and Flannery, Louise, *Merkin and Flannery on the Arbitration Act 1996*, Informa Law from Routledge, 2020.

Merkin, Robert and Hjalmarsson, Johanna, *Singapore Arbitration Legislation*, Informa Law from Routledge, 2016, Annotated, 2nd Edn.

Moffitt, Michael, Three Things to Be Against (Settlement not Included), 2009, *Fordham Law Review*, 78(3), 1203–1245.

Noussia, Kyriaki, *Confidentiality in International Commercial Arbitration: A Comparative Analysis of the Position under English, US, German and French Law*, Springer, 2010.

O'Sullivan, Janet and Hillard, Jonathan, *The Law of Contract*, Oxford University Press, 1998, 7th Edn.

Özdel, Melis, Incorporation of Charterparty Arbitration Clauses into Bills of Lading: Peculiar to Maritime Law? in Malcom Clarke (ed.) *Maritime Law Evolving*, Bloomsbury, 2013.

Pryles, Michale, Limits to Party Autonomy in Arbitral Procedure, 2007, *Journal of International Arbitration*, 24(3), 327–339, Kluwer Law International.

Redfern, Alan, *Law and Practice of International Commercial Arbitration*, Oxford University Press, 2004, 4th Edn.

Scott, Ian Richard, The Courts and Alternative Dispute Resolution, in Julio C. Betancourt and Jason A. Crook (eds.) *ADR, Arbitration and Mediation, a Collection of Essays*, AuthorHouse, September 2014.

Shackelford, Elizabeth, Party Autonomy and Regional Harmonization of Rules in International Commercial Arbitration, 2006, *University of Pittsburgh Law Review*, 67, 897.

Steffek, Felix, Unberbath, Hannes, Genn, Hazel, Greger, Reinhard and Menkel-Meadow, Carrie (eds.) *Regulating Dispute Resolution: ADR and Access to Justice at the Crossroads*, Hart Publishing, 2013.

Sutton, David St John, Gill, Judith and Gearing, Mathew, *Russel on Arbitration*, Thomson, Sweet & Maxwell, 2007, 23rd Edn.

Tang, Zheng Sophia, *Jurisdiction and Arbitration Agreements in International Commercial Law*, Routledge, 2014, 1st Edn.

Tweeddale, Andrew and Tweeddale, Keren, *Arbitration of Commercial Disputes*, Oxford University Press, 2007.

CHAPTER 2

Incorporation of Charterparty Arbitration Clauses into Bills of Lading

2. Shipping and Arbitration

> Why is almost every robust healthy boy with a robust healthy soul in him, at some time or other crazy to go to sea? Why upon your first voyage as a passenger, did you yourself feel such a mystical vibration, when first told that you and your ship were now out of sight of land? Why did the old Persians hold the sea holy? Why did the Greeks give it a separate deity, and own brother of Jove? Surely all this is not without meaning. And still deeper the meaning of that story of Narcissus, who because he could not grasp the tormenting, mild image he saw in the fountain, plunged into it and was drowned. But that same image, we ourselves see in all rivers and oceans. It is the image of the ungraspable phantom of life; and this is the key to it all.[1]

The sea has always been an essential source of sustenance, and the majority of goods are carried by vessels every day. The carriage operations are predominantly conducted by virtue of shipping contracts, such as charterparties and bills of lading indicating the contents of the charterparties. To explain the fundamentals, charterparties contain the terms on which a ship is generally used, whereas bills of lading contain the terms on which goods are carried on a ship. The latter would essentially be made between the carrier and the person, who has an interest in the goods that are being carried (the holder of the bill of lading).

Bills of lading are issued by or on behalf of a carrier of goods by sea to the person with whom the carrier has contracted for the goods to be carried by sea and has an interest in the goods.[2] They reflect the charterparty, which is concluded between the shipowner and the carrier. The alignment of these two separate shipping documents usually constitutes one of the fundamental desires conducting a carriage operation. This is because the parties generally seek carriage operation to be subject to the provisions of shipping documents that are corresponding. Furthermore, the shipowner seeks to be bound by the provisions of a contract, which is known to them. Consequently, bills of lading incorporating charterparties for the purposes of aligning these contracts have been long used as a method of contract drafting.

However, there have been some relevant questions that attracted litigation over many cases. For instance, the scope of incorporation where a bill of lading contains an incorporation clause referring to a charterparty and the sufficiency of the employed words

1 Herman Melville, *Moby Dick*, Penguin Books, first published in 1851, 2012 Edn., 5.
2 Guenter Treitel and Francis Reynolds, *Carver on Bills of Lading*, Sweet & Maxwell, 2005, 1, 1–002.

DOI: 10.4324/9781003268673-3

to incorporate all or merely some of the provisions constitute issues to be assessed. If the words are apt merely to incorporate a few provisions, then which ones would these be? Moreover, what would the incorporation of charterparty arbitration clauses into bills of lading necessitate?

This chapter initially looks at the nature of the bills of lading and their relationship with charterparties under which they are being issued, for the purpose of understanding their specific characteristics. This is because bills of lading, being negotiable documents, are mostly subject to a different level of evaluation dealing with the notion of incorporation. Secondly, the incorporation of charterparty provisions and the comprehensiveness of incorporation within the shipping context is discussed. Under this part, a three-step test is provided for examining the sufficiency of the notion of incorporation. Thirdly, maritime arbitration and charterparty arbitration clauses are looked at taking the usually strict English approach concerning their incorporation into account. Arbitration has served as a common dispute resolution method for several decades, and hence, its incorporation constitutes the focal point of this chapter. To be able to provide a vivid illustration of the matter in English law, a chronological review of the relevant case law is also provided. Finally, the modern approaches concerning the incorporation of arbitration clauses are discussed considering the recent case law.

2.1. Bills of Lading and Charterparties

Bills of lading are unique documents in the sense that they serve multiple purposes:[3] They function as receipts for the goods shipped and describe the condition of these, they evidence the contract of carriage, and they are also documents of title. One of the most significant characteristics of bills of lading is also their negotiability. This particular feature of these documents constitutes

> one of the great legal concepts of the Western world, one that has been with us longer than democracy or human rights. It freed us from our atavistic dependence upon jewelry metal as our basic form of money, carried commerce across physical distances and political divides, and transformed banks from warehouses of valuables into financial intermediaries.[4]

The same peculiarity also constitutes one of the main considerations in dealing with bills of lading incorporating charterparty provisions. Hence, this part examines the background and nature of bills of lading, followed by their conjunction with charterparties.

2.1.1. The Nature and Legal Status of Bills of Lading

As pointed out, bills of lading describe the condition of goods that are shipped, they evidence the contract of carriage between the carrier and the shipper and also function as documents of title. For the purposes of this chapter, the matter of these documents

3 John F. Wilson, *Carriage of Goods by Sea*, Pearson Education Limited, 2010, 7th Edn., 117–142; Arjya B. Majumdar, Incorporation by Reference in Maritime Arbitration, 2013, *Transport Law Journal*, 40, 91–112, 98. Also see Richard Aikens, Richard Lord, Michael Bools, Michael Bolding and Kian Sing Toh, *Bills of Lading*, Informa, 2021, 19: 'Like an elephant, a bill of lading is generally easier to recognize than to define.'

4 Edward L. Rubin, Learning from Lord Mansfield: Toward a Transferability Law for Modern Commercial Practice, 1995, *Idaho Law Review*, 31, 775.

facilitating the transfer of title is not discussed in the following section.[5] This is because the transfer of title constitutes a subaltern concern from the aspect of incorporation of charterparty terms into bills of lading. Therefore, the general position of the holder of the bill of lading is considered regardless of whether them being a current or a subsequent holder.

2.1.1.1. Bills of Lading as Receipts

The general requirement for receipts to verify transactions has been a common practice since the beginning of the written word. For instance, the governing law of Babylon recognized only the transactions, which could be verified by a receipt in writing.[6] The concept of a bill of lading, being one of the vertebral bones of the carriage of goods by sea, has a parallel emergence with the commencement of trade by shipping. The feature of being 'the receipt of goods' still forms one of the substantial functions of the bills of lading in contemporary trade. A remark in the bill indicating that cargo has been shipped or received in apparently good condition likewise evidences the actual condition of the cargo at the time of shipment.[7] Furthermore, statements in the bill regarding the quantity, weight, or number of goods that are shipped have similar evidentiary functions.[8] The bills of lading simply are shipping documents indicating the records of certain goods as

5 The bill of lading represents the goods and possession of the bill of lading is treated as equivalent to possession of the goods covered by it, as stated by Bowen LJ in *Sanders v Mclean* [1883] 11 QBD 327 at 341: 'A cargo at sea while in the hands of the carrier is necessarily incapable of physical delivery. During this period of transit and voyage the bill of lading, by the law merchant, is universally recognised as its symbol and the indorsement and delivery of the bill of lading operates as a symbolic delivery of the cargo. Property in the goods passes by such indorsement and delivery of the bill of lading whenever it is the intention of the parties that the property should pass, just as under similar circumstances the property would pass by an actual delivery of the goods . . . it is the key which, in the hands of the rightful owner, is intended to unlock the door of the warehouse, floating or fixed, in which the goods may chance to be.' Also, an earlier case, *Lickbarrow v Mason* [1787] 2 Term Rep 63, addressed the issue of transfer or title and its relevance with the negotiable nature of bills of lading. It may be regarded one of the cornerstone cases regarding the title issue since it was accepted that the transfer of the bill of lading amounts to the transfer of title 'to' possess in the cargo covered by the bill. In other words, it is settled that the bill of lading is a negotiable instrument indicating the title. Even though it may be said that there is some obscurity on the definition of the terms, such as transferability and negotiability, common law recognizes the acquisition of constructive possession as a result of transfer by delivery, occasionally accompanied by endorsement, of certain sort of things in action which are regarded 'to be locked up in a document; Charles Debattista, *Bills of Lading in Export Trade*, Tottel Publishing, 2009, 3rd Edn., 66, 3.2. Also see Andrew Tettenborn, Transferable and Negotiable Documents – A Redefinition?, 1991, *Lloyd's Maritime and Commercial Law Quarterly*, 542: 'The definition of the concepts of transferability and negotiability is a difficult matter and one on which it is difficult to extract an uncontroversial view from either the decided cases or commentators.' Concerning the remote nature of this matter to the subject this part of the research is addressing, the function of bills of lading as documents of title is not discussed in this chapter.

6 Claude Hermann W. Johns, *Babylonian Law – The Code of Hammurabi: Encyclopedia Brittanica, 1910–1911*, The Avalon Project of Lillian Goldman Law Library of Yale Law School, 11th Edn., available at www.avalon.law.yale.edu/ancient/hammpre.asp (last visited May 28, 2019), 'The carrier gave a receipt for the consignment, took all responsibility and exacted a receipt on delivery. The warehouseman took all risks, paid double for shortage, but no claim could be made unless he had given a properly witnessed receipt.' For a more contemporary evaluation of receipts, also see Emily Farrar, The History of the Receipt, *Around the Box*, June 24, 2014, available at http://blog.shoeboxed.com/the-history-of-the-receipt/ (last visited May 28, 2019).

7 *The Lucky Wave* [1985] 1 Lloyd's Rep 80; *Oceanfocus Shipping Ltd v Hyundai Merchant Marine Co (The Hawk)* [1999] 1 Lloyd's Rep 176, 185.

8 *Smith v Bedouin Steam Navigation Co* [1896] A.C. 70.

having been loaded on a vessel.[9] Accordingly, these may also be considered 'bills of loading'[10] since they evidence that the carrier accepted the shipment of the goods, which are described in the bill, on the stated date, and agreed to transport the relevant goods.

Bills of lading emerged around the 14th century as non-negotiable receipts indicating the cargo has been received, and for the use of merchants, who are not travelling with their goods.[11] At that period, the negotiability of such bills was not really considered a necessity since trade usually did not possess an international and intricate character. Correspondingly, the shipowners essentially desired carriers to follow strict instructions and deliver the cargo to a specific agent at a certain port of destination. Around the 18th century, these bills started to gain their negotiable features due to the commercial desire of the merchants to dispose of the cargo even prior to the arrival of the vessel to its port of destination.[12] For the purposes of maintaining negotiability, bills of lading started to be issued without the name of a consignee, being blank, or in favour of 'bearer' or 'holder.'[13] In any case, the consignee/shipper holder of the bill is able to sell the cargo during its transport by virtue of the endorsement of the bill of lading to the next buyer. This fundamentally bestows negotiability to bills of lading.

The remarks on the bill of lading concerning the description and quantity of the cargo have significant commercial effects.[14] First, the indications on the bill of lading create a basis for any cargo claim of the receiver. An inconsistency between the actual physical condition and the remarks of the bill of lading regarding the quality and quantity of the cargo establishes the fundamentals of the cargo claim. Secondly, in c.i.f. documentary sales,[15] payment for the cargo is made against the delivery of documents and the buyer has the right to reject the documents in case they do not correspond with the specific remarks provided. Thirdly, the bill of lading is usually the only document that is indicating the quality and quantity of the shipped cargo, which is in the possession of the receiver during shipment. In that regard, the bill enables the sale of the relevant cargo during its transport. Hence, the statements on the bill of lading potentially affect the profitability of the cargo/negotiability of the bill because unless a clean bill stating cargo had been shipped in an apparently good condition is provided, 'the goods would not be readily saleable in

---

9 Nicholas Gaskell, Regina Asariotis, and Yvonne Baatz, *Bills of Lading: Law and Contracts*, LLP Professional Publishing, 2000, 2.

10 Thomas E. Johnson, *Export/Import Procedures and Documentation*, AMACOM, 2010, 124. Also see Bernard Eder, Howard Bennet, Steven Berry, David Foxton, and Christopher F. Smith, *Scrutton on Bills of Lading*, Sweet & Maxwell, 2011, 22nd Edn., 2, 1–002.

11 Wilson (n 3) 115.

12 Ibid.

13 Eder et al. (n 10) 2.

14 Wilson (n 3) 118.

15 Ibid. Also see Ewan McKendrick, *Goode on Commercial Law*, Penguin Books, 2010, 4th Edn., 1033–1042: Documentary sales may be classified as strict f.o.b., extended f.o.b., and c.i.f. In a strict f.o.b. contract, the seller is responsible for the cargo conforming to the contract has been put onboard the vessel, which is nominated by the buyer at the port of shipment by the time indicated in the contract and buyer supposed to possess documents which will enable them to obtain possession from the carrier. An extended f.o.b. contract extends the seller's obligations beyond the point of putting the goods over the vessel's rail but without involving him in procurement of the contract of carriage. In a c.i.f. contract, the seller does not undertake that the goods shall arrive but agrees, at his own expense, to procure and tender to the buyer the requisite shipping documents, such as bill of lading, policy of insurance, and commercial invoice and to transfer the property in the goods to the buyer at the due time for such transfer.

transit.'[16] To put it differently, unless a clean bill is provided, the negotiability of the cargo would get seriously compromised since the goods would not be considered fit for sale during their transit.

The holder of the bill of lading depends on the receipt function of the bill and the remarks on it to be indicating the actual good condition of the goods at the time of shipment. They depend on these because these usually constitute the only indicators of the condition of the relevant cargo from their perspective. In this regard, the remarks indicating the receipt is a 'confirming'[17] one may accordingly establish the carrier's liability if the goods are delivered in damaged condition.

The legal position of the bill of lading holder matters concerning the assessment of the allocation of liability. In English law, the bill of lading represents *prima facie* evidence between a carrier and a shipper. Accordingly, it establishes 'evidence which raises a refutable presumption of fact; it stands until rebutted; it, therefore, cannot establish more than probability, but probability which may be displaced by evidence.'[18] Under these circumstances, 'the burden of proof that the statements in the bill of lading are inaccurate falls on the carrier.'[19] However, once the bill of lading is transferred to a third party, the dynamics of this legal structure are modified. In that case, the bill of lading is considered conclusive evidence of the terms of the contract of carriage provided the third-party endorsee acted in good faith and the carrier is estopped from denying the accuracy of statements in a bill of lading against such a transferee.[20]

2.1.1.2. Bargaining Power and Cargo Claims

As stated earlier, negotiability enables the trade of cargo in transit to be conducted rapidly and provides convenience. Facilitating the trade of the relevant cargo through the trade of documents representing its quantity and quality, the negotiable character of the bills of lading, 'carried commerce across physical distances and political divides.'[21] One of the fundamental cases considering the matter of negotiability of bills of lading is *Thomas v Portsea.*[22] The established approach in this case was adopted in many subsequent judgements.

The negotiable character of bills of lading constitutes the underlying reason that their holders lack information concerning the scope and provisions of the charterparty that the bill of lading is issued under. Indeed, the bill of lading ordinarily passes from hand to hand and when it does so, it is seldom for its holder to have information pertaining to charterparty provisions. Accordingly, in *Thomas v Portsea*, the remarks on the bill of

16 Wilson (n 3) 118.

17 Melis Özdel, The Receipt Function of the Bill of Lading: New Challanges, 2017, *International Company and Commercial Law Review*, 28(12), 435–442, 436: buyers usually 'wish to part with their money against the tender of a "conforming" receipt: a receipt covering the contract goods and showing that the goods were in apparent good order and condition at the time of their shipment.'

18 *The Draupner* [1910] AC 450; Stephen Girvin, *Carriage of Goods by Sea*, Oxford University Press, 2011, 2nd Edn., 6.04.

19 Časlav Pejović, *Transport Documents in Carriage of Goods by Sea*, Informa Law from Routledge, 44.

20 Ibid. Also see *Leduc v Ward* [1888] 20 QBD 475.

21 Rubin (n 4).

22 *T W Thomas & Co Ltd v Portsea Steamship Co Ltd, The Portsmouth* [1910] P. 293; [1911] P. 54 (CA); [1912] AC 1 (at the House of Lords the case was referred as *T W Thomas & Co Ltd v Portsea Steamship Co Ltd* instead of *The Portsmouth* as it was referred as at the Divisional Court and Court of Appeal) (*Thomas v Portsea*).

lading were considered to be the sole indicators of the features of the cargo in transit from the perspective of the holder of the bill.

Indeed, the awareness of the subsequent holders of bills of lading is restricted by what is provided on the face of the bill. However, this transfer also means the passing of the title and hence, the contract between the shipper and the carrier to pass.[23] Such transfer necessitates the evaluation of whether the new transferee is expected to be familiar with the full extent and details of the transferred carriage contract. It should be noted that such a transfer is made by virtue of the negotiable character of the bill. This means that the property is accepted in good faith. Negotiability, as a legal concept, diminishes such an expectation to be imposed on the third-party transferee.

The level of power concerning the bargaining of the provisions to govern the carriage operation significantly differs depending on the type of shipping document it is concerned with.[24] Bill of lading, being issued under the charterparty, creates a relatively 'unequal position' concerning such bargaining power. The terms of the charterparty are usually negotiated between parties with equal or similar bargaining powers whereas the terms of carriage under the bill of lading may not be negotiated between the subsequent holder of the bill and the carrier.[25] Although there is a possibility 'for shippers to negotiate with carriers, it is not always possible to see a balance between the bargaining positions of these parties.'[26] Concerning bills of lading, the preponderance of the carrier is usually favoured over the shipper and the latter is generally only given the prepared bill. The shipper (or the subsequent consignee) does normally not have equal bargaining power with the carrier over the terms of the bill.

Pursuant to Section 2(1) of the Carriage of Goods by Sea Act 1992 (COGSA 1992), the lawful holder of the bill has the title to sue under the contract of carriage as if they are an original party to it. The right to sue is vested in the lawful holder of the bill regardless of whether they possess the goods that are indicated in the bill. In other words, a shift between the parties to the contract of carriage takes place through the transfer of the bill of lading to its subsequent holder. Because even the shipper usually lacks equal bargaining power with the carrier concerning the terms of carriage, the subsequent transferee of the bill may not be expected to have much of a saying regarding its terms. Accordingly, the subsequent holders of bills of lading may not expect to fully acknowledge the charterparty provisions as they usually do not contribute to their negotiation.

Bill of lading holders lacking bargaining power concerning the terms of carriage necessitate their protection. If the cargo in transit is sold during its transportation, the subsequent holder of the bill of lading would be subject to the same terms and conditions as the original holder of the bill.[27] In other words, as well as the original holder of the bill of lading, the subsequent holder also lacks the opportunity to examine the contents of the charterparty. Once the bill of lading is transferred to a subsequent holder, regardless of

23 Majumdar (n 3) 99.

24 Carlos Esplugues Mota, Validity and Effects of the Incorporation by Reference of Arbitration Agreements in International Maritime Arbitration: Current Situation and Future Trends, *Social Science Research Network*, May 20, 2012, 9, available at https://ssrn.com/abstract=2063117 (last visited May 28, 2019). See *The Ardennes* [1951] KB 55, 59–60 for the assessment of the imbalance of bargaining power between the shipper and the carrier.

25 Melis Özdel, *Bills of Lading Incorporating Charterparties*, Hart Publishing, 2015, 159.

26 Ibid.

27 Majumdar (n 3) 100.

how many times this particular shipping document is endorsed, the legal status of all of its subsequent *bona fide* holders is considered the same: oblivious to the full scope of the charterparty due to lack of bargaining power and, hence, in need of greater legal protection and commercial certainty. Furthermore, it is historically true that carriers may occasionally try to exculpate themselves from liability for the damage caused by their own negligence by means of abusing their superior bargaining powers.[28] The inequality of the bargaining power between the holder of the bill of lading and the carrier has a direct impact on the terms of the bill of lading[29] as well as cargo claims that may arise.

Bills of lading provide the description, quantity, nature, marks, and packing of the cargo received by the carrier. Therefore, they establish the basis for any claims relevant to the cargo, such as damage or short delivery. English law provides freedom and flexibility to the parties to a contract of carriage pertaining to the negotiation of their own terms. However, it also adopts the Hague/Visby Rules that are created to protect the cargo owners from the excessive implementation of exclusion clauses that waves the liability of the carriers. These essentially necessitate some standard rules to be incorporated into the bills of lading to protect third parties.[30] These rules, due to their imperative nature, are attached to the Carriage of Goods by Sea Act 1971 and constitute an indispensable part of any document relevant to the carriage of goods by sea under English law.

Statements indicating the quantity of the cargo in a bill of lading as well as the ones concerning the apparent order and condition of the cargo are considered conclusive evidence in the hands of a third-party consignee or endorsee who is acting in good faith.[31] It would be unreasonable to expect the shipper/buyer of the cargo to exercise a comprehensive or even a brief examination of the cargo at the port of loading. The port may be in a different country and the shipper/buyer may not have any agents, who may conduct such an investigation at that location. Accordingly, bills of lading save the shipper/buyer from a potential incubus as they provide them with the information pertaining to the quantity and the apparent condition of the shipped cargo,[32] without the need for an on-site investigation of such. Any inaccuracy on a bill of lading regarding the quantity, quality, weight, leading marks, and condition of the cargo potentially causes severely undesired outcomes. Most importantly (as a clean bill of lading would be considered a 'confirming' one for its third-party holder acting in good faith),[33] the remarks on the bill are considered conclusive evidence pertaining to cargo condition from the point of the holder. If there is an inconsistency between the remarks of the bill of lading and the actual physical condition of the cargo in question, the claim of the bill of lading holder usually prevails over any defence that may be set forth by the carrier.[34] Furthermore, it would be most likely that the shipowner to lose their right to limit their liability for the shortage or damage of the goods where such an inconsistency exists.

---

28 Richard L. Kilpatrick, Jr., The Joint and Several Liability of 'Merchants' Under Maritime Bills of Lading, October 2016, *Journal of Maritime Law & Commerce*, 47(4), 423–424.

29 Mota (n 24) 9.

30 Wilson (n 3) 174.

31 Art III Rule 4 of Hague/Visby Rules – The Hague Rules amended by the Brussels Protocol 1968

32 Debattista (n 5) 126, 6.4.

33 Özdel (n 17).

34 *Gard Guidance of Bills of Lading*, March 2011, available at www.gard.no/Content/20651968/Gard%20Guidance%20bills%20of%20lading%20March%202011.pdf (last visited May 28, 2019).

2.1.1.3. Legal Status and Evidence Function of Bills of Lading

Lord Bramwell in *Sewell v Burdick* states, concerning the legal status of bills of lading, 'To my mind there is no contract in it. It is a receipt for goods stating the terms on which they were delivered to and received by the ship and therefore excellent evidence of those terms but it is not a contract.'[35] The bills of lading are vital documents on the part of carriers as they reveal the features such as 'quantity and description of the goods with the condition in which they were received'[36] and, therefore, possibly indicate the damage or loss that occurred subsequent to loading of the goods.

Indeed, bills of lading serve a significant evidentiary purpose. However, Lord Goddard CJ confidently states pertaining to the legal status of bills of lading in *The Ardennes* that

> It is I think well settled that a bill of lading is not, in itself, the contract between the shipowner and the shipper of the goods, though it has been said to be excellent evidence of its terms . . . The contract has come into existence before the bill of lading is signed. The bill of lading is signed by one party only and handed by him to the shipper, usually after the goods have been put on board. No doubt if the shipper finds that it contains terms with which he is not content, or that it does not contain some term for which he has stipulated, he might, if there were time, demand his goods back, but he is not in my opinion thereby prevented from giving evidence that there was a contract which was made before the bill of lading was signed and that it was different from that which is found in the document or contained some additional term. He is not a party to the preparation of the bill of lading, nor does he sign it.[37]

Accordingly, at least for the purposes of this chapter, carriage operations take place subject to the governance of two fundamental documents.

> While the charterparty is that document which embodies the written form of the vessel's charter agreement, containing the terms and conditions which govern the relationship between the shipowner and the charterer, the bill of lading is that transport document which relates to the cargo carriage, governs the relationship between the shipper and the carrier and it is issued either upon the goods being received for shipment (received for shipment bill of lading) or traditionally, upon their shipment on board the ship (shipped bill of lading).[38]

Thus, from a legal perspective, these are indeed disjoint documents with provisions applicable to different parties.

The phrase 'contract of carriage' applies to contracts, which are

> covered by a bill of lading or any similar document of title, in so far as such document relates to the carriage of goods by sea and issued under a charterparty from the moment at which such bill of lading or similar document of title regulates the relations between a carrier and a holder of the same.[39]

---

35 [1884] 10 App. Cas at [105].

36 Wilson (n 3) 118.

37 *The Ardennes* [1951] 1 K.B. 55, 59–60.

38 Evi Plomaritou and Yiannis Voudouris, The Relationship of Bill of Lading, Charterparty and Other Transport Documents, 2019, *Journal of Economics, Management and Trade*, 24(6), 1–8, no. JEMT 51423, 2. Also see Evi Plomaritou and Anthony Papadopoulos, *Shipbroking and Chartering Practice,* Lloyd's Practical Shipping guides, Informa Law from Routledge, 2018, 8th Edn.

39 Art I (b) of Hague/Visby Rules – The Hague Rules amended by the Brussels Protocol 1968.

The involvement of multiple parties to carriage operations creates a 'wide range of permutations as to number of contracts, the parties to them and their rights and obligations.'[40] Accordingly, there may be different contracts of carriage that are made prior to the issuing of the bill of lading as well as there may solely be booking notes[41] reserving a space on the vessel. Because in contemporary trade it is highly likely that a space for the cargo is usually booked well in advance,[42] it is not wrong to say that 'there is almost always an antecedent contract'[43] pertaining to a carriage. However, such a contract would generally have been made without taking any formalities into account and would come into existence at the end of a series of negotiations. Thus, the key issue would be to determine whether the outcome of such negotiations actually matured to form a contract. Each case should be evaluated regarding its own circumstances taking the general principles of contract formation into account. Nevertheless, this may be difficult to assess in the shipping context because the contract contained in or evidenced by the bill of lading often does not contain the signatures of all parties, and this situation makes the analysis of offer and acceptance with regard to contract formation difficult.[44]

Once the contract of carriage is identified, the bill of lading is presumed to be evidencing the terms of this particular contract between the carrier and the shipper. Concerning this evidentiary function, the identification of what is truly evidenced is important. Firstly, it should be evaluated if the parties have actually reached an agreement at the end of the negotiation process and, if they had so, whether that agreement is in compliance with the basic principles of contract law. Secondly, it should be determined if the parties evinced any intention to defer the effect of the agreement until a subsequent point, frequently until they reach an agreement upon further terms[45] or until they pen the agreement.[46]

Concerning the evidentiary function of bills of lading, the shipper may not be asked to accept unexpected or onerous terms that are inconsistent with the bill of lading. In the case of incompatibility or incompleteness in the bill of lading, the shipper has the right to demand their cargo back or as this was the case in *The Ardennes*, and if the cargo had been shipped, the shipper may claim the damages at the vessel's expense. However, if the shipper knows (or ought to have known) that the ship is under charter, then they are not entitled to refuse a bill of lading incorporating charterparty provisions.[47]

---

40 Aikens et al. (n 3) 189.

41 Described by Hobhouse LJ in *Cho Yang v Coral* [1997] 2 Lloyd's Rep 641, 643–644.

42 *The Ardennes* [1951] 1 KB 55.

43 The 'contract' might be in various types such as a contract of carriage, a booking note, a shipping note, a fixture note and other types. *Gulf Steel Co Ltd Al Khalifa Shipping Co (The Anwar Al Sabar)* [1980] 2 Lloyd's Rep 261, 263.

44 Aikens et al. (n 3) 188.

45 *Hofflinghouse & Co Ltd v C-Trade SA (The Intra Transporter)* [1985] 2 Lloyd's Rep 158; affirmed [1986] 2 Lloyd's Rep 132.

46 Eder et al. (n 10) 7, 1–018.

47 *Ralli Brothers v Paddington Steamship Company Ltd.* [1900] 5 Com. Cas. 124. For the arguments on whether this case is still good law or not, see Julian Cooke and Timothy Young, *Voyage Charters*, LLP Professional Publishing, 2007, 3rd Edn., 18.47.

2.1.2. Charterparties and the Need for Alignment of Documents in Shipping

The other fundamental document of carriage of goods by sea is the charterparty. The term originally derives from the Latin *carta partita*, which means a document written duplicate on a singular sheet, cut in two pieces, and given to signatories.[48] A charterparty is a contract of affreightment, where the shipowner puts their vessel or an ascertained part of the vessel at the charterer's disposal for a specific voyage or for a particular period of time.[49]

Thus, the charterparty is concluded between the shipowner and a charterer and essentially pertains to the hire of a vessel whereas bills of lading pertain to cargo carried on the vessel in question. Accordingly, these are indeed disjoint documents. Their disjoint nature is preserved even when the bill of lading incorporates the terms of the charterparty.[50]

Parties often seek to incorporate provisions included in separate or remote documents into a contract and this to create binding results. This practice is especially crucial in shipping. Parties in shipping almost always seek to incorporate the terms of the charterparty into bills of lading. It is particularly important in the shipping industry that the provisions of the indicated documents correspond to avoid any possible conflict that may arise from the operation of inconsistent provisions governing the carriage. Accordingly, it is common practice for the carrier to make the terms and conditions of the charterparty applicable to the bill of lading by stamping on the bill of lading an incorporation clause indicating that the bill shall be subject to the terms and conditions of the charterparty.[51]

If the goods are shipped by a third party, normally the third party remains unaffected by the provisions of the charterparty regardless of their possible awareness of its existence.[52] It is also evident that the third party would not be bound by the provisions of the charterparty that conflict with the terms of the bill of lading. However, shipowners are mostly

> anxious to ensure that their liability as carriers is not extended by the issue of bills of lading by the charterers, and to avoid this, insist on the inclusion in such bills of a clause incorporating the terms of the charterparty.[53]

The failure to align documents may possibly create the result 'that the carrier to become liable for damage to cargo under the bill of lading without being able to invoke agreed exemptions under the charterparty or to seek redress from the charterer.'[54]

Another important issue is the establishment of alignment pertaining to applicable laws and dispute resolution methods. Bills of lading incorporate charterparties simply to align such provisions the shipping operation is subject to so that parties to this multi-layered contractual configuration do not face claims that they are unaware of their potential to arise. Even if these arise, alignment of documents, if done successfully, facilitates disputes to be settled by a certain resolution method and is subject to the application of a certain jurisdiction and rules.

48 Eder et al. (n 10) 5. Or simply, 'divided document.'
49 McKendrick (n 15) 1143.
50 Plomaritou and Voudouris (n 38) 3.
51 Ibid.
52 Wilson (n 3) 247.
53 Ibid.
54 Plomaritou and Voudouris (n 38) 7.

2.2. *The Incorporation of Charterparty Terms into Bills of Lading*

The charterparty and bills of lading of a shipping operation are disjoint in the sense that they predominantly reflect the provisions applicable to different legal aspects of the operation between different parties. On the other hand, they have undeniable conjunction as the bills of lading are issued under the charterparty. In other words, the charterparty constitutes the main source, and therefore, the reference point of the bill of lading. The bill of lading may have multiple subsequent holders due to its negotiable character. The subsequent holders would also be subject to the provisions of the bill of lading, which are reflecting the terms of the charterparty. This contractual setup raises the inevitable question of whether the holder of the bill of lading could be held subject to the provisions of the charterparty that they are not completely familiar with.[55]

Incorporation of charterparty terms into bills of lading by reference as a contract drafting method has been well accepted and efficaciously used in many jurisdictions.[56] In the shipping context, the negotiable character of bills of lading usually necessitates the adoption of a restricted/strict approach concerning the incorporation of charterparty terms that are not particularly pertaining to receipt, carriage, or delivery of cargo and payment of freight. The substantial reasons for such adoption are usually contended to be '(1) the status of bills of lading as negotiable commercial instruments, (2) the jurisdictional consequences of such incorporation, and (3) the significance of promoting certainty in this area.'[57]

The predominant issues to be assessed concerning incorporation as a legal concept are the effectiveness and scope of it. Accordingly, the fundamental examination of whether incorporation takes place should be a twofold one. First, the effectiveness and sufficiency of the incorporation clause should be assessed. Second, if the construction of the clause is considered effective and sufficient, then its scope should be determined next. The latter assessment would help to identify the provisions that truly fall into the scope of the incorporation clause and thus are presumed incorporated. Therefore, in the following section, the concept of incorporation in general and the essential issues concerning the construction of incorporation clauses are explored first. Second, a three-step test which facilitates the assessment of the terms to be incorporated is provided.

2.2.1. Incorporation in Shipping Documents and the Construction of Incorporation Clauses

The assessment of the charterparty terms that are incorporated into bills of lading is a matter of contract construction and a crucial one to make. Such an assessment indicates the legal tools that are at the disposal of the parties against each other in the case a cargo dispute arises. A fundamental desire in shipping operations is the alignment of documents so that the holders of the bill of lading are prevented from bringing claims under provisions, rules, or jurisdictions that are unfamiliar to the shipowner. Accordingly, one of the main objectives of incorporation is the elimination of the risk of having unexpected legal encounters. Harmonization of documents generally facilitates shipping operations to carry out smoothly.

55 *Watkins v Rymill* [1883] 10 Q.B.D 178.
56 Mota (n 24).
57 *Siboti K/S v B P France SA* [2003] EWHC 1278 (Comm), [34]; [2003] 2 Lloyd's Rep 364, 372.

Bills of lading often contain only a number of express terms themselves. Nonetheless, they generally contain an incorporation clause that usually provides some or all charterparty terms to be incorporated into the bill. If successful, such a clause brings the referred terms into the bill of lading and redefines the boundaries of the legal relationship.

A bill of lading incorporation clause may be drafted as a specific (precise) or a general one concerning the rules of construction.[58] It may be drafted in a way involving a particular name or a number that refers to a certain charterparty provision, such as 'destination as per,'[59] 'including clause 30,'[60] or 'law and arbitration clause of'[61] the identified charterparty. This sort of structure indicates that the incorporation clause is a specific one and usually necessitates the assessment of the incorporated charterparty provisions. It would be useful to indicate at this point that, as a common rule, the general words of incorporation usually incorporate 'only those clauses of the charterparty which are applicable to the contract in the bill of lading,'[62] whereas the specific words would usually 'be *prima facie* effective even to incorporate clauses that are not applicable or germane to the receipt, carriage or delivery of the cargo.'[63]

2.2.1.1. Formation and Structure of Incorporation Clauses

Due to different practical necessities and the complex and unique structure of each shipping operation may bring to light, a large variety of incorporation clauses exist. Hence, the structure of the incorporation clause may differ in each document to cater to the wishes of the parties and reflect the needed level of preciseness in different carriage operations. Nevertheless, it is true that shipping law is quite formalistic concerning its requirements of the bare minimum to allow the incorporation of provisions that are not exactly germane to the receipt, carriage, or delivery of the cargo. In that regard, it may be noted that the underlying intention of the parties in drafting a certain incorporation clause may perhaps be considered to a certain level while assessing whether incorporation takes place. However, especially in the shipping context, such an assessment is primarily done so by taking the well-established interpretations of some widely known market phrases of incorporation into account for the sake of promoting legal and commercial certainty.[64]

I. 'Freight and All Other Conditions per Charter'

The phrase 'freight and all other conditions per charter' may be regarded as one of the simplest forms of incorporation clauses in the shipping context. This formation is usually only effective to incorporate the clauses of the charterparty, which are to be performed

---

58 *The Varenna* [1983] 1 Lloyd's Rep 416 at [421].

59 *S.I.A.T. di del Ferro v Tradax Overseas Ltd* [1980] 1 Lloyd's Rep 53.

60 *The Merak* [1964] 2 Lloyd's Rep 527.

61 *The Channel Ranger* [2014] EWCA Civ 1366. The bill of lading involved an incorporation clause indicating 'law and arbitration clause' in the charterparty. However, the charterparty involved an 'English law and court jurisdiction clause' and not a 'law and arbitration clause.' It was held that the phrase 'law and arbitration' was sufficient to incorporate the English law and court jurisdiction clause into the bill of lading.

62 *Gardner v Trechmann* [1884] 15 QBD 154, 157. See *T. W. Thomas & Co. Ltd. v Portsea Steamship Co Ltd, The Portsmouth* [1912] A.C. 1. (*Thomas v Portsea*).

63 Aikens et al. (n 3) 222, 7.100.

64 Ibid 225, 7.109. Also see *Federal Bulk Carriers Inc v C Itoh & Co Ltd (The Federal Bulker)* [1989] 1 Lloyd's Rep 103.

by the holder of the bill of lading or the ones relevant to the discharge of the cargo.[65] Accordingly, it is generally only relevant to the expected liabilities of the consignee and the charterparty terms pertaining to the discharge or receipt of the cargo.

An incorporation clause structured in this way consisting of very simple and straightforward wording usually only suffices to incorporate terms of the charterparty that are supposed to be performed by the consignee. To put it differently, any clause that functions to remove or restrict the liability of the carrier must be specifically referred to as stated in *Diederichsen v Farquharson*.[66] This is because such a function is usually not accepted to be provided by the employment of these sorts of words of incorporation. In the said case, in addition to a deck cargo at the merchant's risk, cargo of timber was also loaded on a vessel under a bill of lading. The bill of lading contained an incorporation clause as 'freight and all other conditions as per charterparty.' However, it did not include any reference to such deck cargo. Shipowners brought an action against the consignees regarding the freight for some part of the cargo that has been carried on deck. Consignees defended the claim indicating damage to their cargo. It was held that, since such an incorporation clause only incorporates the terms, which were to be performed by the consignee, the shipowners are not exempted from their liabilities regarding the deck cargo since there was no reference to such an exemption. The provision concerning the exemption of the carrier's liability held not to be incorporated into bills of lading as such was not referred to.

This formation is presumed to be referring to the features of the shipping operation that are concerned with the receipt or discharge of the cargo. An incorporation clause constructed in this way usually does not apply to the terms, which would not make sense in the context of the bill of lading. To put it differently, incorporation must pass the compatibility test. In *Gullischen v Stewart*,[67] cargo was shipped under two bills of lading, which included the term 'the paying freight and all other conditions as per charterparty.' The charterparty that the defendants were entered into anticipated the liability of the defendants to cease as charterers as soon as the cargo was loaded. The vessel was holding a lien upon the cargo for freight and demurrage. Subsequently, demurrage took place at the port of discharge. The court proceedings due to such delay were initiated by the owners against the charterers. The consignee defendants claimed the validity of the charterparty cesser clause, which indicated the cessation of their liability once the cargo was loaded. Due to the inexplicability and incompatibility a cesser clause would create in the context of a bill of lading, the incorporation of the cesser clause was held ineffective. Consequently, defendants as consignees were held liable for the demurrage that occurred at the port of discharge.

The definitions in the charterparty concerning the identification of the person to whom the freight shall be paid, the terms regarding the rate of freight, and the details of the payment generally fall under the inclusiveness of the simplistic formation of an incorporation clause drafted as such. This specific issue was addressed in *India Steamship Co v Louis Dreyfus Sugar Ltd (The Indian Reliance)*.[68] In this case, the payment that is made by the sub-

65 Eder et al. (n 10) 99, 6–019.
66 [1898] 1 Q.B. 150 (CA).
67 [1883–1884] LR 13 Q.B.D. 317.
68 *The Indian Reliance* [1997] 1 Lloyd's Rep 52.

charterer to the assigned account of the time charterer was considered a valid one, which has been made under the charterparty. Thus, it was held that, although the time charterer had become insolvent before making the payment for time charter hire, the shipowner was not entitled to claim the freight from the sub-charterer.

II. 'All Conditions and Exceptions per Charterparty'

'All conditions and exceptions per charterparty' may be regarded as a more comprehensive incorporation clause as it usually enables the incorporation of charterparty exclusion clauses (and possibly negligence clauses) as long as these are being expressly referred to. In other words, it may be possible for the bills of lading to be subject to the expected perils in the charterparty by virtue of drafting an incorporation clause in the indicated way.

In *The Northumbria*,[69] the issue was whether a crack that eventually led a cargo of linseed to be damaged by the ingress of water occurred due to unseaworthiness or heavy weather. The bill of lading included the phrase 'all other conditions per charterparty including the negligence clause,' and the holders of the bill argued that the damage that occurred due to unseaworthiness was not included in the reference to the negligence clause. The clause further indicated that

> the steamer is no way liable for the consequences of the perils of the seas. Neither is the steamer answerable for losses occasioned by the unseaworthiness or latent defect in the hull, whether existing or not before or after the commencement of the voyage, not resulting from want of due diligence by the owner.

During the voyage, a slight crack on the deck let the water through and caused damage to the cargo. It was claimed by the cargo owners that the unseaworthiness was not covered by the exceptions, which were incorporated into the bill of lading by the phrase 'all other conditions per charterparty including negligence clause.'

It was decided by the County Court that the evidence indicated the existing strain in the structure of the vessel meeting with bad weather led to the deck being cracked. Therefore, it was held that the shipowners were liable for the damage to the cargo as the employed words of the incorporation clause were considered insufficient to incorporate such an exception. Accordingly, the shipowners were held liable for the damage to the cargo. However, the judges of the Divisional Court were not of the same opinion. It was decided by Sir Gorell Barnes and Bargrave Deane J that the negligence clause referred to the charterparty provision in its entirety in a way including the exception of unseaworthiness, and therefore, the decision of the County Court was rejected.

In *The Modena*,[70] the issue was whether the bill of lading containing the term 'all other conditions and exceptions per charterparty' was sufficient to incorporate the charterparty clause including the words 'the steamer to be provided with a deck load, at full freight, at charterer's risk.' Nine hundred barrels of tar were loaded on the defendant's vessel. At the request of the master of the vessel, a clause indicating that the vessel would not be liable for leakage and breakage was included in the bill of lading. Accordingly, the master made the following endorsement: 'the master agrees to load 900 barrels of tar on deck for London at a freight of . . .' At the port of discharge, it was realized that the

69 [1906] P 292.
70 [1911] 16 Com. Cas. 292.

barrels arrived in a damaged condition due to heavy timber being loaded on top of them and a huge number of the barrels were found to be crushed. Accordingly, the cargo was partially or completely lost. In *The Modena*, the true construction of the legal agreement is considered to be one of the most crucial assessments to be made. It was held that the phrase 'at charterer's risk' involved in the charterparty was not incorporated into the bill of lading and the defendants were held liable for the damage that occurred due to their servants' negligence. To put it differently, the words 'all conditions and exceptions' held insufficient to incorporate the phrase 'at charterer's risk' into the bill of lading. Concerning the significance of the allocation of liability in the shipping context, it may not be regarded as an unmerited apprehension from the perspective of the court. This is because allowing such incorporation may possibly enable shipowners, who generally hold a stronger position with more bargaining power, to unfairly exempt themselves from liability without taking their or their servant's negligence into consideration. Consequently, the exemption from liability because of negligence, unless expressed vividly, may not be effectively incorporated by virtue of an incorporation clause simply structured as 'all conditions and exceptions per charterparty.' In *Price & Co. v The Union Lighterage Co.*,[71] the contract of affreightment included an exemption from liability clause for the shipowner and included the words 'for any loss or damage to goods which can be covered by insurance.' The barge sank due to the negligence of the shipowner's servant. It was held that, because the exemption contained general terms and was not clearly related to negligence, the owner of the barge was not exempt from liability for loss or damage resulting from their own servant's negligence.

III. 'All Terms, Provisions, and Exceptions'

A provision including the words 'all terms, provisions, and exceptions' may be regarded as a truly comprehensive incorporation clause. Such a structure usually suffices to bring many elements of the charterparty into the bill of lading[72] if these particular elements make sense in the context of the bill. Furthermore, another criterion for successful incorporation is the consistency of the term to be incorporated with the express terms and provisions of the bill of lading and with its character.[73]

However, the provided flexibility for the parties to shipping operations may sometime pave the way for the incorporation of some incompatible charterparty terms into the bill of lading, provided that the relevant clause purports such incorporation avowedly. However, even such a clear permission of incorporation may not be sufficient to create contractual outcomes that are in contradiction with the fundamental purpose and character of the bill of lading. In *Glyn v Margetson*,[74] a cargo of oranges was shipped under a bill of lading, stating,

71 [1904] 1 K.B. 412.

72 Roche J in *Andreas Vergottis v Robinson David & Co Ltd* [1928] 31 LI.L.Rep Vol. 31, [26]; The words 'All terms, provisions and exceptions contained in which charter are herewith incorporated' were held to be very wide words and wide enough to bring in almost anything and everything which is in the charterparty.

73 *The Varenna* [1983] 1 Lloyd's Rep 416.; *The Mata K* [1998] Lloyd's Rep 614. See also Özdel (n 25) 146: '. . . incorporation should only be permitted to the extent that the application of inconsistent provisions does not defeat ''the main object and intent'' of the bill of lading.' One may argue that the phrase 'the main object and intent' and 'the character of the bill of lading' may be used interchagebly to a certain degree.

74 [1893] AC 351. *See* also *Renton v Palmyra* [1956] 1 QB. 462.

> [L]ying in the port of Malaga, and bound for Liverpool, with liberty to proceed and stay at any port or ports in any station in the Mediterranean, Levant, Black Sea, or Adriatic, or on the coasts of Africa, Spain, Portugal, France, Great Britain, and Ireland, for the purpose of delivering coals, cargo or passengers, or for any other purpose whatsoever.

Additionally, the bill of lading included a clause stating that the shipper has agreed to all the written or printed terms of the bill of lading. After leaving Malaga, rather than heading towards the west, the vessel proceeded to a port on the east coast of Spain and then returned and made her course for Liverpool. Due to the delay resulting from heading to the east first, the perishable oranges were delivered in a damaged condition. Consequently, the shipper brought an action against the shipowner claiming damages for the breach of contract. The shipowners argued that the deviation was justifiable due to the wide construction of the liberty clause, and therefore, they were not liable for the loss. Especially considering the perishable nature of the cargo in question, one may argue that the deviation was not justifiable since it was not coherent with the *raison d'être* of the bill of lading in the first place. In compliance with this, the judges were unanimous in their finding that a possibly very wide scope of liberty clauses had to be read down considering the business realities of contracting for the shipment of perishable goods.

This decision may be regarded as a crucial one as it sets the boundaries for the interpretation of the scope of liberty clauses since it vividly indicates that a liberty clause must be restricted to the ports, which are in the course of the planned voyage. A printed clause usually does not suffice to defeat the main purpose of the contract, which essentially was the shipment of the cargo of oranges to Liverpool. The deviation was not justifiable considering the main purpose and underlying intention of the contract.

IV. 'All Terms, Conditions, Clauses, Liberties, and Exceptions'

Being one of the most comprehensive and common clauses of incorporation, the words 'all terms, conditions, clauses, liberties, and exceptions' should be mentioned at this point.[75] The reach of this particular clause seems to be quite extensive. However, regarding the complex nature of shipping contracts, it has become common practice to insert specific references into the bill of lading to avoid the possible undesirable results of depending on such general words. For instance, the references in *The Varenna*[76] to the negligence clause and in *The Rena K*[77] to the arbitration clause were held to constitute efficient

75 Here are some examples: Congenbill 1978: 'all the terms and conditions and liberties and exceptions of the charterparty, dated as overleaf are herewith incorporated'; Congenbill 1994: 'all terms and conditions, liberties and exceptions of the charterparty dated as overleaf, including the law and arbitration clause, are herewith incorporated'; HIBL Bill: 'All the terms conditions, liberties and exceptions of the said contract of affreightment or charterparty are herewith incorporated, including proper law and arbitration clauses'; Cementvoybill: 'All terms and conditions, liberties and exceptions of the charterparty including the Arbitration clause (Cl.41), dated as overleaf, are herewith incorporated'; Orevoybill: 'All terms and conditions, liberties and exceptions of the charterparty, dated as overleaf, including the war risks clause (Clause 16) and the law and arbitration clause (Clause 23) are hereby expressly incorporated'; Austwheat Bill: 'consigned to . . . assigns, he or they paying freight for the same as per the below mentioned . . . charterparty, as amended, all the terms conditions clauses and exceptions including clause 33 (arbitration) in which charterparty are herewith incorporated'; Intankbill 78: 'pursant and subject to all terms and conditions, liberties and exceptions as per tanker voyage charterparty indicated hereunder, including provisions overleaf.'

76 [1983] 1 Lloyd's Rep 416.

77 [1978] 1 Lloyd's Rep 545.

descriptions.[78] On the other hand, inserting such specific references may possibly pave the way for courts to seek special mention of all other clauses if this application becomes an ordinary part of contract drafting.[79] Accordingly, it is a slippery slope. In *The Emmanuel Coloctronis (No.2)*,[80] the bill of lading included the incorporation clause followed as 'all other conditions, exceptions, demurrage, general average and for disbursements as per above named charterparty.' In this case, the wording of the incorporation clause was held to be restricting the scope of incorporation, and therefore, the reach of the clause was held not extensive enough to include an arbitration clause.[81]

In *The Heidberg*,[82] it was indicated that the rights of the bill of lading holder should be ascertainable from the face of the bill and any charterparty provisions incorporated into it, regardless of them not being brought up to the notice of the shipper, and consequently, a prior awareness on the shipper's part is not created. In the words of Judge Diamond QC, 'What is transferred to the consignee or indorsee consists, and consists only, of the terms which appear on the face and reverse of the bill of lading.'[83] In *Leduc v Ward*[84] it was unsuccessfully argued by the shipowner that the shipper 'knew, at the time when the goods were shipped, that the vessel was intended to proceed to Dunkirk via Glasgow, and in substance agreed to her so proceeding.' However, the bill of lading did not contain any written permission concerning the vessel proceeding to Glasgow. Even though the decision seems compatible with the realities of commerce necessitating the prevention of the 'indorsees being effected by terms of which they are likely to be ignorant, the legal rationale for it is unclear.'[85] Although it is clear that negotiability necessitates the promotion of at least a minimum level of commercial protection, this should be somehow balanced with the realities of the legal relationship and the actual awareness of the third party to avoid the implementation of a dysfunctional approach that may potentially hinder the manifestation of party autonomy. As indicated, the intentions of the parties should be considered in assessing incorporation. However, as indicated, this should be done in light of the well-settled meanings of certain commercial phrases of incorporation.[86] Unless a conceivable amount of awareness of the existence of the charterparty provision can be demonstrated, it would be unreasonable to expect such a provision to be binding for a third-party bill of lading holder. This constitutes a priority, especially in dealing with the incorporation of arbitration clauses. Furthermore, there are substantial requirements concerning the incorporation of charterparty provisions due to the realities of shipping operations. Hence, the substantial requirements for incorporation in the shipping context are examined in the next section.

78 Gaskell, Asariotis and Baatz (n 9) 691.

79 *Spurling v Bradshaw* [1956] 1 W.L.R. 461; the validity of a clause purporting to exclude liability for negligence was examined in this case.

80 *Astro Valiente Compania Naviera v Government of Pakistan (The Emmanuel Colocotronis)* [1982] 1 Lloyd's Rep 286. However, it should be noted that the decision of Staughton J in this case was not followed by Hobhouse J in *The Varenna* [1983] 1 Lloyd's Rep 416; upheld CA [1983] 2 Lloyd's Rep 529.

81 Gaskell, Asariotis and Baatz (n 9) 691.

82 [1994] 2 Lloyd's Rep 287 at [313].

83 [1994] 2 Lloyd's Rep 287 at [301].

84 [1888] 20 Q.B.D. 475, as cited with approval in *The Heidberg* [1994] 2 Lloyd's Rep 287.

85 Aikens et al. (n 3) 199, 7.40.

86 Ibid 225, 7.109.

2.2.1.2. A Three-Step Test: Ascertaining the Eligibility for Incorporation

Predominantly a three-step test may be applied to ascertain which charterparty provisions are incorporated into bills of lading.[87] Firstly, it should be determined whether the incorporation clause is adequately far-reaching to actually enable incorporation. In the case that the incorporation clause is structured inefficiently in the first place, then it would not be possible to argue that the incorporation took place as the reach of the incorporation clause would fall short to target the provision intended to be incorporated. Hence, fundamentally, there should be a certain level of wideness concerning the scope of the incorporation clause. Secondly, a twofold examination should be conducted to assess the reasonableness and relevancy of the provision-to-be-incorporated. This simply means whether it would be legally logical to incorporate the charterparty provision in question into the bill of lading. If the provision that is purported to be incorporated would not make any sense within the context of the bill of lading or if it would be highly unexpected from the point of the holder of the bill of lading to foresee the incorporation of such a provision, then the incorporation is usually not allowed. Thirdly, the provision-to-be-incorporated should be consistent with the rest of the provisions of the bill of lading. As indicated, such consistency is also sought concerning the compatibility of the provision with the characteristics of the incorporating document too.

2.2.1.2.1. The Wideness of the Incorporation Clause

The initial assessment to be made for the purposes of examining if incorporation takes place is whether the structure and wording of the incorporation clause are adequately far-reaching. The general words of incorporation normally only suffice to incorporate more generic provisions. In order to incorporate provisions that are pertaining to more complex issues – for instance, to such as liberties and exceptions – it is usually the approach adopted by the English courts that the employment of some specific words of incorporation is sought. If specific words are chosen, even their manipulation to a certain degree may be permissible to ensure party autonomy does not go astray.

The words selected to form an incorporation clause identify the demarcation lines of its scope. Hence, the comprehensiveness of the incorporation clause may be assessed by evaluating the literal formation of the clause. However, since the wording and construction of various incorporation clauses are analyzed in detail earlier, the issue of wideness is not discussed here again. Nonetheless, it may perhaps be useful to reiterate at this point that the general words merely cover matters concerning receipt, carriage, and delivery of the goods. The incorporation of the charterparty terms regulating the obligations of the shipowner[88] or the obligations of the holder of the bill (other than the promissory ones to be performed during or before the delivery of the cargo)[89] often depends on a specific reference to be made to such provisions. It is generally accepted that specific wording is

87 Stewart C. Boyd, Steven Berry, Andrew S. Burrows, Bernard Eder, David Foxton, and Christopher F. Smith, *Scrutton on Charterparties and Bills of Lading*, Sweet & Maxwell, 2008, 21st Edn., A37. Also see Debattista (n 5) 19, 1.35.

88 For instance, see *S.A. Sucre Export v Northern River Shipping Co Ltd (The Sormovskiy 3068)* [1994] 2 Lloyd's Rep 266 concerning the presentation of the bill of lading.

89 Unlike the requirement in the incorporation clause formed as 'freight & all other conditions as per charter.' Such clauses usually indicate the promissory conditions to be performed by the consignee on or before the delivery of the cargo. See Treitel and Reynolds (n 2) 84.

required 'for the clause to cover jurisdiction and arbitration clauses, which are regarded as matters outside the main contract.'[90]

2.2.1.2.2. Reasonableness and Pertinency

2.2.1.2.2.1. Is the Provision Reasonable to Incorporate?

Where assessed that the words are comprehensive and wide enough to enable incorporation, the second step is to determine whether the incorporation of a certain provision would make sense in the context of the bill of lading. This is purely because the fundamental purpose of this legal concept is to align contracts in a harmonized and corresponding manner. Therefore, any irrelevant terms that would make no sense in the bill of lading context but are only special to the charterparty agreement are usually inapt for incorporation.

For instance, in *Gullischen v Stewart*,[91] the charterparty cesser clause held not to be incorporated, even though an express reference to this specific clause was in place. In this case, a cesser clause mainly providing a lien for the shipowner on the cargo for certain charges relevant to the carriage is held to be irrelevant in the context of the bill of lading.[92] In line with this, an exemption of liability of the shipowner[93] or an agency clause[94] is usually considered inapt for incorporation as these do not constitute obligations to be performed by the bill of lading holder and are substantially regarded irrelevant in the bill of lading context.

It should be noted that the three-step test necessitates a distinction to be made between the *prima facie* wideness of the incorporation clause that primarily exhibits the reach of its inclusiveness of a certain provision, and the aptitude of that particular provision in the context of the bill of lading. Furthermore, legal functions and peculiarities of bills of lading should be considered in assessing the level of reasonableness of incorporating a certain provision into the bill.

2.2.1.2.2.2. Is the Provision-to-Be-Incorporated Pertinent?

The preconditions of potential incorporation furthermore involve pertinency. The provisions of the charterparty that could presumably be incorporated by the employment of general words of incorporation are usually concerned with the following: the receipt function of the bill of lading, carriage or delivery of cargo, or payment of freight. The unawareness of the third-party bill of lading holder of the entirety of charterparty provisions necessitates merely the germane provisions of the bill of lading with the aforementioned concepts to be incorporated by the employment of general words of incorporation.[95] Such third parties

---

90 Francis Reynolds, Time Charterparties and Bills of Lading, in Rhidian Thomas (ed.) *Legal Issues Relating to Time Charperties*, Informa, 2008, 171, 9.33.

91 [1883–1884] LR 13 Q.B.D. 317.

92 Machale A. Miller, Cesser Clause in Charter Party Symposium – Part II, Winter 2001, *Tulane Maritime Law Journal*, 26, 71. The clause is designed to provide the shipowner a lien on cargo for certain charges related to carriage and to concomitantly release the charterer from liability for relevant claims.

93 *Krüger & Co Ltd v Moel Tryvan Ship Co Ltd* [1907] A.C. 272; *Serraino & Sons v Campbell* [1891] 1 Q.B. 283.

94 *Manchester Trust v Furness Withy and Co Ltd* [1895] 2 Q.B. 539.

95 *The Varenna* [1983] 1 Lloyd's Rep 416.

are usually not expected to have further knowledge pertaining to the terms of the referred charterparty since 'they seldom have the right and the chance to see its provisions.'[96]

An arbitration clause is customarily considered a specific clause for the purposes of incorporation. Hence, its incorporation is usually not possible by means of employing general words of incorporation. In other words, courts normally seek a specific reference to be made to an arbitration clause to allow its incorporation since these clauses do not pertain to the carriage and discharge of the cargo and fundamentally govern the issue of dispute resolution instead. Even though the application of the pertinency test may seem quite irrelevant concerning the arbitration clause, one may suggest that this test does not always have a consistent application in the arbitration context. This is because the approach concerning 'what is germane to the bill of lading' may show nuances of interpretation based on the perception of courts.

The main reason this chapter examines the substantial steps of incorporation is to be able to provide a general guideline and reveal the fundamentals of contractual incorporation (including those of arbitration clauses). Therefore, noting that there is some inconsistency among the courts concerning the interpretation of 'pertinency,' the issue to be addressed at this point is whether a specific charterparty provision, such as an arbitration clause may possibly be categorized as a term that is germane to shipment or discharge. As indicated, there are some inconsistent decisions of the courts concerning the evaluation of what is pertinent to shipment and discharge. Such inconsistency is mainly derived from the varying evaluation of the status of some specific provisions such as choice of law and arbitration to possibly fall under the category of 'provisions that are germane to shipment and discharge.' Courts generally seek express reference to the provisions where their pertinency is debatable. This is because 'a great amount of justification'[97] is usually sought since the incorporation of such provisions is most likely to put a tremendous burden on the holder of the bill if the holder is not aware of the possible incorporation and application of these 'distinct' provisions. However, as indicated, the perception of the courts pertaining to the categorization of provisions may have nuances based on the facts of each case.[98]

For instance, in *The San Nicholas*,[99] it was held that the incorporation of a choice of law clause by the employment of general words of incorporation was considered valid even though the clause could not be regarded as more relevant to the bill of lading as a receipt, delivery, or freight than the arbitration clause was. The case was concerned with the incorporation of the provisions of a partially blank charterparty into bills of lading. It was decided that the intention of the parties was to incorporate the relevant charterparty, which was known to exist but not entirely known to the parties due to lack of identification of it. The reasoning of the court was that some parts were left blank because the date and name of the parties to the charterparty were unknown to the master filling the charterparty and that there would be very significant and evident gaps in the bill of lading, which would

96 *Finska Cellulosaforeningen v Westfield Paper Co Ltd* [1940] 2 All ER 473, it was indicated that the seller was not obliged to provide a copy of the charterparty referred to in the bill of lading to the buyer.

97 Liang Zhao and Felix Chan, Incorporating the Charterparty's Applicable Law Clause into Bills of Lading, 2012, *Lloyd's Maritime and Commercial Law Quarterly*, 487–492.

98 See *K/S A/S Seateam & Co v Iraq National Oil Co and Others (The Sevonia Team)* [1983] 2 Lloyd's Rep 640; *Navigazione Alta Italia SpA v Svenska Petroleum AB* (*The Nai Matteini*) [1988] 1 Lloyd's Rep 452.

99 *Pacific Molasses Co and United Molasses Trading Co Ltd v Entre Rios Compania Naviera SA* (*The San Nicholas*) [1976] 1 Lloyd's Rep 8.

amount the bill to fail if there was no incorporation.[100] Consequently, the head charterparty, thus the choice of law clause, was held to be incorporated by general words. *The San Nicholas* illustrates the well-settled principle in English law that a charterparty does not need to be identified in the bill of lading for its successful incorporation.[101]

In *Siboti K/S v BP France SA (The Siboti)*,[102] the issue before Gross J to assess was whether the defendant was to be treated as a party to a bill of lading which claimed to have incorporated by reference to a charterparty, *inter alia*, an exclusive English jurisdiction clause. The incorporation clause in the bill of lading was a general one as follows: 'all the terms whatsoever of the said charter,' and there was no specific reference to the English jurisdiction clause. Gross J, turning on the authorities[103] made the deduction that if the general wording including 'all terms' was insufficient to incorporate an ancillary charterparty arbitration clause into a bill then this would mean that 'the same result must follow with regard to charterparty jurisdiction clauses.'[104] He then went on and stated, 'Does the addition of the word "whatsoever" make all the difference? I do not think it does or should.'[105] The court accordingly held that general words of incorporation are insufficient to incorporate an ancillary term – namely, the jurisdiction clause in this particular case – even though the relevant charterparty provided that the issued bills of lading should incorporate that specific clause and it included the words 'this charterparty shall be governed by and construed in accordance with English law and the English courts have jurisdiction in respect of all disputes arising out of this charterparty.'[106] The insufficiency of the words 'all terms whatsoever' to incorporate a specific charterparty exclusive jurisdiction clause may be considered to be pointing out to the general rule that incorporation is essentially a matter concerning the construction of the incorporation clause in each case.

The Court of Appeal in *The Channel Ranger*[107] considered the permitted level of flexibility of the description test in assessing the provisions of the charterparty that are intended to be incorporated. The concerned charterparty was contained in a fixture recap email message and the bill of lading included the clause as follows 'all terms, conditions, liberties and exceptions of the charterparty including the law and arbitration clause are herewith incorporated.' However, there was no 'law and arbitration clause' in the charterparty, but there was instead an English law and jurisdiction clause. Following the decision of Males J in the first instance,[108] the wording of the bill of lading indicating the incorporation of the charterparty law and arbitration clause held sufficient by the Court of Appeal to incorporate the law and jurisdiction clause of the charterparty in question in *The Channel Ranger*. The judgement departing from

100 Roskill LJ in *Pacific Molasses Co and United Molasses Trading Co Ltd v Entre Rios Compania Naviera SA (The San Nicholas)* [1976] 1 Lloyd's Rep 8, 12.

101 Özdel (n 25) 34. Also see *The Garbis* [1982] 2 Lloyd's Rep 283, 287; *The Ikariada* [1999] 2 Lloyd's Rep 365, 372.

102 *The Siboti* [2003] EWHC 1278; 2 Lloyd's Rep 364.

103 [2003] EWHC 1278, [46] referring to *T. W. Thomas & Co. Ltd. v Portsea Steamship Co Ltd, The Portsmouth* [1912] A.C. 1. at [6] (*Thomas v Portsea*); *Federal Bulk Carriers Inc v C Itoh & Co Ltd (The Federal Bulker)* [1989] 1 Lloyd's Rep 103.

104 [2003] EWHC 1278, [46].

105 Ibid.

106 Ibid [16].

107 *Caresse Navigation Ltd v Zurich Assurances MAROC and Others* [2014] EWCA Civ 1366 (*The Channel Ranger*).

108 *The Channel Ranger* [2014] EWCA Civ 1366.

the traditional approach that dispute resolution clauses may only be incorporated into a bill of lading by virtue of employing words of extremely specific reference faced some criticism as the employment of general words of incorporation was considered sufficient to incorporate an ancillary provision. It was argued by Magklasi that the Court of Appeal 'went astray' from the well-established English approach predominantly promoting the employment of specific words for this kind of incorporation and 'endangered' commercial foreseeability and certainty by means of replacing the arbitration clause with an exclusive jurisdiction clause.[109] The main criticism concerning this decision may be argued to be the court giving effect to the words of the incorporation clause a value that may perhaps not be considered appropriate to be granted. It may be said that incorporating words referring to the 'law and arbitration' clause of a charterparty which instead provides for 'English law and jurisdiction' to be interpreted as sufficient to incorporate the latter to possibly mean an inappropriate intervention of the court. Furthermore, one may also consider that the inappropriate interpretation of the referring words may have the potential to impair the anticipated contractual outcomes that reflect the codetermination of the parties.[110]

Nevertheless, it should be noted that the Court of Appeal in *The Channel Ranger* gave significant scrutiny to the wording of the bill of lading and considered these with the understanding of a reasonable person as a whole in their context. Citing Gross J in *The Siboti*, who stated that 'in every case, the court is seeking the ascertain the intention of the parties and, when construing the language, it is necessary to have regard to the individual context and commercial background,'[111] the Court of Appeal in *The Channel Ranger* concluded that the overall context was suitable to include the relevant charterparty provision. The reasoning provided was that the court had to seek what the parties should reasonably understand from the words 'law and arbitration clause' and analyzing that it was established that the parties would understand and expect at least one kind of ancillary clause to be incorporated. Even though there is some criticism of *The Channel Ranger*, Özdel considers it

> a welcome decision, as it provides the desired degree of flexibility to the description test. It should now be possible to incorporate a charterparty arbitration clause into a bill of lading without having to use of the word 'arbitration' in the incorporation clause. Thus, it now seems that even a reference to 'litigation' as opposed to arbitration in the incorporation clause should be sufficient to incorporate an arbitration clause into the bill of lading.[112]

Accordingly, the decision may be regarded to have struck a balance between commercial certainty and party autonomy by assessing that the parties ordinarily assume that this to be the typical application as may be understood from the construction of the contract in accordance with the commercial purpose of incorporation as a contract drafting method.

---

109 Eleni Magklasi, *A new channel to the heart of incorporation clauses: Caresse Navigation Ltd v Zurich Assurances MAROC (The Channel Ranger)* [2014] EWCA Civ 1366 (CA), JIML [2014] 20, (6), 397, 2014, JIMW, 20(6), 398.

110 Felix Chan, Specific Words of Incorporation in Bills of Lading, 2015, *The Law Quartetly Review*, 131, 372–376.

111 *Siboti K/S v B P France SA* [2003] EWHC 1278 (Comm), [36]; [2003] 2 Lloyd's Rep 364, 372. *Caresse Navigation Ltd v Zurich Assurances MAROC and Others (The Channel Ranger)* [2014] EWCA Civ 1366 at [28]. The Court of Appeal in *The Channel Ranger* also found the red ink principle stated by Lord Hoffmann in *Chartbrook Ltd v Persimmon Homes Ltd* [2009] UKHL 38, reported at [2009] 1 AC 1101 at [25] applicable (as also followed in the first instance: [2013] EWHC 3081).

112 *Dr Melis Ozdel discusses the impact of the Channel Ranger at the LMAA Spring Seminar*, July 1, 2015, UCL, available at www.ucl.ac.uk/laws/news/2015/jul/dr-melis-ozdel-discusses-impact-channel-ranger-lmaa-spring-seminar.

2.2.1.2.3. *Consistency with the Rest of the Terms*

The potential difficulty in assessing the legal position of the parties to the bill of lading is provided as the top 'principal disadvantage of incorporating clauses' in the UN Bills of Lading Report dated 1971.[113] Indeed there is a general principle of promoting the legal protection of the *bona fide* third-party holder of the bill of lading and, accordingly, the attempts to incorporate an inconsistent term with the rest of the provisions of the bill usually fail. In case of incoherency, the provisions of the bill of lading generally prevail over the charterparty term,[114] despite the latter may perhaps be considered comprehensive enough to bind the parties to the bill of lading as 'incorporation does not lead to mechanical application of the charterparty terms under the bill of lading.'[115] The overall assessment of the terms that prevail and be effective is vital as it indicates the legal leverage that the parties have against each other in the case of a cargo dispute arising. This primarily set the boundaries of their rights and liabilities.

The charterparty clause that is purported to be incorporated must not be inconsistent[116] with the express terms of the bill of lading. An incorporation clause may, on its true construction, cover a specific charterparty provision.[117] The referred charterparty provision will nevertheless not be incorporated into the bill of lading to the extent that it is inconsistent with an express term of the bill.[118] For instance, if the freight indicated in the bill of lading is lower than that payable under the charterparty, the incorporation clause follows as 'other conditions per charterparty' does not make a shipper liable for more than the bill of lading freight as such incorporation would not be effective.[119] In other words, the incorporation clause would not be sufficient to incorporate the charterparty freight if the actual freight clause in the bill of lading is indicating a lower amount.[120] If there is any inconsistency regarding freight, the charterparty freight provision may be incorporated so far as they relate to the method of payment[121] but so far as they relate to the amount, the provision may not be incorporated. Whilst incorporating words such as 'freight payable per charterparty' is *prima facie* effective, it is crucial to assess what obligations concerning freight, in terms of rate, amount or payee, and so on, are incorporated in each individual case.[122]

Giving effect to a charterparty term which the bill holder has no awareness of may impair the commercial certainty and legal foreseeability that the courts seek to provide. Therefore, the relevant provision included in the bill usually prevails[123] if the charterparty

---

113 See United Nations Conference on Trade and Development, *Report on Bills of Lading*, 1971, New York, 51–52, available at https://unctad.org/en/PublicationsLibrary/c4isl6rev1_en.pdf.

114 *The Miramar* [1984] AC 676.

115 Özdel (n 25) 143.

116 Staughton J in *The Emmanuel Colocotronis (No.2)* [1982] 1 Lloyd's Rep 286 at [289].

117 Treitel and Reynolds (n 2) 88, 3–023.

118 *Tradigrain S.A. v King Diamond Shipping S.A. (The Spiros C)* [2000] 2 Lloyd's Rep 319 at [335].

119 *Gardner v Trechmann* [1884] 15 QBD 154: the words 'other conditions per charterparty' were not given effect to incorporate the charterparty provisions concerning freight that were inconsistent with a provision in the bill of lading for freight. Brett MR stated that 'those clauses of the charterparty cannot be brought in which would alter the express stipulations in the bill of lading' at 157.

120 [1884] 15 QBD 154, 157.

121 *India Steamship Co Ltd v Louis Dreyfus Sugar Ltd (The Indian Relience)* [1997] 1 Lloyd's Rep 52. (*The Indian Reliance*).

122 Aikens et al. (n 3) 223, 7.101. *The Indian Reliance* [1997] 1 Lloyd's Rep 52, 57–58; *The Spiros C* [1999] 2 Lloyd's Rep 91, reversed on other grounds [2000] 2 Lloyd's Rep 319, *The Bulk Chile* [2013] 2 Lloyd's Rep 38.

123 *The Miramar* [1984] AC 676.

provision creates inconsistency and such incorporation would generally be considered void. It may be argued that the inconsistency argument is somewhat disregarded in *The Channel Ranger* as Beatson LJ stated: 'it is only after a meaning is attributed to it that one can consider whether there is a problem of inconsistency.'[124] Nonetheless, it may be suggested that by shifting the actual time of the consistency test, arbitration was firstly given a meaning and then interpreted in the context of the case as an element of which meaning to be construed and not one to be examined from the perspective of incorporation. Accordingly, the charterparty provision providing for 'English law and jurisdiction' was held to be incorporated despite the incorporation clause referring to the charterparty 'law and arbitration clause.' The justification for shifting the timing for the consistency test may be debatable. However, what is not much debatable is that the approach of the Court of Appeal illustrates a departure from the strict rule of using express reference for the incorporation of some ancillary provisions. *The Channel Ranger* reflects that a reference to a 'law and arbitration provision' may be sufficient to incorporate a charterparty 'law and jurisdiction clause' and, accordingly, paves the way for the *vice versa* argument concerning a reference to a jurisdiction clause in the bill of lading to possibly create the result of a charterparty arbitration clause to be incorporated into the bill.[125]

2.2.1.3. Examining the Necessity: Strict Requirements for Incorporation and the Underlying Reasons They Exist in the Shipping Context

If general words of incorporation are employed and the intention of the parties regarding the incorporation of ancillary terms is ambiguous, the courts would generally be reluctant to allow incorporation. There are several reasons that courts are usually inclined to seek further assurance concerning the manifestation of the intention of the parties to incorporate such provisions from another contract by reference.

- First, a charterparty includes provisions that are not particularly concerned with the bill of lading holder. General words of incorporation normally only enable the incorporation of terms that are concerning receipt, carriage, or delivery of the cargo or the payment of the freight.[126] In other words, merely the pertinent charterparty terms, which are governing the issues covered by the bill of lading, are incorporated by means of a generally structured incorporation clause. Such an implementation seems to be in line with the necessity for the preservation of flexibility and credibility in commercial shipping.[127]
- Second, regarding the transferable nature of the bills of lading, it should be considered that the bill might be in the hands of a third party, who is not aware of the terms of the charterparty. Concerning the interpretation of a bill of lading, the starting point

124 *Caresse Navigation Ltd v Zurich Assurances MAROC and Others (The Channel Ranger)* [2014] EWCA Civ 1366.

125 Melis Özdel, *Incorporation of Arbitration Clauses into Bills of Lading*, London Maritime Arbitrators Association, 2015.

126 *T. W. Thomas & Co. Ltd. v Portsea Steamship Co Ltd, The Portsmouth* [1912] A.C. 1. at [6] (*Thomas v Portsea*); *Excess Insurance Co Ltd v Mander* [1997] 2 Lloyd's Rep 119 at [125].

127 See *Tradigrain S.A. v King Diamond Shipping S.A. (The Spiros C)* [2000] 2 Lloyd's Rep 319 at [355]: It may be argued that the decision of the Court of Appeal is in line with the realities of commercial shipping practice and that the court respected the need for flexibility in commercial shipping.

is generally the bill itself and the wording of the charterparty is usually considered immaterial. In accordance with this, in *The Siboti*, it was held that general words of incorporation are not sufficient to incorporate an ancillary term – namely, the jurisdiction clause – even though the relevant charterparty provided that the bills issued under that particular charterparty should incorporate that specific clause.[128]

- Third, as it was considered in the *Manchester Trust v Furness Withy*,[129] it is a matter of concern whether allowing incorporation by virtue of employing general words would have an analogous impact that may create the introduction of the doctrine of constructive notice,[130] which is usually regarded as a concept of company law, into commercial law.[131] In the *Manchester Trust*, this issue was considered where a clause in the charter providing that the master should sign the bills of lading as an agent of the charterer did not bind the holder of the bill who had no awareness of the charter. The mere reference in the bill of lading to the charterparty did not provide the holder with any constructive notice of the contents of the charterparty as held that the holder could not be taken to have notice of the charterparty provisions in their entirety. Furthermore, *Manchester Trust* sets the authority that the equitable doctrine of constructive notice would not apply in commercial transactions[132] as observed by Lindley LJ that 'if we were to extend the doctrine of constructive notice to commercial transactions we should be doing infinite mischief and paralyzing the trade of the country.'[133]
- Fourth, bills of lading are inherently issued for the particular parts of the cargo while the charterparties generally are pertinent to the entire cargo.[134] In other words, parties to the charterparty are generally aware of or have the means to discover, the features of the cargo in question, which is specified in the bills of lading, as it constitutes a part of the whole cargo. On the other hand, the holders of the bills of lading usually have no ready means of discovering the charterparty terms – in other words, the provisions applicable to the carriage of the rest of the cargo that is being carried with theirs. In an equitable sense, it is usually unreasonable to hold the parties with varying levels of bargaining power (parties to the charterparty being familiar with almost all aspects of the carriage operation and thus holding a stronger position, and the parties who are just aware of the aspects of the bill of lading, who hold a relatively weaker position) liable to the same extent. Thus, in *The Miramar*, the imposition of financial liability of unknown extent on the holder of the bill of lading was held inequitable, and consequently, the bill of

128 [2003] 2 Lloyd's Rep 364 at [34]. See Özdel (n 25) 143.

129 [1895] 2 Q.B. 539 at [545]. Also see *Serraino & Sons v Campbell and others* [1891] QB 283, in which the incorporation of a charterparty exclusion clause, which purported to relieve the carrier of liability for the loss or damage to the cargo due to the negligence of the master, was ruled against. Also see Aikens et al. (n 3) 218, 7.88.

130 'Knowledge that the law presumes a person to have even if he is actually ignorant of the facts.' Constructive Notice, *Oxford Dictionary Online*, available at www.oxfordreference.com/view/10.1093/oi/authority.20110803095634980.

131 Treitel and Reynolds (n 2) 79, 3–012.

132 See Melis Özdel, *Incorporation of Charterparty Clauses into Bills of Lading: Peculiar to Maritime Law?*, Chapter 8 in Malcom Clarke, *Maritime Law Evolving*, Hart Publishing, 2013, 181–195, 191.

133 *Manchester Trust v Furness Withy* [1895] 2 Q.B. 539, [545].

134 Treitel and Reynolds (n 2) 79.

lading holders were held not personally liable for the demurrage payable under the terms of the charterparty.[135]

- Fifth, the courts value the promotion of certainty and uniformity concerning the meaning of particular phrases of incorporation in contracts and documents of commercial shipping. To express it differently, if the specific phrase of incorporation before the court had been defined and its implementation is well established by former decisions, the courts would usually be reluctant to seek another divergent meaning of the clause as that may compromise the certainty of commerce and the law of precedent. It was stated in *The Varenna* that

  > the commercial customers, shipowners, shippers and receivers, attach supreme importance to certainty, and where particular phrases have established meanings and effects it is not the policy of the law to seek to change them even if, in the absence of precedent, there would be a case for so doing.[136]

  Thus, courts are usually inclined to follow precedents that are transparentizing the meaning of a particular phrase of incorporation.[137]

The reluctance of the courts to adopt a flexible approach concerning the incorporation of 'ancillary' charterparty provisions by general reference in the bill of lading may be understandable if the intention of the parties regarding the incorporation of such a particular provision is ambiguous. However, generally speaking, if such an intention is vivid, adopting a timid approach concerning incorporation may be precarious as it may possibly overbalance the relationship between commercial realities and the consistency of law. This issue becomes much more significant especially when the dispute involves the possible incorporation of an arbitration clause, and the courts possibly sacrifice the concept of party autonomy for the sake of promoting persistence.

It is hardly an overstatement that shipping law, being concerned with negotiable shipping documents that almost constantly incorporate provisions from other sources, provides us with incredibly extensive case law on the issue of incorporation. More specifically, it is very common for relevant shipping contracts to incorporate arbitration clauses from other contracts and documents. Accordingly, the examination of maritime arbitration and the incorporation of charterparty arbitration clauses into bills of lading constitutes a necessity in evaluating the incorporation of arbitration clauses.

2.3. Maritime Arbitration and the Incorporation of Charterparty Arbitration Clauses

2.3.1. Maritime Arbitration

Arbitration has served as an ordinary, familiar, and convenient tool for the settlement of maritime disputes for decades.[138] Some of the reasons for arbitration to remain the preferred method of dispute resolution in the maritime industry may be argued to be the

---

135 *Miramar Maritime Corp v Holborn Oil Trading Ltd (The Miramar)* [1984] A.C. 676.

136 Sir John Donaldson in *The Varenna* [1983] 2 Lloyd's Rep 592, 594.

137 See *Diederichsen v Farquharson* [1898] 1 Q.B. 150 (CA).

138 Patrick Martin, *Why Is Arbitration Getting Much too Legalistic? Can the Old Method Be Reviewed?*, 8th International Congress of Maritime Arbitration, 1987, 1. Also see Majumdar (n 3) 98.

involvement of often-lower costs,[139] the ability it provides to shape the dispute resolution process in accordance with the needs of the parties involved, and the confidentiality it facilitates for the parties, who wish the details of their dispute to remain private.[140] Parties in arbitration may choose a neutral, or at least a trusted, jurisdiction rather than one linked to one of the parties to the dispute. Another reason is the enforceability of this dispute resolution method. The Convention on the Recognition and Enforcement of Foreign Arbitral Awards 1958, commonly known as the New York Convention, provides a scheme of international enforcement, which is often easier than trying to enforce court judgements.

Charterparties commonly include arbitration clauses. The arbitration proceedings are mostly handled by experts, who focus on commercial customs and general shipping practices. Unlike court litigation, which is immensely subject to statutory and procedural rules and to the doctrine of precedent, the rules of arbitration are generally set forth in a way reflecting the mutual wishes of the parties concerning arbitration proceedings. Arbitral awards are 'tailor-made' and they are not necessarily accompanied by any detailed legal reasoning. Consequently, unlike courts that are predominantly inclined to promote certainty and legal foreseeability, arbitral tribunals do not promote the establishment of a foreseeable legal pattern as their awards neither create precedent nor are published often. Nonetheless, one would perhaps hope to see some consistency with arbitral awards.

Maritime disputes[141] constitute the vast majority of the disputes that referred to *ad hoc* arbitration.[142] The preferred method of arbitration being *ad hoc* also shows that maritime disputes, due to their unique characteristics and the tailor-made solutions that they require, may be classified as special disputes that are in need of special treatment.

The results of the 2021 International Arbitration Survey that explores the responses of the participants in international arbitration to the changing circumstances and market realities indicate that 'international arbitration is the preferred method of resolving-cross border disputes for 90% of respondents.'[143] The survey also suggests that even for the first time it shares its position with Singapore as a result of both arbitration hubs getting

139 It may perhaps be difficult to argue that arbitration always involves lover costs than litigation nowadays. However, considering the fact that its proceedings being tailor-made and rapid, arbitration still remains the favourable method of dispute resolution in the maritime industry. Michael Marks Cohen, A New Yorker Looks at London Maritime Arbitration, 1986, *Lloyd's Maritime and Commercial Law Quarterly*, 57: 'arbitration in maritime disputes is on average 60 to 70% cheaper than litigation.' Furthermore, see Christopher R. Drahozal, Arbitration Costs and Forum Accessibility: Empirical Evidence, Summer 2008, *University of Michigan Journal of Law Reform*, 41(4).

140 Kyriaki Noussia, *Confidentiality in International Commercial Arbitration – A comparative Analysis of the Position under English, US, German and French Law*, Springer, 2010.

141 Also, various commodity market disputes. See Jason Clapham, Recent Trends in Commodities Arbitrations, 2013, *Journal of International Arbitration*, 30(6), 665–688.

142 *2018 International Arbitration Survey: The Evolution of International Arbitration*, Queen Mary University of London, 15, available at www.arbitration.qmul.ac.uk/media/arbitration/docs/2018-International-Arbitration-Survey-report.pdf (last visited May 15, 2019).

143 'This edition saw the widest-ever pool of respondents. With 1218 questionnaire responses received and 198 interviews conducted. Views were sought from a diverse pool of participants in the international arbitration sphere, including in-house counsel from both public and private sectors, arbitrators, private practitioners, representatives of arbitral institutions and trade associations, academics, experts and third-party funders': *2021 International Arbitration Survey: Adapting Arbitration to a Changing World*, Queen Marry University of London and White & Case, available at https://arbitration.qmul.ac.uk/media/arbitration/docs/LON0320037-QMUL-International-Arbitration-Survey-2021_19_WEB.pdf.

in the top-five picks of %54 of the respondents,[144] London still remains one of the most attractive venues for commercial arbitration and in particular maritime arbitration, even after Brexit.[145] It is also expected that the impact of Brexit on London maritime arbitration to be limited[146] because even if international regulations concerning the determination of the law applicable[147] would no longer form a part of English law, since London tribunals have not been obliged to follow these regulations in the first place, they would be able to determine questions of applicable law in the same way as they did pre-Brexit.[148] The availability of experienced and specialized arbitrators and the fruitfulness of the case law on English maritime arbitration in this jurisdiction may be considered as the essential elements reinforcing London's position.[149]

2.3.2. Arbitration Agreement: The Role and Significance in the Maritime Industry

A few intertwined concepts regarding arbitration are examined to understand some of the basics of implementing this method in the maritime context. An arbitration agreement constitutes the core element of any maritime dispute that is purported to be referred to as arbitration. Party autonomy concerning the decision of the parties to arbitrate is usually mirrored in the arbitration agreement and the law generally requires such to be manifested in certain ways. The relevant criteria of the law are predominantly pertaining to the formal aspects of arbitration agreements, which would clearly reflect that the 'declaration' of the parties of their wish to arbitrate is meeting the 'legal threshold of formality' to refer their dispute to this method of resolution.

An arbitration agreement constitutes the origin of any arbitration proceeding as such an agreement echoes the intention of the parties to refer their existing or future disputes to arbitration. With arbitration meaning a crucial divergence from the traditional adjudicatory process,[150] English courts have always sought to assess whether it is the true intention of the parties to prefer this method of dispute resolution over litigation. Courts have usually

144 Ibid: 'The rise in popularity of key Asian arbitral hubs demonstrated by Singapore's success is mirrored by Hong Kong, which takes third place (50%). Paris comes in fourth (chosen by 35% of respondents) followed by Geneva in fifth place (13% of respondents).'

145 See *The Maritime Arbitration Universe In Numbers: Will Brexit Impact London's Standing?, HFW Shipping Insight: Who Rules the Waves?*, March 2018, available at www.hfw.com/downloads/HFW-The-maritime-arbitration-universe-in-numbers-March-2018.pdf.

146 Clare Ambrose, Karen Maxwell and Michael Collett, *London Maritime Arbitration*, Informa Law from Routledge, 2018, 19, 1.58.

147 Mainly Rome I and II Regulations: The Rome I Regulation (EC) No 593/2008); The Rome II Regulation (EC) No 864/2007.

148 Ambrose, Maxwell, and Collett (n 146) 19, 1.58. According to Section 46 of the Arbitration Act 1996 as follows:

> Rules applicable to substance of dispute. (1) The arbitral tribunal shall decide the dispute – (a) in accordance with the law chosen by the parties as applicable to the substance of the dispute, or (b) if the parties so agree, in accordance with such other considerations as are agreed by them or determined by the tribunal. (2) For this purpose the choice of the laws of a country shall be understood to refer to the substantive laws of that country and not its conflict of laws rules. (3) If or to the extent that there is no such choice or agreement, the tribunal shall apply the law determined by the conflict of laws rules which it considers applicable.

149 *Ian Gaunt Explains the Benefits of London Arbitration*, Marine Strategy, June, 10, 2018, available at www.maritime-executive.com/features/ian-gaunt-explains-the-benefits-of-london-arbitration (last visited May 16, 2019).

150 Majumdar (n 3) 95.

been timid to grant a stay of their proceedings where the application for a stay is made based on an arbitration, of which agreement is considerably obscure, not completely known, or perhaps in need of exploration to affirm its true existence. The selection of arbitration as a dispute resolution method prevents parties from exercising their natural right to apply to a court. Accordingly, the intention to arbitrate must be unambiguous and without reservation. The ascertainment of this actual intention becomes particularly crucial in dealing with negotiable shipping documents. Therefore, English law establishes some formal requirements concerning the formation and validity of arbitration agreements.

An arbitration agreement to be in writing usually constitutes an essential requirement to establish its validity. This legislative requirement is fundamentally derived from the pursuit of courts to be ensured that this is the preferred method over court litigation, and such a preference is manifested in a written agreement, which is holding more evidentiary value than an oral agreement. Nevertheless, the meaning of 'being in writing' is broader than it may initially be perceived. The phrase, in light of the Arbitration Act 1996, suggests that the agreement is to be made in writing (disregarding it is being signed by the parties), by exchange of communications in writing, or to be evidenced in writing.[151] There is a fundamental requirement that the element of writing be reflected in one of the ways that the law indicates for the purposes of an arbitration agreement to be considered valid. However, there is clearly some room for flexibility as the law does not impose strict requirements of formality but rather sets some minimal thresholds. The requirement of an arbitration agreement to 'be in writing' can be interpreted as aiming 'both to assess the real will of the parties to submit their disputes to arbitration and to endorse the existence of a valid and efficient arbitration clause as regards third parties.'[152]

Maritime arbitration necessitates the issue of negotiability to be evaluated from the aspect of incorporation due to the involvement of negotiable documents in the equation. Fundamentally, an arbitration agreement pertaining to maritime disputes is subject to the same formal requirements as any arbitration agreement. On the other hand, the peculiar characteristics of shipping documents give rise to certain complications in assessing the fulfilment of the formal requirements for the valid formation of an arbitration agreement.[153] A bill of lading containing an incorporation clause referring to the charterparty arbitration provision may be transferred to a third party, who does not have awareness or knowledge of the scope and details of the provision referred to. Due to the potential involvement of oblivious/unaware third parties, courts mostly adopt a timid approach in assessing the incorporation of arbitration clauses and usually require strict criteria to meet. Accordingly, the incorporation of an arbitration agreement in the shipping context is generally subject to an examination that is more painstaking than it is conducted in determining whether incorporation is considered valid in another context than shipping.

2.3.3. Incorporation of Charterparty Arbitration Clauses

The performance of shipping operations is usually governed by provisions that are set out in various documents and contracts involving multiple parties. One of the main objectives

151 Section 5(2) of the Arbitration Act 1996. Also see '1.3.2. Arbitration Agreement to be in Writing' in Chapter 1, 'The Foundations of Incorporation and Arbitration Clauses.'

152 Mota (n 24) 5.

153 Ibid 7.

of the parties to shipping is generally to provide conformity between such various instruments. The desire for aligning the relevant documents and contracts mainly derives from the reluctance of the parties to possibly face and be held liable for some contractual terms or jurisdictions that are unfamiliar to them.

Even though it is quite usual for charterparties to contain an arbitration clause,[154] it is not very likely for bills of lading to include such a provision. Rather than including an arbitration clause, bills of lading generally contain an incorporation clause that enables the incorporation of the arbitration clause of the charterparty, under which the bill is issued.[155] Arbitration differs from litigation as the former does not apply to every kind of dispute arising since a prior agreement pertaining to a particular dispute is required for it to be referred to this certain method of dispute resolution.[156] On the other hand, if the dispute falls into the scope of the arbitration agreement, the relevant claim enables the parties to seek a stay of court proceedings as the right to refer the dispute to arbitration prevails.[157] Furthermore, aside from the arbitration agreement being void, inoperative, or incapable of being performed, the stay of proceedings to be granted would be compulsory.[158]

The assessment of whether the charterparty arbitration clause is incorporated into the bill of lading is crucial. When the incorporation of the arbitration clause of a distinct contract is in question, the establishment of precise and clear reference[159] to it is generally the initial requirement of English courts for such a provision to be considered incorporated and to form a part of the bill of lading. On the other hand, some examples of recent case law reveal the adoption of a more contemporary and flexible approach.[160]

2.3.3.1. The General Requirements Concerning the Incorporation of the Charterparty Arbitration Clause

Even though some flexibility is perceived as a necessity for the incorporation of arbitration clauses in modern shipping, evidently, some default formal requirements exist. These are

154 Michael J. Mustill and Stewart C. Boyd, *Commercial Arbitration*, LexisNexis Butterworths, 2001, 2nd Edn.

155 Wilson (n 3) 335.

156 However, see *NB Three Shipping Ltd v Harebell Shipping Ltd* [2005] 1 Lloyd's Rep 509, where, for just one of the parties, the prior agreement restricted the right to opt for arbitration.

157 Section 9(1) of the Arbitration Act 1996. Also see *Fiona Trust v Privalov* [2007] UKHL 40; [2008] 1 Lloyd's Rep 254.

158 Section 9(4) of the Arbitration Act 1996: 'On an application under this section the court shall grant a stay unless satisfied that the arbitration agreement is null and void, inoperative, or incapable of being performed.' The court may also exercise its discretion to grant a stay under its inherent jurisdiction: *Lombard North Central plc and another v GATX Corporation* [2012] EWHC 1067 (Comm).

159 To see an example of a high-costed litigation due to uncertainty concerning incorporation; *Johnson Matthey Bankers Ltd v The State Trading Corporation of India Ltd* [1984] 1 Lloyd's Rep 427, 430–434.

160 Simon Allison and Kanaga Dharmananda, Incorporating Arbitration Clauses: The Sacrifice of Consistency at the Altar of Experience, 2014, *Arbitration International*, 30(2), 265–282, LCIA. Also by allowing the reference to a charterparty law and arbitration clause where the charterparty providing a law and jurisdiction provision, to incorporate the English jurisdiction clause, *The Channel Ranger* [2014] EWCA Civ 1366, paves the way for questioning whether this would work the other way around and if it would be possible to incorporate a charterparty arbitration provision into the bill of lading where the bill is simply referring to a charterparty law and jurisdiction clause: Özdel (n 125). Furthermore, see *Sea Trade Maritime Corporation v Hellenic Mutual War Risks Association (Bermuda) Ltd, The Athena (No 2)* [2006] EWHC 2530; *Habas Sinai ve Tibbi Gazlar Isthisal Endustri AS v Sometal SAL* [2010] 1 Lloyd's Rep 661.

essentially no different than the requirements of the 'three-step test' for the incorporation of the general provisions of the charterparty.

First, the bill of lading is expected to include effective words of incorporation to incorporate the charterparty arbitration provision. Accordingly, one of the fundamental elements of incorporation is structural and concerns the wording and structure of the bill of lading itself. Accordingly, any visible intention of the charterparty concerning the incorporation of charterparty terms into the bill of lading issued under it is normally irrelevant. This is because such an agreement may only be substantiated by the parties to the bill. Thus, the words of incorporation should ordinarily be found on the bill of lading itself.[161]

Second, words of incorporation should be sufficient to describe the charterparty arbitration provision that is purported to be incorporated.[162] In other words, these words must be properly targeting the provision to be incorporated. Thus, especially when the concerned charterparty provision is an arbitration clause, a general incorporation clause consisting of the words 'all conditions, exceptions of the charterparty' is normally not considered adequate to 'target' such a substantial provision.[163] On the other hand, it should be noted that the description issue is a matter of construction of the incorporation clause, and the parties may overcome the relevant strict rules of incorporation by means of establishing a different construction that may be more suitable to their needs.

Third, evidently, the targeted charterparty provision must be consistent with the express terms of the bill.[164] Ordinarily, if there is no indication on the bill of lading of a potential incorporation of the charterparty arbitration clause, then incorporation usually fails. Furthermore, an existing incorporation clause may at first glance seem sufficient, but perhaps, for instance, due to lack of room for manipulation, incorporation may not be successful. Provisions that are clearly set out in the bill of lading normally prevail. For instance, if there is a clearly structured jurisdiction clause in the bill of lading, then incorporation of the charterparty arbitration clause would normally not be possible as this would create inconsistency.

Similarly, a sufficient reference in the bill of lading to a non-existing charterparty arbitration clause would also create an inconsistent situation. Indicated previously, this issue was considered by the Court of Appeal in *The Channel Ranger*, and the submission that the reference to a 'law and arbitration clause' was inconsistent with the incorporation of the charterparty 'English law and jurisdiction clause' was rejected considering the circumstances of the case.[165] The Court of Appeal considered the meaning attributed to the words of incorporation and the timing of such an attribution and concluded that the incorporation clause containing the words 'law and arbitration' to incorporate charterparty 'law and jurisdiction clause' did not create inconsistency, because this was

161 Sir John Donaldson MR in *The Varenna* [1983] 2 Lloyd's Rep 592 at [594] (appeal). Overruling, Staughton J in *The Emmanuel Colocotronis (No.2)* [1982] 1 Lloyd's Rep 286 at [289].

162 Wilson (n 3) 248.

163 *The Varenna* [1983] 1 Lloyd's 416. Furthermore, in *Siboti K/S v B P France SA* [2003] EWHC 1278 (Comm); [2003] 2 Lloyd's Rep 364 at [372] the incorporation clause involving the phrase 'all terms whatsoever' was held insufficient to incorporate a charterparty jurisdiction clause into the bill of lading.

164 Staughton J in *The Emmanuel Colocotronis (No.2)* [1982] 1 Lloyd's Rep 286, [289].

165 [2014] EWCA Civ. 1366.

essentially an issue of how the meaning was construed and not truly an assessment pertaining to incorporation.

The bill of lading provided that all terms and conditions, liberties, and exceptions of the charterparty, including the English law and arbitration clauses, are incorporated. The charterparty provided for an express choice of English law and an exclusive jurisdiction clause designating courts of England. To put it differently, the charterparty dispute resolution clause provided not for English law and arbitration but for English law and court jurisdiction. It was relied on by the defendants that the ordinary and natural meaning of the words of incorporation to the 'law and arbitration clause if any' was not sufficient to submit disputes to the exclusive jurisdiction of English courts. However, it is stated by Beatson LJ that the issue in this particular case was concerning 'the effect of a specific reference in the bill to one kind of charterparty ancillary provision and the construction of the words "law and arbitration clause" in the bill of lading, in particular the word "arbitration."'[166] The court assessed, in the context of the case, that the reliance on the principle about the insufficiency of general words was misplaced provided that the clause in the bill of lading was effective to incorporate one kind of ancillary clause meaning another kind of ancillary clause, such as a jurisdiction clause could be incorporated instead.[167]

One may argue that the court allowing the words 'law and arbitration' contained in the bill of lading to effectively incorporate the charterparty provision providing for 'law and English jurisdiction' constitutes an excessive intervention. *The Channel Ranger* has indeed attracted some criticism. Nonetheless, one may also argue that the court intervened in such a way that is eliminating inconsistency as it established a certain consistency by making the following deduction: If parties have agreed that at least one ancillary provision of the charterparty provision concerning dispute resolution to be incorporated by means of operating the words of the bill of lading incorporation clause, then it could be presumed that the parties may be considered to have been willing to incorporate another kind of ancillary provision of the charterparty too. It is rejected, considering the circumstances of the case that the reference to an arbitration clause was inconsistent with the incorporation of the jurisdiction clause.[168] The fundamental reasons for this may be said to be twofold. First, the timing of attributing meaning to a phrase was considered by the court. It was decided that this case was concerning the question of construing the meaning of the words and not of incorporation and therefore the assessment of whether there is a problem of inconsistency held solely to be done after meaning is attributed to the word.[169] The second issue was concerning the meaning that the parties attributed to the phrase in question. It was considered by the court that, particularly because the original parties to the bill of lading themselves chose to repeat the wording of the clause (1) of the printed conditions of the Congenbill form in the typed clause in the face of the bill, they were presumed to know or must be taken to have known of the charterparty provisions and, hence, that it did not contain an arbitration clause.[170] An otherwise approach was considered to possibly create uncommercial results.[171] Accordingly, it may be argued

166 Ibid [27].
167 Ibid.
168 Ibid [30].
169 Ibid.
170 Ibid [31].
171 [2014] EWCA Civ. 1366, [31].

that *The Channel Ranger* was more concerned with the timing of attributing meaning to a phrase and the actual commercial meaning that is attributed to it from the aspect of construing the true meaning of the words and not very much with 'inconsistency' as the timing of such attribution was held to be ruling out that possibility.

As indicated, the requirements regarding the incorporation of charterparty arbitration clauses are fundamentally not much different from the ones for the incorporation of general clauses. The three-step test also finds application in the context of the incorporation of arbitration clauses, and accordingly, there are similar boxes to be ticked in dealing with the incorporation of these. Nevertheless, the evaluation of whether arbitration clauses are incorporated is subject to a more detailed examination than of more generic charterparty provisions pertaining to shipment and delivery of the cargo since the incorporation of arbitration agreements may create more substantial outcomes. Accordingly, different approaches concerning their incorporation have been adopted over time and various concerns found voice in the expression of these divergent perspectives. In the following sections, some crucial examples of the inevitably accumulated fruitful case law are accordingly investigated chronologically to understand how various approaches adopted in English law concerning the incorporation of charterparty arbitration clauses are reflected in the practical implementation of shipping law over time.

2.3.3.2. A Chronology of the Case Law Regarding the Incorporation of Charterparty Arbitration Clauses into Bills of Lading

Once the bill of lading meets its third-party holder, the provisions of it prevail as its holder usually has no other means than reading these provisions to discover the rules that are applicable to their legal position. At this point, the 'special and possibly unique'[172] issue of the incorporation of charterparty arbitration clauses into bills of lading comes into prominence.

Traditionally, in the context of bills of lading incorporating charterparty provisions, English courts follow some 'peculiar and sophisticated rules which have grown out of a large body of English maritime case law'[173] rather than evaluating the implementation of the contractual doctrine of notice in maritime law. To put it differently, generally, a higher threshold for incorporation is established in this branch of law, and there are more elaborate and stricter criteria to meet to allow incorporation in comparison to what applies in contract law. However, some contemporary decisions of English courts[174] are in fact signalizing the adaptation of more flexible and modern approaches that validate what is known to the parties concerning contract terms, and such an implementation may perhaps be considered to show similarities with the application of a contractual doctrine of notice. Some relevant

172 *AIG Europa (UK) Ltd v The Ethniki* [2000] Lloyd's Rep IR 343 at [38]. The incorporation of a charterparty arbitration clause into the bill of lading did not constitute the main concern of this case, but the incorporation of the jurisdiction clause of an insurance contract into a reinsurance contract was essentially concerned with.

173 Özdel (n 132) 206.

174 Specifically, see *Sea Trade Maritime Corporation v Hellenic Mutual War Risks Association (Bermuda) Ltd, The Athena (No 2)* [2006] EWHC 2530; *Habas Sinai ve Tibbi Gazlar Isthisal Endustri AS v Sometal SAL* [2010] 1 Lloyd's Rep 661. It should be noted that these cases are, in fact, non-marine cases. However, these decisions lay the essential groundwork to be able evaluate how incorporation works in different branches of law and what the takeaways that may possibly be for a 'cross-fertilized' implementation: Merkin and Flannery (n 191) 6.2.2.

contemporary non-maritime cases[175] are analyzed at the end of this very chapter to evaluate the possibility of adopting the principles that are set out in these cases in the shipping context.

Despite providing some room for flexibility, English courts usually tend to adopt a narrow and restricted approach concerning the incorporation of ancillary provisions in the shipping context. The principles regarding the incorporation of charterparty arbitration clauses into bills of lading are predominantly turned to by courts settling disputes concerning the incorporation of provisions between chain contracts in branches of law other than shipping, such as reinsurance and construction. Therefore, in order to analyze the incorporation of arbitration clauses more comprehensively, some important examples of English case law are chronologically evaluated below to also include some decisions given before Arbitration Act 1996 came into force. Subsequently, the impact of the Act on the relevant case law is also discussed. Following this, the current standpoint and the mollification of the strict approach concerning the incorporation of arbitration clauses are considered. Now we turn to the chronological evaluation of English case law on the incorporation of charterparty arbitration clauses into bills of lading.

I. Hamilton & Co v Mackie Sons – *The Origin Story*

The relevant examination of the incorporation of charterparty arbitration clauses into bills of lading starts with *Hamilton & Co v Mackie Sons.*[176] The bill of lading, which the Court of Appeal was concerned with in this case, included the words 'all other terms and conditions per charterparty.' It was indicated by Lord Esher MR that concerning the purpose of incorporating charterparty terms into the bill of lading, the charterparty terms 'must be read *verbatim* into the bill of lading . . . Then if it was found that any of the conditions of the charterparty on being so read were inconsistent with the bill of lading were insensible, and must be disregarded.' It was held by the Court of Appeal that the relevant words of incorporation were inapt to incorporate the charterparty arbitration clause into the bill of lading as it was not applicable to a dispute between the shipowner and the endorsee of the bill of lading, who was not the charterer. The possible inconsistency that the incorporation would create in this case led the Court of Appeal to disallow the incorporation of the charterparty arbitration clause into the bill of lading and accordingly, the decision of the Divisional Court to uphold the stay of the proceedings was reversed.

II. Weir v Pirie – *Arbitration Clause in a Third-Party Guarantee*

Ten years after *Hamilton v Mackie*, the issue before the court was again the incorporation of a charterparty arbitration clause in *Weir & Co v Pirie & Co.*[177] Charterers were sued by shipowners for damages arising out of the delivery of coal under a charterparty providing that 'vessel to be loaded as customary, but subject in all respects to the colliery guarantee.' The said third-party guarantee dated a day later than the charterparty providing any question under the guarantee should be referred to arbitration and the decision to be binding and

175 Ibid.
176 [1889] 5 TLR 677.
177 [1898] 6 Comm Cas 263.

final by all interested. Such guarantees are regarded to be trite as they 'almost invariably incorporated in this way into charterparties' and any person interested in the relevant trade is deemed to be 'perfectly familiar with' them. Accordingly, Smith LJ considered the relevant guarantee in its entirety. With respect to the incorporation of the arbitration clause, the learned judge emphasized that such a clause should not be treated differently from the rest of the terms of the colliery guarantee. He pointed out that the wording of the arbitration clause indicating the shipowner, the charterer, and the colliery proprietor, it was not sensible to construe the true meaning of the scope of the incorporation between these two business contracts to exclude the arbitration clause. In other words, a third-party guarantee, including the arbitration clause it contained, was held to be incorporated in its entirety into the charterparty.[178]

III. Thomas v Portsea – *A Milestone Decision*

In *Thomas v Portsea*,[179] a strict approach regarding the incorporation of charterparty arbitration clauses was adopted. The case was concerned with claimed demurrage payments by the bill of lading holders to the shipowners due to a delay that occurred during the discharge of a cargo of timber at the port of arrival. The bill of lading included an incorporation clause indicating that 'other conditions per charterparty' and had a further margin endorsement that read 'all other terms and conditions and exceptions of the charter to be per charterparty including negligence clause.' The charterparty provided that 'any dispute or claim arising out of the conditions of this charterparty shall be adjusted at the port where it occurs, and same shall be settled by arbitration.' Following a dispute arising pertaining to the demurrage alleged to be payable to the shipowners, an arbitration against the holders of the bill of lading was initiated pursuant to the arbitration clause included in the charterparty. Due to some complications regarding the identification of the arbitrators, the arbitral proceedings could not be completed, but it was evident that arbitration was the primary method of dispute resolution sought by the shipowners. As this issue could not be resolved, the shipowners applied to the court to initiate court proceedings instead, which led to the defendant bill of lading holders to seek a stay of these proceedings. Initially, the stay was granted due to the comprehensiveness of the incorporation clause as it referred to disputes 'arising out of the conditions' and the relevant dispute considered to be falling into this category. The decision was subsequently rejected by the Court of Appeal, and the stay of the proceedings was dismissed. It was clear to Vaughan Williams LJ

> that the parties did not mean or assume that every clause in the charterparty which was applicable as between ship and charterer was to be incorporated and used as part and parcel of the bill of lading, so as to govern the relations between the ship and the bill of lading holder.[180]

In other words, the words included in the bill of lading held not to be clearly indicating the intention of the parties to assume that every charterparty provision was applicable to the relationship between the shipowner and the bill of lading holder.

178 This case was cited in argument before the Court of Appeal in *Thomas v Portsea* but hardly mentioned in any of the later authorities.

179 *Thomas v Portsea* [1912] AC 1.

180 [1911] P. 54, at [63].

The matter was eventually taken to the House of Lords,[181] where it was settled by means of a landmark judgement. The incorporation clause was held insufficient to incorporate the charterparty arbitration clause. One of the main underlying reasons for the rejection of incorporation held to be the specific and negotiable nature of these particular shipping documents.[182] It was indicated that it would pose danger to hold a general reference in a bill of lading to a charterparty to amount to incorporate the charterparty as a whole due to the amount of money passing by the transfer of bills of lading.[183]

The decision of the House of Lords sets out some ground rules as it indicates while a bill of lading is concerning the receipt, carriage, and delivery of the cargo, the charterparty is dealing with some other issues between the shipowner and the charterer and not the third-party holder of the bill. Furthermore, it is a landmark decision indicating that for the incorporation of provisions that are not relevant to the cargo or shipment (the ones that are 'not germane to the subject matter of the bill of lading'), very clear language is required. Since no holder of a bill of lading would desire any unknown provision to potentially require them to arbitrate at a location that they have no connection with, a vivid expression of intention to incorporate an arbitration clause is normally required. Truly, no one may be ousted from the jurisdiction of the courts against their wishes, and also, no one may be compelled to arbitrate. However, the incorporation of an arbitration clause functions as an indicator of the wishes of the parties to arbitrate, and thus, the language revealing such a wish is required to be very clear.[184]

Over some 100 years ago, it is settled in this milestone case that the incorporation of arbitration clauses is too serious of a business to be left to the employment of general words of incorporation, and hence, the intention to incorporate such has to be reflected in a specific way. Although it is true that a purely maritime-centric approach that is highlighting the peculiarities of shipping contracts and somewhat differentiating marine cases from non-marine ones, was adopted in *Thomas v Portsea*, it is also true that this particular landmark decision of the House of Lords had set an example for many subsequent cases, being marine or not, concerned with the issue of incorporation of arbitration clauses between chain contracts over the years. The fundamental concern leading to the adaptation of this approach was the negotiable nature of the incorporating document – namely, the bill of lading – and the potential risk of depriving an oblivious third-party holder of the document of their right to go to a court due to the transferability of this document. To put it differently, some concerns that led courts to seek some reassurance in the form of specific use of incorporating language were in fact purely relevant to some peculiarities of carriage of goods by sea and shipping law. Nevertheless, interestingly, this particular approach was also subsequently adopted in non-marine cases that are concerned with reinsurance and construction contracts. This juxtaposition is examined in the following chapters. However, setting up some ground rules, the significance of *Thomas v Portsea* is undeniable.

181 [1912] A.C. 1 (HL).
182 [1912] A.C. 1 (HL), [4].
183 [1912] A.C. 1 (HL), [4].
184 [1912] A.C. 1 (HL), [9].

IV. Elizabeth H – *Contractual Vary or Waiver of Arbitration After 18 Months?*

One of the issues before the court in *Elizabeth H*[185] was whether parties litigating could be perceived either as an alteration or the annulment of the arbitration agreement, and it was consequently decided that the relevant conduct of the parties was indicating that they accepted the jurisdiction of the court by means of varying the arbitration clause.[186]

The defendant shipowner applied for a stay, so the dispute arising out of damage and short delivery of the cargo of lard could be taken to arbitration. The charterparty included 'any dispute to shall settle in New York,' and the bill of lading provided that 'all the terms whatsoever of the said charterparty except the rate and payment of freight specified therein apply to and govern the rights of the parties.' This was a matter of New York law and not English law and the only relevant English case that was touched upon in *Elizabeth H* was *Thomas v Portsea*. Subsequent to short delivery, the vessel was arrested. The shipowners obtained a release as their P&I Club provided a letter of undertaking to pay the amount of which owners might be held liable to pay and the promise that 'if called upon to instruct solicitors to accept on behalf of owners service of proceedings' was given. Under these circumstances, the letter of undertaking was considered a bargain, for which there was a consideration for the solicitors to accept service on behalf of the owners of any proceeding. Hewson J pointed out that this undertaking was an evident invitation to continue the action, without a hint of arbitration. Furthermore, by staying in silence for 18 months before bringing the application to stay, the defendant shipowners were presumed to have accepted the court's jurisdiction. These facts accepted sufficient to depict that the defendant shipowners, or their agents, had impliedly accepted the court's jurisdiction by allowing the alteration in the arbitration clause by remaining silent. In *The Elizabeth H*, the court emphasized the magnitude of the acts and what is genuinely known to the parties. The 18 months long silence of the defendant shipowners and their failure to indicate their wish to refer present or future disputes to New York arbitration is considered by the court as reflecting the knowledge and intention of the parties, which constitute vertebral bones of arbitration as a dispute resolution mechanism. Accordingly, Hewson J was of the view that there were no sufficient grounds for granting a stay of proceedings and therefore, the first instance decision of Kerr J was overturned.

V. The Merak – *A Mistake with Contractual Enumeration*

It was considered in *The Merak*[187] whether the charterparty arbitration clause was incorporated into bills of lading since the charterparty arbitration clause applied to 'any dispute arising under this charterparty or any bill of lading issued hereunder' despite the fact that there was a mistake with the enumeration of contract clauses. The bill of lading included the words 'all the terms, conditions, clauses and exceptions including Clause 30 contained in the charterparty.' Clause 30 of the charterparty had no bearing on the bill of lading and had nothing to do with arbitration. The charterparty arbitration clause was in fact drafted under Clause 32. Charterparty included an express stipulation that it was to

185 [1962] 1 Lloyd's Rep 172.

186 See Peter Gillies and Andrew Dahdal, Waiver of a Right to Arbitrate by Resort to Litigation, in the Context of International Commercial Arbitration, 2007, *Journal of International Commercial Law and Technology*, 2(4), 221–230, 222.

187 [1965] P 223; [1965] 2 WLR 250; [1965] 1 All ER 230; [1964] 2 Lloyd's Rep 527.

be incorporated into any bill of lading issued under the charterparty. In other words, there was an indication in the charterparty that 'including Clause 32' (arbitration clause), the provisions of the charterparty were to be incorporated into the bills of lading issued under the charterparty.

It was considered by Sellers LJ that the incorporating clause could be read as referring to Clause 32 instead of Clause 30 as a matter of construction. However, Davies and Russel LJ, leading to the same result, adopted a different approach considering the indication in Clause 32 of the charterparty, which refers not only to disputes arising under the charterparty but also the ones arising under any bills issued under the charterparty, paramount. *Thomas v Portsea*, being concerned with a reference merely to disputes arising under the charterparty, was distinguished by the Court of Appeal in *The Merak* on the basis that Clause 32 was extensive enough to include disputes arising under bills of lading that were issued under the charterparty. On these grounds, Russel LJ distinguished the case from *Thomas v Portsea*, stating,

> I think a true view of [*Thomas v Portsea*] is that it shows that clauses which are directly germane to shipment, carriage and delivery may be incorporated by general words though the fact that they are found in a charterparty may involve a degree of verbal manipulation to fit exactly a bill of lading: but that where there is a clause whose subject-matter is not thus directly germane, such as an arbitration clause, it is not permissible to construe general words of incorporation as extending to a clause which does not in terms relate to a bill of lading.[188]

Furthermore, it was unacceptable for Davies LJ that the reference to Clause 30 to be considered to mean Clause 32 of the charterparty. Nonetheless, he regarded the 'all embracing' words of the bill of lading incorporation clause, as indeed embracing to extend the incorporation to charterparty arbitration clause provided that the words 'including Clause 30' considered 'surplusage.'[189] Moreover, it was also considered that since the scope of the word 'clauses' was wider than that of the word 'conditions,' which was clearly more comprehensive read together with the express reference in the charterparty arbitration clause to any bills issued under the charterparty, incorporation of the arbitration clause was held permissible.[190]

It was evident that there was a mistake concerning enumeration as the intention of the parties to refer their disputes to arbitration was clear, but they failed to properly do it so. However, the intervention of the court to rectify this would be considered excessive, and hence, the court refrained from such an intervention. Accordingly, a rectification was avoided, and the court instead sought other possible ways for allowing incorporation. Accordingly, the circumstances (the employment of the word 'clauses' and charterparty arbitration clause containing the words 'arising under bills of lading') which are indicating the intention of the parties to incorporate the arbitration clause were found convincing to allow incorporation in *The Merak*. The Court of Appeal was of the view that the parties were unsuccessful to reflect their true intention on the shipping documents merely because of a mistake they made in contract drafting and feeling 'unable to put right the mistake by

188 [1965] P 223, 260.
189 [1964] 2 Lloyd's Rep 527, 533.
190 Ibid 536 charterparty language was in 'ample width.'

rectifying the bill, it instead gave effect to the evident common intention of the original parties to the bill.'[191]

It should be noted that in light of the statements made by Beatson LJ in *The Channel Ranger*[192] concerning *The Merak*, the case would perhaps be decided differently today. In the opinion of the learned judge, *The Merak*, in which the Court of Appeal by a majority found that they could not correct an error in the bill of lading that referred to an incorrect clause number of the charterparty arbitration clause, predated the modern contextual approach to construction and implication.[193] The learned judge provided a detailed analysis of *The Merak* and regarded the approach of Davies and Russel LJ, considering the interpretation of the incorporation clause, 'very old fashioned and outdated,' to modern eyes particularly considering the red ink rule that is developed in *Chartbrook Ltd v Persimmon Homes Ltd.*[194] This particular rule establishes that there is no visible limit to the red ink the court could use to correct a contractual mistake detected in the process of interpretation, provided that both the mistake and the true meaning are apparent to a reasonable person. To put it differently, in light of the modern contextual approach to construction and implication, such a mistake could have been corrected during the interpretation phase without necessarily rectifying the relevant contract.

vi. The Annefield – *Exceptions Based on the Construction of Charterparty Arbitration Clause*

In *The Annefield*,[195] a few years later, the explicitness of the incorporation clause to refer to any ancillary provision and the scope of the arbitration agreement were hinged on. The vessel of the defendant owners was let out under a voyage charterparty for the transportation of the cargo of maize to Mediterranean ports. Clause 39 of the charterparty contained the provision as follows: 'all disputes from time to time arising out of this contract should be referred to London arbitration and that any claim must be made within 3 months of final discharge.' The payment for the delivery of the cargo was made by the buyers and the bills of lading were taken up by them. Subsequently, they sold part of the cargo to a French company and some of the bills are also endorsed by this company. Each bill stated that 'all terms, conditions, exceptions of which charterparty, including the negligence clause, are incorporated herewith.' The cargo was allegedly discharged in bad condition and subsequently, within three months of the final discharge, the buyers, as charterers, and the French company, as the holder of the bills, claimed arbitration. However, arbitration was not proceeded with. Later on, an action *in rem* was brought against the shipowners for damages as a result of the breach of contract. Shipowners applied for a stay on the basis that the dispute ought to be submitted to arbitration.

The Court of Appeal dicta in *The Annefield* supports the existence of an exception to the strict rule for the incorporation of the charterparty arbitration provision, 'where the arbitration clause in the charterparty is wide enough on its true construction and without

191 Robert Merkin and Louis Flannery, *Merkin and Flannery on the Arbitration Act 1996*, Informa Law from Routledge, 2020, 6.2.2. (ix).
192 [2014] EWCA Civ 1366, [32–39].
193 Ibid.
194 [2009] UKHL 38.
195 [1970] 2 Lloyd's Rep 252; [1971] 1 Lloyd's Rep 1 (CA); [1971] P 168.

any verbal manipulation to include disputes under the bill of lading and between parties to it.'[196] It should be noted that Lord Denning, holding that the charterparty arbitration clause was not incorporated into the bill of lading by the employment of general words, accepted that the manipulation test adopted in *The Merak* could be 'adapted slightly.'[197] The learned judge stated,

> I would follow the test laid down by Russel LJ in *The Merak* [1965] P. 223, 260, but I would adapt it slightly. I would say that a clause which is directly germane to the subject-matter of the bill of lading (that is to shipment, carriage and delivery of goods) can and should be incorporated into the bill of lading contract, even though it may involve a degree of manipulation of the words in order to fit exactly the bill of lading.[198]

It should perhaps be noted, it was indicated in *The Annefield* that the argument before the Court of Appeal was different than the one in *The Merak* as the latter was an unusual case and it was established in *The Annefield* that incorporation is a concept that is concerned with contract construction.[199] However, the Court of Appeal acknowledged the possible incorporation of a charterparty arbitration clause by virtue of an incorporation clause that is not formed in a specific style. However, for such incorporation to be applicable, there are further requirements such as the arbitration clause itself to be constructed in a more inclusionary manner and this was not held to be the case in *The Annefield*. Accordingly, incorporation was not allowed and a stay was not granted.

vii. The Rena K – *Intention to Arbitrate and Sufficient Incorporation*

The Rena K[200] exhibits a successful example of the incorporation of a charterparty arbitration clause into bills of lading. The relevant incorporation clause was formed as follows 'all the terms, clauses, conditions and exceptions including the arbitration clause . . . are hereby incorporated.' The charterparty provided 'any disputes . . . to be settled by Arbitration in London. Two bills of lading were issued . . . both containing . . . all terms, clauses, conditions and exceptions including the Arbitration Clause . . . are hereby incorporated.' The ways that the arbitration clause and the incorporation clause were structured were found sufficient for the incorporation of the charterparty arbitration clause by Brandon J, and consequently, the stay was granted. Indeed, the particular addition of the words 'arbitration clause' in the bills of lading may considered to be illustrating the intention of the parties to refer their disputes to arbitration, which was governed under the charterparty arbitration clause.[201] It

196 Ambrose, Maxwell, and Collett (n 146) 56, 4.42.

197 [1971] P 168, 184. Also see Merkin and Flannery (n 191) 6.2.2. (xi).

198 [1971] P 168, 184.

199 [1971] 1 Lloyd's Rep 1 at 5. However, it should be noted that the Court of Appeal in *The Merak* [1964] 2 Lloyd's Rep 527 refrained from rectifying the obvious mistake with referencing but instead gave priority to the true and ascertainable intention of the parties to refer their disputes to arbitration. In other words, the validation of incorporation was achieved not by means of rectification but instead by means of prioritizing the intention of the parties. The result, anyways, was incorporation to be held sufficient. Nevertheless, see *Caresse Navigation Ltd v Zurich Assurances MAROC and Others (The Channel Ranger)* [2014] EWCA Civ 1366 for some arguments why *The Merak* would perhaps be decided differently today in light of modern contextual approach to construction and implication: See *Chartbrook Ltd v Persimmon Homes Ltd* [2009] UKHL 38.

200 [1978] 1 Lloyd's Rep 545.

201 Ibid [546].

was stated by Brandon J that, since the intention of the parties to incorporate the charterparty arbitration clause into their bills of lading was clear, if some degree of manipulation of the wording of the arbitration clause was needed to give effect to this intention, then he was clearly of the view that this manipulation should have been done. Brandon J indicated,

> The present case is, in my view, clearly distinguishable, in that there are added to the usual general words of incorporation in the two bills of lading the further specific words 'including the arbitration clause.' The addition of these words must, as it seems to me, mean that the parties to the bills of lading intended the provisions of the arbitration clause in the charterparty to apply in principle to disputes arising under the bills of lading; and, if it is necessary, as it obviously is, to manipulate or adapt part of the wording of that clause in order to give effect to that intention, then I am clearly of opinion that this should be done.[202]

However, it was emphasized that there was well-established authority that general words of incorporation would usually not be sufficient to incorporate an arbitration clause into the bills of lading, as well as a distinction between charterparty clauses that are 'directly germane to the shipment, carriage and delivery of the goods covered by the bill of lading and other clauses which are not directly germane to such matters.'[203] *The Rena K* may be considered significant in the sense that it highlights the distinction[204] between the charterparty clauses that are 'directly germane to the shipment, carriage and delivery of the goods covered by the bill of lading and other clauses which are not germane to such matters.'[205] The distinction being acknowledged, the circumstances in *The Rena K* did not seem to be falling under one of these categories as there was a clear illustration of the intention to arbitrate because the incorporation clause simply included the words 'arbitration clause.'

VIII. The Varenna – *Conditions v Ancillary Terms*

In *The Varenna*,[206] a bill of lading was issued regarding the shipment of crude oil from Syria to Germany. The bill indicated that 'all conditions and exceptions of the charterparty including the negligence clause are deemed to be incorporated.' The charterparty specifically set forth its terms and conditions, including the London arbitration clause, to be incorporated into any bills of lading issued under.[207] The bill of lading did not include any specific reference to the charterparty arbitration clause. One of the main issues to be addressed was whether the word 'conditions' in the bill of lading was sufficient to incorporate the charterparty arbitration provision.

It was emphasized in *The Varenna*, 'On no view is an arbitration clause such a condition. An arbitration clause is a collateral provision . . . It is a clause or a term. It is not a condition.'[208] It was stated that because the arbitration clause was not a 'condition' but

202 Ibid [551].

203 [1978] 1 Lloyd's Rep 545, [550]. *Hamilton v Mackie* [1889] 5 TLR 677, *Thomas v Portsea* [1912] AC 1, *The Annefield* [1970] 2 Lloyd's Rep 252; [1971] 1 Lloyd's Rep 1 (CA); [1971] P 168 were among the cited cases.

204 Merkin and Flannery (n 191) 6.2.2. (xii).

205 [1978] 1 Lloyd's Rep 545 at [550].

206 [1983] 1 Lloyd's Rep 416; affd. [1983] 2 Lloyd's Rep 592.

207 Same requirement in the charterparty existed in *The Merak* [1964] 2 Lloyd's Rep 527.

208 [1983] 1 Lloyd's Rep 416 at [422].

rather 'a clause or a term,' the incorporation of it was not possible by the employment of the indicated words of incorporation.[209]

The promotion of commercial certainty was regarded as an issue by the Court of Appeal in *The Varenna* that would prevail and it was stated that

> the commercial customers – shipowners, shippers and receivers – attach supreme importance to certainty and where particular phrases have established meanings and effects it is not the policy of the law to seek to change them even if, in the absence of precedent, there would be a case for so doing.[210]

The court in *The Varenna* did not differentiate the phrases 'all terms and conditions' and 'all conditions' and concluded that neither of these phrases was sufficient to incorporate the arbitration clause.[211]

IX. THE FEDERAL BULKER – *DIFFERENTIATING CLAUSES AND TERMS*

In *The Federal Bulker*,[212] the relevant bill of lading included that 'all terms, conditions and exceptions per charterparty to be considered as fully incorporated.' Bingham LJ, by rejecting the incorporation, followed the general authority set out in *Thomas v Portsea*[213] and stated that the general words do not suffice to incorporate an arbitration clause. It was emphasized by the Court of Appeal that, although, the employment of general words is sufficient to incorporate the charterparty clauses, which are germane to the carriage and discharge of the cargo, for the incorporation of ancillary clauses that mainly govern the relationship between the owner and the charterer, stricter and thus more specific and clear rules are needed. This is highlighted on the following grounds:

> This is indeed a field in which it is perhaps preferable that the law should be clear, certain and well understood than that it should be perfect. Like others, I doubt whether the line drawn by the authorities is drawn where a modern commercial lawyer would be inclined to draw it. But it would, I think, be a source of mischief if we were to do anything other than try to give effect to settled authority as best we can.[214]

To put it differently, the desired predictability of the law is considered to be prevailing over the reflection of the true selection of the parties of the resolution method that would be applicable to their dispute. It is stressed by Bingham LJ that if the parties do not like to be subject to the well-settled strict English principle that necessitates the employment of specific words for the incorporation of an arbitration provision, then they can spell arbitration out in the context of the bill of lading.[215]

Moreover, the classification of arbitration clauses was further discussed in *The Federal Bulker* since the incorporation clause in the bill of lading contained the words 'all terms and conditions,' and it was considered necessary to identify whether an arbitration provision

209 Ibid [421]. The decision was upheld on appeal. *The Varenna* [1983] 2 Lloyd's Rep 592 at [595].
210 [1983] 2 Lloyd's Rep 592, [594].
211 Ibid 597. Also see Merkin and Flannery (n 191) 6.2.2. (xv).
212 *Federal Bulk Carriers Inc v C Itoh & Co Ltd (The Federal Bulker)* [1989] 1 Lloyd's Rep 103.
213 [1912] A.C. 1.
214 [1989] 1 Lloyd's Rep 103, [105].
215 Ibid.

falls into the scope of such a category. For such an identification to be made it was necessary to clarify the classification of the arbitration clause. It was found beyond doubt that the charterparty arbitration clause was indeed 'a term, even if not a condition.'[216] *The Federal Bulker* draws a line between the approach adopted in *The Merak*[217] and the well-settled approach adopted in *Thomas v Portsea*[218] indicating that the keyword in *The Merak* was 'clauses,'[219] and there was a vivid illustration of the intention of the parties to refer to their disputes to arbitration. This was not the case in *The Federal Bulker*. Consequently, the Court of Appeal in *The Federal Bulker* was convinced that specific words of incorporation were needed for the incorporation of the charterparty arbitration clause.

X. THE OINOUSSIN PRIDE – *FOLLOWING* RENA K

The Oinoussin Pride[220] was concerned with an application by Taiwanese bill of lading holders for a stay of proceedings that were initiated by Liberian/Greek shipowners on the grounds that parties were bound to arbitrate. Reading together the bill of lading incorporation clause indicating the incorporation of all terms of the charterparty including the arbitration clause, and the charterparty arbitration clause stating the arbitration to apply to disputes between the charterer and the shipowner, the court found similarities between the case in hand and *The Rena K*.[221] Similarly, some degree of manipulation considered to be required for the arbitration clause to apply to disputes that may arise under the bill of lading due to the restricted construction of the charterparty arbitration clause. The manipulation of the words of the charterparty arbitration clause was considered necessary in *The Oinoussin Pride* due to the similarity it showed with *The Rena K*. The stay was granted because Webster J was convinced that there was reciprocal assurance concerning the intention to arbitrate reading these interconnected shipping documents together, and therefore, manipulation to some degree was permitted.

XI. THE NERANO – *INCONSISTENCY AND RECONCILIATION*

The convenient circumstances in which a charterparty arbitration clause may be incorporated into a bill of lading were considered in *The Nerano*.[222] The charterparty arbitration clause read as follows: 'That should any dispute arise between the Owners and the Charterers the matter in dispute should be determined in London, England . . . and English law to govern.' The bill of lading contained an endorsement by virtue of the words 'conditions as per relevant Charter Party . . . are incorporated in this Bill of Lading and have precedence if there is a conflict. English law and jurisdiction applies.' However, the first clause on the back of the bill of lading provided, 'All terms and conditions, liberties, exceptions and arbitration clause of the Charter Party . . . are herewith incorporated.' Accordingly, there was obvious inconsistency.

216 Merkin and Flannery (n 191) 6.2.2. (xviii).
217 [1964] 2 Lloyd's Rep 527.
218 [1912] A.C. 1.
219 [1989] 1 Lloyd's Rep 103, [108].
220 [1991] 1 Lloyd's Rep 126.
221 [1978] 1 Lloyd's Rep 545.
222 [1994] 2 Lloyd's Rep 50.

The Nerano was concerned with the application of Italian shipowners to stay proceedings, allegedly brought in breach of the arbitration clause by the bill of lading holders. The application was based on the claim that the charterparty arbitration clause was incorporated into the bills of lading. The 'exception test' that was developed in *The Annefield*[223] *is* considered inapplicable due to the restricted construction of the charterparty arbitration clause and the impossibility of it to apply to disputes under the bill of lading without verbal manipulation. Furthermore, like *The Oinoussin Pride*,[224] the potential necessity of reading the bill of lading and charterparty together was also considered in *The Nerano*. However, the issue with the latter was the existence of contextual inconsistency within the bill of lading as it was considered to include conflicting terms. The court indicated that the term at the front of the bill of lading indicating the incorporation of charterparty conditions was not sufficient to incorporate the charterparty arbitration clause because, first, the term did not specifically refer to the arbitration clause, and second, the charterparty arbitration clause did not have a wide scope to include the disputes under the bill of lading. On the other hand, the inconsistent incorporation clause, which is located on the back, included a specific reference to the charterparty arbitration clause.

All in all, reading two provisions together, the wording of the bill of lading was held to be referring to the charterparty arbitration clause. Accordingly, Clarke J allowed the reconciliation of the words by construing the reference to English jurisdiction as one to the residual supervisory jurisdiction of the English courts over all arbitrations seated here.[225] To put it differently, the phrase 'English jurisdiction' was held not to be inconsistent with the expressly referred charterparty arbitration clause. Consequently, the incorporation was allowed, and the stay was granted.

xii. The Heidberg – *Charterparty Not Being Reduced into Writing*

The High Court in *The Heidberg*[226] considered the potential incorporation of the arbitration clause of an unidentified charterparty. The main issue before the High Court to consider was that the charterparty had not been reduced into writing at the time that the bill of lading was issued under this charterparty. In other words, there was solely an oral agreement regarding the terms of the charterparty. However, the bill of lading contained a reference to this unidentified charterparty and an incorporation clause indicating its terms, including the charterparty arbitration clause, to be incorporated into the bill of lading. It was decided by HHJ Diamond QC that an oral agreement that was not evidenced in writing was not capable of being incorporated into a bill of lading, as a matter of construction.[227]

To be able to analyze *The Heidberg*, we can make some deductions. Fundamentally, the incorporation of the charterparty arbitration clause was held insufficient not because the approach in *Thomas v Portsea*[228] was adopted in *The Heidberg.*[229] Even though there was insufficient information to identify the charterparty in the latter, there was still a

223 [1970] 2 Lloyd's Rep 252; [1971] 1 Lloyd's Rep 1 (CA); [1971] P 168.
224 [1991] 1 Lloyd's Rep 126.
225 [1994] 2 Lloyd's Rep 50, [55].
226 [1994] 2 Lloyd's Rep 287.
227 [1994] 2 Lloyd's Rep 287, [311].
228 [1912] A.C. 1.
229 [1994] 2 Lloyd's Rep 287 at [311]. Merkin and Flannery (n 191) 6.2.2. (xxv)

specific reference to the charterparty arbitration clause. The main problem pertaining to incorporation was the vagueness of the charterparty and not the employment of the general words of incorporation. Hence, although incorporation was not allowed, the rejection of the notion was based on the structural features of the relevant bills of lading, and not on the approach adopted in *Thomas v Portsea*. Hence, the decision may not necessarily be regarded to be reflecting the *Thomas v Portsea* approach. Another issue that was considered in *The Heidberg* was the negotiable character of the bills of lading and its unbalancing impact on the bargaining power of the parties to shipping operations. The potential risk of subsequent holders of the bill, who are not aware of charterparty terms that may potentially be incorporated,[230] to be subject to the governance of the terms of such a distant contract was considered to create a 'commercially unsound'[231] situation in *The Heidberg*.

It should be noted that *The Heidberg* was one of the last judgements concerning the incorporation of charterparty arbitration clauses prior to the enactment of the Arbitration Act 1996. This point is of significance as the Arbitration Act 1996 adopts a more flexible approach regarding the matter of incorporation and contains provisions that particularly regulate the incorporation of arbitration clauses by reference.

2.3.3.3. The Arbitration Act 1996 and Incorporation of Arbitration Clauses

Prior to the enactment of the Arbitration Act 1996, predominantly the strict approach concerning the incorporation of arbitration clauses was preferred and applied over time. The main reasoning for this, among other concerns, has usually been propounded to be the cruciality of promoting the security of the third parties who do not have any knowledge (or the means of finding out) of the charterparty provisions and their scope. To subject the oblivious holder of the bill to the terms of an arbitration agreement they are unaware of has been perceived as unfair, and thus, specific words of incorporation to be employed are established as a fundamental requirement of the courts to allow the incorporation of the charterparty arbitration clause. The relevant judgements of English courts 'form a clear and developed line of authority, which is well-known and recognized in the shipping trade and which has been endorsed in modern case law.'[232] It is indeed true that the promotion of third-party protection is primary to ensure law and commerce go hand in hand so that there is a certain level of foreseeability. Nonetheless, it should also be noted that the wide usage of arbitration clauses may not completely be overlooked, and it would somewhat be naive to contend the true unawareness of the contracting party of the 'remote' possibility of the charterparty to contain an arbitration clause provided that the party in question is an experienced actor of the shipping market and is familiar with the ways shipping transactions are conducted. Arbitration clauses are contained in shipping contracts 'too often.'

The Arbitration Act 1996 explicitly regulates the matter of incorporation of arbitration clauses. Section 6(2) stipulates, 'The reference in an agreement to a written form of the arbitration clause or to a document containing an arbitration clause constitutes an arbitration agreement if the reference is such as to make that clause part of the agreement.' In other words, the legal concept of incorporation by reference found itself a statutory place in

230 Treitel and Reynolds (n 2) 75, 3–008.
231 [1994] 2 Lloyd's Rep 287, [310].
232 Ambrose, Maxwell, and Collett (n 146) 54, 4.39.

the Arbitration Act 1996 and one may think such involvement has cleared the air. One would be mistaken. The Act indeed lays out some ground rules. However, the wording of Section 6(2), in fact, is far from being instructive and contains vague terms such as 'the reference is such as to make that clause part of the agreement.' Such wording in the legal sense neither provides any instruction for the parties regarding the formulation of an incorporation clause nor gives any indications concerning how to evaluate the phrase 'as to make that clause part of the agreement.'

There are also other issues regarding incorporation such as the way of illustrating the true and ascertainable intention to arbitrate that the legislation is silent on. The Report of the Departmental Advisory Committee on Arbitration Law (DAC Report) openheartedly admitted that the section pertaining to the incorporation of arbitration clauses was deliberately left open to the interpretation of the courts. The reason provided was that there was a need for each case to be considered on its own facts. Accordingly, it was provided in the DAC Report that, taking the facts of the cases and the requirements of the Act into consideration, the decision regarding the incorporation of arbitration clauses was one of the courts to make.[233]

Over time, the application of the strict approach and some underlying concerns that have been contended to justify its implementation got subjected to some elaborate examination.[234] Some of the suggested justifications are considered in the following section to evaluate whether these still find reasonable applications in implementing incorporation or simply create evitable obstacles on the way to the promotion of party autonomy.

2.3.3.4. Is the Strict Approach of Incorporation Justifiable?

The restrictions concerning the incorporation of arbitration clauses are fundamentally derived from some legal concerns. One of the essential concerns pertaining to such restrictions has been contended to be the necessity of providing fairness.[235] For the purpose of ensuring such is provided to the subsequent holders of the negotiable bill of lading, who are possibly unfamiliar with the charterparty arbitration clause, the incorporation of these particular provisions has been restricted to circumstances where a specific reference is made to them. However, the strict application of incorporation is eventually extended even to non-marine transactions[236] that do not include the element of negotiability.

The restricted approach concerning the incorporation of arbitration clauses fundamentally finds its merits more or less in three concerns that are laid out in *Aughton*.[237] The first

233 DAC Report, [42].

234 See specifically *Sea Trade Maritime Corporation v Hellenic Mutual War Risks Association (Bermuda) Ltd, The Athena (No 2)* [2006] EWHC 2530 (Comm); *Habas Sinai ve Tibbi Gazlar Isthisal Endustri AS v Sometal SAL* [2010] 1 Lloyd's Rep 661. Furthermore, also see Chapter 5, 'Singapore Law and Incorporation of Arbitration Clauses.'

235 Section 11 of the Unfair Contract Terms Act (UCTA) 1977 provides that a term 'shall have been a fair and reasonable one to be included having regard to the circumstances which were, or ought reasonably to have been, known to or in the contemplation of the parties when the contract was made.' Also, list of factors set out in Section 2 are considered in determining whether a term is reasonable.

236 Masood Ahmed, Arbitration Clauses: Fairness, Justice and Commercial Certainty, 2010, *Arbitration International*, 26(3), 412. LCIA.

237 Sir John Megaw applying the strict approach of incorporation outside the shipping context (construction) in *Aughton Ltd v M F Kent Services Ltd.* [1991] 57 Build LR 1. (This case is analyzed in more detail in Chapter 4, 'Construction Contracts and the Incorporation of Arbitration Clauses.') The case concerned whether the arbitration

concern that is expressed in this case was the empowerment of the arbitral tribunal over the court and accordingly, the impediment of the latter's jurisdiction. A second concern is 'the unclear' requirement concerning arbitration agreements to be 'in writing' and the form requirements to show fundamental differences under different conventions and legal systems. The third concern that is expressed by Sir John Megaw in *Aughton* is one of contractual entirety concerned with the fact that arbitration agreements usually remain effective regardless of the invalidity of the primary contract they may be contained in.

2.3.3.4.1. The Impediment of Court's Jurisdiction

> Arbitration agreements may potentially impede[238] the jurisdiction of the court.[239] However, as a rule of common law, the mere existence of an arbitration agreement do not prevent parties from initiating court proceedings as they may not agree to oust the jurisdiction of the court.[240] This is because the comprehensive and fair legal protection is considered an essential right that the courts provide for the parties. Therefore, the arbitration agreement (and not the arbitration award) does not suffice to supplant the jurisdiction of the court, but it may lead it to decide to stay.[241]

The Arbitration Act 1996 regulates that a party to an arbitration agreement against whom legal proceedings are brought in respect of a matter – which under the agreement is to be referred to arbitration – may apply to the court, in which the proceedings have been brought, to stay the proceedings so far as they concern that matter.[242] According to the Act, the court shall stay its proceedings unless the relevant arbitration clause is inoperative,

---

clause in a building subcontract was incorporated into the sub-subcontract by general wording. It was stated by Ralph Gibson LJ in 20 that even though the words, in terms of construction, were sufficient to incorporate the clause, the arbitration agreement itself failed to meet the statutory requirement to be in writing. Sir John Megaw applied a strict approach and set forth reasons that justify the adoption of such dealing with the incorporation of arbitration clauses. He set forth that, first, an arbitration agreement may preclude the parties to it from bringing a dispute before a court of law. Second, an arbitration agreement has to be 'a written agreement.' Third, the arbitration clause differs from other types of clause because it constitutes a 'self-contained contract collateral or ancillary to' the substantive contract. *Aughton* is analyzed in more detail in the following chapters. Also see Paul Todd, Incorporation of Arbitration Clauses into Bills of Lading, 1997, *Journal of Business Law*, 331, 337; Allison and Dharmananda (n 160) 273–275.

238 Under English law, an *in rem* (*in rem:* describing a court action that is directed against an item of property rather than against a person or group of people. Actions *in rem* are a feature of Admiralty Court, *Oxford Dictionary of Law*, Oxford University Press, 2015, 8th Edn.) action may be brought despite an arbitration agreement, but if the dispute is submitted to arbitration, then the proceedings will be stayed and the arrested vessel retained as security; *The Andria Now Renamed Vasso* [1984] QB 477, 489–490. See Section (11) of the Arbitration Act 1996.

239 See Moses Oruaze Dickson, Party Autonomy and Justice in International Commercial Arbitration, 2018, *International Journal of Law and Management*, 60, 114.

240 Robert Merkin and Johanna Hjalmarsson, *Singapore Arbitration Legislation*, Informa Law from Routledge, 2016, 27.

241 For an excellent evaluation of how courts 'give up' their jurisdiction and grant stay of legal proceedings, see Merkin and Flannery (n 191) 9.0–9.21.

242 Section 9(1) of the Arbitration Act 1996. The distinction between the duty to stay and power to stay should be drawn here. This division would be provided regarding the domestic or non-domestic character of the arbitration agreement, therefore by Section 3 of the Arbitration Act 1996, which regulates 'the seat of arbitration.' If the seat of arbitration is in England, Wales, or Northern Ireland, then Section 9 would apply, and therefore, the court 'shall' grant a stay if the arbitration agreement meets the provided criteria. However, if the seat of arbitration is in somewhere else or there has been no seat designated, then the stay rules would apply as Section 2(2) and the Courts of England must stay proceedings before them on such non-domestic arbitration disregarding the seat of arbitration.

void, or incapable of being performed.[243] The word 'shall' in the Act may be evaluated to understand the position of the courts in granting stay. It is safe to say that courts retain a decision-making function because 'shall' only kicks in once the court has freely decided that there is a valid arbitration agreement. Therefore, the operation of the word 'shall' comes subsequent to the decision-making of the court regarding the justification of its operation.

Once stay is granted, this creates the result of the relevant action to 'stay forever.'[244] Although arbitration agreements preclude the avenues of judicial recourse,[245] the common law courts shall stay their action for the prominence of the arbitration process provided that legal preconditions are met.[246] The courts are usually not reluctant to decide in favour of arbitration (and to stay their proceedings) if they are convinced that the promotion of such would accurately reflect party autonomy.

In an insurance case, *Sea Trade Maritime Corporation v Hellenic Mutual War Risks Association (Bermuda) Ltd (The Athena)*,[247] the perpetual application of the well-established strict rule was evaluated, and it was indicated that the question of whether an arbitration clause included in standard terms to be incorporated by the employment of general words was one of contractual construction. Subsequently, the court found, based on the configuration of contracts, that standard terms, possibly including arbitration clauses, ought to be incorporated by the employment of such words. In this case, the concerned words were held sufficient to incorporate the arbitration clause in the defendant Mutual War Risks Association's Rules into the contract of insurance because the knowledge of the claimant shipowner Sea Trade was irrelevant since brokers as its agents were aware of the arbitration clause.[248] The knowledge of the brokers held is attributable to their principal, Sea Trade, under English law. The court in *The Athena* distinguished the contractual situation in hand from a 'two-contract situation,' under which bills of lading incorporating charterparties generally fall and therefore be subject to stricter rules of incorporation.

With regard to this first concern about arbitration impeding the jurisdiction of the courts, it may be argued that it would be senseless to ignore the emerging global pro-arbitration climate,[249] which diminishes the prospect disputes of competing jurisdictions[250] and reduces

243 Section 9(4) of the Arbitration Act 1996.

244 Merkin and Flannery (n 191) 9.20–9.21: In *Inco Europe Ltd v First Choice Distribution* [2000] 1 WLR 586, it was decided that the right of appeal existed. The court held that the right to appeal to the Court of Appeal against a decision to refuse a stay had not been removed by the Arbitration Act 1996.

245 Simon Greenberg, Christopher Kee, and Romesh Weeramantry, *International Commercial Arbitration: An Asia-Pacific Perspective*, Cambridge University Press, 2010, 152.

246 *Channel Tunnel Group Ltd. v Balfour Beatty Construction Ltd.* [1993] AC 334, 351–352 (HL).

247 *The Athena* [2006] EWHC 2530 (Comm). As it is analyzed under '2.4. Mollification of the Strict Approach and the Current Standpoint,' this does not apply to two-contract scenarios. *The Athena* was concerned with an insurance and the question was whether the arbitration agreement incorporated. It was held that the general words of incorporation was sufficient for the incorporation of the arbitration clause since the case included a single-contract scenario. It was stated that as long as between the established players in a well-known market, general words would be sufficient for the incorporation.

248 [2006] EWHC 2530 (Comm), [70]. In the context of all the exchanges over the years of cover, frequency of explicit references to the rules in question, and the knowledge of the agencies involved, Langley J considered the submission of the claimant as a 'hopeless' one: [68].

249 Hamblen J in *Stellar Shipping Co Llc v Hudson Shipping Lines* [2010] EWHC 2986 at [63].

250 James Spigelman, *Law and International Commerce: Between the Parochial and the Cosmopolitan*, Speech delivered at the New South Wales Association, Sydney, June 22, 2010. Also see Allison and Dharmananda (n 160) 273–274.

the avoidable formality and expenses on the parties' benefit. Nevertheless, arbitration as a dispute resolution method both reflects the need for the promotion of party autonomy in commercial disputes and provides efficient protection by foreseeing a possible judicial intervention if circumstances in the future make such necessary in order to ensure fairness is restored.[251]

On the other hand, as clearly illustrated by Gerold Herrmann, even without the slightest hope of reaching a consensus, the views concerning the role the courts should play in the arbitration process are highly diversified.[252] Herrmann provides a spectrum, which has arbitration turning into an inadmissible theatre of absurdity if not monitored and assisted by the court at one end, and the arbitration process as a good play, which would suffer and get ruined as a result of the intervention of the court since the artistic freedom of the players would be hindered, at the other.[253] However, one may argue that the eminence of providing a wider autonomy to the arbitrating parties, and thus, minimizing the judicial intervention has been more and more prioritized over the years[254] since the rules of arbitration sprout out from party autonomy. Accordingly, it has been stated in the general principles of the Arbitration Act 1996 that 'the parties should be free to agree how their disputes are resolved, subject only to such safeguards as are necessary for the public interest and the court should not intervene except as provided in the Act.'[255] Furthermore, it has also been provided in the UNCITRAL Model Law that in the matters governed by (the Model) law, no court shall intervene except where so provided in the Model Law.[256] In other words, the law generally does not endorse the intervention of the courts in the process of arbitration unless circumstances make it crucially necessary for its fair conduct.

International commercial parties, who are subject to cross-border commercial relationships, may prefer to resort to arbitration due to the potential unpredictability of the application of different jurisdictions to a dispute that may arise from their cross-border transactions. This is because one of the fundamental wishes of the parties to a commercial transaction of international character would be to avoid both facing an unfamiliar jurisdiction and being subject to the rules of an unknown legislation. Accordingly, the concern regarding arbitration agreements impeding the jurisdiction of the courts seems quite unmerited, especially in the context of international commercial disputes and their practical realities. Specifically, in the shipping context, London handled 1,737 maritime arbitrations in 2019, which equates to around 83% of all international maritime arbitrations that year.[257] This demonstrates that London is usually the preferred jurisdiction, and arbitration is a highly popular resolution method that applies to shipping disputes.

---

251 Ahmed (n 236) 409.

252 Gerold Herrmann, The Role of the Courts Under the UNCITRAL Model Law Script, in Julian DM Lew (ed.) *Contemporary Problems in International Arbitration*, Springer Science + Business Media, 1987, 164.

253 Ibid.

254 Mary E. McNerney and Carlos A. Esplugues, International Commercial Arbitration: The UNCITRAL Model Law, 1986, *Boston College International and Comparative Law Review*, 9(1), Article 3, 55.

255 Section 1(b), 1(c) of the Arbitration Act 1996.

256 UNCITRAL Model Law 1985 amended in 2006, Art. 5.

257 *The Maritime Arbitration Universe in Numbers: London Remains Ever Dominant*, July 2020, HFW, available at www.hfw.com/downloads/002203-HFW-Maritime-Arbitration-in-Numbers-July-2020.pdf.

Concerning international commercial transactions, arbitration reduces 'the uncertainty arising from the existence of competing jurisdictions with claims to settle the disputes.'[258] Also, the words of Hamblen J in the *Stellar Shipping Co Llc v Hudson Shipping Lines* are worth mentioning as they profoundly reflect the actual situation regarding the decision of the courts to grant a stay concerning international commercial disputes: 'In the modern pro-arbitration climate I cannot accept that the fact that the court's jurisdiction is being ousted remains a consideration of weight.'[259] Indeed, the policy considerations of the courts in our century are significantly 'different from those that may have motivated judges at the end of the nineteenth.'[260] Furthermore, one of the reasons for 'courts being less jealous of their jurisdiction than the past'[261] is perhaps because arbitration nowadays, if regarded to be perfectly suitable for the resolution of international commercial disputes and the entire referral of these to courts instead, would create a massively heavy burden on legal systems.

2.3.3.4.2. Formality of Arbitration Agreements

The requirement of arbitration agreements to be in writing has been considered an element that induces the adoption of stricter rules for the incorporation of arbitration clauses. Indeed, the Arbitration Act 1996 only applies to agreements in writing.[262] Notwithstanding, being 'in writing' has a broader scope than it may initially be perceived. The Arbitration Act 1996 does not necessitate strict formality criteria to be met as it neither requires the written agreement to be signed nor it to exist as a separate document as the relevant provision of the Act simply states that 'the agreement can be evidenced in writing.'[263] The Act also indicates that the writing requirement is satisfied if the agreement is made by the exchange of communications in writing to be recorded by any means,[264] which includes emails and other types of electronic documentation.[265]

The first concern regarding the impediment of the court jurisdiction may be said to be predominantly intertwined with this form requirement. It is usually contended that unless it is expressly agreed, as a written statement would clearly indicate, no one should be deprived of their right to recourse to the court for obtaining a judgement. Therefore, the main approach is that if a mere oral agreement would not be qualified as a sufficient one, then it would follow that a depending agreement would not suffice either.[266]

In 1958 the Convention on the Recognition and Enforcement of Foreign Arbitral Awards (the New York Convention), which provides a set of rules concerning the enforcement

258 Spigelman (n 250) 4.

259 Hamblen J in *Stellar Shipping Co Llc v Hudson Shipping Lines* [2010] EWHC 2986 at [63].

260 Merkin and Flannery (n 191) 6.2.3.

261 Adrian Baron, The International Arbitration Act, the Fiction of Severability and Claims for Restitution – Part Two, 2000, *Arbitration International*, 16(2), 159–188, 183. See Peter Sallman, The Impact of Caseflow Management in the Judicial System, 1995, *University of New South Wales Law Journal*, 18, 193.

262 Section 5(1) of the Arbitration Act 1996.

263 Section 5(2)(c) and Section 5(4) of the Arbitration Act 1996.

264 Section 5(6) of the Arbitration Act 1996.

265 Merkin and Flannery (n 191) 6.1.5. Also see *The Epsilon Rosa* [2002] 2 Lloyd's Rep 701, affirmed in [2003] 2 Lloyd's Rep 509.

266 See *Aughton Ltd v M F Kent Services Ltd.* [1991] 57 Build L R 1 (this case is analyzed in more detail in Chapter 4, 'Construction Contracts and the Incorporation of Arbitration Clauses). Also see Martin Davies, Litigation Fights Back: Avoiding the Effect of Arbitration Clauses in Charterparty Bills of Lading, 2004, *Journal of Maritime Law and Commerce*, 35(4), 617, 640. It may be said that there is not really a consensus concerning the outcomes of invalidity and if the orally concluded arbitration agreement may still be enforced.

of foreign arbitral awards, was adopted by a United Nations diplomatic conference. The convention is further adopted by the United Kingdom in 1975. Moreover, the UNCITRAL Model Law (the Model Law) was designed in 1985 for the purpose of assisting jurisdictions in reforming and modernizing their laws on the arbitral procedure. Both the Model Law[267] and the New York Convention[268] require arbitration agreements to be in writing. Similar to the New York Convention, the Model Law has more or less the same requirements that the agreement in writing to include an arbitration clause in a contract or an arbitration agreement, signed by the parties or contained in an exchange of letters or telegram.[269] Furthermore, the 2006 amendments to the Model Law somewhat smoothened some strict formalities and provided that because drafting a written document in numerous situations would not be possible (or practical), as long as the readiness and intention of the parties are clear, the arbitration agreement should be considered valid.[270] It may be argued that nowadays a somewhat more flexible approach that reflects the realities of contemporary and digitized commerce is being adopted concerning the incorporation of arbitration clauses.[271] On the other hand, the formality requirements and their potential impact on the incorporation by reference may be said to remain quite unclear as the international conventions and recommendations do not really provide clear stipulations, under which arbitration agreements may be incorporated. Nonetheless, one thing is certain that the relevant international conventions 'accord parties broad autonomy to agree upon the substantive laws and procedures applicable to "their" arbitration.'[272]

The Arbitration Act 1996 'provides all agreements relating to arbitration should be made or evidenced in writing.'[273] Furthermore, the 'being in writing' stipulation that the Act provides has quite a broad scope. According to the provisions of the Act, an agreement in writing would be found in any of the following circumstances where an agreement (1) is made in writing (it being signed or not being irrelevant, any regular written contract); (2) is made by an exchange of communications in writing (Section 5(6) of the Act refers to anything being in writing and recorded by any means);[274] and (3) is evidenced in writing (includes oral agreements that are recorded by one of the parties or by a third party).[275]

A division in English law concerning the position of arbitration agreements that are subject to the provisions of the Arbitration Act 1996, and the ones that are not, should be provided. Clearly, it is possible for arbitration agreements to be concluded in a way that

267 Article 7(2) of the UNCITRAL Model Law 1985. It should be noted that the 2006 amendment of Article 7, Option II, does not require the arbitration agreement to be in writing.

268 Article II(1), II(2) of the New York Convention 1958.

269 Article 7(2) of the UNCITRAL Model Law 1985.

270 UNCITRAL Model Law on International Commercial Arbitration 1985, with amendments as adopted in 2006, United Nations Publications, Sales No. E.08.V.4 [2008], 28.

271 See Felix Sparka, *Jurisdiction and Arbitration Clauses in Maritime Transport Documents: A Comparative Analysis*, Springer, 2010.

272 Gary Born, *International Commercial Arbitration*, Kluwer Law International, 2021, 81.

273 Ambrose, Maxwell, and Collett (n 146) 48, 4.20.

274 *Zambia Steel & Building Supplies Ltd v James Clark & Eaton Ltd* [1986] 2 Lloyd's Rep 225 (CA): A case which was also referred to in the DAC Report with approval, in which it was held that an oral assent was sufficient where the clause was a written arbitration agreement within the meaning of the applicable arbitration legislation. To put it differently, to show a written assent to a term which was already in writing was considered unnecessary. The case was later followed by *Abdullah M Fahem v Mareb Yemen Insurance Co* [1997] 2 Lloyd's Rep 738 (Comm).

275 Ambrose, Maxwell, and Collett (n 146) 49, 4.20.

would not be subject to the provisions of the Arbitration Act 1996. As Section 5(1) of the Act provides, 'the provisions . . . apply only where the arbitration agreement is in writing.' If it is not made in a way falling into the broad 'being in writing' category, then the arbitration agreement would not be subject to the provisions of the Act as it would rather be subject to the general rules of incorporation under English law, in which the formality requirements are much more severe than the ones that are set forth in the Arbitration Act 1996. This is because such agreements do not benefit from the 'shortcuts of formality' that the arbitration legislation provides. As indicated, the Arbitration Act 1996 specifies that any recording of the arbitration agreement,[276] as long as the recording refers to terms that are in writing, constitutes a written arbitration agreement regardless of the arbitration agreement itself being completed 'unwritten.'[277] On the contrary, concerning the strict rules of incorporation under English law, the charterparty is required to be in writing, and an oral charterparty,[278] for instance, regardless of being recorded or not, will not be suitable for incorporation.[279] It should also be noted that there is a difference between, on the one hand, arbitration agreements being in writing so as to fall within the Arbitration Act 1996 and the New York Convention 1958 and, on the other hand, the need for specific writing if an arbitration clause is to be incorporated into a bill of lading. These are also two different motivations.

Nevertheless, it should be noted that once an arbitration agreement is incorporated into the bill of lading, it will be binding upon the holder of the bill of lading regardless of the holder not being an 'original' party to the agreement. In that regard, the notion of incorporation turns the arbitration agreement into an indestructible one that is enforceable against a third party.[280] In *The Nerano*,[281] the Court of Appeal allowed the manipulation of the arbitration clause in the charterparty to fit the context of the bill of lading. Despite the clause referring to 'any dispute arising between the owners and charterers' and that the reference to 'charterers' was not appropriate, the intention of the parties to incorporate the arbitration clause held clear from the specific wording of the incorporation clause in the bill of lading.[282] Furthermore, it was also indicated in *The Delos*[283] that, as long as properly incorporated, the holders of the bill are deemed to have accepted to arbitrate as they were the original parties to the agreement.

The requirement of formality does not seem to have the same prominence that it had in the past.[284] One may argue that the contemporary trend is the promotion of party autonomy[285] over the satisfaction of some very strict formal requirements that may truly impair the manifestation of such autonomy, which forms the basis for commercial arbitration. Section 5(5) of the Arbitration Act 1996 provides that an agreement constituted by the

276 Section 5(6) of the Arbitration Act 1996.

277 Section 5(3) of the Arbitration Act 1996.

278 Özdel (n 25) 65.

279 See *The Heidberg* [1994] 2 Lloyd's Rep 287; an oral agreement which was not evidenced in writing was held insufficient to incorporate the charterparty arbitration clause.

280 See Özdel (n 25) 69.

281 [1994] 2 Lloyd's Rep 50, confirming *The Rena K* [1978] 1 Lloyd's Rep 545.

282 Incorporation clause provided 'all terms and conditions, liberties, exceptions and arbitration clause of the Charterparty, dated as overleaf, are herewith incorporated.'

283 [2001] 1 Lloyd's Rep 703.

284 Sparka (n 271).

285 Emmanuel Gaillard and John Savage (eds.), *Fouchard Gaillard Goldman on International Commercial Arbitration*, Kluwer Law International, 1999, 9–62, 27.

exchange of written submissions in arbitral or legal proceedings, in which the existence of the agreement is asserted by and not denied by the other is also an agreement 'in writing.' By providing this so, the legislation 'represents a notable widening of the category of agreements in writing.'[286] Since arbitration promotes the amicable resolution of disputes, its implementation should serve that purpose too. Accordingly, even though each case will turn on its own facts, the incorporation of arbitration clauses by reference should be enabled provided that the intention to arbitrate is clear.[287]

2.3.3.4.3. Separability of Arbitration Agreements

Another concern that fundamentally led to the development of the strict rule of incorporation over time is the separable nature of arbitration agreements. In the traditional sense, the term 'separability'[288] means that an arbitration clause contained in a contract is to be treated as a separate contract from the main one. The Arbitration Act 1996 indicates,

> Unless otherwise agreed by the parties, an arbitration agreement which forms or was intended to form part of another agreement (whether or not in writing) shall not be regarded as invalid, non-existent or ineffective because that other agreement is invalid, or did not come into existence or has become ineffective, and it shall for that purpose be treated as a distinct agreement.[289]

As reflected in the Act, separability as a legal doctrine allows an arbitration agreement to be considered separate from the contract in which it is contained. The legal effect of the implementation of separability gains importance where the enforceability of the underlying agreement is questionable. In other words, the doctrine prevents the automatic invalidation/termination of an arbitration agreement due to the invalidity or termination of the contract, of which the arbitration agreement constitutes a part.[290]

The scope and meaning of the said doctrine are unfortunately commonly confused, and therefore, its implementation has been considered an obstacle to the adoption of more flexible rules for the incorporation of arbitration clauses.[291] As mentioned, the doctrine of separability illustrates the ability of the arbitration agreement to prevail over the possible invalidity of an underlying agreement that contains the former. The argument that suggests 'because arbitration agreements are separate, as a matter of construction, their incorporation may not take place without the employment of words of specific reference' may be regarded to be an 'ill-founded one.' This fundamentally seems problematic since the doctrine of separability and the incorporation by reference, in fact, constitute two distinct concepts of law.

The doctrine of separability finds its foundations in more or less four justifications.[292] Firstly, the undeniably distinct character of the arbitration clause to the primary agreement may be said to be establishing the fundamental justification. The moment parties enter into an agreement

286 Ambrose, Maxwell, and Collett (n 146) 50, 4.27.

287 Allison and Dharmananda (n 160) 274.

288 Doctrine of 'separability' or 'severability' or 'autonomy.' Born (n 272) 375–505.

289 Section 7 of the Arbitration Act 1996.

290 Phillip Capper, *International Arbitration: A Handbook*, Informa Legal Publishing, 2004, 12; cited at *Jorge Gonzales et al. V Climax Mining Ltd., et al.* GR No. 161957, January 22, 2007 (a decision of the Supreme Court of Philippines).

291 Born (n 272) 889.

292 Stephen Schwebel, *International Arbitration: Three Salient Problems*, Grotius Publications, 1987, 3–6.

which involves an arbitration provision, this amounts to the conclusion of not one but two agreements as 'the arbitral twin would survive any birth defect or acquired disability of the main agreement.'[293] To be able to illustrate this, it would be useful to note *Paul Smith v H&S International Holding*[294] since in this case, the arbitration provision in the contract stated to be a self-contained agreement providing for the disputes to be referred to arbitration. If there is an arbitration and a jurisdiction clause in the same contract, and if there is no indication that these apply to different disputes, it is now settled by *Paul Smith v H&S International Holding* that the arbitration clause takes priority.[295] The court's interpretation in this case of the clause was that it constituted an agreement to arbitrate with a provision for the courts of England to retain supervisory function. Accordingly, English courts usually take a liberal approach to interpreting contractual construction if there is a hybrid court and arbitration charterparty clause as well as a specific bill of lading reference to arbitration.[296] For instance, it was held that the dispute had to be referred to arbitration provided that the charterparty contained a law and litigation clause and the bill of lading included a law and arbitration clause in *The YM Saturn*.[297]

Furthermore, the arbitration agreement usually prevails even in the case where the underlying contract is terminated due to fraud or bribery as long as such conducts have not been committed relating particularly to the arbitration agreement. *The Fiona Trust*, being particularly concerned with this issue, vividly depicts that the arbitration agreement is a distinct one from the underlying agreement.[298] It is indicated in this case that if the underlying contract is invalid, for instance, due to bribery, the arbitration agreement would survive and the validity of the contract would be determined by the arbitrator and not by the court as long as the bribery was not pertaining to the formation of the arbitration agreement. The contemporary legitimate assumption is that the parties would intend to keep the arbitration agreement effective, irrelevant of the actual or purported invalidity of the rest of the contract *ab initio*.[299] This approach seems in line with the legal twin agreement fiction[300] and the commercial expedience.[301]

---

293 Ibid 5.

294 [1991] 2 Lloyd's Rep 127.

295 [1991] 2 Lloyd's Rep 127, [130]. Also: *Shell International Petroleum Co v Coral Oil Co Ltd (No 1)* [1999] 1 Lloyd's Rep 72; *Axa Re v Ace Global Markets Ltd* [2006] 1 Lloyd's Rep IR 683 (Gloster J); *Sul América Cia Nacional de Seguros SA v Enesa Engenharia SA* [2012] 1 Lloyd's Rep 275 (Cooke J), *Interserve Industrial Services Ltd v ZRE Katowice SA* [2012] EWHC 3205 (Comm) (HHJ David Grant); *British-American Insurance (Kenya) Ltd v Matelec Sal* [2013] EWHC 3278 (Comm); *Exmek Pharmaceuticals SAC v Alkem Laboratories Ltd* [2016] 1 Lloyd's Rep 239 (Burton J).

296 Jonatan Echebarria Fernández, Incorporation of Dispute Resolution Clauses Contained in the Charterparty into Bill of Lading, in Jonatan Echebarria Fernández (ed.) *Jurisdiction and Arbitration Agreements in Contracts for the Carriage of Goods by Sea: Limitations on Party Autonomy*, Informa Law by Routledge, 2021, 61.

297 *YM Mars Tankers Ltd v Shield Petroleum Co (Nigeria) Ltd (The YM Saturn)* [2012] EWHC 2652. Even though, English cases mostly follow *Paul Smith v H&S International Holding*, see *MH Alshaya Company WLL v Retek Information Systems Inc* [2001] MCLR 99 in which clauses providing for both arbitration and litigation are viewed as being untidy and litigation provision prevailed.

298 *Fiona Trust v Privalov* [2007] UKHL 40; [2008] 1 Lloyd's Rep 254.

299 Latin for 'from the beginning.' If a contract is void *ab initio*, this has the consequence that no innocent third parties can acquire rights under any subsequent contract; *Oxford Dictionary of Law*, 2015, 8th Edn. See *Bell v Lever Bros* [1932] AC 161 HL. A recent case on the matter: *Enka Insaat ve Sanayi AS v OOO Insurance Company Chubb* [2020] UKSC 38; [2020] 1 WLR 4117 discusses how convincing to say arbitration agreement is separable. Nevertheless, its convenience is evident when the main contract is said to be void.

300 Schwebel (n 292) 5.

301 Baron (n 261) 183.

Secondly, arbitration clauses are significant as they form the arbitration agreement, which reflects the mere and ascertainable intention of the parties concerning the selected method of dispute resolution. Where the arbitration clause is constructed in a broad way, this usually indicates the intention of the parties regarding all existing and future relevant disputes that may arise to be referred to arbitration. The general assumption would be that the employment of such a broad wording includes the entirety of the disputes and not merely a part of them.[302]

Thirdly, without the concept of separability, the integral nature of arbitration would be cramped as one party wishing to ward off the arbitration process may simply contend that the main contract was invalid and propound their supposed right to go to the court. This could also delay the resolution of the dispute as under such circumstances the court would also have to decide whether the contract is valid. Consequently, this would potentially deprive the benefits such as speed and minimal costs that the arbitration process provides.

Fourthly, in line with the third justification, in the absence of the separability doctrine, the court would find itself in an unwanted position of being required to consider the substance of the dispute.[303] This would extend to the ascertainment of the arbitrator's findings on the validity of the agreement and purported jurisdiction of the tribunal. Such an implementation would have the potential to impair the credibility of the arbitration practice and arbitral awards.

The doctrine of separability has its own critics. For instance, it is argued that such a fictional concept may not be accepted by default as it validates commercial convenience more than it validates logic.[304] This argument supports the idea of the invalidity of the contract *ab initio* and therefore propounds that if the underlying contract would be invalid, then the arbitration agreement would be too, as this would mean that the latter also never had legal effect.[305] Overlooking the word 'fiction' and the elusive perception it creates, the doctrine of separability is a concept that 'secures practical and common-sense results in the great majority of cases.'[306] Nonetheless, 'the cruciality of incorporation not to be confused with the doctrine of separability.'[307] These constitute completely different concepts of law. Indeed, the separability of arbitration agreements does not have much relevance since the separability of an arbitration clause 'is retained even after incorporation.'[308] As it is accurately emphasized in *Habas Sinai v Sometal* by Clarke J,

> A commercial lawyer would probably understand that an arbitration clause is a separate contract collateral to another substantive contract and that the expression 'arbitration clause'

302 Andrew Rogers and Rachel Launders, Separability – the Indestructible Arbitration Clause, 1994, *Arbitration International LCIA*, 10(1).

303 Ibid 80.

304 Adrian Baron, Arbitration and the Fiction of Severability, November 1999, *Australian Bar Review*, 19, 49–66.

305 Ibid. See also Baron (n 261).

306 *Ferris v Plaister* [1994] 34 NSWLR 474, at 485–491 (an Australian case). The case involved the allegation of fraud result in the vitiation of the contract and the separability of the arbitration agreement was in question. It was held that the arbitration clause was severable, notwithstanding the allegation that the contract was void *ab initio*.

307 Greenberg, Kee, and Weeramantry (n 245) 151.

308 Merkin and Flannery (n 191) 6.2.3.

> is, on that account, something a misnomer for 'the arbitration contract which is ancillary to the primary contract.

But a businessman would have no difficulty in regarding the arbitration clause (as he would call it) as part of a contract and as capable of incorporation.'[309]

2.4. Mollification of the Strict Approach and the Current Standpoint

According to English law, the Arbitration Act 1996 only applies to existing or future disputes of the parties, who agreed in writing to submit their disputes to arbitration.[310] Therefore, it is crucial to determine if the arbitration agreement has, in fact, been sufficiently incorporated since this sets out whether the parties are required to proceed to resolve their dispute by arbitration rather than by court proceedings. Pursuant to the fundamental doctrine of the freedom of contract, parties have the general liberty to choose whom to contract, whether to contract or not, and on which terms to contract. Even prior to the Arbitration Act 1996, it was well-established that the parties to an arbitration agreement did not need to spell out the arbitration provision in their written contract, and the incorporation of the arbitration clause by reference was possible.[311] Following this, the Arbitration Act 1996 particularly regulates that matter and states that 'the reference in an agreement to a written form of the arbitration clause or to a document containing an arbitration clause constitutes an arbitration agreement if the reference is such as to make that clause part of the agreement.'[312] Although by its wording, the Arbitration Act 1996 seems like providing some flexibility concerning the contracting method since it indicates that 'incorporation by reference' is permissible, it anyways does not provide clarity regarding the application of such a method. In other words, the actual meaning of 'to make that clause part of the agreement' and a clear methodology to ensure effective incorporation are not elements provided in the Arbitration Act 1996. Concerning these elements, some relevant requirements and methods are developed by the English courts over time. Concerning bill of lading cases, the predominant requirement has been the employment of specific words of incorporation targeting the arbitration clause as the bill of lading holder is usually deemed to neither have knowledge of the terms of the underlying contract[313] nor the power to negotiate the terms of carriage.

Accordingly, the protection of the oblivious third-party holders of the bills has usually been the prime concern of the courts dealing with the issue of incorporation in the shipping context, and thus, the employment of express words of incorporation has been strictly required to reinforce commercial certainty. Nonetheless, the very straightforward adoption of such a strict approach sometimes induces third-party security to outbalance party autonomy. To put it differently, a blindfolded implementation of such strict criteria may occasionally mean the party autonomy is being swept under the rug. Accordingly, the

---

309 Clarke J in *Habas Sinai ve Tibbi Gazlar Isthisal Endustri AS v Sometal SAL* [2010] 1 Lloyd's Rep 661, 672, 51. This case is comprehensively analyzed in the following parts as it provides quite a ground-breaking approach concerning contractual categorization and, accordingly, for the examination of incorporation.

310 Section 5(6) of the Arbitration Act 1996.

311 Merkin and Flannery (n 191) 6.2.

312 Section 6(2) of the Arbitration Act 1996.

313 *T. W. Thomas & Co. Ltd. v Portsea Steamship Co Ltd, The Portsmouth* [1912] A.C. 1 (*Thomas v Portsea*); *The Varenna* [1983] 1 Lloyd's Rep 416; *The Federal Bulker* [1981] 1 Lloyd's Rep 103.

overlooking of the delicate balance between the indicated concepts may cause dysfunction depending on the circumstances of a dispute.

Going back to basics, it would be useful at this point to reiterate what incorporation means after all. The basics of incorporation as a concept of law are hinged on in the classical non-marine case of *Olley v Marlborough Court.*[314] A room was booked by the claimant at the defendant hotel. The booking was completed at the reception, and later in the room, the claimant found a notice indicating the exclusion of the defendant's liability for the personal belongings of its guests. Subsequently, the fur coat of the claimant got stolen. It was argued by the defendant hotel that they were not liable due to the notice in the claimant's room, indicating the exclusion of liability. However, it was held by the Court of Appeal that such notice was not sufficiently incorporated as it was brought to the attention of the claimant after the conclusion of the contract at the reception. Consequently, it was emphasized that for the incorporation of a standard term of one of the contracting parties – exclusion of liability of the hotel for the stolen personal belongings in this case – a reasonable and sufficient notice must have been given of the existence of the terms to be incorporated.[315] *Olley v Marlborough Court* is quite a straightforward case that set up the precedent concerning the link between the concept of incorporation and the element of relevant contractual acknowledgement and the timing of its obtainment.

Attitudes towards arbitration clauses and their incorporation are transformed quite remarkably over the years. As indicated, the essential concerns pertaining to the incorporation of arbitration clauses by the employment of general words may be stated to be the possible impediment of the court's jurisdiction, the 'confusion' regarding the form requirement, and the mistaken approach towards the doctrine of separability. Consequently, particularly in the shipping context, English law promoted the application of the strict approach, which does not welcome the incorporation of arbitration clauses by the employment of general words. *Thomas v Portsea*[316] quite clearly reflects the position of the English courts on the strict rule of incorporation. The arbitration clause that was concerned in this case was held insufficient to be incorporated into the bill of lading since there was no express reference to this clause. It was indicated that because arbitration provisions do not deal with the typical aspects of shipping, receipt, and delivery, and since such an arbitration clause should have been indicated explicitly to make it clear for the holder of the bill that a potential dispute would be settled by arbitration, the incorporation was not allowed. The essential incentive of the court in *Thomas v Portsea* was indeed the protection of the third party, who is oblivious of the terms of the charterparty due to its contractual remoteness, from the potential imposition of arbitration on them. This motive was further adopted in many subsequent cases, and commercial certainty and predictability have been considered the initial necessities to prevail. With the justification for its harsh implementation in each case being open to debate, the complexity and volume of commercial transactions may seem to be justifying the purposefulness of this rationale, especially in the shipping context. However, one thing is for sure – the main approach of the courts regarding this issue has generally been 'if it is not broken, do not fix it.'

314 [1949] 1 KB 532.

315 See *Parker v South Eastern Railway Co.* [1877] LR 2 CPD 416, CA.

316 [1912] A.C. 1.

However, some contemporary examples of case law are signalling that courts may give weight to the configurational assessment of contract structure that truly reflects the characteristics of the legal relationship. Accordingly, for the purposes of understanding and evaluating the changes that pertain to the notion of incorporation of arbitration clauses and to be able to provide a relevant analysis, the next part examines two ground-breaking cases: *The Athena*[317] and *Habas Sinai v Sometal.*[318] These contemporary cases made undeniably significant contributions to the development of English case law pertaining to the concept of incorporation.

It was essentially provided in *The Athena* that there are two fundamental categories that the contracts would fall under in English law and the assessment of the way that the incorporation is implemented would be done according to the determination of to which category the contract belongs. Langley J highlighting the relevant categories indicated that a particular contract in English law would fall either under a single-contract scenario or a two-contract scenario.[319] Accordingly, the 'scenarios theory' that is highlighted in *The Athena* enables a contractual classification to be made for the purposes of testing to which criteria an attempt of incorporation should be subject, depending on the class of contract this notion is concerned with.

Furthermore, the 'scenarios theory' that was provided in *The Athena* was further developed as other supporting categories were created for the purpose of establishing a much more comprehensive guideline concerning the assessment of incorporation depending on the contractual configuration in *Habas Sinai v Sometal.*[320]

It should be noted at this point that neither *The Athena* nor *Habas Sinai v Sometal* is concerned with bills of lading incorporating charterparties. These cases are in fact pertaining to disputes that arose from an insurance agreement and a sale agreement, respectively. However, both ways the issue regarding the notion of incorporation was handled in these cases establish quite neat guidelines concerning the assessment of contractual classification. In the interest of brevity, both cases promoted the necessity of evaluating the rationale behind the structural formation of contracts pertaining to the notion of incorporation rather than following the 'strict rule.' The adopted incentive of the courts in the indicated cases seems to be accommodating the contemporary realities of international commerce. We first turn to *The Athena* and its 'scenarios theory' to have a better understanding of the fundamentals of incorporation of arbitration clauses and the divisions that the relevant contracts would substantially fall under.

2.4.1. The *Athena* and the Common Law 'Scenarios Theory'

2.4.1.1. THE *ATHENA*

The *Athena* was a vessel insured against war risks. A claim was made following an explosion allegedly caused by a militant organization in Sri Lanka. Only part of the claim was paid due to insurers exercising their discretion. After two proceedings were commenced in New York and Greece by the insured, the insurers sought to enforce the arbitration clause set out in their standard terms, which refers the existing and prospective disputes to London

317 [2006] EWHC 2530 (Comm).
318 [2010] 1 Lloyd's Rep 661.
319 [2006] EWHC 2530 (Comm) at [62].
320 [2010] 1 Lloyd's Rep 661.

arbitration. The validity of the arbitration clause was challenged by the insured on the basis that the incorporation of the said clause did not take place. Langley J implementing the 'scenarios theory test' concluded that this was a single-contract scenario, and thus, general words of incorporation were sufficient to incorporate the arbitration clause contrary to the express reference requirement that would apply to a two-contract scenario. Reaching this decision, the court avoided adopting the 'strict rule' that necessitates the employment of specific wording referring to the arbitration clause. However, it is also noted that such a requirement would still apply in a two-contract scenario. Furthermore, the attempt of the claimants to draw an analogy between the case in hand and *Thomas v Portsea*[321] was found unsuccessful because relevant contracts held to constitute a single-contract structure. The court was of the view that this was a 'hopeless' argument and an otherwise assessment of it would cause 'the exception swallowing the rule and would put a weight on the *Thomas v Portsea* which could not begin to be born.'[322] The actual knowledge of the parties and their actual 'privity' to the contract were regarded to be the fundamental points of consideration in *The Athena*. The court was of the opinion that this particular case involved parties who were familiar both with each other and the ways the insurance market functions. Accordingly, the assessment of the court was that the contractual situation in *The Athena* was one of single-contract scenario, and therefore, a reference to an arbitration clause included in some standard terms did not particularly necessitate some specific reference to be made to it. The decision is of great significance as the relevant contracts were perceived from a 'structural' point of view rather than one that is 'numerical,' which could unmeritedly necessitate the employment of specific words of incorporation. To put it differently, the court gave weight to the true structure and configuration of the contracts rather than conducting a numerical evaluation of them.

2.4.1.2. The Scenarios Theory

The significance of incorporation that functions as a tool providing immense convenience is not difficult to grasp particularly considering the multitude of parties involved in complex international commercial transactions. Since flexibility is an element of momentous need for international commerce, the strict rule of incorporation may sometimes be perceived as a drawback as it potentially exposes transactions to some very rigid formalities to comply with. Although it is clear that there should be some degree of formality for the promotion of commercial certainty, there should also be room for the contractual manifestation of party autonomy. Accordingly, the fundamental issue is about striking a balance. Consequently, one of the essential issues to be addressed is whether the promotion of the protection of third parties truly justifies the rigidity and formal burdens that are imposed on commercial transactions. To be able to make the relevant assessment, Langley J in *The Athena* investigated the true configuration of the contractual structure and accordingly provided the 'scenarios theory.'[323]

321 [1912] A.C. 1.
322 [2006] EWHC 2530 (Comm), [68].
323 Ibid [62]. Also see Jason Chuah, *Law of International Trade: Cross-Border Commercial Transactions*, Sweet and Maxwell, 2009, 4th Edn.; Ahmed (n 236) 409; Andrew Tweeddale and Keren Tweeddale, Incorporation of Arbitration Clauses Revisited, November 2010, *Arbitration*, 76(4), Chartered Institute of Arbitrators. Also see *Stellar Shipping Co Llc v Hudson Shipping Lines* [2010] EWHC 2986, [64].

2.4.1.2.1. Single-Contract Scenario

The single-contract scenario comprises the situation where the arbitration agreement does not constitute a part of the same physical documentation of the underlying contract,[324] but due to the nature of the contractual configuration at hand, its incorporation would not be subject to the strict rule of incorporation. This specifically applies where there are only two contracting parties. In this situation, one of the parties may require the contract (i.e. a sales agreement) to incorporate their standard terms. In such a case, presuming that the standard terms include an arbitration clause, a two-layered structure of the contractual relationship is created. However, due to the number of parties involved in such a contractual relationship, this two-layered contractual structure would, in fact, establish one solid monolithic setup as the standard terms would merge with the sales contract in this 'melting pot' situation. The strict requirement of specific and express language to be employed to incorporate the arbitration clause would usually be inappropriate in this scenario because the contractual situation generally does not involve a third party, their protection by virtue of employing specific words of incorporation would be irrelevant. In a single-contract scenario, the presumed contractual awareness of the parties is generally perceived as a justification for allowing general words of incorporation to be more inclusive than they are perceived in a two-contract scenario. The parties to such a contractual structure would either be assumed to know the provisions of this monolithic contractual set-up or would have the means to discover these and their potential of being incorporated. In other words, as both parties would be 'privy' to the contractual structure, an argument based on 'lack of awareness' would highly likely be a futile one. Consequently, under the single-contract scenario, the employment of the general words of incorporation normally suffices for the incorporation of an arbitration clause, which is contained in the standard terms.[325]

2.4.1.2.2. Two-Contract Scenario

Two-contract scenario, being composed of a multi-layered contractual structure, is a much more convoluted concept than the single-contract scenario. In this situation, there are two or more self-reliant contracts, with just one of them containing an arbitration clause or two autonomous contracts involving one mutual party. To illustrate, after the conclusion of an initial contract between A and B, A later contracts with C and wishes to incorporate the terms of the initial contract with B into this subsequent contract with C. Moreover, a second sub-division of the two-contract scenario consists of the situation where the term of the contract between A and B to be incorporated into a contract between C and D. The most common examples of the two-contract structure are seen in the areas of shipping, insurance, and construction. Merging in these contexts often takes place by virtue of the incorporation of charterparty terms into bills of lading, terms of the insurance contract into reinsurance contract, and terms of construction contracts into the construction subcontracts.

In the two-contract scenario involving more than two parties, privity of contract constitutes a fundamental consideration in evaluating this contractual configuration. With respect to the negotiable nature of the bill of lading, the holder of it will not be privy to the underlying charterparty contract, of which terms are to be incorporated. Accordingly,

324 Ahmed (n 236) 413.
325 *Parker v South Eastern Railway Co.* [1877] LR 2 CPD 416, CA.

the holder of the bill would neither be aware of the charterparty provisions (that include an arbitration clause) nor be expected to know what they entail. The strict rule requiring specific words of incorporation to be employed for the incorporation of arbitration clauses may be said to be deriving from the 'unawareness' of the current or prospective holder of the bill of lading. To tackle the potentially unfair imposition of charterparty arbitration provision on the unaware third-party holder of the bill, courts usually adopt the strict approach that requires a specific reference to be made to the arbitration clause or the clear manifestation of the intention of the parties to incorporate a charterparty arbitration clause.[326] However, imposing a quantitative and literal restriction, the test does not seem fairly applicable to each occasion involving more than two contracting parties because the true assessment of contractual configuration would instead reveal the privity or remoteness of the contracting parties to the multiple contracts that are concerned with, and accordingly, show what should be the level of strictness implementing incorporation.

The scenarios theory, indeed, provides a substantial guideline pertaining to the notion of incorporation as it dismantles the potentially complex structure of commercial contracts and establishes some very valuable ground rules. Subsequently, Christopher Clarke J in *Habas Sinai v Sometal*[327] took the matter even further and provided sub-divisions to the scenarios theory.[328] After *Habas Sinai v Sometal*, the elements that should be taken into account by the courts in examining the incorporation of arbitration clauses are more clear now.[329]

2.4.2. *Habas Sinai v Sometal*

The classification of contractual configuration provided in *The Athena*[330] was further detailed in *Habas Sinai v Sometal* from an analytical perspective. Habas, the claimant, was a Turkish company, which formerly contracted with Sometal for the sale of steel scrap on 14 occasions between January 23, 2004, and June 9, 2008. Some of the former contracts contained clauses providing for London arbitration, some provided for Istanbul arbitration, and the rest were silent concerning dispute resolution. Following the failure of Habas to take delivery of the commodity during the 15th contract period, Sometal commenced London arbitration contending that the arbitration clause was incorporated[331] because the contract included the words 'All the rest will be same as our previous contracts' and claimed $5 million from Habas for repudiating the contract. Habas challenged the jurisdiction of the London Court of International Arbitration (LCIA) Tribunal, arguing that the incorporation of an arbitration clause required an express reference to being made to it, and the words employed in the present case were inapt for such purpose. The Tribunal found in favour of Sometal and decided that the relevant contract was 'a single contract,' so the general words were sufficient to incorporate the arbitration clause. Habas applied to the Commercial Court, arguing the insufficiency of the indicated general words to incorporate the arbitration

326 Ahmed (n 236) 414.
327 [2010] 1 Lloyd's Rep 661.
328 Christopher Clarke J in *Habas Sinai ve Tibbi Gazlar Isthisal Endustri AS v Sometal SAL* [2010] 1 Lloyd's Rep 661.
329 Ahmed (n 236) 409.
330 [2006] EWHC 2530 (Comm) at [62].
331 For further information on commodities arbitrations, see Clapham (n 141) 665–688.

clause, and sought for the dismissal of the award based on the lack of jurisdiction of the LCIA Tribunal.[332] To put it differently, Habas argued that the case was one of two-contract and not of a single-contract, and accordingly, specific words of incorporation had to be employed to incorporate the arbitration provisions.

The two main considerations of the Commercial Court were whether the general words of 'all the rest will be same as our previous contracts' were capable of incorporating *an* arbitration clause and whether they were capable of incorporating 'the London arbitration clause.'[333] Habas sought the dismissal of the incorporation of the London arbitration clause on the basis that the incorporation of such would require the employment of express words of incorporation. The submissions of Habas were found inconsistent with previously revealed considerations of Langley J in *The Athena* regarding contractual structure.[334]

Concerning the assessment of whether the contractual structure is one of single contract, the characteristics of the transactions between parties may be evaluated. These transactions concerned parties that contracted 15 times regarding the sale of the same type of commodity and accordingly, they had a mutual understanding of how their agreements, which are enshrined in contracts often incorporating an arbitration agreement, are conducted. Similarly, Clarke J, finding the multiplicity of the relevant contracts irrelevant, instead hinged on the familiarity of the parties with each other and their mutual understanding of the way in which their transactions are conducted, and concluded that this was a case to be regarded as a single-contract case.[335] Therefore, the learned judge, in compliance with the relatively milder requirements of incorporation in a single-contract scenario, indicated that the employment of general words of incorporation sufficed for the incorporation of the arbitration clause. In his view, it would be unexpected for a businessperson to consider the phrase 'all terms of the previous contract to apply' to exclude the arbitration clause.[336]

Furthermore, while the necessity of bringing the onerous and unusual terms to the attention of the contracting parties was highlighted by Clarke J, it was also emphasized that an arbitration provision is genuinely regarded as neither onerous nor extraordinary under a single-contract situation.[337] Moreover, it was noted by the learned judge that, particularly in the context of a single-contract case, the potential of an arbitration clause to oust the jurisdiction of the court does not necessarily 'mean that it requires some extraordinary methods of incorporation.'[338] It may indeed be considered a wonder why the arbitration provision is treated differently implementing incorporation between acquainted parties who are familiar with the well-established market practice and their own 'highly repetitive' contractual relationship with one another. *Habas Sinai v Sometal* is immensely prominent as the 'divisional guideline' it provides presents the courts with the opportunity to consider the implementation of the incorporation of arbitration clauses more thoroughly.

332 Based on Section 67 of the Arbitration Act 1996, which states, '(1) A party to arbitral proceedings may (upon notice to the other parties and to the tribunal) apply to the court (a) challenging any award of the arbitral tribunal as to its substantive jurisdiction; or (b) for an order declaring an award made by the tribunal on the merits to be of no effect, in whole or in part, because the tribunal did not have substantive jurisdiction.'

333 [2010] 1 Lloyd's Rep 661; [2010] EWHC 29 (Comm).

334 [2010] EWHC 29 (Comm), [36].

335 Ibid [52].

336 Ibid [51].

337 Ibid [47].

338 Ibid.

Now we turn to a more detailed evaluation of the fundamental issues concerning arbitration that were addressed in *Habas Sinai v Sometal*. The issues to be determined were essentially twofold. The first matter was whether the general words of incorporation were sufficient to incorporate an arbitration clause. The second was whether these were in fact effective to incorporate the provisions concerning London arbitration.

2.4.2.1. Creating Further Divisions: Whether the General Words of Incorporation Suffice to Incorporate 'An Arbitration Clause' Found in Previous Contracts

Pertaining to the first issue to determine, Clarke J, further developed the approach that was fundamentally put forward in *The Athena* and presented four divisions of possible legal scenarios concerning the incorporation of arbitration clauses in a 'multiple-contract configuration':[339]

Division 1: 'A and B make a contract in which they incorporate standard terms.'

This first division constitutes the most straightforward version of incorporation from one contract to another. In this scenario, A and B get into a contract and intend to incorporate some set of standard terms into it. Clarke J in *Habas Sinai v Sometal* went further to explain the scope of the first division and indicated these contracts may be (1) the standard terms of one party set out on the back of an offer letter or order, (2) some standard terms included in another document to which reference is made, (3) terms embodied in the rules of an organization of which A or B or both are members, or (4) terms perceived as standard in a particular trade or industry.[340]

The employment of general words of incorporation ordinarily suffices for the incorporation of standard provisions that include an arbitration clause under this division. This is fundamentally because such standard terms are usually visible or accessible to contracting parties. These may have been set out on the back of an offer letter or perhaps an order and thus generally be apparent. However, the containment of these provisions in a different document to which the reference is made may also be inferred as them being visible in the legal sense. Accordingly, what the word visible entails should be interpreted as 'something becoming visible if the minimal effort to make it so is made.' However, expecting a toilsome effort to ascertain the provisions would understandably not be convenient for the purposes of Division 1.

Division 2: 'A and B make a contract incorporating terms previously agreed between A and B in another contract or contracts to which they were both parties.'

'Ordinary course of dealing' constitutes another division of the multi-layered contractual scenario.[341] It was indicated in *Habas Sinai v Sometal* that 'the present case may be regarded as falling within the second of the categories.'[342] Pertaining to Division 2 (similar to Division 1), the employment of general words of incorporation often suffices for the incorporation of the arbitration clause by reference. This is because, similar to the first division, 'the sought level of effort to ascertain the provisions to be incorporated' would play the dominant role in determining whether the words of incorporation are sufficient. Regarding the 'ongoing business relationship' of the involved parties in this scenario, the provisions to be incorporated are ordinarily familiar to them as these are generally the terms of their former agreements. Even

339 Ibid [13].
340 Ibid.
341 See Chapter 1, 'The Foundations of Incorporation and Arbitration Clauses.'
342 [2010] EWHC 29 (Comm), [35].

if the parties are actually not familiar with these provisions, they are generally easily available and discoverable to them if the parties are willing to find out more concerning their scope.

The first and second divisions presented by Clarke J in *Habas Sinai v Sometal* are pertaining to 'the single-contract scenario' division of the 'scenarios theory' provided in *The Athena*.[343] The 'monolithic contractual structure' that is formed in Division 2 usually necessitates the actual number of contracts involved to be disregarded and the implementation of incorporation to accordingly be subject to more flexible rules. To put it differently, multiple contracts that fall under Division 2 are generally treated to constitute a 'one-piece contractual structure' for incorporation purposes provided that the established nature of the parties' dealing indicates that it is one of regular and consistent.

The other two divisions (Division 3 and Division 4) are pertaining to the 'two-contract scenario' category of *The Athena*'s 'scenarios theory.' The two-contract scenario mostly emerges in the contexts of shipping, reinsurance, and construction as these areas of law are typically concerned with multi-layered chain contracts. The bills of lading incorporate the provisions of a charterparty, where the reinsurance contract incorporates the provisions of the underlying insurance contract, and a construction subcontract incorporates the provisions of the construction contract. The well-settled practice suggests that the alignment of these contracts constitutes a fundamental goal to be achieved pertaining to contract drafting in these branches of law.

Division 3: 'A and B make a contract incorporating terms agreed between A (or B) and C.'

The third division is concerning the incorporation of the provisions of an agreement made between one of the contracting parties and a third party. This particular division usually includes the bill of lading cases, in which the consignee is not the charterer,[344] the reinsurance contracts where the terms of the initial underlying insurance are incorporated,[345] and building or engineering subcontracts incorporating the terms of a main contract or sub-subcontracts incorporating the terms of a subcontract.[346] To put it differently, Division 3 is usually concerned with incorporation in the subcontract context and it illustrates a motion from top to bottom picturing the contractual structure in a vertical way.

Concerning the third division, the general requirement for the incorporation of arbitration clauses by reference is usually the employment of specific wording, as this division involves multi-layered contracts and multiple parties. However, indeed, this may not be the issue concerning all sorts of chain contracts and the actual contractual structure may instead need to be explored depending on the facts of the case and the realities of the contractual structure it is concerned with.

Division 4: 'A and B make a contract incorporating terms agreed between C and D.'

Similar to the third division, shipping, reinsurance, and construction subcontracts may also fall under the fourth category. However, this division includes the situation where a subcontractor seeks to incorporate the arbitration clause that is included in the main contract into a sub-subcontract. Hence, also the fourth category illustrates a motion from top to bottom if the contractual chain may be visualized in a vertical way. Nonetheless, the motion of incorporation

343 [2006] EWHC 2530 (Comm), [62].

344 And hence in the cases where the consignee is remote to the charterparty.

345 Also, the excess insurance contracts where the terms of the primary layer insurance are incorporated.

346 *Aughton Ltd v MF Kent Services* [1991] 57 BLR 6. The second case that the Court of Appeal decided on incorporation by reference in a building contract. The first English building case was *Modern Building Wales Ltd v Limmer & Trinidad Co Ltd.* [1975] 1 WLR 1291; included an application to stay of proceedings.

> under this category extends relatively further as the number of the concerned contracts is usually higher than it is under the other divisions of 'the scenarios theory.'
>
> The fourth division may involve a third party to the underlying contract who is willing to incorporate the provisions of the underlying contract into a sub-subcontract. This division generally necessitates the employment of specific words of incorporation for the incorporation of arbitration clauses due to the involvement of third parties in the contractual configuration. The involvement of third parties that are concerned with sub-levels of the contractual chain and their protection is also considered in *Habas Sinai v Sometal*, as Clarke J stated, 'Bills of lading may come into the hands of those who will neither know nor have the means of knowing about the arbitration clause in the charterparty to which they would be unlikely to assent. They will not therefore appreciate that by becoming a party to the bill they became parties to a contract precluding access to the courts.'[347] One may consider the grounds for applying a stricter approach concerning the incorporation of arbitration clauses quite appropriate and justifiable under this division. Moving from the first division to the fourth, an increase in the required level of strictness that applies to the incorporation of arbitration clauses becomes clear as the additional layers of contracts possibly increase the remoteness of the parties to the substantial contract and necessitate the scope of incorporation to be restricted more.

Indeed, the third and the fourth categories may be distinguished from the first two concerning the incorporation of arbitration clauses because it would be perceived unfair to subject the holder of the bill of lading to terms of an arbitration clause of which they are not aware of.[348] At the same time, contracts that are pertaining to the first two categories are usually anticipated to be subject to a higher degree of flexibility due to the familiarity of the limited number of contracting parties with each other and their transactional patterns.

In the particular case before the Commercial Court, there were merely two contracting parties who were privy to the contractual relationship established for the sale of a certain commodity that was manifested on 14 occasions. Accordingly, Clarke J considered the number of contracts irrelevant and instead gave weight to the promotion of the actual characteristics of the contractual relationship.[349] Consequently, it was held that this was a single-contract case, and therefore, the general words of incorporation were sufficient to incorporate the standard form contract terms that included an arbitration clause without expressly referring to it. It should be kept in mind that the relevant dispute involved parties contracted more than a dozen times and they understood some of their previous contracts included arbitration provisions by which they were previously bound. In other words, this case hinged on the realities of the commercial relationship of the contracting parties.

2.4.2.2. A Consuetudinary Practice – Were the Words of Incorporation Effective to Incorporate the Provision Pertaining to London Arbitration?

As a first step, the wording was held appropriate to incorporate 'an arbitration clause.' The second issue to be addressed was whether the wording was appropriate to incorporate the provisions of London arbitration. The contract before the Commercial Court included words such as 'our' and 'same as our previous contracts.' The Commercial Court had the view, under the light of such references, that the concerned contract was a Sometal-prepared

347 [2010] EWHC 29 (Comm), [34].
348 Ambrose, Maxwell, and Collett (n 146) 54, 4.39.
349 [2010] EWHC 29 (Comm), [52].

contract and not a Habas-prepared one, based on the existing pattern of contract drafting that was established between the parties. This was because the previous contracts, which included the provisions of London arbitration, were the ones drafted by Sometal. However, the ones drafted by Habas included dispute resolution clauses, which were referring to other venues and not London, or they did not include any dispute resolution clauses at all. This consuetudinary practice of the parties is held to be illustrating a certain pattern and in particular, their awareness of the potential application of the London arbitration clause. Accordingly, the intended reference to London arbitration was accepted to be a clear one due to this settled practice between the parties. Thus, the words were held operative to incorporate the London arbitration provision.

2.4.2.3. Salutation to Clarke J: Clarke J to the Rescue

The judgement in *Habas Sinai v Sometal* is momentous as Clarke J took the initiative to reshape and redefine methods of contractual interpretation, particularly concerning the assessment of the incorporation of arbitration clauses.

This was a case that concerned parties who contracted on 15 occasions on similar subject matters. Hence, they were familiar with the ordinary provisions of their contracts and arbitration was one of them. It is indeed true that even in the case of such a repetitive contractual relationship to be established, a provision of a previous contract should still be referred to properly. Accordingly, Clarke J stated,

> Whenever some terms other than those set out in the incorporating document are said to be incorporated it is necessary to be clear what those terms are. Since arbitration clauses are not terms which regulate the parties' substantive rights and obligations under the contract but are terms dealing with the resolution of disputes relating to those rights and obligations it is also necessary to be clear that the parties did intend to incorporate such a clause. But, if a contract between A and B incorporates all the terms of a previous contract between them other than the terms newly agreed in the later contract, there should be no lack of clarity in respect of what is to be incorporated.[350]

He went further and emphasized the need for clarity and indicated,

> There is a particular need to be clear that the parties intended to incorporate the arbitration clause when the incorporation relied on is the incorporation of the terms of a contract made between different parties, even if one of them is a party to the contract in suit. In such a case it may not be evident that the parties intended not only to incorporate the substantive provisions of the other contract but also provisions as to the resolution of disputes between different parties, particularly if a degree of verbal manipulation is needed for the incorporated arbitration clause to work. These considerations do not, however, apply to a single contract case.[351]

There was indeed no express reference to the arbitration clause in *Habas Sinai v Sometal*. Nevertheless, Clarke J was of the view that the way contracts were configurated was congruent with the contractual form of single-contract cases, and accordingly, the intention to arbitrate did not need to be manifested by the employment of express words of incorporation. It is well-settled in English law that the employment of some specific

---

350 Ibid [48].
351 Ibid [49].

words of incorporation is required for the purposes of incorporating an arbitration clause, especially in two-contract scenarios. However, the true assessment of contract configuration may eventually indicate that a legal relationship consists of multiple contracts to possibly constitute a single-contract scenario in reality. Accordingly, the timing of assessing the intention of the parties may fundamentally affect the 'contractual division' that the contract may fall under. Accordingly, it may be possible for such a clear manifestation of party autonomy to outweigh and diminish strict formalities. Where the intention is ascertainable and clear, the incorporation of an arbitration clause by the employment of general words of incorporation may possibly be allowed. Assessing the true intention of the parties regarding the applicable dispute resolution method would also prevent parties from hiding behind strict formalities to compel others to a method that in fact does not reflect the mutual wishes of the contracting parties pertaining to the settlement of their disputes.

Clarke J, in *Habas Sinai v Sometal*, by taking the facts of the case into consideration, decided that the incorporation was successful. This was because the parties were contracted on 14 occasions in the past regarding the sale of the same commodity. The incorporation of arbitration clauses perhaps requires some special attention to be drawn to them dealing with two-contract scenarios. However, taking the facts of the case into consideration, the learned judge indicated that the structural formation of the contracts did amount to a single-contract scenario in *Habas Sinai v Sometal*. He concluded,

> I do not accept that, in a single-contract case, the independent nature of the arbitration clause should determine whether it is to be incorporated. A commercial lawyer would probably understand that an arbitration clause is a separate contract collateral to another substantive contract and that the expression 'arbitration clause' is, on that account, something of a misnomer for 'the arbitration contract which is ancillary to the primary contract.' But a businessman would have no difficulty in regarding the arbitration clause (as he would call it) as part of a contract and as capable of incorporation, by appropriate wording, as any other term of such a contract; and it is, as it seems to me to a businessman's understanding that the court should be disposed to give effect. A businessman who had agreed with his counterparty a contract with 10 specific terms under various headings and then agreed with the same counterparty terms 1 to 5 under the same headings as before and, as to the rest, that all the terms of the previous contract should apply, would, I think, be surprised to find that 'all' should be interpreted so as to mean 'all but the arbitration clause.'[352]

The alignment of contracts by means of incorporation and disputes arising from international transactions to be referred to arbitration have been ordinary applications of international commercial transactions. Accordingly, the possibility of facing the incorporation of an arbitration clause may hardly be considered astonishing provided that international parties are familiar with usual business practices. It is indeed true that commerce needs certainty and predictability. Nonetheless, commercial certainty should not outweigh party autonomy provided it is obviously manifested. At this point, Clarke J comes to the rescue. It is now more translucent after *Habas Sinai v Sometal* that the assessment of the category under which a contract would fall is simply a matter of applying a logical test of its structural interpretation.

352 Ibid [51].

2.5. Concluding Remarks

The nature of bills of lading and their conjunction with charterparties constitute significant aspects of the concept of incorporation between these two shipping documents. Bills of lading, by their nature, are transferable. This peculiarity has an undeniable impact on the bargaining power that the holder of the bill of lading is vested with. The bill of lading refers to the charterparty under which it is issued. The protection of third-party holders of bills of lading and the lack of bargaining power they have over the terms of the carriage operation necessitate the terms of the bill as reflected on its face to prevail over charterparty terms in the occasion of inconsistency.

Bills of lading and charterparties are considered disjoint as they substantially reflect and govern the contractual relationships of different parties. However, they also have an irrefutable conjunction as the bill of lading is issued under the charterparty, and hence, the charterparty constitutes the fundamental source of this contractual chain. This conjunction mainly comes to light as a structural formation of the shipping documents that are usually desired to be aligned. The parties generally anticipate the carriage operation to be subject to the corresponding provisions of shipping documents. Consequently, the incorporation of charterparty terms into bills of lading by reference has been a well-established and efficaciously implemented method of contract drafting. There are some essential requirements for incorporation to be successful: Incorporation clause should be wide enough to include a charterparty provision purported to be incorporated, the provision should be reasonable in the context of the incorporating bill, and the provision should be consistent with the rest of the bill of lading terms.

It would not be wrong to say that these requirements are initially concerned with the structural side of incorporation as they necessitate the incorporation clause to be structured wide enough to sufficiently target and include the charterparty provision. Further requirements mostly concern the compatibility of the provision-to-be-incorporated with the rest of the terms of the bill of lading. Indeed, if the charterparty term does not make any sense in the bill of lading context or if it causes inconsistency with the rest of its terms, then, as the incorporation would be illogical and inappropriate, the provisions of the bill prevail. Not many complications arise in dealing with the incorporation of general charterparty terms provided that the essential requirements for the notion of incorporation are met. However, the situation gets more complex when the issue is the incorporation of charterparty arbitration clauses. The requirements for the incorporation of such fundamentally not being very different than the ones for the incorporation of the other provisions of the charterparty, due to some peculiarities of arbitration agreements, courts are mostly inclined to adopt a strict approach in assessing their incorporation. The relevant case law illustrates that this has been a well-settled approach in English law, especially before the enactment of the Arbitration Act 1996. The main reasons for a restrictive approach to be adopted are more or less as follows:[353] arbitration clauses not being germane to the subject matter of the contract, and thus, the propounded necessity that incorporation clause should include an express reference to the arbitration clause;[354] these clauses being

353 See *Habas Sinai v Sometal* [2010] EWHC 29 (Comm), [34] for the list of these reasons.
354 *Thomas v Portsea* [1912] A.C. 1; *The Annefield* [1971] 1 Lloyd's Rep 1.

ancillary;[355] the potential of an arbitration clause to oust the jurisdiction of the courts if incorporated;[356] the possibility of the new holder of the bill of lading to be unaware of the charterparty arbitration clause due to the negotiable nature of bills of lading;[357] the potential ineptitude that incorporated charterparty terms would create in the context of bills of lading;[358] and the need for certainty in this (particularly shipping) branch of law.[359]

The Arbitration Act 1996 regulates incorporation by reference. However, the Act, in fact, does not provide a clear guideline concerning how the method of incorporation suffices. The Act leaves this matter to courts to decide on each individual case. Therefore, some fundamental issues pertaining to the incorporation of arbitration clauses by reference prior to the Arbitration Act 1996 remained unresolved also after the Act was passed. One of the main reasons for courts to adopt a strict approach in the shipping context is that the layout of the bills of lading and charterparties constitutes a two-contract scenario situation in terms of contractual structure. The two-contract structure usually necessitates the adoption of a strict approach concerning the incorporation of arbitration clauses.

Bills of lading incorporating charterparties, indeed, constitute a two-contract scenario. In fact, considering the contractual categories provided in *Habas Sinai v Sometal*,[360] they fall under the division of two-contract scenario where 'A and B make a contract incorporating terms agreed between A (or B) and C' or 'A and B make a contract incorporating terms agreed between C and D.' It is reasonable to expect courts adopt a strict approach where the case in hand is concerned with a two-contract scenario. However, the significant contribution of *Habas Sinai v Sometal* to the case law is the fresh perspective it brings to the contract interpretation concerning the manifestation of party autonomy. Even though this particular case is concerned with parties who contracted on 15 occasions and hence, there was a multiple-contract structure, the facts of the case led the Commercial Court to decide these were in fact parts of one solid contractual configuration and the situation was one of a single-contract scenario. Hence, it may be argued that *Habas Sinai v Sometal*, by improving the contractual division system provided in *The Athena*, created a guideline laying out the structural formation of the contracts and the actual scope of the contractual relationship of the parties in light of party autonomy. *Habas Sinai v Sometal* is concerned with multiple contracts of sale and, therefore, is not pertaining to a shipping dispute. However, it evidently paved the way for some critical thinking on contract drafting and interpretation.

Bills of lading incorporating charterparty arbitration clauses will understandably always be subject to some restrictions due to the characteristic features of shipping documents and arbitration agreements. However, a hypothetical situation in the shipping context might include parties who, on many repetitive occasions, contract on a similar subject matter and are well aware of the almost certain existence of a charterparty arbitration clause. Assuming the bill of lading is not transferred to a third party who is not involved in this well-defined hypothetical circle, would the very straightforward implementation

355 *The Federal Bulker* [1989] 1 Lloyd's Rep 103; *The Varenna* [1983] 1 Lloyd's Rep 416.
356 *Thomas v Portsea* [1912] A.C. 1.
357 Ibid; *The Federal Bulker* [1989] 1 Lloyd's Rep 103.
358 *Thomas v Portsea* [1912] A.C. 1.
359 *The Federal Bulker* [1989] 1 Lloyd's Rep 103.
360 [2010] EWHC 29 (Comm).

of the strict requirements for incorporation of the charterparty arbitration clause be truly justifiable? With this perhaps being a bit of a far-fetched consideration, the negotiability of the bills of lading, the inequality of the bargaining power that the consignee and the shipper have, and the necessity of the third-party protection are indeed crucial issues concerning the carriage of goods by sea. Also, predictability and clarity in this area of law have always been (and will be) a substantial requirement for shipping operations to carry on smoothly and for the promotion of commercial foreseeability for the parties involved in shipping transactions. On the other hand, *Habas Sinai v Sometal*, visualizing the significance of contractual awareness and intention of the parties by virtue of providing a contractual structure diagram, brings a fresh perspective and paves the way for questioning the necessity of applying the utmost level of restriction to the incorporation of arbitration clauses in each relevant shipping case.

Bibliography

2018 International Arbitration Survey: The Evolution of International Arbitration, Queen Mary University of London, available at www.arbitration.qmul.ac.uk/media/arbitration/docs/2018-International-Arbitration-Survey-report.pdf.

2021 International Arbitration Survey: Adapting Arbitration to a Changing World, Queen Marry University of London and White & Case, available at https://arbitration.qmul.ac.uk/media/arbitration/docs/LON0320037-QMUL-International-Arbitration-Survey-2021_19_WEB.pdf.

Ahmed, Masood, Arbitration Clauses: Fairness, Justice and Commercial Certainty, 2010, *LCIA, Arbitration International*, 26(3), 412.

Aikens, Richard, Lord, Richard, Bools, Michael, Bolding, Michael and Toh, Kian Sing, *Bills of Lading*, Informa, 2021.

Allison, Simon and Dharmananda, Kanaga, Incorporating Arbitration Clauses: The Sacrifice of Consistency at the Altar of Experience, 2014, *LCIA, Arbitration International*, 30(2), 2014.

Baron, Adrian, Arbitration and the Fiction of Severability, November 1999, *Australian Bar Review*, 19, 49–66.

Baron, Adrian, The International Arbitration Act, the Fiction of Severability and Claims for Restitution – Part Two, 2000, *Arbitration International*, 16(2), 159–188.

Born, Gary, *International Commercial Arbitration*, Kluwer Law International, 2021.

Boyd, Stewart C., Berry, Steven, Burrows, Andrew S., Eder, Bernard, Foxton, David and Smith, Christopher F., *Scrutton on Charterparties and Bills of Lading*, Sweet & Maxwell, 2008, 21st Edn.

Capper, Phillip, *International Arbitration: A Handbook*, Informa Legal Publishing, 2004.

Chan, Felix, Specific Words of Incorporation in Bills of Lading, 2015, *The Law Quartetly Review*, 131, 372–376.

Chuah, Jason, *Law of International Trade: Cross-Border Commercial Transactions*, Sweet and Maxwell, 2009, 4th Edn.

Clapham, Jason, Recent Trends in Commodities Arbitrations, 2013, *Journal of International Arbitration*, 30(6), 665–688.

Cohen, Michael Marks, A New Yorker Looks at London Maritime Arbitration, *Lloyd's Maritime and Commercial Law Quarterly*, 57, 1986.

Cooke, Julian and Young, Timothy, *Voyage Charters*, LLP Professional Publishing, 2007, 3rd Edn.

Davies, Martin, Litigation Fights Back: Avoiding the Effect of Arbitration Clauses in Charterparty Bills of Lading, 2004, *Journal of Maritime Law and Commerce*, 35(4), 617.

Debattista, Charles, *Bills of Lading in Export Trade*, Tottel Publishing, 2009, 3rd Edn.

Dickson, Moses Oruaze, Party Autonomy and Justice in International Commercial Arbitration, 2018, *International Journal of Law and Management*, 60, 114.

Dr. Melis Ozdel Discusses the Impact of the Channel Ranger at the LMAA Spring Seminar, July 1, 2015, UCL, www.ucl.ac.uk/laws/news/2015/jul/dr-melis-ozdel-discusses-impact-channel-ranger-lmaa-spring-seminar.

Drahozal, Christopher R., Arbitration Costs and Forum Accessibility: Empirical Evidence, Summer 2008, *University of Michigan Journal of Law Reform*, 41(4).

Eder, Bernard, Bennet, Howard, Berry, Steven, Foxton, David and Smith, Christopher F. Scrutton, *Bills of Lading*, Sweet & Maxwell, 2011, 22nd Edn.

Farrar, Emily, *The History of the Receipt, Around the Box*, June 24, 2014, available at http://blog.shoeboxed.com/the-history-of-the-receipt/.

Fernández, Jonatan Echebarria (ed.), *Jurisdiction and Arbitration Agreements in Contracts for the Carriage of Goods by Sea: Limitations on Party Autonomy*, Informa Law by Routledge, 2021.

Gaillard, Emmanuel and Savage, John, *Fouchard Gaillard Goldman on International Commercial Arbitration*, Kluwer Law International, 1999.

Gard Guidance of Bills of Lading, March 2011, available at www.gard.no/Content/20651968/Gard%20Guidance%20bills%20of%20lading%20March%202011.pdf.

Gaskell, Nicholas, Asariotis, Regina and Baatz, Yvonne, *Bills of Lading: Law and Contracts*, LLP Professional Publishing, 2000.

Gillies, Peter and Dahdal, Andrew, Waiver of a Right to Arbitrate by Resort to Litigation, in the Context of International Commercial Arbitration, 2007, *Journal of International Commercial Law and Technology*, 2(4), 221–230.

Greenberg, Simon, Kee, Christopher and Weeramantry, Romesh, *International Commercial Arbitration: An Asia-Pacific Perspective*, Cambridge University Press, 2010.

Herrmann, Gerold, The Role of the Courts Under the UNCITRAL Model Law Script, in Julian DM Lew (ed.) *Contemporary Problems in International Arbitration*, Springer Science + Business Media Dordrecht, 1987, 164.

Ian Gaunt Explains the Benefits of London Arbitration, *Marine Strategy*, June, 10, 2018, available at www.maritime-executive.com/features/ian-gaunt-explains-the-benefits-of-london-arbitration.

Johns, Claude and Hermann Walter, Babylonian Law – The Code of Hammurabi, in *Encyclopedia Brittanica, 1910–1911*, in The Avalon Project of Lillian Goldman Law Library of Yale Law School, 11th Edn., available at www.avalon.law.yale.edu/ancient/hammpre.asp (last visited May 28, 2019).

Johnson, Thomas E., *Export/Import Procedures and Documentation*, AMACOM, 2010

Kilpatrick, Jr., Richard L., The Joint and Several Liability of 'Merchants' Under Maritime Bills of Lading, October 2016, *Journal of Maritime Law & Commerce*, 47(4).

Magklasi, Eleni, A New Channel to the Heart of İncorporation Clauses: Caresse Navigation Ltd v Zurich Assurances MAROC (The Channel Ranger) [2014] EWCA Civ 1366 (CA) JIML [2014] 20, (6), 397, 2014, *Journal of International Maritime Law*, 20(6), 398.

Majumdar, Arjya B., Incorporation by Reference in Maritime Arbitration, 2013, *Transport Law Journal*, 40, 91–112.

The Maritime Arbitration Universe in Numbers: Will Brexit Impact London's Standing?, *HFW Shipping Insight: Who Rules the Waves?*, March 2018, available at www.hfw.com/downloads/HFW-The-maritime-arbitration-universe-in-numbers-March-2018.pdf.

The Maritime Arbitration Universe in Numbers: London Remains Ever Dominant, *HFW*, July 2020, available at www.hfw.com/downloads/002203-HFW-Maritime-Arbitration-in-Numbers-July-2020.pdf.

Martin, Patrick, *Why Is Arbitration Getting Much Too Legalistic? Can the Old Method Be Reviewed?*, 8th International Congress of Maritime Arbitration, 1987.

McKendrick, Ewan, *Goode on Commercial Law*, Penguin Books, 2010, 4th Edn.

McNerney, Mary E. and Esplugues, Carlos A., International Commercial Arbitration: The UNCITRAL Model Law, 1986, *Boston College International and Comparative Law Review*, 9(1), Article 3, 1986, 55.

Melville, Herman, *Moby Dick*, Penguin Books, first published in 1851, 2012 Edn., essay copyright 1956, the Estate of Alfred Kazin.

Merkin, Robert and Flannery, Louis, *Merkin and Flannery on the Arbitration Act 1996*, Informa Law from Routledge, 2020.

Merkin, Robert and Hjalmarsson, Johanna, *Singapore Arbitration Legislation*, Informa Law from Routledge, 2016.

Miller, Machale A., Charter Party Symposium – Part II: Cesser Clause, Winter 2001, *Tulane Maritime Law Journal*, 26, 71.

Mota, Carlos Esplugues, Validity and Effects of the Incorporation by Reference of Arbitration Agreements in International Maritime Arbitration: Current Situation and Future Trends, May 20, 2012, *Social Science Research Network*, 9, available at https://ssrn.com/abstract=2063117.

Mustill, Michael J. and Boyd, Stewart C., *Commercial Arbitration*, LexisNexis Butterworths, 2001, 2nd Edn.

Noussia, Kyriaki, *Confidentiality in International Commercial Arbitration – A Comparative Analysis of the Position Under English*, US, German and French Law, Springer, 2010.

Özdel, Melis, Incorporation of Charterparty Clauses into Bills of Lading: Peculiar to Maritime Law?, Chapter 8 in Clarke, Malcom (ed.) *Maritime Law Evolving*, Hart Publishing, 2013.

Özdel, Melis, *Bills of Lading Incorporating Charterparties*, Hart Publishing, 2015.

Özdel, Melis, *Incorporation of Arbitration Clauses into Bills of Lading*, Maritime Arbitrators Association, 2015.

Özdel, Melis, The Receipt Function of the Bill of Lading: New Challanges, 2017, *International Company and Commercial Law Review*, 28(12).

Pejović, Časlav, *Transport Documents in Carriage of Goods by Sea*, Informa Law from Routledge, 44.

Plomaritou, Evi and Voudouris, Yiannis, The Relationship of Bill of Lading, Charterparty and Other Transport Documents, 2019, *Journal of Economics, Management and Trade*, 24(6), 1–8, no. JEMT 51423.

Plomaritou, Evi and Papadopoulos, Anthony, *Shipbroking and Chartering Practice,* Lloyd's Practical Shipping Guides, Informa Law from Routledge, 2018, 8th Edn.

Reynolds, Francis, Time Charterparties and Bills of Lading, in Rhidian Thomas (ed.) *Legal Issues Relating to Time Charperties*, Informa, 2008.

Rogers, Andrew and Launders, Rachel, Separability – the Indestructible Arbitration Clause, 1994, *LCIA, Arbitration International*, 10(1).

Rubin, Edward L., Learning from Lord Mansfield: Toward a Transferability Law for Modern Commercial Practice, 1995, *Idaho Law Review*, 31, 775.

Sallman, Peter, The Impact of Caseflow Managemenet in the Judicial System, 1995, *University of New South Wales Law Journal*, 18, 193.

Schewebel, Stephen, *International Arbitration: Three Salient Problems*, Grotius Publications, 1987.

Sparka, Felix, *Jurisdiction and Arbitration Clauses in Maritime Transport Documents: A Comparative Analysis*, Springer, 2010.

Spigelman, James, *Law and International Commerce: Between the Parochial and the Cosmopolitan*, Speech delivered at the New South Wales Association, Sydney, June 22, 2010.

Stephen Girvin, *Carriage of Goods by Sea*, Oxford University Press, 2011, 2nd Edn.

Tettenborn, Andrew, Transferable and Negotiable Documents – A Redefinition?, 1991, *Lloyd's Maritime and Commercial Law Quarterly*, 542.

Todd, Paul, Incorporation of Arbitration Clauses into Bills of Lading, 1997, *Journal of Business Law*, 331.

Treitel, Guenter and Reynolds, Francis Carver, *Bills of Lading*, Sweet & Maxwell, 2005.
Tweeddale, Andrew and Tweeddale, Keren, *Incorporation of Arbitration Clauses Revisited*, November 2010, *Arbitration, Chartered Institute of Arbitrators*, 76, 4.
Wilson, John F., *Carriage of Goods by Sea*, Pearson Education Limited, 2010, 7th Edn.
Zhao, Liang and Chan, Felix, Incorporating the Charterparty's Applicable Law Clause into Bills of Lading, 2012, *Lloyd's Maritime and Commercial Law Quarterly*, 487–492.

CHAPTER 3

Incorporation of Arbitration Clauses into Reinsurance Contracts

3. Incorporation of Arbitration Clauses and Reinsurance

English law provides us with a categorization system that classifies contracts depending on their structural formation and nature. The fundamental categorization is twofold: The first division is of 'single-contract cases,' and the second is of 'two-contract cases.'[1] The first category is essentially concerned with a single-layered contractual structure. Therefore, it is a straightforward category that deals with a single contract and, accordingly, with a singular contractual relationship deriving from a single contract between A and B.[2] The second division, on the other hand, would involve two different contracts a contract between A and B and a different contract between B and C, and B seeking to incorporate by reference into its contract with A the arbitration agreement contained in the agreement with C. As a matter of fact, the involvement of D in such a contractual structure is also not a rare occasion. Thus, the second division containing multiple contractual relationships, evidently, has more complex features. The examples of this sort of contractual structure are commonly seen in shipping, insurance, and construction contracts.[3] For example, bills of lading would usually be incorporating the terms of the underlying charterparty, reinsurance contracts the terms of the insurance contract, and construction subcontracts the terms of the construction contract. Shipping cases dealing with the incorporation of charterparty terms into bills of lading have long established an authority regarding the implementation of incorporation. However, the 'cross-fertilization'[4] of these branches of law and, thus, the provided derivatives may not be overlooked. Therefore, this chapter focuses on the meaning, types, and nature of reinsurance and its relationship with the said areas of law in terms of methods of incorporation. One of the essential issues to be addressed is whether and the extent to which, if any, it is a legal necessity to follow the settled implementations of the said branches of law in the reinsurance context.

The second chapter discusses the relevant legal issues concerning the incorporation of charterparty arbitration clauses by reference into bills of lading. Because the bill of lading is a transferable document, the holder of it may not be aware of the scope or perhaps even of the existence of a charterparty arbitration clause. Therefore, it follows from the above

1 Such a distinction is made by Langley J in *Sea Trade Maritime Corporation v Hellenic Mutual War Risks Association (Bermuda) Ltd, The Athena (No 2)* [2006] EWHC 2530 (Comm), [62] (*The Athena*).

2 Notwithstanding, the reference may have been made to another document containing an arbitration clause.

3 Robert Merkin and Louis Flannery, *Merkin and Flannery on the Arbitration Act 1996*, Informa law from Routledge, 2020, 6.2.2.

4 Ibid.

DOI: 10.4324/9781003268673-4

that, the main approach has been oriented towards the promotion of third-party protection in the shipping context. The long line of shipping authorities on the matter have usually adopted a restricted approach in assessing the incorporation of charterparty arbitration clauses for that reason. Nevertheless, insurance and construction cases dealing with the same matter usually do not require the implementation of such strict requirements because of the absence of the element of negotiability in these contexts. Despite this, it is quite frequent for cases concerned with the incorporation of arbitration clauses in insurance and construction contexts to refer to bills of lading cases and vice versa.[5]

The said branches of law affect each other concerning the implementation of the legal concept of incorporation. It is clear that relevant shipping cases provide very valuable guidelines for reinsurance cases concerned with incorporation. However, it must be highlighted that reinsurance cases are much different from bills of lading cases. The necessities for incorporation may show differences in different contexts due to the peculiarities of different branches of law.

Courts considering bills of lading cases, due to dealing with negotiable documents, mostly prioritize the certainty of law and commercial foreseeability. By virtue of applying a stricter test of incorporation, courts usually subordinate flexibility in this area of law. Nonetheless, reinsurance does not particularly deal with negotiable documents. It is true that these areas of law may affect each other concerning the application of legal principles developed under each other. However, characteristic features and different realities of these areas should be considered in assessing the scope of such an effect.

In light of this approach, the following part explores the legal concept of reinsurance and the nature of reinsurance contracts under the category of 'two-contract structure.' Then, the correlation between insurance and reinsurance contracts is evaluated from the perspective of incorporation. This would essentially illustrate how the applicability of the legal concept of incorporation shows nuances in different branches of law.

3.1. What Is Reinsurance?

Encapsulating the way in which reinsurance works, Lord Mance stated in *Wasa International Insurance Co Ltd v Lexington Insurance Co*,[6]

> Reinsurance is a settled business conducted worldwide by experts, often possessing very considerable legal knowledge and expertise. The well-recognized analysis which neither side gainsaid before your Lordship is that a reinsurance such as the present is an independent contract, under which the subject matter reinsured is the original subject matter. The insurable interest which entitles the insurer to reinsure in respect of that subject matter is the insurer's exposure under the original insurance.[7]

Insurance is the United Kingdom's second-largest invisible export, of which reinsurance forms a large part and amounted to at least £1.2 million in 2007.[8] The relevant statistical

5 Ibid.

6 [2007] EWHC 896 (Comm); [2009] 2 Lloyd's Rep 508; [2009] UKHL 40. (*Wasa v Lexington*).

7 [2009] 2 Lloyd's Rep 508; [2009] UKHL 40, 925, [33].

8 *Wasa v Lexington* [2009] UKHL 40, [55] Lord Collins of Mapesbury citing the Office for National Statistics, *United Kingdom Balance of Payments*, The Pink Book, 2008, 52.

bulletin published in 2021 indicates that the reinsurance export of the UK amounted to at least £548 million.[9] In the indicated period of 13 years, the market had a whooping growth of over 450%.

Reinsurance is the insurance of the insurance. However, it is still an elusive concept in terms of providing a sufficient and comprehensive definition. In fact, no English legislation defines reinsurance.[10] An approach from a literal perspective to the word 'reinsurance' in the English language seems to reveal the most fundamental obstacle to overcome to be able to provide a definition of this legal concept. The employment of prefixes such as 're' potentially creates confusion as they may be attached to various verbs and would ordinarily indicate a repetitive action. To put it differently, the employment of this particular prefix usually creates the perception that something is 'being done again.' Accordingly, the use of the word initially creates the predominant complication concerning the nature of reinsurance as it may be perceived as the insurance being done again.[11] However, reinsurance is neither repetitive nor retrospective.[12]

A reinsurance contract would include the insurer, who insured the underlying risk, and the reinsurer, who reinsured the liability of the initial insurer that may arise from the underlying initial insurance. In this sense, indeed, reinsurance finds its merits in the underlying insurance and, therefore, cannot exist without such initial insurance. However, this would not mean that the initial insurance is repeated. Since the assured is not taking out two different policies on the same risk of theirs, reinsurance may not be considered double insurance. Indeed, there would be two policies on risk, but the policies come with different policyholders. Furthermore, concerning the time that these separate contracts become effective, the reinsurance contract comes into existence when it is concluded, irrelevant of the time that the underlying insurance policy is concluded. Thus, reinsurance is not retrospective, and it covers the liability of the reinsured when it becomes effective as a contract. The periods that the reinsurance covers are determined by the parties and be indicated in the contract. However, this would not mean that the reinsurance contract is retrospective in the legal sense. Using the prefix 're' simply presents convenience. It does not suggest that the underlying insurance contract is doubled, or reinsurance has a retrospective effect.

Indeed, there is an issue with the terminology of *re*insurance. However, the wording should be regarded to provide convenience rather than causing complexity. A reinsurance merely suggests that the reinsured settles the original claims and seeks to find coverage from their reinsurer. The concept of reinsurance further indicates that reinsurance and insurance contracts are back-to-back covered. Indeed, the insurance contract and the relevant reinsurance contract would have similarities as the latter would have been derived from the former. However, this by no means suggests that the latter is repetitive or retrospective.

The clarification of the terminology concerning reinsurance is an essential first step to take in analyzing how incorporation works in the reinsurance context. This is because the

9 Office for National Statistics, *United Kingdom Balance of Payments*, The Pink Book, 2021, '3.4. Insurance and Pension Services.'

10 Terry O'Neill and Jan Woloniecki, *The Law of Reinsurance in England and Bermuda*, Sweet & Maxwell, 2015, 4th Edn., 36, 1–044.

11 Ibid 3, 1–001.

12 Ibid 36, 1–044.

prefix 're' provides us with a starting point concerning the exploration of the nature of reinsurance contracts. The assessment concerning the nature of reinsurance contracts has a direct impact on the implementation of incorporation in the reinsurance context because it bares great potential to affect the contractual outcome.

The nature of reinsurance and the effect of its assessment are concepts analyzed later in this chapter. The next part initially provides a distinction between the types of reinsurance as this matter constitutes significance in dealing with incorporation.

3.2. Types of Reinsurance

In the most straightforward way possible, reinsurance is a form under which the insurers, who agreed to indemnify the insured against a specific loss, enter into a reinsurance agreement with a reinsurer to cover their own potential liability that may arise from the first policy.[13] There are indeed different versions of reinsurance policies that may be drafted to meet certain requirements for specific risks and coverage. Nevertheless, the evaluation of incorporation in the reinsurance context necessitates the examination of some fundamentals.

There are essentially two types of reinsurance contracts: facultative and treaty. Unlike facultative reinsurance contracts, it is likely for reinsurance treaties to contain arbitration clauses and incorporation of such to be brought before the court as an issue to be considered. Treaties deal with a number of risks for a period of time, whereas facultative reinsurance covers a single individual risk instead. Facultative reinsurance often contains the words 'as original,' which purport to incorporate the terms of the original insurance policy. Treaties, by contrast, deal with the 'specifics of incorporation' as they are usually concerned with the incorporation of arbitration clauses.

However, to finely delineate how incorporation works in the insurance context one must first start exploring the fundamentals of this branch of law. Perhaps an essential issue to be addressed is the sufficiency of the phrase 'as original' in facultative reinsurance for incorporation purposes and the extent of how far it stretches. In other words, the incorporation of arbitration clauses first needs to be set aside to clarify how incorporation generally works in insurance. Accordingly, facultative insurance is explored below from the aspect of incorporation. Functions of incorporation in reinsurance treaties are rather different, given that multiple risks are at stake and reinsurance covers many underlying contracts some with and some without arbitration clauses. However, the wording and the fundamental meaning of an incorporation clause either in a facultative or treaty setup are usually similar. Accordingly, the incorporation of provisions in the facultative reinsurance context creates a baseline and provides a guideline. Hence, both types of reinsurance contracts are explored in the following sections.

3.2.1. Facultative Reinsurance

A reinsurance policy in the most straightforward and simplest form is a 'facultative' one.[14] In facultative reinsurance, the right to choose to accept a specific risk or not lies

13 Kyriaki Noussia, *Reinsurance Arbitrations*, Springer, 2013, 4.

14 Reinsurance may also be proportional or non-proportional. However, with this issue not constituting an equally significant aspect of the subject for the purposes of incorporation, it will not be considered in detail.

with the reinsurer. Facultative reinsurance is straightforward as it consists of a distinct agreement that considers each risk individually and provides the choice to choose to enter a reinsurance relationship in respect of each separate risk.[15] In other words, the facultative method entails the reinsurance of a single risk covered in a specific reinsurance policy.[16] The reinsured usually has the right to select the risks to be ceded in facultative reinsurance.

Because offer and acceptance constitute the fundamental elements of facultative reinsurance, this may be regarded as 'take it or leave it insurance.' These elements spawn individual stages of contracting and there is no obligation for making or accepting the offer. In that regard, facultative reinsurance differs significantly from reinsurance treaties as the latter cover a number of risks for a determined period of time. Therefore, the reinsurer accepts the risks as a whole or does not accept them at all. Going through the details of the risks undertaken with a fine-tooth comb would usually not be possible in reinsurance treaties. Accordingly, the reinsurer may possibly not be able to displace some of the risks, which they may not prefer to cover because they would accept the risks of a predetermined class of policies, and these certain risks may be falling into the scope of an accepted class.

Each offer, in terms of facultative reinsurance, is a unique one as each includes a different particular risk on a different subject matter, which is to be insured by a particular proportion. In facultative reinsurance, the offeree is entitled to judge each individual risk that they are offered. To put it differently, the potential reinsurer in facultative reinsurance has the right to require detailed underwriting information[17] and to appraise the risk in a way that they would invest if they were instead offered the same risk as a direct insurer under the original insurance policy.[18]

It is necessary to indicate at this point that all early examples of reinsurance were influenced by facultative methods. In the early instances of reinsurance, this was generally the only acceptable method by reinsurers and the cover was required for each individual case because the reinsurers mainly wished to consider each case on their own merits.[19] Facultative reinsurance is indeed the earliest form of reinsurance and still forms simply on its own a large field within the reinsurance industry and the London insurance market. However, the developments in trade and commerce emerged the need for a greater number of risks to be covered by contemporary reinsurance methods and accordingly, reinsurance treaties came into play.

3.2.2. Reinsurance Treaties

Treaty reinsurances cover a number of risks. Thus, the main distinction to be drawn between facultative and treaty reinsurance is that the latter means the ceding of multiple risks whereas the former cedes a single risk.[20] In a reinsurance treaty, a standing offer is made by the reinsurer to the (potential) reinsured that all accepted risks that

15 Colin Edelman, *The Law of Reinsurance*, Oxford University Press, 2013, 2nd Edn., 13, 1.41.

16 Michael Mendelowitz, Reinsurance, in *Insurance Handbook*, Barlow Lyde & Gilbert LLP, Tottel Publishing, 2007, 3rd Edn., 288.

17 The relevant underwriting information would mainly include the details of the original assured, the interest or the property insured, the risks insured and the time period coverage, the agreed premium to be paid, and the total sum insured. See Robert Kiln, *Reinsurance in Practice*, Witherby & Co., 1991, 8.

18 Ibid 7.

19 Cecil Edward Golding, *The Law and Practice of Reinsurance*, Witherby & Co. Ltd., 1987, 5th Edn., 3.

20 O'Neill and Woloniecki (n 10) 21, 1–018.

potentially fall within preconcerted financial limits and fit a given description to be covered by the treaty.[21]

It is a prominent feature of reinsurance treaties that the reinsurer is deprived of the right to refuse individual liabilities, which are already accepted by the reinsured. In this sense, this type of reinsurance may be regarded as an 'automatic' one because 'Reinsurance treaties are usually renewable on an automatic basis, unless one of the parties wants new renewal terms. This characteristic ("automatic renewal") of the treaties makes them relatively easy to implement and cheaper to operate.'[22]

In the first reinsurance case in Singapore, *Hanwha Non-Life Insurance Co Ltd v Alba Pte Ltd*,[23] the issue before the High Court of Singapore was to identify the type of a reinsurance contract to assess whether it was facultative or an 'obligatory/automatic' treaty. On the basis of its brief terms concerning a fixed premium, monthly declarations, a limit of cover, and the way of construction of such indicated terms,[24] it was held that the reinsurance was an obligatory one.[25] Hence, in this type of reinsurance, the reinsurer becomes obliged to accept the risks that are included in the treaty, whereas the reinsured becomes obliged to cede to the reinsurer those risks that are within the class specified in the treaty. Therefore, one may further suggest that treaty reinsurance is an automatic one. However, the employment of the word 'automatic' should be interpreted cautiously. Indeed, the reinsurance contract, once completed and agreed, obliges the reinsurer to all the risks for a period of time that is agreed upon. The fact that the reinsurer becomes obliged to accept the risks that they are covering does not mean that they are obliged to get involved in a reinsurance relationship in the first place. Accordingly, the word 'automatic' simply indicates that once a risk is ceded to the reinsurer by the reinsured, it would be treated as 'automatically accepted' by the reinsurer. It is also not necessary or plausible to anticipate that the reinsurer would take the whole of the underlying risk on their own. It is common practice that the reinsurance is limited to a proportion of the reinsured's liability, where both the reinsurer and the reinsured have a common interest in obtaining the lowest possible compromise with the assured in the event of a relevant claim arising.[26] This is fundamentally how reinsurance functions.

Given the fact that the matter of incorporation of arbitration clauses constitutes the focal point of this chapter, and it is predominantly the reinsurance treaties and not the facultative reinsurance policies that contain an arbitration clause, the weight of our discussion and analysis will be given to the former. A reinsurance treaty may be proportional or non-proportional in a way reflecting the wishes of the parties to the insurance. Under a proportional treaty, the reinsurer would offer to reinsure an agreed proportion of any risk

21 Mendelowitz (n 16) 288.

22 Dănilă Ştefan Matei, Reinsurance from the Perspective of Property Insurance Contract, 2018, *Challenges of the Knowledge Society*, 12, 262–269, 267. Also see Gary S. Patrik, Reinsurance, in *Foundations of Casualty Actuarial Science*, Casualty Actuarial Society, 2001, 4th Edn., 343–484, 347, available at www.casact.org/library/studynotes/ch7.pdf (last visited October 5, 2022).

23 [2011] SGHC 271 (a Singapore case).

24 Edelman (n 15) 16, 1.50.

25 The contextual approach that has set forth in *Investors Compensation Scheme Ltd v West Bromwich Building Society* [1998] 1 WLR 896, 912 was also adopted in this case. The contextual approach is explored under the '5.4.4. The Ascertainable Objective Intention of the Parties and Contextual Interpretation.'

26 Robert Merkin, *Colinvaux's Law of Insurance,* Sweet & Maxwell, 1997, 181–182.

accepted by the reinsured provided such risk falls within a class specified in the treaty.[27] The limits of the treaty may be set in relation to the risk, its nature, and its amount. Nevertheless, with this sort of reinsurance being 'automatic,' the insurer is obliged to cede, and the reinsurer is obliged to accept all the risks that are within the scope of the relevant treaty.[28] Proportional treaties are usually in either quota share or surplus form. In the former, the insurer and the reinsurer are obliged to cede and accept an agreed proportion of every risk that falls within the scope of the treaty.[29] In the latter, 'the reinsurer agrees to accept the liability above that which the insurer wishes to retain for itself.'[30] Accordingly, in a surplus proportional reinsurance treaty, the insurer decides the sum that they wish to cede to the reinsurer.[31]

Treaties may also be non-proportional. In this case, the reinsurer has sole liability as the aggregate loss reaches an agreed figure, the ultimate net loss. These treaties are called 'excess of loss' treaties. It should be noted that the back-to-back assumption is only presumed in proportional reinsurance and, therefore, not in an excess of loss treaty. Non-proportional treaties are not presumed back-to-back covered with the underlying insurance policy.

3.3. Reinsurance Relationship and Structure of Reinsurance: The Back-to-Back Assumption

Under a contract of insurance, the insurer normally has an insurable interest in their risk and, hence, may seek reinsurance in respect of it. Unless the policy otherwise provides, the original assured would have no right or interest in respect of such reinsurance. With a more far-reaching definition, a reinsurance contract may be regarded as an agreement merely between the reinsured (or the ceding company) and the reinsurer, in which the reinsurer does not become a joint insurer of the initial liability of the reinsured for the original assured. Such an agreement illustrates the acceptance of the reinsurer to share the insured's risk to a certain fixed share.[32]

Concerning contractual formation and interpretation, the general principles of contract law also apply to reinsurance contracts.[33] Moreover, since reinsurance contracts also fall under the general category of insurance contracts, the dominant principles of insurance, such as insurable interest and good faith,[34] are also fully applicable in the formation of reinsurance contracts.[35] This is important to note as these principles constitute fundamentals

27 Ibid 238.
28 Noussia (n 13) 5.
29 Ibid 57.
30 Ibid 5.
31 Ibid.
32 Golding (n 19).
33 GS Staring, *Law of Reinsurance*, CBC, 1993, 13:3.
34 This matter is considered along with the concept of honourable agreement in the following parts due to the relevancy of these two concepts. Concerning the delicate nature of 'good faith in English contract law,' the exhaustive number of debates on the issue, and the concept being outside of the scope of this chapter, 'good faith' is not analyzed in detail but is merely mentioned alongside the 'honourable engagement' aspect of reinsurance arbitration in the following parts of this chapter.
35 See *Pan Atlantic Insurance Co Ltd v Pine Top Insurance Co Ltd* [1994] 3 All ER 581. One of the leading cases on reinsurance, non-disclosure, and good faith.

for the evaluation of some other specific issues in reinsurance law such as the nature of reinsurance and the concept of honourable agreement. Both these issues, constituting special features of reinsurance, help us to differentiate reinsurance contracts from contracts in other branches of law. Accordingly, they are important indicators illustrating reinsurance contracts are different from shipping contracts. As indicated before, when it comes to the incorporation of provisions between contracts, different branches of law 'cross-fertilize'[36] and affect each other. Some peculiarities of reinsurance contracts are beneficial to explore at this point as these may give us an idea concerning the appropriate application of some main principles of incorporation in this branch of law. Due to these peculiarities, it may not be feasible to adopt the same approaches in reinsurance and shipping contexts. Accordingly, we now turn to the structure of reinsurance contracts by giving a particular focus on their back-to-back assumption.

The formation 'being subject to the same terms and conditions as original' is a time-honoured market shorthand and is often used in reinsurance contracts.[37] The shorthand is presumed to be indicating that reinsurance and insurance contracts are back-to-back.[38] In other words, this formation is accepted to be an indicator of the intention for the terms of the insurance contract to be incorporated into the reinsurance contract, and thus, the reinsurers are liable to pay to the full extent that their reinsured was liable to pay.[39] It was stated by Lord Griffiths in *Foskringasaktieselskepat Vesta v Butcher*[40] that

> in the ordinary course of business reinsurance is referred to back-to-back with insurance, which means that the reinsurer agrees that if the insurer is liable under the policy, the reinsurer will accept liability to pay whatever percentage of the claim he agreed to reinsure.[41]

The back-to-back assumption is a reality of reinsurance and is derived from the necessities and customs of the reinsurance market. It is a special feature of proportional reinsurance contracts that differentiates them from other types of contracts, such as bills of lading and construction subcontracts.

The correlation between reinsurance and its underlying insurance constitutes one of the fundamental aspects of insurance law. When it comes to reinsurance, two different contracts come into play: (1) the original insurance between the insurer (reinsured) and the original insured and (2) the reinsurance contract between the reinsured and the reinsurer. In other words, the reinsurance contracts constitute the extremities of the original insurance and may not come into existence without an original insurance policy.

The wording of reinsurance contracts may not be ascertained outside of their contexts for the purposes of their interpretation. By doing so, the realities of the reinsurance market and customs should be considered. For instance, dealing with a dispute that arose from a

36 Merkin and Flannery (n 3) 6.2.2. Also, construction contracts are included in this cross-fertilization. See Chapter 4, 'Construction Contracts and the Incorporation of Arbitration Clauses.'

37 O'Neill and Woloniecki (n 10) 146, 4–004.

38 See Özlem Gürses, *Marine Insurance Law*, Routledge, 2015, 315–319 for a detailed evaluation of the presumption of back-to-back cover. Also see O'Neill and Woloniecki (n 10) 144, 146, 4–004.

39 This concept also paves the way for the implementation of 'follow the settlements' as the back-to-back cover may also be interpreted as 'pay as may be paid thereon.' See O'Neill and Woloniecki (n 10) 5–005.

40 [1989] 1 Lloyd's Rep 331 (*Vesta v Butcher*).

41 Ibid 336.

proportional treaty, one should keep in mind there is a presumption that the insurance and reinsurance contracts are back-to-back. Therefore, the manipulation of the wording to some extent may accordingly be presumed to be allowed. In *CNA International Reinsurance Co Ltd v Companhia de Seguros Tranquilidade SA*,[42] a point indicated was that the terms of the insurance contract and the relevant reinsurance contract to be treated in the same way if they were making sense with some level of necessary manipulation in the context of the reinsurance contract. The grounds for this are considered to be the necessity of maintaining a good back-to-back cover. Accordingly, the manipulation of the word 'insurer' to read 'reinsurer' was found permissible.

The structure of reinsurance contracts is a layered one containing similar contracts with similar subject matters. However, from a legal perspective, these in fact cover the risks of different parties by facilitating the transfer of the risk originally covered. This makes these two contract types completely different. However, in the reinsurance context, there is room for flexibility and manipulation to allay literal differences.[43]

The back-to-back assumption does not always apply. Undeniably, to be able to presume as such is appealing as it evidently provides convenience where the reinsurance is covering an ascertainable singular risk and construed in a facultative manner. However, for the said assumption to apply, the related reinsurance would need to be of proportional nature. For reinsurance to be rightfully presumed back-to-back with the underlying insurance, fundamentally, the reinsurance should be either a proportional treaty or a proportional facultative reinsurance. This issue was settled in *AXA Reinsurance (UK) Plc v Field*.[44] Considering a dispute arising from an excess of loss treaty, it was set forth by Lord Mustill that

> where a reinsurer writes an excess of loss treaty for a layer of the whole account of the reinsured, there was no reason to assume that aggregation clauses in one were intended to have the same effect as aggregation clauses in the other; the insurances were not in any real sense back-to-back.[45]

It should be noted that although back-to-back presumption generally does not operate in non-proportional reinsurance, the contracts with non-proportional character may be interpreted in the same way with the underlying insurance by the courts only if these are worded in the same manner as the original.[46]

The distinction concerning the types of contracts that may be presumed back-to-back is an important one because such an assessment potentially clarifies some issues about incorporation. For instance, parties to proportional reinsurance are more or less in the same position as co-adventurers.[47] It would evidently not be possible to presume that the contracts are back-to-back if the terms of the contracts are fundamentally different. That being said, such a presumption does not apply in the context of non-proportional reinsurance. This is

42 [1999] Lloyd's Rep IR 289. (*CNA International v Companhia de Seguros*).

43 *HIH Casualty & General Insurance v New Hampshire Insurance* [2001] EWCA Civ. 735 at [170] (*HIH Casualty v New Hampshire*).

44 [1996] 2 Lloyd's Rep 233.

45 Ibid 238.

46 Gürses (n 38) 316–317. Also see *Tokio Marine Europe InsuranceLtd v Novae Corporate Underwriting Ltd* [2013] EWHC 3362 (Comm).

47 Robert Carter, Nigel Ralph and Leslie Lucas, *Carter on Reinsurance*, Witherby, 2013, 5th Edn., Vol. 1, 121.

because the relationship between the insurer and the reinsurer is not considered similar to that of co-adventurers and the reinsurance premium is assessed irrelevant of the amount paid as premium by the original insured to the reinsured.[48]

3.3.1. The Scope of Back-to-Back Cover

The historical reasoning provided for this well-accepted market shorthand – namely, the presumption of back-to-back cover – is set forth in *Re Eddystone Marine Insurance Co*.[49] It was stated that there is always the possibility of the original policies being effected at various places and therefore not being at hand or copied. Thus, the incorporation of the terms of the original policy, in compliance with the back-to-back presumption, is a common application in Lloyd's market. The postulated approach is that insurance and reinsurance are presumed back-to-back, and these need to be interpreted in a similar manner. Furthermore, such an assumption may still prevail even where the contracts are governed by different laws. *Vesta v Butcher*,[50] in that regard, sets an example. In this case, both insurance (governed by Norwegian law) and reinsurance (governed by English law) contracts included the warranty that a 24-hour watch be kept over the premises insured. There was a breach of warranty as the watch was not kept. Had the watch been kept, the loss would have been prevented from occurring. Because the legal concept of 'breach of warranty' had different meanings and interpretations under English and Norwegian laws,[51] the issue concerning the assessment of the applicable law was subsequently raised. The insurer was liable under Norwegian law and the reinsurance contract included the phrase 'as original.' However, the reinsurance was governed by English law, and if the meaning of 'breach of warranty' were to be interpreted under English law, the reinsurers would not have been liable. However, since the reinsurance cover was intended to be back-to-back with the underlying insurance and because there was no explicit declaration suggesting otherwise, the warranty held to be creating the same effect in both policies. Therefore, it was held that the reinsurers could not avoid liability.

Pine Top Insurance v Unione Italiana Anglo Saxon Reinsurance Co Ltd[52] was concerned with the scope of the words 'all terms.' It was indicated in this case that the incorporation clause containing the words 'all terms' was, in fact, not referring to all the terms of the insurance policy but to the terms, which defined the risk, such as the ones concerned with the period and geographical limits. Considering the scope of the words 'all terms,' *Pine Top Insurance* provides us with an assessment pertaining to the scope of coverage. It is settled in this case that the phrase 'all terms and conditions as original' is not to be read as indicating in fact 'all' terms of the original policy. Gatehouse J in *Pine Top Insurance* was not convinced that the general words of incorporation were appropriate to incorporate the terms of the reinsurance contract, including an arbitration clause, into the retrocession

48 Ibid.

49 Joseph Walton QC in *Re Eddystone Marine Insurance Co* [1892] 2 Ch. 423, 425.

50 [1989] 1 Lloyd's Rep 331.

51 Under Norwegian law, a breach of warranty could not be relied upon by the insurers to avoid liability unless there is a casual link between the breach and the damage whereas under English law the breach of warranty by the insured entitled reinsurers to avoid payment.

52 [1987] 1 Lloyd's Rep 476. (*Pine Top Insurance*).

contract. It also bears importance to note that the learned judge 'was not persuaded that the line of bills of lading cases were confined to such contracts.'[53] In that regard, the case also illustrates the interaction of shipping cases with insurance cases, and this issue is explored in detail in the following paragraph.

Parties to a proportional reinsurance contract are regarded as 'co-adventurers' despite, as a matter of law, merely being contracting parties.[54] The application of the back-to-back principle facilitated the settlement of the dispute in *Vesta v Butcher*[55] in which the reinsurance and insurance contracts contained the same terms but were governed by different laws. Last but not least, regarding the back-to-back cover as a principle of construction,[56] *Groupama Navigation et Transports Ors v Catatumbo Seguros* takes the scope of this implementation further and suggests that the principle may possibly override the express terms of reinsurance.[57] The Court of Appeal in this case was of the view that even though reinsurance contained an express warranty, due to the back-to-back presumption, 'the reinsurance cover was to be construed so as to produce the same effect as the underlying warranty.'[58]

It may furthermore be questionable whether the reinsurer was in fact completely aware of the terms of the underlying insurance that they were agreeing to reinsure at the time of drafting the reinsurance contract for it to provide back-to-back cover. In this sense, one may argue that the reinsurer may have actually drafted the reinsurance contract without fully acknowledging the terms of the original insurance, and in that regard, the reinsurer has drafted the reinsurance agreement 'blindly.'[59] However, even if the contract is being drafted in such a manner, the reinsured still has the duty of disclosing the unusual terms to the reinsurer. Therefore, the drafting process may not be considered 'blind.' In the context of reinsurance treaties, the parts of the reinsurance that perhaps may be at the 'blind spot' of the overall cover are usually the parts that the reinsurer neither requires nor needs to be informed of as these constitute the ordinary parts of any reinsurance contracts. Therefore, the 'blindfolded' presumption of the reinsurer that the contracts are back-to-back does not impair the reinsurer's right to have knowledge of the terms because the unusual terms of the insurance are disclosed to the reinsurer anyway.

3.3.2. Difficulties that the Back-to-Back Cover Assumption May Create

It may be argued that whether inserting the phrase 'subject to the same terms and conditions as original,' or sometimes abbreviated to 'as original,' would work flawlessly and bring the reinsurance and insurance contracts back-to-back without potentially creating any

53 Merkin and Flannery (n 3) 6.2.2. (xvi).

54 John Lowry, Philip Rawlings and Robert Merkin, *Insurance Law: Doctrines and Principles*, Hart Publishing, 2011, 3rd Edn., 502.

55 [1989] 1 Lloyd's Rep 331.

56 See *Wasa v Lexington* [2007] EWHC 896 (Comm); [2009] 2 Lloyd's Rep 508; [2009] UKHL 40, where it was emphasized that the back-to-back cover is a matter of construction of the wording used by the parties and not a rule of law.

57 [2000] EWCA Civ 220. (*Groupama v Catatumbo*).

58 Özlem Gürses, *Reinsuring Clauses*, Informa, 2014, 36.

59 See O'Neill and Woloniecki (n 10) 4–004 and 6–072 to 6–076. *HIH Casualty v New Hampshire* [2001] EWCA Civ 735; *Marc Rich & Co v Portman* [1997] 1 Lloyd's Rep 225.

problems. In fact, the requirements to create a back-to-back cover may sometimes not be easily complied with due to the following reasons.

First, the assumption that the reinsurance and the original insurance policies are back-to-back does not always apply. Undeniably, the back-to-back presumption is appealing where the reinsurance is covering an ascertainable singular risk and is construed in a facultative manner, providing convenience. In the absence of express words stating the contrary, the risks covered by these two contracts would be consistent.[60] However, for the said assumption to apply, the related reinsurance would need to be of proportional nature. The cover is presumed to be back-to-back in non-proportional reinsurance contracts. This was settled by Lord Mustill in *AXA Reinsurance (UK) Plc v Field.*[61] The requirement for reinsurance to be proportional for the purposes of creating a back-to-back structure was later affirmed in *Municipal Mutual Insurance Ltd v Sea Insurance Ltd.*[62] It was clarified that for a realistic back-to-back assumption to be made, the contracts should be similar in character. In *Municipal Mutual Insurance v Sea Insurance*,[63] the period of risk coverage was considered a characteristic feature of reinsurance. Because the periods covered by the relevant three annual facultative contracts were different, these contracts were held not to be back-to-back.

Second, due to the different purposes of creation, there would be terms of the original insurance contract that cannot be incorporated appropriately into the reinsurance contract, even with some sort of manipulation or substitution.[64] It may be permissible to incorporate a term referring to the 'insurer' by manipulating it to read 'reinsurer'[65] in some cases. However, a simple substitution of the word 'insurer' with 'reinsurer' and the word 'insured' with 'reinsured' may not always be sufficient to 'do the trick' as simply such manipulation may possibly be unfit to the context of the incorporating contract. In *Vesta v Butcher*,[66] the appropriateness of incorporating a stock control clause into the reinsurance was examined. The original insurance policy provided as follows: 'underwriters reserve the right to replace the stock lost, for the claim is made, with similar stock of like species.' It was remarked by Lord Griffiths that

> is it seriously to be supposed that it was the intention of the parties that London underwriters were to have the option of discharging their liability to Vesta by delivering a load of live fish to them?[67]

In assessing the eligibility of the stock control clause, the court held its incorporation unsuitable even being subject to some degree of manipulation. As seen in *Groupama v*

60 See *American International Marine Agency of New York Inc v Dandridge* [2005] Lloyd's Rep IR 643; *Toomey v Banco Vitalico De Espana SA de Seguros* [2004] Lloyd's Rep IR 354; *HIH Casualty v New Hampshire* [2001] EWCA Civ 735; *Mann v Lexington Insurance Co* [2001] Lloyd's Rep IR 17.

61 [1996] 2 Lloyd's Rep 233. See also *American Centennial Insurance Company v Insco Limited* [1996] LRLR 407; *Municipal Mutual Insurance Ltd v Sea Insurance Ltd* [1998] Lloyd's Rep I.R. 421; *Goshawk Syndicate Management Ltd v XL Speciality Insurance Co* [2004] Lloyd's Rep IR 683.

62 [1998] Lloyd's Rep I.R. 421.

63 Ibid.

64 O'Neill and Woloniecki (n 10) 144, 4–004.

65 See *CNA International v Companhia de Seguros* [1999] Lloyd's Rep IR 289.

66 [1989] 1 Lloyd's Rep 331.

67 Ibid 337.

Catatumbo,[68] the back-to-back presumption being a rule of construction that potentially may override the express terms of reinsurance, and some level of manipulation is still required to be allowed to make contracts back-to-back. *Vesta v Butcher* did not provide a back-to-back cover as such an alignment did not hold to be making sense in the reinsurance context to discharge a liability by delivering fish. Furthermore, as it is analyzed under '3.4. The Function of Incorporation in Reinsurance and the Assessment of the Eligibility of the Clauses to Be Incorporated' the matter of the permissible level of manipulation is considered a principle of incorporation and it is formulated in *HIH Casualty v New Hampshire*.[69] It would indeed be unreasonable to expect the presumption of back-to-back cover to constantly override the express provisions of the reinsurance contract.[70] The manipulation of the term to be incorporated must essentially be possible and the term should make sense in the reinsurance context.[71]

Third, the incorporation of some special clauses by the employment of some general words of incorporation may not be permissible by the courts, such words being contained for example in some of the following clauses, i.e. clauses relating to time limits,[72] jurisdiction,[73] choice of law,[74] or arbitration.[75] This is fundamentally because courts may consider these clauses irrelevant concerning the definition of the undertaken risk and inappropriate to disputes, which may arise from the reinsurance contract.[76] With regard to the 'survival skills' – that is, the notion of separability – of the arbitration clauses, they are classified as ancillary agreements in their own right, and as such, they are held as not being a term or a condition. Furthermore, the indicated provisions may have substantial consequences for parties, for instance; an arbitration clause may be depriving the parties to it of access to state courts and may hence be putting them in a potentially difficult position. Therefore, generally speaking, courts are inclined to seek a clear manifestation of party autonomy concerning the incorporation of provisions of this kind.

---

68 See *Groupama v Catatumbo* [2000] EWCA Civ 220. The issue of express warranties of the reinsurance contracts that are in contadiction with the terms of the insurance contract was considered in this case. It was held that, as indicated earlier, even though there was an express warranty in the reinsurance contract, due to the supposition that insurance and reinsurance policies to be back-to-back, the reinurance warranty assumed to have the same effect and cover with the insurance warranty. In LJ Mance's words at [32], 'Here too it seems to me that the reinsurance warranty must respond to and reflect the interpretation put on the equivalent warranty . . . in the original insurance.'

69 [2001] EWCA Civ 735.

70 *Wasa v Lexington* [2007] EWHC 896 (Comm); [2009] 2 Lloyd's Rep 508; [2009] UKHL 40.

71 Robert Merkin, Incorporation of Terms into Reinsurance Agreements, in Rhidian Thomas (ed.), *The Modern Law of Marine Insurance*, Informa, 2002, Vol. 2, 67–70.

72 *Home Insurance Co of New York v Victoria-Montreal Fire Insurance Co* [1907] A.C. 59; the incorporation of the 12-month time bar into the retrocession contract was in question and the action was commenced more than 12 months after the fire. Also see *OK Petroleum AB v Vitol Energy SA* [1995] 2 Lloyd's Rep 160.

73 *AIG Europe (UK) Ltd v The Ethniki* [2000] Lloyd's Rep I.R. 343; *Cigna Life Insurance Co of Europe SA-NV v Intercaser SA d Seguros y Reaseguros* [2001] Lloyd's Rep IR 821; [2001] CLC 1356 (*Cigna Life Insurance v Intercaser*); *AIG Europe SA v QBE International Insurance Ltd* [2002] Lloyd's Rep I.R. 22; *Assicurazione Generali SpA v Ege Sigorta AS* [2002] Lloyd's Rep I. R. 480.; *Prifti v Musini Sociedad Anonima de Seguros y Reaseguros* [2004] Lloyd's Rep IR 528.

74 *Gan Insurance Co Ltd v Tai Ping Insurance Co Ltd* [1999] Lloyd's Rep IR 229, affirmed [1999] Lloyd's Rep IR 596.

75 *Pine Top Insurance* [1987] 1 Lloyd's Rep 476; *Excess Insurance Co Ltd and Home and Overseas Insurance Co Ltd v C J Mander* [1997] 2 Lloyd's Rep 119 (*Excess Insurance v Mander*); *Trygg Hansa Insurance Co Ltd v Equitas* [1998] 2 Lloyd's Rep 439 (*Trygg Hansa Insurance v Equitas*).

76 *Excess Insurance v Mander* [1997] 2 Lloyd's Rep 119.

Fourth, where a retrocession contract (a subsequent reinsurance contract down the contractual chain) includes the words 'as original' by means of incorporation, the question arises whether this would amount to a reference to the primary insurance or to the reinsurance.[77] Accordingly, the assessment of what is 'original' may be considered to constitute a contractual matter in reinsurance to tackle.

3.4. The Function of Incorporation in Reinsurance and the Assessment of the Eligibility of the Clauses to Be Incorporated

The reinsurance market may be regarded as quite a practical one concerning the brevity of reinsurance contracts and thus, reinsurance contracts may not be extensive. The insurance policy may indeed include some details regarding the express terms of the agreement. However, the usual practice would be the implementation of terms and conditions of the reinsurance, which are to be found in standard Lloyd's form.

Furthermore, it is highly likely for a reinsurance contract to include the phrase 'subject to the same terms and conditions as original'[78] and to refer to the underlying insurance that the reinsurance is 'derived' from. Because reinsurance draws its vitality and entity from insurance – and, thus, cannot exist without an underlying insurance – in practice, reinsurance contracts include the phrase 'as original,' which indicates that the terms of the reinsurance contract are the same as those of the underlying insurance contract. Furthermore, generally speaking, there would be a strong assumption that these two contracts to be back-to-back, and therefore, there would be consistency between these contracts. The key element, to provide compatibility, is the concept of incorporation, which simply means the incorporation of the original insurance terms into the reinsurance contract. However, concerning the complexity of reinsurance practice and the possibility that these contracts are governed by different laws, the incorporation of terms becomes a delicate issue in the reinsurance market and practice, especially in dealing with the incorporation of arbitration clauses.

Evidently, for the incorporation of any term or condition to be successfully achieved, the document containing that term or condition to be incorporated should be properly defined and ascertained. Failure to do so would blur the actual intention of the parties to incorporate the relevant document.[79] The question regarding the lack of identification of the document to be incorporated was considered in *Cigna Life Insurance v Intercaser SA de Seguros y Reseguros.*[80] It was held that the proceedings were not to stay because when the slip was scratched, it was found that the terms of the reinsurance contract, which included an arbitration clause, has not even been agreed upon.

Furthermore, for a term or a condition to be eligible for incorporation, such a term or condition needs to make sense in the context of the reinsurance contract. Indeed, many reinsurance contracts include the phrase 'all terms, clauses and conditions as

77 In *Pine Top Insurance* [1987] 1 Lloyd's Rep 476 it was indicated that the 'as original' clause in the retrocession slip referred to provisions of the insurance policy and not of the reinsurance policy.

78 Should be noted that retrocession contracts may include the phrase 'as original' as well. This usually refers to the original insurance and not to the reinsurance: *Pine Top Insurance* [1987] 1 Lloyd's Rep 476.

79 Edelman (n 15) 66–67, 3.39.

80 [2001] CLC 1356.

original.' However, it may not be plausible to expect all of the underlying policy terms to be completely appropriate and make sense in the reinsurance context. In the simplest terms, they involve different parties and different obligations to be fulfilled. Therefore, simple manipulation of the words may not always create the effect of the contracts becoming back-to-back if such manipulation does not make any sense in the context of reinsurance. The ascertainment of the terms that are actually eligible for incorporation may be regarded as a question of construction.[81] *In CNA International v Companhia de Seguros*[82] the main issues were whether Lloyd's wordings referred to on the slip and conditions precedent of the original insurance were incorporated into the reinsurance contract and whether there existed the possibility of giving room for manipulation of the words of a referred document to be incorporated. It was held in this particular case that it may be permissible to manipulate the word 'insurer' to read it as 'reinsurer.' Accordingly, *CNA International v Companhia de Seguros* is important as it assesses the allowed level of manipulation.

Manipulation is a delicate matter, and it should be implemented carefully. However, as long as the involved business entities are familiar with the customs and practices of reinsurance, and perhaps are in a position to be aware of the possibility and effects of manipulation, then incorporation by means of manipulation should be considered possible. Manipulation, indeed, facilitates the alignment of contracts and provides convenience where necessary.

Now we turn to the assessment of eligibility of the terms to be incorporated into the reinsurance contract. This is because the term to be incorporated should be eligible for this in the first place even if some degree of manipulation of it may be needed.

The examples of commercial transactions whereby general words of incorporation are used to refer to another contract are various. This is simply because such a practice facilitates flexibility and speeds up relevant transactions. Incorporation in the insurance context is usually implemented by the employment of the words 'as original' to indicate the underlying insurance terms to be incorporated into the subsequent contract in the relevant contractual chain. However, the actual scope of incorporating phrases may not be completely clear. In other words, the limits of their contractual reaching may be subject to examination.

One of the leading cases shedding light on this scope issue is *HIH Casualty v New Hampshire*.[83] The case was concerned with the scope of the incorporation clause formed as 'subject to all terms, clauses and conditions as original.' Accordingly, the reaching of such a clause to incorporate the terms of the underlying insurance was regarded. The principles concerning the assessment of eligibility of a term for incorporation established in *HIH Casualty v New Hampshire* were highlighted by Steel J as whether the clause being (1) germane to the reinsurance, (2) making sense in the context subject to permissible manipulation, (3) being consistent with the express terms of reinsurance, and (4) being apposite or appropriate for incorporation.

81 Clarke J in *CNA International v Companhia de Seguros* [1999] Lloyd's Rep IR 289, 299. Clarke J considered the incorporation as a question of construction.

82 [1999] Lloyd's Rep IR 289.

83 [2001] EWCA Civ 735, [2001] 2 Lloyd's Rep 161. The criteria as to the incorporation of a specific term into the reinsurance contract are listed in the first instance judgement by Steel J, and referred to by Rix LJ.

It is indicated in Chapter 2, 'Incorporation of Charterparty Arbitration Clauses into Bills of Lading,' that the general rule is that merely the terms that are concerned with shipment, carriage, and discharge of cargo are to be incorporated by the employment of general words of incorporation. In other words, the general approach of the courts in the shipping context would be to seek specific words to allow the incorporation of any provisions that are concerned with issues different from the ones indicated earlier.

The assessment of the terms that are eligible for incorporation may not be that straightforward in the insurance context. To put it differently, the question of 'which terms are eligible for incorporation?' does not have a straightforward answer such as 'the terms that are concerned with coverage.'[84] This is because reinsurance practice contains various types of contracts some of which show fundamental differences when it comes to the concept of 'coverage.' On the other hand, the classification of insurance types may provide us with some patterns. Where facultative reinsurance is concerned with the extent of coverage and the limits entailed, treaty reinsurance would be concerned with the class that the business is involved in – that is, the coverage issue – as well as the limits and premium entailed. The indicated concerns in both cases bear relation to the possible extent of exposure of the reinsurer to the risk. However, with regard to the underlying insurance policy, it would be highly unlikely for the reinsurer to take the time and put in the effort to check its wording, even more so in the case of a treaty reinsurance. In other words, when the reinsurer agrees that the reinsurance will contain the terms 'as original,' the reinsurer may, in fact, not have detailed knowledge of the insurance terms. Hence, it may not be plausible to expect the reinsurer to be able to ascertain which of the terms of the original policy are eligible for incorporation. The reinsurer under a reinsurance treaty is usually obliged to accept the risks that fall within the class specified in the treaty. Therefore, merely the risks that fall under the specified classes trigger the liability of the reinsurer. Accordingly, the mere knowledge of the reinsurer of the substantial classes of risks they are covering is sufficient and they are generally not expected to be aware of all insignificant details of the underlying policy.

That being said, such unawareness of the reinsurer does not discredit the principles of incorporation established in *HIH Casualty v New Hampshire.*[85] The relevant principles established are briefly looked into to formulate the implementation of incorporation in the insurance context. This also provides a basis for analyzing the incorporation of arbitration clauses in reinsurance.

Concerning the germaneness of a term, *Pine Top Insurance* establishes that terms are concerned with risk, period, and geographical limits would be the ones that are germane to insurance. Accordingly, a reference to 'all terms' usually indicates the incorporation of terms pertaining to these issues.

It is clear a certain level of manipulation of words may be allowed and each reinsurance contract usually has a threshold until which the manipulation would be permissible so that the nature and meaning of the contract remain intact. This understandably makes the assessment of the 'permissible level of manipulation' necessary. It was indicated by Rix LJ sitting at the Court of Appeal in *HIH Casualty v New Hampshire*[86] that 'there

84 O'Neill and Woloniecki (n 10) 146, 4–005.
85 [2001] EWCA Civ 735.
86 Ibid.

was nothing unusual about a manipulation, provided that it could be done simply and deftly as a matter of language, where everything pointed to the incorporation of the term in question.'[87] Although the Court of Appeal allowed the incorporation of the waiver clause, it did not allow this to take place by manipulation of the clause. This was because doing this so considered to possibly go beyond the assumed underlying 'intention of incorporation, which was to bring two insurance covers back-to-back, and because it would significantly modify the important common law duty on the reinsured to make a fair presentation to the reinsurer.'[88] Accordingly, the manipulation seems essentially concerned with the elimination of literal barriers that are created by the contractual language. Furthermore, the extent of manipulation would be subject to the test of consistency and appositeness. Manipulated or not, the clause to be incorporated essentially needs to make sense in the context of the incorporating contract. Otherwise, incorporation would not create results that are compatible with the characteristics and essence of the contract.

Another critical point of consideration is that there is a need for insurance terms to be incorporated in such a way that they do not contradict an express provision of the reinsurance contract. 'The notion of back-to-back cover cannot operate to strike out or override those express terms of the reinsurance agreement which are inconsistent with the underlying terms.'[89] An inconsistency with the terms of the reinsurance may prevent the incorporation of insurance terms into the former.

The criterion of apposition somewhat overlaps with the question as to whether a clause makes sense in another context. However, 'the criterion affords the courts the ability to have regard to the general purpose and commercial realities of a contract in determining whether a clause should be deemed to be incorporated.'[90]

All in all, there are some fundamental elements delimiting the scope of incorporation and manipulation of insurance clauses, and some of these show resemblance to ones that are applicable in the shipping context. This is because both these reflect some general principles of contract law, and also these branches of law, being concerned with chain contracts have a considerable impact on each other. The law on the incorporation of insurance terms that are not concerned with special aspects of insurance such as arbitration but rather dealing with relatively generic terms, is more or less settled.[91] If the provision makes sense in the context of the incorporating contract, is consistent with the express terms of reinsurance, and its inclusion would be apposite in the reinsurance context, then its incorporation would usually be permissible in the reinsurance context. Concerning the incorporation of some more general provisions, the relevant criteria are quite basic and predictable. However, the implementation of incorporation is usually subject to more restrictive criteria concerning

87 Ibid [170].

88 Reynolds Porter Chamberlain, UK: In or Out, Incorporation of Direct Policy Terms in Reinsurance Contracts, *Mondaq*, January 8, 2002, available at www.mondaq.com/article/15106/in-or-out-incorporation-of-direct-policy-terms-in-reinsurance-contracts (last visited October 7, 2022).

89 Lowry, Rawlings and Merkin (n 54) 501 citing *Reinsurance Corporation v New Hampshire Insurance Co* [2004] Lloyd's Rep IR 404.

90 Edelman (n 15) 69, 3.45.

91 Robert Merkin, *Recent Developments in Reinsurance Law*, Chartered Insurance Institute, May 17, 2016, available at www.cii.co.uk/fact-files/law-and-regulation/recent-developments-in-reinsurance-law/ (last visited June 4, 2019, updated by Samantha James).

arbitration clauses. Accordingly, reinsurance arbitration and the incorporation of arbitration clauses in the reinsurance context are examined in the following section.

3.5. Reinsurance Arbitration

Arbitration, being one of the dominant resorts for dispute resolution in reinsurance, has a history going back to the time when the whole concept of insurance finds its origins.[92] At present, it remains a highly preferred method of dispute resolution for reinsurance. However, its application may not always be seen as beneficial in dealing with different types of reinsurance covering singular risks and involving individual insureds especially concerning facultative reinsurance contracts. It is much more common to come across arbitration provisions in treaty reinsurance contracts instead. In reinsurance treaties covering numerous risks, it is considered a convenient market practice to refer these all together to arbitration under quite a simple provision such as 'all disputes to be referred to arbitration.'

Reinsurance arbitration clauses are usually brief with a scope not matching their brevity.[93] This is because a reinsurance treaty would already have a broad cover dealing with multiple risks. Accordingly, arbitration clauses are usually drafted in a broad way too so that they virtually can refer to any existing or future dispute concerning the interpretation or application of reinsurance to arbitration.[94]

3.5.1. Why Arbitration Rather than Court Jurisdiction?

Essentially, there are not many differences between trial by court and arbitration from the aspect of their legal foundations as both involve the binding decision of a third-party decision-maker. However, from a procedural point of view, they have very little in common.

Reinsurance treaties usually contain an honourable engagement clause that is included in the arbitration provision, which typically follows as

> the arbitrators and umpire shall interpret this reinsurance as an honourable engagement and they shall make their award with a view to effecting the general purpose of this reinsurance in a reasonable manner rather than in accordance with a literal interpretation of the language.[95]

The honourable engagement clause sets the requirement for the arbitrators to interpret the contract as an honourable engagement and not solely as a legal obligation.[96] Nevertheless, the existence of an arbitration clause in an honourable agreement form does not directly create the effect of a reinsurance contract to be binding in honour only.[97] An arbitration clause in an honourable agreement form indicates that the arbitrators are expected to consider the contract and dispute arising from it not by following the strict rule of law but as an honourable engagement.[98]

---

92 *Butler and Merkin's Reinsurance Law*, 1999, Kluwer, C-0677.

93 Noussia (n 13) 132.

94 Ibid.

95 Merkin (n 26) 256.

96 Noussia (n 13) 81.

97 *Home Insurance Co v Administratia Asigurarilor De Stat* [1983] 2 Lloyd's Rep 674. See O'Neill and Woloniecki (n 10) 36, 1–044.

98 Noussia (n 13) 81.

Furthermore, Section 46 of the Arbitration Act 1996 pertaining to rules applicable to the substance of dispute establishes,

> The arbitral tribunal shall decide the dispute – (a) in accordance with the law chosen by the parties as applicable to the substance of the dispute, or (b) if the parties so agree, in accordance with such other considerations as are agreed by them or determined by the tribunal.

The construction and meaning of Section 46 may be interpreted to indicate a statutory validation of the honourable engagement clauses, and accordingly, it may be argued that this particular piece of legislation has codified the concept.[99] Accordingly, alongside being an accustomed concept of insurance, honourable engagement also has a statutory reflection in arbitration legislation.[100]

Arbitration has since long been globally adopted as the traditional method for settling disputes that may arise from reinsurance treaties.[101] The reasons for which reinsurers are opting for arbitration instead of legislation are not that difficult to comprehend. One of the main reasons is that disputes that are referred to arbitration are to be settled by experts in the reinsurance industry, who may even be experts on the specific subject of the dispute in question. In other words, the experts of the industry hold the title of being 'the deciders' of the dispute. The arbitral tribunals are often formed of three members, with two of the arbitrators being 'players' of the market, for example, underwriters, and a third arbitrator acting as a chairperson, usually a lawyer.[102]

The dispute to be settled by the experts constitutes an essential element of the 'honourable engagement.' This particular concept imposes on the arbitrators the duty of determining the issues by extensively applying the necessities of equity, fairness, and common sense.[103] In other words, while moderating the strict rules concerning the formality of law, the honourable engagement concept, on the other hand, sets the bar of expectations at a higher level. There is indeed vagueness concerning what the limits of expectations are and how these could be set. However, the main interpretation that is adopted under English law is that the honourable engagement requires 'an arbitrator to be impliedly required to disregard technical constructions than to disregard the general law.'[104] Arbitration may understandably be preferred to court proceedings, especially in the reinsurance treaty context, because the former facilitates that the reinsurance dispute is to be settled based on industry business practices and by industry experts, whereas the latter contains the possibility of the involvement of a judge that would treat a very complex and comprehensive reinsurance treaty just as another regular commercial contract.[105]

Another reason is that the arbitration process usually provides speedier results. In a reinsurance dispute, as long as the parties to the arbitration are acting in good faith and are

---

99 Stephanie T. Dunn, Todd Corey and Leah M. Quadrino, A Gentlemen's Agreement: The Impact of Honorable Engagement Clauses in U.S. and English Reinsurance Agreements and Arbitration Today, April 6, 2006, *Mealey's Litigation Report: Reinsurance*, 16, 23.

100 See Lyde Barlow, *Reinsurance Practice and the Law*, Informa, 2009, 26.

101 *Butler and Merkin's Reinsurance Law* (n 92) C-0677.

102 Noussia (n 13) 134.

103 *Butler and Merkin's Reinsurance Law* (n 92) C-0705.

104 Ibid.

105 Larry Schiffer, *Expert Commentary: Reinsurance – Arbitration: A Primer*, IRMI, 2006, available at www.irmi.com/articles/expert-commentary/reinsurance-arbitration-a-primer (last visited October 5, 2018).

willing to cooperate with the arbitration panel, then the possibility exists for the dispute to be resolved relatively and significantly faster than it would be in the court proceedings.

Moreover, arbitration provides flexibility. Due to strict procedural rules that are to be followed in state court proceedings, there is usually not much flexibility. Arbitrators, on the other hand, are vested with wide powers[106] concerning procedural and evidential issues unless some restrictions pertaining to the scope of such powers have mutually been agreed upon by the parties to the arbitration.[107] For instance, within the arbitration process, the parties may set their own timetable that they think would be the most fitting for the resolution of the dispute in question as well as they can decide that the arbitration proceedings be held in different locations. Allowing the parties to privately create their own unique methods and procedures that they think best suit the dispute is the fundamental reason for the emergence of the concept of commercial arbitration.[108]

Arbitration further provides confidentiality. A court hearing is generally open to the public for anyone to watch. However, arbitration proceedings are confidential. The proceedings in the latter remain private due to the decisions normally not being published so that the subject matter of the dispute remains confidential.[109] Alongside the wish of keeping arbitral decisions and awards private, the parties may also seek to ensure the confidentiality of all the relevant documents and communications to the dispute. On the other hand, the possibility of a leak always exists.[110] This may happen where the court appoints the same arbitrator to more than one similar case hoping to get consistent results and for that purpose making all of the related documents from the initial proceeding available in the next.[111] Furthermore, such a leak may result due to 'the industry rumor mill.'[112] Also, in case an arbitral award is being challenged, any relevant decision that the court gives evidently becomes public due to the public nature of court proceedings.[113] However, ordinarily, all of the relevant documents and evidence produced within the context of commercial arbitration would solely be open to the parties and the tribunal of the arbitration.[114]

Now that the dominant reasons that have encouraged the widespread adoption of arbitration in the reinsurance context have been mentioned, we now turn to examine some possible drawbacks of opting for this specific dispute resolution method.

Due to arbitral proceedings being private and flexible, legal inconsistency concerning these becomes unavoidable. The sincere adaptation of the 'honourable engagement' and the fact that reinsurance arbitrators follow the extensive and, debatably, elusive principles of fairness instead of conducting the arbitration process in line with the strict provisions of the law, may inarguably create inconsistency. Such inconsistency often arises as a result of different arbitrators deciding on similar matters in different ways.[115] However, it may be

106 However, those powers would still derive from the contract under which they appointed.

107 Noussia (n 13) 137.

108 Schiffer (n 105).

109 Kyriaki Noussia, *Confidentiality in International Commercial Arbitration: A Comparative Analysis of the Position Under English, US, German and French Law*, Springer, 2010, 20.

110 Noussia (n 13) 132.

111 Urs Martin Laeuchli, Civil and Common Law: Contrast and Synthesis in International Arbitration, August 2007, *Dispute Resolution Journal*, 62, 81–85.

112 Schiffer (n 105).

113 *Abu Dhabi Gas Liquefaction Co v E. Bechtel Corp.* [1982] 2 Lloyd's Rep 425, 427.

114 Ibid.

115 *Butler and Merkin's Reinsurance Law* (n 92) C-0677.

said that this freedom is compatible with the main aim of the arbitrator of deciding a case based on the customs and practices of the parties to that particular reinsurance treaty.[116] Even though it may be argued that this lack of uniformity may make it difficult for the parties to give business decisions about an existing or a future dispute, it should be kept in mind that as a rule of thumb, providing such convenience or foreseeability is neither the purpose nor the assertion of arbitration as a dispute resolution mechanism.[117]

A further issue regarding arbitral awards pertains to their bindingness. The awards are solely binding on the parties to the arbitration. In the reinsurance context, this may possibly cause a problem if there is an arbitration award against one subscribing reinsurer because it would remain necessary to bring separate proceedings against the others. The effect of the findings in one arbitration on a subsequent one was considered in *Sun Life Assurance Co of Canada v Lincoln National Life Insurance Co.*[118] The nature of arbitration was considered in this particular case and it was emphasized that this method constitutes a consensual private affair between particular parties to a specific arbitration agreement.[119] The fact that other parties cannot be joined and connected arbitrations cannot be heard together held to mean that 'different arbitrations on closely inter-linked issues may as a result lead to different results, even where, as in the present case, the evidence before one tribunal is very largely the same as that before the other.'[120] Indeed, if there is an arbitration award against one of the reinsurers, this would not be binding for the other reinsurers to the contractual chain, and it would be necessary to bring separate actions against them. This necessity also prevents the other reinsurers to gain some unjustifiable benefit from an award given concerning an arbitration, to which they are not a party. Nonetheless, the existence of circumstances for a joinder to arbitration and the legal concept of quasi-contractual anti-suit injunctions should be noted.[121]

It should be kept in mind that arbitration and litigation have fundamental differences. In litigation, different parties may be joined, and trials heard together. However, in arbitration, due to the consensual nature of the process, combining different parties or handling connected matters together would usually not be possible. Therefore, unavoidably, there would always be the possibility of reaching different conclusions on similar matters that are settled by different tribunals. Arbitration is a private process and it only binds the parties to the arbitration agreement. Undoubtedly, if there are multiple subscribing reinsurers, it would be necessary to bring separate proceedings to the others. Even though this would create the result of having multiple arbitration proceedings based on the same evidence concerning the same subject matter of the underlying insurance, parties would still be different as there would possibly be different reinsurers involved. In other words, the source of the disputes being the same or similar would not be sufficient to eliminate the element of the remoteness of different reinsurers to a specific arbitration. The private and consensual nature of arbitration removes the possibility of combining different proceedings

116 Noussia (n 13) 23.

117 John J. McDonald Jr., Reinsurance Arbitration 2001: Will the New Ways Cripple the "Arbitration Clause"?, 2001, *Defense Counsel Journal*, 68, 328–338.

118 [2005] 1 Lloyd's Rep 606.

119 Ibid.

120 Ibid 610.

121 See Part II, 'Not Incorporation – but a Close Analogy: Arbitration Clauses Binding Third Parties.'

for the sake of creating convenience. Allowing the involvement of different parties merely because the disputes share the same or similar subject matter would undeniably and irreparably damage the private and consensual nature of the arbitration. Therefore, this matter may not really be considered a drawback but should instead be perceived as an inherent result of the implementation of arbitration.

3.5.2. Reinsurance Arbitration Clause

In the global reinsurance market, it is highly likely for reinsurance contracts, mainly reinsurance treaties, to include an arbitration clause. The parties, due to freedom of contract, may choose the law applicable to their agreements. The law applicable to a reinsurance arbitration clause may be the same law that is applicable to the reinsurance contract. Nevertheless, where the wording of express choice of law governing the reinsurance contract is absent, it would strongly be presumed that the applicable law upon which the arbitrator's decision should be based, will be that of the place chosen for the arbitration.[122] There is neither a law requiring reinsurance to be arbitrated nor reinsurance treaties to contain certain arbitration clauses. Furthermore, there are usually no restrictions concerning the formation of a reinsurance arbitration clause.[123] The courts generally order a dispute to be referred to arbitration provided that an agreement in writing to do so is ascertainable.

An arbitration clause would manifest the existence of an arbitration agreement that indicates any existing or future dispute to be referred to arbitration. Accordingly, arbitration clauses reflect the intention and consensus of the concerned parties. Nonetheless, the international and complex character of the reinsurance market may occasionally blur such manifestation. With the market being international, it is highly likely for the parties to a reinsurance agreement to be from different countries and the agreement to be settled to be performed in a completely different country.[124] Accordingly, the industry itself created institutions such as the International Insurance Law Association (AIDA), which aims to facilitate the promotion and development of international and national insurance law.[125] Furthermore, to allay difficulties that may arise from the variety of laws and jurisdictions that may be chosen applicable to reinsurance, some arbitration clause templates have been created for purposes of practicality and convenience.

In practice, whether institutional or not, reinsurance arbitration clauses should be covering the fundamental issues concerning the implementation of the arbitration process. Some fundamental issues are the assessment of the agreed number of arbitrators and the method regarding their appointment. Furthermore, such provisions may also be including the method to be followed by the arbitral tribunal in reaching its decision – that is, whether the strict rule of law will be followed or whether the decision will be given in an amicable way. Also, one of the crucial things to be considered in drafting a reinsurance arbitration

122 Carter, Ralph, and Lucas (n 47) 121.

123 Excluding the main restriction on the enforceability of 'any' arbitration clause, such as being contrary to public policy: Section 103 of the Arbitration Act 1996.

124 *The Arbitration Clause In Insurance & Reinsurance*; EMEA Legal Counsels, Lexology, October 20, 2017, available at www.lexology.com/library/detail.aspx?g=58de2c07-29dd-4bee-a7a2-29fa262220d5 (last visited October 8, 2018).

125 AIDA, *Overview*, available at https://aidainsurance.org/about-aida/overview.

clause is the precision of the wording because clear drafting facilitates easier and more effective implementation of this dispute resolution method.

3.6. Incorporation of Arbitration Clauses in the Reinsurance Context

With arbitration being a common method of dispute resolution in the reinsurance context, its incorporation comes into prominence in insurance law. Especially in the reinsurance treaty context, it is highly likely for an underlying insurance contract to include an arbitration clause that is intended to be incorporated into the reinsurance contract.

Similar to shipping cases, also in the insurance context, courts usually abstain from allowing the incorporation of arbitration clauses into reinsurance and retrocession contracts by the employment of general words of incorporation. One of the fundamental grounds for such abstinence has been provided, similarly to the ones in the shipping context, as the ancillary and separable nature of arbitration agreements to the substantive agreement.[126] Accordingly, it is also generally accepted in the insurance context that there should be an express reference in the reinsurance contract to an arbitration provision that is contained in the underlying insurance contract to facilitate its incorporation. On the other hand, the authorities on this point are numerous and not fully consistent. Thus, analyzing the case law on the matter of incorporation of arbitration clauses in the reinsurance context in chronological order would provide a vivid illustration of the existing authorities. Hence, laying down the benefits and disadvantages of adopting a strict requirement of express reference to incorporate an arbitration clause, a backdrop is provided to discuss whether finding a compromise between the relevant implementations of the indicated branches of law would be possible.

i. *Pine Top Insurance v Unione Italiana Anglo Saxon Reinsurance* – an Old Flame

In the 1987 case of *Pine Top Insurance*,[127] the insurer issued travel policies which covered medical expenses. The policies contained arbitration clauses setting out the arbitral procedures to be followed in the case of a dispute. Insurers then reinsured their liabilities with the defendant reinsurers under a slip provided 'all terms, clauses and conditions as original.' Furthermore, the defendants retroceded their relevant liability under a retrocession agreement, which again included similar words and followed as 'all terms and conditions as original.' The underlying insurance policy included an arbitration clause that was referring the disputes that may arise between the assured and the original insurer to arbitration. The reinsurance arbitration clause was referring to disputes between the reinsured (the original insurer) and the reinsurer. With regard to the third layer of this contractual formation, the retrocession contract between the reinsurer and the retrocessionaire did not include an express reference to an arbitration clause but merely included the words 'as original.' Following the objection to paying the retrocessionaire, the reinsurers commenced arbitration proceedings indicating the retrocession contract incorporated the terms of the reinsurance contract, which included an arbitration clause. The retrocessionaire sought

126 *Pine Top Insurance* [1987] 1 Lloyd's Rep 476; *Excess Insurance v Mander* [1997] 2 Lloyd's Rep 119; *American International Speciality Lines Insurance Co v Abbott Laboratories* [2003] 1 Lloyd's Rep 267; *Cigna Life Insurance v Intercaser* [2001] CLC 1356; *OK Petroleum AB v Vitol Energy SA* [1995] 2 Lloyd's Rep 160.

127 [1987] 1 Lloyd's Rep 476.

declarations to affect that the arbitration clause was not incorporated and, thus, was not binding on them.

The assessment of the contract, to which the words 'as original' were referring to, and of whether the terms of the assessed contract, including the arbitration clause were actually incorporated, were the two main issues considered in this case.[128] Gatehouse J was of the view that the words 'as original' should be read as referring to the initial contract of this multi-layered formation and, therefore, the travel insurances were held to be the 'original contract.' It was emphasized that in a retrocession contract, wording that is indicating the 'original' contract could be referring to the underlying insurance, in other words, to the origin of the layered contractual structure that exists.[129] In addition, it was settled that the words 'all terms' were in fact not referring to all of the terms of the underlying (origin) policy but to the terms which defined the risk – namely, the period, the geographical limits and with regard to *Pine Top Insurance*, medical and other expenses. Therefore, the incorporation of such terms by general words of incorporation was allowed. It was indicated that only the insuring provisions are allowed to be incorporated by the employment of general words of 'all terms and conditions as original' and nothing else.

It should also be noted that it is necessary to properly assess the terms of the underlying insurance that are incorporated in the subsequent contract. Evidently, the provision that is referred to needs to be suitable for identification. For instance, in *HIH Casualty v New Hampshire*,[130] the contract included a reference to a 'cancellation clause,' but there was actually no such clause in the underlying contract meeting this description.[131] Furthermore, the incorporation of the original insurance policy provisions is usually only permissible as long as such incorporation does not create inconsistency in the context of the incorporating contract.[132] At this point, it is also necessary to distinguish the incorporation of terms from the underlying policy and from other sources. This is because in the latter case, the probability of facing inconsistencies is higher,[133] where in the former this is less likely as the underlying policy constitutes the main source of the reinsurance contract.

Concerning the second part of the assessment – the incorporation of the arbitration clause – the court followed the well-settled authority of bills of lading cases that there should have been a clear reference as to make that clause a part of the agreement due to the private nature of arbitration agreements.[134] It was also stated that the construction of the arbitration clause was not suitable for 'manipulation' because the arbitration provision included 'the insured' and 'the insurer,' it would not be appropriate to read them as 'the reinsurer' and 'the retrocessionaire.' Concerning the nature of the contract,[135] such a degree

128 Merkin (n 71) 94.

129 Ibid.

130 [2001] EWCA Civ 735.

131 [2001] EWCA Civ 735 as stated by Rix LJ at [146]: 'clause 8 was not identified by the words "Cancellation Clause," since clause 8 was neither entitled as a cancellation clause, nor dealt with cancellation . . . nor was regarded . . . as a cancellation clause rather than a non-cancellation clause.'

132 See *Home Insurance Co of New York v Victoria-Montreal Fire Insurance Co* [1907] A.C. 59.

133 See *Axa v Ace Global Markets* [2006] Lloyd's Rep IR 683 in which Gloster J allowed the reconciliation of the arbitration clause in standard wording with the English choice of law and jurisdiction clause in the reinsurance slip to avoid conflict. For a more detailed analyze of the case, see Noussia (n 13) 65–66.

134 Edelman (n 15) 72, 3.51. However, Article 7(2) of the Model Law does not specifically require an express reference to be made to the arbitration clause. Also see O'Neill and Woloniecki (n 10) 95–986, 14–047.

135 However, see *CNA International v Companhia de Seguros* [1999] Lloyd's Rep IR 289, 300.

of manipulation anticipating a change in the names of the parties is considered to fall beyond the permissible degree.[136] The dispute resolution clauses, including arbitration provisions, are usually categorized as ancillary or collateral to the contract of reinsurance.[137] This classification is reinforced by many decisions.[138]

A crucial issue to be taken into account in *Pine Top Insurance* is that this particular case followed the settled authority in the relevant bills of lading cases. In other words, *Pine Top Insurance* did not consider the nature of reinsurance contracts and, accordingly, did not provide an approach that originated solely from the reinsurance context. However, the judgement was 'one formulated in broad terms and cannot be lightly dismissed.'[139] *Pine Top Insurance* is a significant case that considers the matter of incorporation of arbitration clauses in the reinsurance context. This is particularly because even though the judgement, at the end of the day, was given by adopting the principles in the bills of lading context, it may be argued to have paved the way for questioning the authority of bills of lading cases in the reinsurance context.

ii. *Excess Insurance Co Ltd v C J Mander* – Are Bills of Lading Cases the Sole Authority? A Melting Pot of Bills of Lading, Reinsurance, and Construction Cases

Excess Insurance v Mander[140] is a case of great significance, as it was set forth for the first time that bills of lading cases had to be treated as being a category of their own and not to be regarded as being the sole authority concerning the issue of incorporation. It was suggested that there should not be a solid rule of construction affecting the capability of general words as to incorporation.[141] In other words, the fairness of holding bills of lading as the sole authority was questioned in *Excess Insurance v Mander*. Furthermore, a predominant construction case on the concept of incorporation *Aughton Ltd v MF Kent Services*[142] was also taken into consideration by the court. In this respect, *Excess Insurance v Mander* provides a combined illustration of the approaches adopted before the enactment of the Arbitration Act 1996, demonstrating the viewpoint of three different branches of law (shipping, reinsurance, construction) concerning the incorporation of arbitration clauses.

The issue before the court was whether the full reinsuring clause following 'all terms, clauses, conditions and warranties as original' was effective to incorporate the reinsurance arbitration clause into the retrocession contract relating to it. One of the initial matters addressed was whether having to resort to the well-settled authority of bills of lading cases on the concept of incorporation was in fact inevitable considering the suggestion that there should not be a solid rule of construction derived from solely one branch of law.[143]

---

136 *Pine Top Insurance* [1987] 1 Lloyd's Rep 476, 481.

137 Ibid. Also see Noussia (n 13) 64.

138 *Aughton Ltd v MF Kent Services* [1991] 57 BLR 1 (*Aughton*); *Excess Insurance v Mander* [1997] 2 Lloyd's Rep 119; [1995] LRLR 358. See also *Trygg Hansa Insurance v Equitas* [1998] 2 Lloyd's Rep 439 endorsed in *Cigna Life Insurance v Intercaser* [2001] CLC 1356.

139 Merkin (n 71) 94.

140 *Excess Insurance v Mander* [1995] LRLR 358; [1997] 2 Lloyd's Rep 119. The judgement was handed down in May 1995, and thus, it is one of pre-Arbitration Act 1996.

141 Merkin and Flannery (n 3) 6.2.2. (xxvii).

142 [1991] 57 BLR 6; [1991] 31 Con LR 60.

143 Reliance was placed on the judgement of Ralph Gibson LJ in *Aughton*.

Generally, an express reference in the bill of lading to the charterparty is sought in order to incorporate the charterparty arbitration provision into the bill of lading. Nevertheless, where the bills of lading are not satisfying this condition, the incorporation would also possibly be achieved by the employment of certain words drafting the charterparty arbitration clause providing that this particular clause is also applicable to disputes under bills of lading.[144] What was predominantly questioned in this case was the justification for the adoption of a settled approach in a different branch of law even if such an adoption is creating somewhat of a consistency in commerce.[145] It is suggested that the need to refer to the bills of lading authority was irrefutable since this branch of law provided an extensive amount of case law. However, it was also indicated by Colman J that

> in order to ascertain whether the same rule of construction applies in the context of reinsurance contracts, it is necessary to identify the considerations which have led the Courts to adopt that rule in the bill of lading cases and then to see whether those considerations also apply in a different contractual environment.[146]

Taking the authority of the bills of lading cases on the issue into account, it may be said that there is a strong precedent that the general words of incorporation are deemed insufficient to incorporate charterparty arbitration clauses. One of the main grounds for this is given as an arbitration clause that is contained in the charterparty and, therefore, effective on the relationship between the shipowner and the charterer, to not to be 'germane' to the contractual rights and obligations that arise under bills of lading contracts.

In *Excess Insurance v Mander*, the key issue to be settled in order to determine whether the words of incorporation were sufficient was considered to be

> whether it was equitable to adopt the same rule of construction in a reinsurance case, by identifying the considerations which had led the courts in those cases – which were concerned with bills of lading and construction subcontracts – to adopt the rule in question and see whether those considerations were applicable in a reinsurance context.[147]

Colman J, painstakingly analyzing the authority of bills of lading on the incorporation of arbitration clauses, indicated that the arbitration clause was not a condition but in fact was a self-contained, separate contract. Consequently, it was held that the incorporation of such a 'self-contained' and separate document was not successfully achieved by the employment of general words of incorporation.

The requirement concerning the employment of specific reference to arbitration in the shipping context fundamentally derives from two issues: The arbitration is private to the parties, and the negotiability of bills of lading has an impact on the concept of incorporation.

First, with arbitration being essentially private to the parties to the incorporated contract, the employment of general words of incorporation is usually not presumed sufficient to incorporate the arbitration provision. This is because the general words of incorporation in the bill of lading context are commonly assumed to indicate the mutual intention of the parties to incorporate merely the issues relevant to the subject matter of the contract, such

144 See *The Merak* [1964] 2 Lloyd's Rep 527.
145 *The Annefield* [1971] 1 Lloyd's Rep 1; *The Federal Bulker* [1989] 1 Lloyd's Rep 103.
146 *Excess Insurance v Mander* [1997] 2 Lloyd's Rep 119, 124.
147 Merkin and Flannery (n 134) 6.2.2. (xxvii).

as shipment, carriage, or delivery. The arbitration clause not governing any of the said aspects of the contractual relationship, such a clause usually necessitates the employment of specific words for its effective incorporation.[148]

Second, concerning the negotiable nature of bills of lading, Colman J also considered the possible intention of the bill of lading holder to endorse it. He emphasized that it is highly likely even for the shipper not to have seen the charterparty that includes an arbitration clause. Thus, if there are no express words of incorporation, it would be unfair to bind an endorsee to such a contract, which is precluding their resort to the courts by means of the incorporation of an arbitration clause that they are probably not even aware of.[149]

Subsequent to analyzing the relevant case law on bills of lading, Colman J then considered a construction case, *Aughton*.[150] He drew attention to the indication in *Aughton* pertaining to the nature of arbitration clauses, suggesting that these should be considered ancillary to the subject matter of the incorporated contract where the contracts are not related to affreightment.[151] The learned judge concluded that

> the incorporated contract does not exist at the time when the incorporating contract is entered into, the arbitration clause of the incorporated contract will not generally be incorporated by general words of incorporation. Unless perhaps there were particular background circumstances, such as a course of dealing, which would outweigh the consideration that the arbitration clause was merely collateral to the subject-matter of the incorporated contract, the general words of incorporation will not be construed as wide enough to cover any provision which is not part of the subject-matter of the incorporated contract and certainly not the arbitration clause.[152]

Furthermore, *Pine Top Insurance*[153] was also considered in *Excess Insurance v Mander*.[154] The settled principles of the bills of lading cases were held to be applicable in this case due to the absence of express words of incorporation in the slip. Thus, the arbitration clause in the reinsurance contract was held not to be incorporated into the retrocession contract in *Pine Top Insurance*.[155] In this case, the reinsurance slip contained both the words 'terms, clauses and conditions as original' and also a detailed arbitration clause not found in the direct policy. The reinsurer's retrocession agreement also contained the words 'all terms and conditions as original' and it made no reference to the reinsurance arbitration clause. The court by applying the settled principles of the bills of lading, held in the absence of express incorporation in the slip, the reinsurance arbitration clause is not incorporated into the reinsurance contract.[156] It was found that the only intention attributable to incorporation was the concerned period, geographical limits, and the nature of the risk.

Excess Insurance v Mander, despite comparing adopted approaches of different branches of law on the incorporation of arbitration clauses, does not consider the matter further

148 *Excess Insurance v Mander* [1997] 2 Lloyd's Rep 119, 124.
149 [1997] 2 Lloyd's Rep 119, 125.
150 [1991] 57 BLR 1; [1991] 31 ConLR 60, 88.
151 [1991] 31 ConLR 60, 88.
152 [1997] 2 Lloyd's Rep 119, 127.
153 [1987] 1 Lloyd's Rep 476.
154 [1997] 2 Lloyd's Rep 119, 127.
155 [1987] 1 Lloyd's Rep 476.
156 Ibid 481.

since the nature of reinsurance contracts was not considered in this case.[157] Indeed, the case evaluates the well-settled approaches pertaining to the incorporation of arbitration clauses that apply in shipping and construction contexts. Nonetheless, the evaluation of the matter does not include the nature of reinsurance and its potential impact on incorporation. However, the more recent case law[158] signalizes that the consideration of the nature of reinsurance contracts may play a significant role in determining the incorporation of arbitration clauses.

iii. The Arbitration Act 1996 and the DAC Report

Pine Top Insurance predates the English Arbitration Act 1996. This particular piece of legislation aims to refine the already existing system and provide coherence rather than radically reform arbitration law.[159]

The Arbitration Act 1996 provides that 'the reference in an agreement to a written form of arbitration clause or to a document containing an arbitration clause constitutes an arbitration agreement if the reference is such as to make that clause part of the agreement.'[160] Concerning the wording of the provision it is clear that the incorporation of an arbitration clause from one document to another is statutorily allowed. However, the Departmental Advisory Committee on Arbitration Law (DAC) Report, which was published in February 1996, left the decisions pertaining to its implementation to the courts to decide. The Report frankly indicates that 'this was really a matter for the court to decide' and 'the wording we have used certainly leaves room for the adoption of the charterparty rules in all cases, since it refers to references to a document containing an arbitration clause as well as a reference to the arbitration clause itself.'[161] Regarding the statement 'this was really a matter for the court to decide,' it may perhaps be argued that the Report is not supporting the strict approach of incorporation in all branches of law.[162] Two years after the publication of the DAC Report, this issue was taken into consideration in *Trygg Hansa Insurance v Equitas*, and the need for clarity and certainty in this field of law was emphasized. The debate on the issue continues as later authorities demonstrate.[163] Given that the aim of the Arbitration Act 1996 is 'to refine the system and provide coherence and not to radically reform arbitration law,' it may be argued that the DAC Report provided a compatible approach concerning the incorporation issue, leaving the issue to the courts rather than

157 Merkin (n 71) 95, 2.58.

158 Specifically see *Wasa v Lexington* [2009] 2 Lloyd's Rep 508.

159 David St. John Sutton, Judith Gill, and Matthew Gearing, *Russel on Arbitration*, Sweet & Maxwell, 2015, 24th Edn., 1–003.

160 Section 6(2) of the Arbitration Act 1996.

161 Paragraph 42 of the DAC Report.

162 DAC Report referred to indicated approaches in *Aughton*; whether an arbitration clause could be regarded as incorporated only if it was expressly referred to in the words of incorporation or whether the test was lesser one of whether an intention to incorporate could be gleaned from the words used. The wording was certainly leaving room for the adoption of the charterparty rule in all cases since it refers to references in a document containing an arbitration clause and a reference to arbitration clause itself. Thus, the wording was not confined to cases where there is a specific reference to the arbitration clause, which was considered by Sir John Megaw in *Aughton* as a requirement for effective incorporation by reference.

163 Merkin and Flannery (n 3) 6.2.2. (xxix). Furthermore, the review of the Law Commission pertaining to the Arbitration Act 1996, which was published in September 2022, does not consider the matter: Law Commission, *Review of the Arbitration Act 1996 A Consultation Paper*, Law Com No 257, 2022. Also see '6.5. The Review of The Arbitration Act 1996 by the Law Commission and Third Parties.'

attempting to radically reform the law. One may argue that the silence of the Report on the incorporation of arbitration clauses could be interpreted as the 'non-endorsement' of the Committee of the very straightforward application of shipping authorities on other branches of law. Whatever the reason might have been, the Committee seems to have felt obliged to prioritize the decision-making process of the courts rather than radically reforming the law and intervening into the assessment process of courts regarding the matter.

iv. *Trygg Hansa Insurance v Equitas* – What Has Changed?

In *Trygg Hansa Insurance v Equitas*,[164] a post–Arbitration Act 1996 case, it was considered whether this new piece of legislation entitled the courts to disregard the former authorities on the incorporation of arbitration clauses in the reinsurance context and whether it formed a basis for creating a relatively liberal and flexible approach regarding the incorporation of arbitration clauses.[165]

The applicant reinsurer T reinsured Lloyd's syndicate E in respect of layers of excess of loss. The primary insurance was referring any dispute arising to London arbitration. The reinsurances had the same construction and provided 'except as otherwise provided herein this policy is to follow the same terms, exclusions, conditions, definitions and settlements as the policy of the primary insurers.' T avoided reinsurances on the grounds of alleged non-disclosure and misrepresentation. Respondent E brought actions against T. T applied to stay proceedings under Section 9 of the Arbitration Act 1996 on the grounds of arbitration provision included in the underlying policies to be incorporated into the reinsurance contract. The two fundamental issues to be settled were (1) whether the general words of incorporation in the general conditions to the excess and loss policies effective to incorporate the arbitration clause were to be found in the general conditions of the primary insurance and, (2) if so, whether the general words of incorporation used in the reinsurance slips were effective to incorporate the arbitration agreement into the reinsurance contracts.

One of the substantial arguments concerned with the incorporation of the arbitration clause was that Section 6(2) of the Arbitration Act 1996[166] had a redefining and modifier nature as it provided the grounds for creating a valid arbitration agreement by means of referring to an existing one. Therefore, it was suggested that the earlier authorities were to be disregarded and, thus, general words of incorporation to be held sufficient for the incorporation of an arbitration clause. HHJ Jack QC, reviewing the authorities, commented that some approaches outside the shipping context may be considered to be facilitating the incorporation of arbitration clauses by employing general words of incorporation if the field is one where arbitration is common and there are no contraindications.[167] However, he also acknowledged the dominancy of the bills of lading cases as an authority. The learned judge concluded that, indeed, there was a liberal approach, as opposed to the strict approach,[168]

164 [1998] 2 Lloyd's Rep 439.

165 O'Neill and Woloniecki (n 10) 146, 4–012.

166 Section 6(2) of the Arbitration Act 1996: 'The reference in an agreement to a written form of arbitration clause or to a document containing an arbitration clause constitutes an arbitration agreement if the reference is such as to make that clause part of the agreement.'

167 [1998] 2 Lloyd's Rep 439, 447.

168 *The Annefield* [1998] 1 Lloyd's Rep 1.

which is set out in the bills of lading cases; nevertheless, the 'charterparty cases embodied the strict approach.'[169] Concerning the argument suggesting that Section 6(2) of the Arbitration Act 1996 had a redefining and modifier nature, HHJ Jack QC, by interpreting the wording of the DAC Report, stated that

> an arbitration clause is of a special nature different to majority of clauses in a contract and the parties to the contract are not to be taken to have intended to incorporate it along with other clauses unless there is some express indication that they have intended to do so. That idea lies at the heart of charterparty cases.[170]

Paragraph 42 of the DAC Report[171] indicates the somewhat existing expectation of the Report to clarify the law on the subject matter. Acknowledging this, the Report, however, establishes that this being a delicate issue with the need for tailor-made solutions, was left to the courts to decide. Therefore, HHJ Jack QC, pointing out that this was a field in which the law should be clear, certain, and well understood, concluded that the Arbitration Act 1996 Section 6(2) did not change the settled view, and hence, he concluded 'in the absence of special circumstances, general words of incorporation are not to be treated as effective for the purposes of section 6(2).'[172]

v. *Cigna Life Insurance Company v Intercaser SA de Seguros y Reseguros* – Following *Pine Top* and *Excess Insurance*

Pine Top Insurance and *Excess Insurance* may be considered to be the leading authorities on the incorporation of arbitration clauses in the reinsurance context not permitting the incorporation by means of employing general words. These decisions were confirmed also in *Cigna Life Insurance v Intercaser SA de Seguros y Reseguros* as the court refused the incorporation of arbitration clauses by the employment of general words of incorporation.

In *Cigna Life Insurance v Intercaser SA de Seguros y Reseguros*,[173] the issue before the court was whether the terms of an underlying policy and the reinsurance wording were incorporated into the reinsurance policy. The conditions included in the policy slip solely indicated that the reinsurance was to follow the terms of the original policy and another clause stated that 'all other terms and conditions as more properly defined in the Intercaser

169 [1998] 2 Lloyd's Rep 439, 447.

170 Ibid.

171 DAC Report para 42: 'The second subsection (The Arbitration Act 1996 s.6(2)) reflects Article 7(2) of the Model Law. In English law there is at present some conflicting authority on the question as to what is required for the effective incorporation of an arbitration clause by reference. Some of those responding to the July 1995 draft Clauses made critical comments of the views of Sir John Megaw in *Aughton* [1991] 57 B.L.R. 1 (a construction contract case) and suggested that we should take the opportunity of making clear that the law was as stated in the charterparty cases and as summarised by Ralph Gibson L.J. in *Aughton*. (Similar disquiet has been expressed about decisions following Aughton, such as *Ben Barrett v Henry Boot Management Ltd* [1995] Constr. Ind. Law Letter 1026). It seemed to us, however, that although we are of the view that the approach of Ralph Gibson L.J. should prevail in all cases, this was really a matter for the court to decide. The wording we have used certainly leaves room for the adoption of the charterparty rules in all cases, since it refers to references to a document containing an arbitration clause as well as a reference to the arbitration clause itself. Thus, the wording is not confined to cases where there is specific reference to the arbitration clause, which Sir John Megaw (but not Ralph Gibson L.J.) considered was a requirement for effective incorporation by reference.' Approach adopted in the DAC Report is discussed further analyzing *Aughton* under '4.6.(v) The Arbitration Act 1996 and the Departmental Advisory Committee (DAC) Report.'

172 [1998] 2 Lloyd's Rep 439, 447.

173 [2001] Lloyd's Rep IR 821.

Reinsurance Contract.' Accordingly, it should be noted that in *Cigna Life Insurance v Intercaser SA de Seguros y Reseguros*, the issue before the court was not incorporation from insurance to reinsurance but rather from other terms, which had not at that stage been agreed to. Furthermore, the original insurance was itself incomplete at the time that the reinsurance contract was concluded. Following a dispute, Intercaser was required to proceed to arbitration on the grounds that the reinsurance contract included an incorporated arbitration clause. Cigna Life contended that an arbitration clause could not be incorporated into a separate reinsurance contract by means of general words of incorporation, and also, that the slip did not include any express reference to the said reinsurance contract. It was held that the arbitration clause had not been incorporated into the reinsurance slip, the arbitration clauses were private to the parties involved, and when the slip was scratched, terms of the Intercaser Reinsurance Contract had not even been agreed on, so the clause in that contract could not have been incorporated into the slip.[174] It was indicated that it would evidently be unfair to accept that the claimants were bound to arbitrate as they did not accept such an agreement. The wording of the incorporation clause was held not to be sufficient. Also, it is decided that compelling a party to arbitrate solely because the document, including the arbitration provision, was signed by the lead underwriter would not be justifiable.

vi. What Deductions May Be Made from the Reinsurance Case Law on the Incorporation of Arbitration Clauses?

Even though the considerations in shipping that have led to the creation of strict rules of incorporation (such as negotiability and the protection of third parties) do not apply in insurance, the same rules have also found application in the context of the latter. Accordingly, one may question exactly how the same principles find application in reinsurance. Moreover, if shipping cases accepted the prevailing authority, then a further issue to be assessed is the extent of the application of the strict rule in the insurance context.

To address these issues, a two-step analysis should be performed. First, the nature of reinsurance contracts and their differences from shipping contracts should be set forth. The question regarding the true nature of reinsurance may still be regarded as a delicate and complex one as there are contradicting decisions on this matter. Providing an illustration of the differences between these two different contexts would therefore be useful to examine the rationality of adopting the strict approach in reinsurance. Considering that there is not much debate on the legal nature of bills of lading, the nature of reinsurance instead is looked into to be able to compare both.

Second, regarding the fact that bills of lading cases are the predominant authority on the incorporation of arbitration clauses, it is necessary to analyze what would actually happen if we remove these from the equation. Accordingly, the following questions should be posed, in that case: Which rules of law and methods would apply in implementing incorporation? What other methods of law are there to facilitate incorporation? Considering these questions, we start with the evaluation of the nature of reinsurance contracts and their evident differences from bills of lading.

---

174 See Noussia (n 13) 69; O'Neill and Woloniecki (n 10) 145–146, 4–004.

3.7. Nature of Reinsurance and Its Effect on Incorporation

Marine Insurance Act 1906 provides that 'the insurer under a contract of marine insurance has an insurable interest in his risk and may re-insure in respect of it. Unless the policy otherwise provides, the original assured has no right or interest in respect of such re-insurance.'[175] With a more far-reaching definition, a reinsurance contract may be regarded as a mere arrangement between the reinsured and the reinsurer, in which the reinsurer does not become a joint insurer of the initial liability of the reinsured for the original assured.[176] Moreover, since reinsurance is considered a type of insurance, the general requirements for the establishment of insurance such as the insurable interest and good faith[177] apply in full effect to the creation of reinsurance contracts. The Marine Insurance Act 1906 predates the Insurance Act 2015 and some of its provisions have been abolished or amended. However, the provided definition of the Marine Insurance Act 1906 is still useful to bear in mind. The Insurance Act 2015 mentions the phrase, 're-insuring,' only once in section 5 followed by the statement that 'the persons connected with a contract of insurance are – (a) the insured and any other persons for whom cover is provided by the contract, and (b) if the contract re-insures risks covered by another contract, the persons who are (by virtue of this subsection) connected with that other contract.'[178]

Facultative reinsurance policies are clearly categorized as insurance contracts as they possess characteristics of a classic insurance contract: They contain a simple promise to indemnify the reinsured for their liability under a specific original policy.[179] The risk undertaken by the reinsurer in this context is foreseeable and agreed upon. In essence, the reinsurer exactly acknowledges what they have signed up for.

Reinsurance treaties not possessing the general characteristics of typical reinsurance, the problem of assessing the nature of these comes into prominence. For instance, in treaty reinsurance, it would not be possible for the reinsurer to acknowledge all the exact risks covered by the reinsurance in advance.[180] In practice, it is assumed by the courts that such forms of reinsurance constitute insurance, and as an outcome, they attract the duty of utmost good faith.[181] Therefore, the principle of utmost good faith has an impact on the incorporation of arbitration clauses. Nevertheless, the effectiveness of this principle is evidently not sufficient to clarify the nature of reinsurance contracts and there is some unclarity. Concerning the nature of reinsurance contracts the main issue to be addressed is whether reinsurance is a further insurance on the subject matter originally insured or an insurance of liability of the reinsured under the original policy.[182]

---

175 Section 9(1) of the Marine Insurance Act 1906.

176 See Andrew McGee, *The Modern Law of Insurance*, LexisNexis Butterworths, 2018, 4th Edn.

177 See *Pan Atlantic Insurance Co Ltd v Pine Top Insurance Co Ltd* [1994] 3 All ER 581. The case may be regarded as one of the leading ones on reinsurance concerning non-disclosure and good faith. Nevertheless, the matter of 'good faith' is a complex one, especially under English law, and, therefore, is not discussed in detail. For an in depth analysis of the concept, see Özlem Gürses, What Does 'Utmost Good Faith' Mean?, 2016, *Insurance Law Journal*, 27, 124–134.

178 Section 5 of the Insurance Act 2015.

179 *Delver v Barnes* [1807] 1 Taunt 48.

180 Merkin (n 26) 239, 12.

181 *Forsikringsaktieselskabet National (of Copenhagen) v Attorney General* [1925] AC 639: Viscount Cave LC, sitting at the House of Lords, stated that 'by a contract of reinsurance the reinsuring party insures the original party against the original loss.'

182 Özlem Gürses, The Construction of Terms of Facultative Reinsurance Contracts: Is Wasa v Lexington the Exception or the Rule?, January 2010, *The Modern Law Review*, 73(1), 119–140, 123.

3.7.1. *Wasa v Lexington*: A Dealbreaker

The House of Lords in *Wasa v Lexington*[183] was concerned with the presumption of back-to-back cover and the exceptional circumstances in which the presumption may not be applicable.[184] The House of Lords accepted the ordinary commercial purpose of proportional facultative reinsurance policies is to provide back-to-back cover but where policies are governed by different laws, they were of the opinion that this raises the necessity to assess the construction of both contracts concerning what risk is assumed. Indeed, 'there are no special conflict of laws rules which govern the consequences of any inconsistency.'[185]

Lexington, a US insurer, insured Alcoa for three years from July 1977 under an all-risks property damage and business interruption policy. Lexington, then, purchased a facultative reinsurance policy covering the same period in respect of all risks of physical loss or damage. Wasa and AGF were the reinsurers in the present litigation and the reinsurance was placed in the London market and, hence, according to the English common law principles, was subject to English law. There was not a formal contract, and the terms of the reinsurance were set out in the slip. The reinsurance was stated to be a contributing facultative reinsurance covering 'all risks of physical loss or damage . . . as original.' Furthermore, the coverage period was stated to be for '36 months . . . pro rata to expiry of original.' The full reinsurance clause was not identified but the early versions of the reinsurance clause stated 'warranted all terms and conditions as original' and the main issue to be addressed was pertaining to the capability of these words to incorporate insurance provisions into the reinsurance.

The US Environmental Protection Agency required Alcoa to clean the pollution and contamination at various of its manufacturing sites. Based on the timeline that has been provided by an investigation pertaining to the time and scope of the pollution, Alcoa, initiated proceedings against insurers, who provided cover during the period of the 1940s to 1990. The Washington Supreme Court found that there was a reasonable basis on which to allocate to each policy year the costs related to the property damage that has been occurred by the pollution. It was decided by the Court that the development of the contamination had gotten steady over the years and, hence, dividing the total damage by the number of years that the pollution and contamination occurred was found reasonable. Accordingly, the Court ruled that Lexington was liable for the damage that occurred during the three-year policy period starting from July 1977. That meant that Lexington was jointly liable for the damage that occurred before and after the policy coverage as well.

Alcoa's claim was settled by Lexington and Lexington made its own claim against its reinsurers, Wasa and AGF. The reinsurers sought declarations in England that they were not liable. As indicated, reinsurance was placed in the London market and, hence, according to the English common law principles, was subject to English law. The reinsurers sought the declaration that the coverage period was governed by English law, and therefore, the liability would only arise pertaining to the coverage period.[186] In other words, the reinsurers

183 [2007] EWHC 896 (Comm); [2009] 2 Lloyd's Rep 508; [2009] UKHL 40.

184 Gürses (n 38) 335.

185 Joanne Jolly and Tracey Anderson, *UK: Wasa v Lexington – The Repercussions for Reinsurers*, Barlow Lyde & Gilbert LLP, August 5, 2009, available at www.mondaq.com/uk/reinsurance/84212/wasa-v-lexington--the-repercussions-for-reinsurers (last visited August 16, 2022).

186 *Knight v Faith* [1850] QB 649.

contended that this specific settlement was not suitable to be followed by them as they were not obliged to indemnify the reinsured unless the occurred loss fell within the scope of the insurance cover and, accordingly, within the scope of the reinsurance cover.

It is quite common for reinsurance contracts to include a 'follow the settlements clause' that would stipulate the reinsurer to follow all settlements that are made by reinsured. If the reinsurance includes such a clause, then, the reinsured would not have to prove that the loss fell within the scope of the insurance policy but anyways that they acted with due diligence and took all proper and business-like steps in settling the claim, as Lexington did in this case. The main question to be answered was whether the claim fell within the scope of the reinsurance as a matter of law. To be able to answer this question, the initial issue to be assessed was whether the time coverage of the insurance and reinsurance contracts could be construed as overlapping.

Concerning the ascertainment of the coverage period, it was indicated by the court that reinsurers agreed to reinsure Lexington for the period between July 1977 and July 1980 and the coverage did not pertain to damage occurring before or after this particular period. Therefore, it was held that the claims did not fall within the scope of the reinsurance and hence, the reinsurers were not obliged to follow the settlement of the reinsured.

One of the most significant aspects of *Wasa v Lexington* is Simon J ruling that reinsurance is not a liability cover but, in fact, a further insurance on the subject matter insured, and hence, the interpretation of the insurance and reinsurance contracts pertaining to the law that these contracts are subject to should be done independently.[187] Even though the contracts were intended to be back-to-back, the period coverage and, hence, the interpretation of contracts and the law that they were subject were held to be prioritized. Accordingly, these contracts were held not to be overlapping, and therefore, the reinsurers were held not to be liable for the losses that occurred outside the coverage period.

Following the appeal of Lexington, the Court of Appeal[188] decided that even though the applicable laws may be different, the interpretation of the time coverage of the insurance and reinsurance should be considered overlapping due to the back-to-back nature of these types of contracts. However, the House of Lords[189] allowed the judgement of Simon J, and it was stated that 'reinsurance is not liability insurance and discussing the nature of reinsurance would make no difference to the disposition of the appeals if it were.'[190] Accordingly, interpreting the contracts separately, the reinsurers were entitled to rely upon the English law to restrict their liability with the 36-month period reinsurance coverage.

Wasa v Lexington was a deal-breaker in the sense that it was accepted by the House of Lords that 'reinsurance is a contract whereby the subject matter of the original insurance is insured by the reinsurer and it is not a contract under which the reinsurer agrees to indemnify the insurer for its liability arising under the primary insurance.'[191] This may be argued to be in contradiction with the generally adopted approach accepting that reinsurance

187 [2007] EWHC 896 (Comm).

188 [2008] EWCA Civ 150. For an evaluation of the view of the Court of Appeal pertaining to *Wasa v Lexington*, see Özlem Gürses and Robert Merkin, Facultative Reinsurance and the Full Reinsurance Clause, 2008, *Lloyd's Maritime and Commercial Law Quarterly*, 3, 366–388.

189 [2009] UKHL 40.

190 Ibid 114.

191 Gürses (n 182).

would constitute a separate insurance covering the liability of the reinsured and would not constitute a limb of the original insurance. Observing the conspicuous impact of assessing the nature of reinsurance contracts on the contract interpretation and contractual structure, it becomes clear that this is an issue that is intertwined with the issue of incorporation. The assessment pertaining to the nature of the reinsurance contract has the inevitable effect on the determination of issues pertaining to incorporation. Accordingly, the concept of incorporation in the reinsurance context is evaluated in the following section, considering the nature of reinsurance contracts.

3.7.2. The Antagonist of Reinsurance: Is Reinsurance a Further Insurance on the Subject Matter Originally Insured?

In an early case, *Delver v Barnes*, reinsurance was defined as 'a new assurance effected by a new policy on the same risk which was before insured in order to indemnify the underwriters from their previous subscriptions.'[192] Similarly, in some subsequent cases, it was plainly rejected that 'reinsurance is a distinct insurance,' and instead decisions were signalling that 'reinsurance is a further insurance' on the original subject matter. Nevertheless, with Section 9(1) of the Marine Insurance Act 1906 stating that reinsurance is an insurance under which 'the insurer insuring his risk,' the compatibility of the 'further insurance' approach with the legislation seems highly questionable. In other words, the relevant section seems to be indicating the 'liability insurance' approach instead.

Furthermore, the law changed after the Insurance Act 2015 came into force on August 12, 2016. The impact of this new piece of legislation on reinsurance contracts may be considered debatable as the Insurance Act 2015 does not really say much about these contracts. However, it is clear that the Act applies to reinsurance since 'reinsurance is a contract of insurance' and, Insurance Act 2015, applies to contracts of insurance. The status of reinsurance and retrocession contracts was confirmed by the Law Commission later as being 'contracts of insurance at common law[193] and non-consumer insurance contracts for the purpose of the Act.'[194]

The silence of the Insurance Act 2015 concerning the issue of reinsurance may be interpreted as the Act leaving the assessment of the nature of reinsurance contracts to the courts and, therefore, referring to the resolution of issues that may arise from such an assessment to the case law. The case law that is suggesting reinsurance is a further insurance on the subject matter is mostly dated and merely constitutes a minority of the cases dealing with the nature of reinsurance. Nonetheless, *Wasa v Lexington*, being a case which is settled only a few years before the Insurance Act 2015 came into force and substantially contradicting the Act on this matter, makes it crucial to address the nature of reinsurance contracts in light of this particular judgement and the Act.

Wasa v Lexington was a dealbreaker. Before it, the law concerning the nature of reinsurance contracts was more or less settled as it was widely accepted that reinsurance would be considered insurance of the liability and not further insurance of the original

192 Mansfield CJ in *Delver v Barnes* [1807] 1 Taunt 48 at [51]; *Uzielli v Boston Marine* [1884] 15 Q.B.D. 11; *British Dominions General v Duder* [1915] 2 K.B. 394.

193 See *Delver v Barnes* [1807] 1 Taunt 48.

194 Explanatory Notes, *Insurance Act 2015*, Chapter 4, para 36, available at www.legislation.gov.uk/ukpga/2015/4/pdfs/ukpgaen_20150004_en.pdf.

subject matter of the initial insurance. Some of the main concepts that are considered intertwined with the 'liability insurance' approach have generally been accepted to be the following: privity of contract, insurable interest, and the issues of double insurance and co-insurance. The validity of these is examined later in this chapter. However, one may argue that these are very fundamental concepts to insurance, and accordingly, they indicate the compatibility of the 'liability insurance approach,' rather than of the 'further insurance' approach, with the realities of the reinsurance market. Nevertheless, the latter in a way resurrected as manifested in *Wasa v Lexington.*[195] The House of Lords decided not to follow the conventional approach on the matter and held that reinsurance is further insurance on the subject matter originally insured. However, the decision is indeed an exceptional one, and accordingly, its accuracy may be discussed. The decision may be considered a highly significant one because it reveals the importance of assessing the nature of reinsurance as such an assessment may profoundly alter the outcome of the implementation of incorporation.

3.7.3. The Protagonist of Reinsurance: Is Reinsurance the Insurance of Liability of the Reinsured?

In *Home Insurance Company of New York v Victoria-Montreal Fire Insurance Company*, the substance of a reinsurance contract was stated to be 'against the liability, or a portion of the liability, undertaken by the original insurer or the insurer covering the original insurer's direct liability.'[196] Consequently, it was held that a direct insurance notice term under the original policy was not applicable to the reinsurance policy as such a clause would only be applicable in the original policy where the assured may sue immediately on incurring a loss. The term was not applicable as the insured was unable to sue until the direct loss was ascertained between the parties over whom they have no control. In compliance with the 'liability insurance' approach, the term held insufficient to trigger the reinsurance coverage. Furthermore, in the modern form of reinsurance, it is not even mandatory for the underlying contract to be one of insurance[197] as stated in *Travelers Casualty & Surety v Commisioners of Customs and Excise.*[198] The case was concerned with various bonds, which themselves were not insurance contracts even though issued by insurers. This case also signalizes the adoption of the 'liability insurance' approach rather than the 'further insurance' approach.

3.7.4. Some Criticized Points of the Further Insurance Approach

The 'further insurance' approach was expressly rejected by Adrian Hamilton QC in *D.R. Insurance v Seguros America Banamex.*[199] The criticized points about the approach are more or less concerned with the following: privity of contract, insurable interest, and double insurance and co-insurance. Accordingly, these issues are evaluated below concerning their correlation with the nature of reinsurance contracts.

---

195 [2009] UKHLR 40.
196 [1907] AC 59, 63.
197 Jonathan Gilman, Robert Merkin, Claire Blanchard, and Mark Templeman, *Arnould: Law of Marine Inurance and Average,* Sweet & Maxwell, British Shipping Laws, 2013, 18th Edn., 1707, 33.
198 [2006] Lloyd's Rep I.R. 385.
199 [1993] 1 Lloyd's Rep 120, 129.

3.7.4.1. Privity of Contract

One of the fundamental problems with accepting reinsurance is a 'further insurance' on the subject matter originally insured is regarding the implication that the word 'further' creates about the contractual relationship. This potentially implies that a contractual relationship is established between the original insured and the reinsurer as the word 'further' may potentially suggest such an establishment. It is stated in *English Insurance Co v National Benefit Assurance Co* that

> whether or not the reinsurers or the alleged reinsurers have assumed a contractual liability to the original assured, for such an original contractual liability is not an incident of reinsurance, and if such an original liability had been assumed then there would have been a contract of insurance.[200]

In reinsurance contracts, there would inherently be no privity between the original assured and the reinsurer unless the policy otherwise provides.[201] Therefore, the insured would normally not be entitled to bring claims against the reinsurer as the insured would not have a right or interest in respect of such reinsurance.

On the other hand, it should be noted that the reinsurance contract might contain a cut-through clause that may be defined as 'a provision in a contract of insurance which typically purports to afford protection to a policyholder against the insolvency of its insurer.'[202] Such a clause entitles the original assured to make a direct claim against the reinsurer in the case of the original insurer – namely, the reinsured becomes liquidate and also enables the reinsurers to settle the claim of the original assured directly.[203] The cut-through clause may be considered a shortcut that provides the insured to bring a claim against the reinsurer, despite there being no privity of contract between these parties.[204] The concept may also be argued to find statutory reflection in the Contracts (Rights of Third Parties) Act 1999.[205] In the absence of such a clause, privity is also usually absent. It was pointed out by the Court of Appeal in *Gouriet v Union of Post Office Workers*[206] that the reinsurer is external to the contractual relationship between the original assured and the reinsured. Because the special interest of the reinsurer was absent in this case, they were not entitled to initiate proceedings themselves.

3.7.4.2. Insurable Interest

The consideration of 'further insurance' may create the assumption that the reinsurer has an insurable interest on the subject matter originally insured under the direct policy.[207]

---

200 [1929] AC 114, 124.

201 This is also consistent with Section 9(2) of the Marine Insurance Act 1906, stating that the original assured would not have a right or interest in respect of reinsurance unless otherwise provided. Gürses (n 182) 129: 'Although in fact they may be if the insurers are acting as a front for the reinsurers and the reinsurance cover is 100 per cent.'

202 Christopher Braithwaite, Cut-Through Clauses, 1997, *BILA Journal*, 22.

203 See *Grecoair Inc v Tilling* [2005] Lloyd's Rep IR 151.

204 Gürses (n 38) 311.

205 Section 1(1) of the Contracts (Rights of Third Parties) Act 1999 provides that 'a person who is not a party to a contract (a "third party") may in his own right enforce a term of the contract if the contract expressly provides that he may.' Accordingly, the concept has statutory reflection.

206 [1978] AC 435, 501.

207 *Feasey v Sun Life Assance Co of Canada* [2002] 2 All ER (Comm) 492.

Under an insurance contract, the insurer would have an insurable interest that establishes the foundation for the reinsurance of the insurer's liability.[208] Accepting that reinsurance constitutes a 'further insurance' may potentially be understood as the reinsurer having a similar insurable interest where, in fact, they do not. Where the insurer/reinsured does not have an underlying insurable interest, the liability of the reinsurer would not arise because the insurer/reinsured would not have an insurable interest to support the reinsurance.[209] In other words, in such a case neither policy would be enforceable.[210] Consequently, the insurable interest of the assured and the reinsured coexist or do not exist at all.

Hobhouse LJ stated in *Toomey v Eagle Star* that the extent of the reinsured's insurable interest has to be defined referring to the direct policy, as the reinsurer should also be entitled to benefit from any protection, which the reinsured is entitled to by means of the original policy.[211] Accordingly, the reinsured's interest should be circumscribed by the scope of the liability, which has been undertaken under the original policy.[212] Indicatively, just because it establishes the liability of the reinsured, the insured risk is a concern of the reinsurers, but not because it forms the subject matter originally insured under the direct policy.

If reinsurance is assessed as the insurance of the reinsured's liability, then the usual rules according to the insurable interest would apply to liability. On the other hand, assuming reinsurance as a further insurance would raise the requirement of conformity with the rules of insurable interest[213] concerning that particular class of direct insurance.[214]

3.7.4.3. Double Insurance and Co-Insurance

Reinsurance is neither co-insurance nor double insurance. While a co-insurance may be defined as two or more insurers subscribing to a contract[215] or an insurance contract arranged in layers,[216] a double insurance may be defined as more than one policy, which the assured takes out on the same subject matter, interest, and also risk.[217] Accepting reinsurance as 'further insurance' would inevitably raise the question of whether this constitutes a type of co-insurance since the same risk would presumably be assumed to be insured both by the original insurer (the reinsured) and the reinsurer. However, since no contract would exist between the original insured and the reinsurer, it may clearly be understood that reinsurance does not form co-insurance. Furthermore, conversely to the principle of mutuality of interest between the insurers in co-insurance,[218] the reinsured settles the original claims and seeks to pass them on to their reinsurer in the context of reinsurance. Moreover, reinsurance may also not be categorized as double insurance as it does not involve an assured that is taking out two different policies on the same risk

208 *Mackenzie v Whitworth* [1875] 1 Ex.D. 36.

209 *Colonial Insurance Co of New Zeland v Adelaide Marine Insurance* [1886] 12 App. Cas. 128.

210 *Re Overseas Marine Insurance Co Ltd* [1930] 36 LI L Rep 183.

211 *Toomey v Eagle Star Insurance Co* [1994] 1 Lloyd's Rep 516, 522–523.

212 See Robert Merkin (ed.), *What Is Reinsurance*, LLP Professional Publishing, 1998, 77 (AIDA Reinsurance Working Party Report).

213 *Dalby v India and London Life* [1854] 15 C.B. 365.

214 Merkin (n 26) 240, 12–05.

215 Ibid C-0630.

216 Lowry, Rawlings and Merkin (n 54) 502.

217 Merkin (n 26) C-0600.

218 *Roar Marine Ltd v Bimeh Iran Insurance Co* [1998] 1 Lloyd's Rep 423.

of theirs. Even though the contractual configuration of the reinsurance structure includes two different policies existing on such a risk, the fact that policies come with different policyholders makes them completely different in the legal sense.

3.7.5. The Battle of Theories: *Antagonist v Protagonist*

The discussion concerning the nature of reinsurance contracts predominantly revolves around two arguments: One suggesting reinsurance is a further policy on the subject matter originally insured, and the other suggesting reinsurance is alike liability insurance, where the reinsured becomes indemnified in case of facing liability to the assured, who is originally insured. Regarding the identified shortcomings of the further insurance theory, it looks clear that reinsurance has greater similarities with the features of liability insurance, which is usually effected against the risk of incurring tortious liability to a third party.[219] In reinsurance, the liability of the reinsurer would also be triggered by the establishment and quantification of the loss similar to that of the insurer being triggered under a liability policy.

The assessment of the nature of reinsurance is of great significance, especially considering the situation in which the terms of reinsurance and underlying insurance contracts have identical wording. The adoption of theories on the nature of reinsurance is significant as the adopted theory may alter the contractual outcome. This chapter argues that reinsurance is the insurance of liability of the reinsured that is being triggered by the liability of the reinsured to the original insured under the original insurance.

First, liability insurance and reinsurance are similar because liability insurance may be defined as a contract of indemnity covering the risk of the assured incurring liability to third parties.[220] As such agreements provide indemnity, the assured is not entitled to recover until the loss and the liability for the relevant loss are established and ascertained.[221] In other words, provided that the reinsured's liability is established and quantified, the obligation of the reinsurer to indemnify the assured arises.[222] Moreover, the liability of the reinsured must be established by means of a court judgement, an arbitration award, or a binding settlement.[223] Furthermore, as it is possible in liability insurance contracts, the reinsurance contracts may include claims co-operation clauses, which oblige the reinsured to not settle a claim or undertake liability without the initial consent of the reinsurer.

Second, even though *Delver v Barnes*[224] set forth that reinsurance is further insurance on the subject matter originally insured, at the time this case was decided, the allowed level of manipulation of the words was perhaps more flexible than it currently is. It was common for parties to manipulate the word 'insured' into 'reinsured' in a way in accordance with the 'further insurance' approach. This may essentially impair the promotion of the privity of contract and fail to reflect the contemporary practice in the London market.[225]

---

219 Peter Cane, *Tort Law and Economic Interests*, Clarendon Press, 1991.

220 Fletcher Moulton LJ in *British Cash and Parcel Conveyors v Lamson Store Service* [1908] 1 KB 1006, 1014.

221 *Cox v Bankside Members Agency Ltd* [1995] 2 Lloyd's Rep 437.

222 Sedley LJ in *Wasa v Lexington* [2008] 1 CLC 340, 362.

223 *Insurance Co of Africa v Scor (UK) Reinsurance Co Ltd* [1985] 1 Lloyd's Rep 312.

224 *Delver v Barnes* [1807] 1 Taunt 48.

225 John Birds, Ben Lynch, and Simon Milnes, *MacGillivray on Insurance Law*, Sweet & Maxwell, 2012, 12th Edn., 33–3.

Third, the further insurance approach may also fail to facilitate a workable calculation method for the limitation period. If reinsurance is accepted as 'further insurance,' this would potentially necessitate the limitation period to run from the same date for the assured and the reinsured. Nonetheless, reinsurance practice applies differently.

Fourth, the loss incurred is established once the liability of the insured is clearly ascertained. Accordingly, in compliance with the 'liability insurance' approach, the date of the assured's loss is regarded to be the date that the liability of the assured to a third party is established and ascertained.[226] Moreover, as it was stated by the Privy Council in *Home Insurance v Victoria-Montreal*,[227] the reinsurers are not entitled to Act until the assessment of the direct loss incurred between the parties to the direct insurance policy as they have no control over the parties or the proceedings, which the parties to the direct policy are involved.

This relatively brief investigation elucidates that the nature of reinsurance bears a great number of similarities with liability insurance.

It should be further noted that the notion of incorporation in the reinsurance context is mostly derived from wordings that were commonly used in the Victorian period[228] and at the time, the general assumption pertaining to the nature of these contracts was that these constituted 'further insurance.'[229] The contemporary considerations in the reinsurance market are evidently different from the ones that were in the Victorian period. The subject matter of direct insurance may be something that is exposed to loss or damage, or some potential liability that is insured by the insurer. Thus, the subject matter of the insurance contract is the financial interest of the policyholder in that property, choice in action, or liability.[230] The subject matter of the reinsurance that is placed to cover this underlying interest is the liability of the insurer/reinsured, which had been accepted by the insurer/reinsured under the original insurance, and therefore, all contracts that are reinsuring such liability should be considered as contracts of liability insurance. *Wasa v Lexington* should accordingly be considered 'exceptional.'[231]

3.7.6. The Aftermath of *Wasa v Lexington* and the Notion of Incorporation

The nature of reinsurance, as *Wasa v Lexington* vividly illustrates, is crucial. The assessment of nature has a direct impact on the way incorporation is implemented in this branch of law. The adoption of the 'further insurance' approach would mean the terms of the insurance contract to be incorporated into the reinsurance contract in an easier way as the latter would be considered an extension of the former. A 'further insurance' would in a way mean that there is an extension to the original insurance on the original subject matter, even though there would be no privity between the reinsurer and the original insured. This sort of formation may potentially create a perception that the contractual structure in the reinsurance context forms a single-contract scenario. A single-contract scenario may involve two situations: (1) A and B make a contract in which they incorporate standard terms or (2) A and B make a contract incorporating terms previously agreed between A and B in another contract or contracts to which they were both parties.

226 *Sphere Drake Insurance plc v Basler Versicherungs-Gesellschaft* [1998] Lloyd's Rep IR 35.
227 [1907] A.C. 59.
228 Merkin (n 71) 99, 2.65.
229 Ibid.
230 Carter, Ralph, and Lucas (n 47) 103–104.
231 Gürses (n 182).

Considering the contractual structure that is established in the reinsurance context, it may not be plausible to suggest that the single-contract scenario generally covers a reinsurance relationship. This is because the divisions that this scenario provides are usually not appropriate for the reinsurance relationship to fall under. However, accepting reinsurance as an extension of the initial insurance – in other words, a 'further insurance' – would in fact suggest that there is a single-contract scenario. Concerning incorporation, such an acceptance would therefore amount to general words of incorporation to be held sufficient for the incorporation of the insurance arbitration clause into the reinsurance contract.

On the other hand, accepting that reinsurance is the insurance of liability of the reinsured would limit the scope of 'what is reinsured.' Accordingly, the terms to be incorporated from the insurance contract would be subject to elimination for the purposes of ascertaining the terms that are directly concerned with the liability of the reinsured.

The categorization of arbitration clauses and the assessment of where they fall under this equation constitute issues to be addressed. Would these be considered something easily transferable between contracts if the 'further insurance' theory is adopted? Furthermore, what would be the situation if the 'insurance of liability' approach is preferred?

To reiterate, if the 'further insurance' theory is found applicable, the reinsurance and insurance contracts would possibly be categorized under the single-contract scenario, and potentially, no express references to the insurance arbitration clause would be sought for its successful incorporation. On the other hand, if the 'liability insurance' theory is adopted, the reinsurance and insurance contracts would be categorized as distinct and, to a certain level, separate, and accordingly, they would fall under the two-contract scenario. This category involves two situations: (1) A and B make a contract incorporating terms agreed between A (or B) and C or (2) A and B make a contract incorporating terms agreed between C and D. This second scenario evidently provides a more feasible structure for reinsurance.

Generally, a reinsurance contract needs to specifically refer to the insurance arbitration clause for such a clause to be incorporated. However, this may not always be the case and the facts of the cases may alter the division that a contractual structure may possibly fall under.[232] The categorization of contractual structure and its direct impact on the notion of incorporation may be argued to have a close correlation with shipping cases, which fundamentally adopt a strict approach concerning incorporation and deal with contracts of different nature than the ones in the reinsurance context. Nonetheless, they greatly influence reinsurance cases. Accordingly, a crucial issue to be addressed is the permitted level of the implementation of such a strict approach in a different branch of law dealing with different types of contracts.

3.8. *Assessing the Nature of Reinsurance Contracts and Removing Bills of Lading Cases from the Equation of Incorporation*

The case law on bills of lading incorporating charterparties has predominantly been the main authority to follow implementing incorporation in chain contracts. Accordingly, the strict rule of incorporation in the shipping context, requesting the employment of specific

232 *Habas Sinai ve Tibbi Gazlar Isthisal Endustri AS v Sometal SAL* [2010] 1 Lloyd's Rep 661 (*Habas Sinai v Sometal*).

words to incorporate arbitration clauses, was also adopted in the reinsurance context in a blindfolded manner. Nevertheless, this was until the authority of bills of lading on the matter was questioned in *Excess Insurance v Mander*,[233] following *Pine Top Insurance*[234] paving the way. What was considered in these cases was the justification for reflecting this 'shipping-oriented approach' on insurance law. Even though it was found necessary to follow this in order to have some clarity on this aspect of the law, these decisions paved the way for questioning the 'unquestionable' authority of bills of lading cases on other branches of law concerned with chain contracts. Accordingly, one may criticize this 'blindfolded adoption' and pose the following questions: What would happen if we did not have relevant case law on bills of lading? How would law fill such a gap?

3.8.1. Characteristic Tools in Reinsurance Arbitration

The courts that are facing the task of assessing the incorporation would usually have the tendency to resort to relevant bills of lading cases as they establish the predominant authority on the matter. However, reinsurance has its own peculiarities that need to be taken into account.

In the reinsurance context, usually, a specific reference to the insurance arbitration clause would be sought to make such a clause part of the reinsurance contract. As a rule of thumb, the courts facing the task of assessing whether the incorporation of arbitration clauses was successful in the reinsurance context have also been following the bills of lading cases as the principal guideline.

Providing authority that goes back to the late 19th century,[235] bills of lading cases undeniably shed light on the issue of incorporation of arbitration clauses. To reiterate, the fundamentally applicable approach in the shipping context has been the adoption of the 'strict rule' that stipulates the employment of specific words of incorporation for charterparty arbitration clauses to be incorporated into bills of lading. The essential justification of the adoption of the 'strict rule' has usually been provided as bills of lading being negotiable, their holder likely being oblivious of the terms of the charterparty, and accordingly, the possible unfairness of holding the new holder of the bill subject to arbitration with a party they do not know and under an arbitration agreement that they are not a party to but is somehow incorporated into their contract. This justification seems compatible with the traditional commercial principle of third-party protection. Nevertheless, as the realities and necessities of the market evolved over time, certain implementations should also evolve to accommodate contemporary circumstances and necessities. For instance, the promotion of party autonomy has come into prominence over the last half-century.[236] Accordingly, there is a fine balance between commercial certainty and party autonomy.

Unavoidably, the 'strict rule' of incorporation applies to the implementation of incorporation of arbitration clauses in the shipping context.[237] On the other hand, reinsurance contracts

233 [1997] 2 Lloyd's Rep 119.

234 [1987] 1 Lloyd's Rep 476.

235 *Hamilton & Co v Mackie & Sons* [1889] 5 TLR 677 is the first bills of lading case that is concerned with the incorporation of arbitration clauses.

236 For instance, see *Habas Sinai v Sometal* [2010] 1 Lloyd's Rep 661.

237 John F. Wilson, *Carriage of Goods by Sea*, Pearson Education Limited, 2010, 7th Edn., 248: 'A strict contra profentem approach has been adopted towards such attempts since, while arbitration clauses are common in charterparties, they are rarely found in bills of lading.'

bear almost no similarities with bills of lading and the reinsurance market has fundamentally different practices and customs. Then why the courts dealing with the incorporation of arbitration clauses in the reinsurance context are by default resorting to the methods that are essentially accepted in the bills of lading context on the matter? For instance, reinsurance contracts are not negotiable documents, unlike bills of lading. Therefore, the potential jeopardy of the rights of unaware third parties may not be truly reflected as a concern in the insurance context. Accordingly, it does not seem fully justifiable to hold reinsurance contracts subject to the same level of protection that is required in the shipping context.

It should further be noted that there has been some inconsistency even among the decisions concerned with bills of lading incorporating charterparties. There have been occasions in which the transferable nature of bills of lading seemed insufficient for the by default adoption of the 'strict rule.' Numerous times the courts indicated that there would be room for verbal manipulation[238] and interpretation of the construction of the bills of lading[239] if circumstances allow. Furthermore, the true intention of the parties has also been promoted in many cases that have dealt with the incorporation of arbitration clauses.[240] It may be argued that there is now a more delicate balance between third-party protection and the promotion of party autonomy.

This brings us to the point of questioning the reasons for adopting 'the strict rule of incorporation' in the reinsurance context. Reinsurance contracts may be argued to possess their secret weapons concerning incorporation: the back-to-back coverage and the honourable engagement clauses. In other words, incorporation in reinsurance may be evaluated in its own context purified from the interventions of bills of lading cases.

3.8.1.1. A Structural Tool: The Back-to-Back Cover

Reinsurance contracts, at least the proportional ones, are presumed back-to-back with the underlying insurance contract. The word 'presumption' should be emphasized at this point. Indeed, these contracts are presumed back-to-back and have the same meaning if there are no remarks indicating the contrary. In other words, there is already a functioning presumption in practice that the terms are by default 'incorporated.' Therefore, the general assumption, unless otherwise stated, is that the liability of the reinsurer is matched with the liability of the insurer, who is also the reinsured.[241] One may argue that the reinsurance practice already has its default method of incorporation. Nonetheless, parties may rule out this presumption by employing additional wording specifying its elimination.

This presumption usually does not apply when it comes to ancillary clauses and, therefore, to arbitration clauses. It is somewhat settled that, to successfully achieve the incorporation of an insurance arbitration clause into a reinsurance contract, the words of incorporation should expressly be referencing such clause. Employing merely general words that are not specific, such as the words of a full reinsurance clause, 'as original,' is often not sufficient

---

238 *The Merak* [1964] 2 Lloyd's Rep 527, 537.

239 *The Nerano* [1994] 2 Lloyd's Rep 50.

240 *The Merak* [1964] 2 Lloyd's Rep 527. See *Pacific Molasses Co and United Molasses Trading Co Ltd v Entre Rios Compania Naviera SA (The San Nicholas)* [1976] 1 Lloyd's Rep 8. *See* also *K/S A/S Seateam & Co v Iraq National Oil Co and Others (The Sevonia Team)* [1983] 2 Lloyd's Rep 640; *Navigazione Alta Italia SpA v Svenska Petroleum AB (The Nai Matteini)* [1988] 1 Lloyd's Rep 452. However, also see *The Heidberg* [1994] 2 Lloyd's Rep 287.

241 *Butler and Merkin's Reinsurance Law* (n 92) B-0180.

to incorporate an arbitration clause. The back-to-back cover presumption would still be valid if there is an arbitration clause in the underlying insurance policy. The requirement that the arbitration clause specifically be referred to does not deprive the parties of the satisfying amenities that the reinsurance practice presents. This usually just means that the incorporation of an arbitration clause is not among the amenities that the back-to-back presumption provides and, therefore, requires special treatment. For a more detailed analysis of the back-to-back cover please see '3.3. Reinsurance Relationship and Structure of Reinsurance: the back-to-back assumption.'

3.8.1.2. An Inherent Feature: The Honourable Engagement

Reinsurance is, genuinely, a self-sufficient branch of law. However, it is true that the case law concerning different branches of law, such as shipping, set significant authorities regarding the implementation of incorporation that is also followed in the reinsurance context. Nonetheless, reinsurance has its own specific features, such as the back-to-back presumption, which facilitates the alignment of the contractual structure.

Indeed, a number of disputes arising out of reinsurance go through English courts. However, the case law on the matter is quite limited.[242] An overwhelming majority of the disputes arising out of reinsurance are referred to arbitration. Considering the limited number of cases that are referred to courts, it may be argued that the general preference in the market is to keep the disputes confidential and, accordingly, to refer them to arbitration rather than to the jurisdiction of the courts. This brings us to another peculiarity of reinsurance, which has a long tradition.

Honourable engagement is a long-standing concept of reinsurance. This generally necessitates reinsurance disputes to be handled in the same manner as what the settlement of an honourable engagement entails, and thus, reinsurance arbitration is to be conducted in the same manner, provided the arbitration agreement is in honourable engagement form.

Reinsurance contracts may contain an exclusive type of arbitration clause. The reinsurance arbitration clause often contains words that require arbitrators to determine issues in accordance with notions of equity, fairness, or market practice rather than according to the strict rules of law[243] and as solely as a legal obligation.[244] This type of construction of the clause suggests that arbitrators, who are considering a reinsurance dispute, have relatively more 'elbow room' than arbitrators considering different types of disputes. This is simply a market convenience.

The honourable engagement has not always been welcomed by the courts. However, considering the general unwelcoming attitude of courts to arbitration in the past, the reasons that the concept of honourable engagement was taken with a grain of salt seem

242 Some important examples are *Pine Top Insurance* [1987] 1 Lloyd's Rep 476; *Excess Insurance v Mander* [1997] 2 Lloyd's Rep 119; *Trygg Hansa Insurance v Equitas* [1998] 2 Lloyd's Rep 439; *Cigna Life Insurance v Intercaser* [2001] CLC 1356.

243 *Butler and Merkin's Reinsurance Law* (n 92) C-0705; Carter, Ralph, and Lucas (n 47) 136; the words 'the arbitrator or umpire, as the case may be, shall interpret this treaty rather as an honourable engagement than as a merely legal obligation' and 'the arbitrators and umpire are relieved from all judicial formalities and may abstain from following the strict rules of law' were not upheld by the court, and the former words inclined the court to the view that the clause invalidated the whole contract on the grounds that the parties did not intend it to have legal effect.

244 Noussia (n 13) 81, 261.

quite comprehensible. In the past, arbitration was regarded as a threat to the authority of the courts, and hence, there was generally an unfavourable attitude towards this method of dispute resolution. 'Arbitration was viewed disdainfully as an inferior process of justice.'[245] Accordingly, the hostility of the courts in the past to the 'honourable engagement' seems understandable since it probably made some judges, who were not even completely satisfied with the idea of arbitration, exasperated. This is because, although the concept of arbitration was considered secondary to litigation by most, it was still regulated. The possible results of implementing a concept as vague as 'honourable engagement' were likely to be found worrying. Accordingly, the wish of the judges to have a full understanding of the scope of such an engagement causing undeniable legal haziness was perhaps one of the main reasons preventing them from welcoming the implementation of it in reinsurance arbitration.

In *Orion Compania Espanola de Seguros v Belfort Mattschappij Voor Algmene Verzekgringeen*,[246] this unwelcoming attitude was in clear display. The arbitration clause before the Court that is constructed in an honourable agreement form is as follows:

> The Arbitrators and Umpire are relieved from all judicial formalities and may abstain from following the strict rules of the law. They shall settle any dispute under this Agreement according to an equitable rather than a strictly legal interpretation of its terms and their decision shall be final and not subject to appeal.

The arbitration clause was clearly indicating an honourable agreement. It was stated that the policy of the law in England pertaining to arbitration was that the arbitrators must apply a fixed and recognizable system of – normally and primarily English – law and that they would not be allowed to apply some different criteria such as the promotion of the view of the arbitrator(s) on abstract justice or equitable principles.[247] The honourable engagement element in the arbitration clause, in this case, was treated as a factor that invalidates the legality of the contract, therefore self-destroying its legal validity as an arbitration clause. Thus, it was stated that an arbitration award given according to implementations of the 'honourable engagement' would not be an award, which the law would recognize.[248] This was quite a straightforward approach that was illustrating the intolerance towards arbitration, especially when it comes to the honourable engagement form within reinsurance arbitration. The arbitration clause in honourable engagement form, just because it included elements that were compatible with the realities of the reinsurance market, was perceived as a clause that put the legality of the whole contract at risk. Accordingly, it may be suggested that there was no tolerance for arbitration unless its scope and construction were applying the fixed and recognizable system of English law.

More than 15 years later, in *Eagle Star Insurance Co Ltd v Yuval Insurance Co Ltd*,[249] some tolerance to the concept seemed to have been developed. The arbitration clause of the reinsurance treaty, in this case, indicated that 'the arbitrators and umpire shall not be by the strict rules of law but shall settle any difference referred to them according to an

245 Merkin (n 3) 6.2.3. Tables are now turned. See Chapter 5, 'Singapore Law and Incorporation of Arbitration Clauses.'

246 [1962] 2 Lloyd's Rep 257 (*Orion Compania*).

247 Ibid 264.

248 Ibid.

249 [1978] 1 Lloyd's Rep 357.

equitable rather than a strict legal interpretation of the provisions of this agreement.' It was held by Lord Denning that this expression was neither invalidating the contract nor ousting the jurisdiction of the courts but was merely removing the need for applying the technicalities and strict constructions of law.[250] Indeed, it would be unreasonable to conclude that such words are invalidating a perfectly good contract. They were considered by Lord Denning as functioning 'in the way that equity did in the old days, but also arbitrators would do under such a clause, in the current context, nowadays.'[251] In other words, the function of a reinsurance arbitration clause that is including an 'honourable engagement' element was considered a factor which is establishing equity in modern practice.

This is a significant decision as it lays emphasis on the distinctive characteristic of reinsurance arbitration clauses and it highlights that these may include the element of 'honourable engagement.' Furthermore, the decision also indicates that this element functions in a way ensuring equity in the reinsurance relationship is established. In other words, the decision promotes the realities of reinsurance arbitration. Moreover, the selection of the word 'equity' and the phrase 'a perfectly good contract' seem to be indicating a clear departure from the adopted approach in *Orion Compania*.[252]

In *Home Insurance Co and St Paul Fire and Marine Insurance Co v Administratia Asigurarico de Stat*,[253] the concerned reinsurance included an arbitration agreement followed as

> the award of the arbitrators or the umpire . . . shall be final and binding upon all parties without appeal. This treaty shall be interpreted as an honourable engagement rather than as a strict legal obligation and the award shall be made with a view to effecting the general purpose of this treaty rather than in accordance with the literal interpretation of the language.

The defendant reinsurers argued that the agreement was binding in honour only and not in law. Following the ruling in *Eagle Star Insurance Co v Yuval Insurance Co*, the characteristic and supplementary functions of the reinsurance arbitration being an 'honourable one' were reiterated, and it was indicated that the underlying intention of this function was merely 'to free the arbitrators to some extent from following the strict rules of law.'[254] It was held that the clause did create a legally binding agreement to arbitrate and to abide by an award, and if and in so far as the arbitration clause went further than the law permits, it could be struck out in whole or in part without affecting the validity of the reinsurance treaty. 'Honourable engagement' clauses are neither invalid themselves nor invalidate the whole contract due to their 'offensive'[255] nature. They are simply special elements that function as flotation rings uplifting characteristic principles applicable in a reinsurance arbitration. This approach subsequently received further support.[256]

---

250 [1978] 1 Lloyd's Rep 357, 362.
251 Ibid. Also see Noussia (n 13) 20.
252 [1962] 2 Lloyd's Rep 257.
253 [1983] 2 Lloyd's Rep 674.
254 Ibid 677.
255 Carter, Ralph, and Lucas (n 47) 136.
256 *Overseas Union Inc v AA Mutual International Ltd* [1988] 2 Lloyd's Rep 63; and the Court of Appeal's decision in *Home and Overseas Insurance Co Ltd v Mentor Insurance Co (UK) Ltd.* [1989] 1 Lloyd's Rep 473.

As indicated, this peculiarity of reinsurance arbitration has some legislative roots too. Section 46(1)(b) of the Arbitration Act 1996 provides for arbitrators to decide the dispute 'if the parties so agree, in accordance with such other considerations as are agreed by them or determined by the tribunal.'[257] Indeed, the arbitrators are obliged to Act within the boundaries of their power, which is drawn by the parties, and unless allowed by the parties, they may not decide in contradiction with the provisions of the agreement as agreed by the parties. The case law further sets forth that reinsurance arbitration clauses may be in honourable engagement form.[258]

Honourable engagement, either being a stand-alone provision or an agreement that falls within the terms of the reinsurance arbitration clause, simply reiterates the traditional reinsurance concept of utmost good faith.[259] An honourable engagement in the reinsurance context fundamentally indicates that the parties to a reinsurance contract have entered it with 'the highest integrity and in utmost good faith.'[260] The evolvement of utmost good faith in reinsurance has different roots than ordinary commercial good faith.[261] The concept of good faith in reinsurance harkens back to the past when reinsurance contracts were being concluded by a handshake, which was considered an indication of good faith, thus finding its roots outside courts.[262] Good faith in reinsurance necessitates parties to perform their contractual obligations in a businesslike manner, compatible with the realities and customs of the reinsurance market, and thus, any dispute arising from the reinsurance contract to be resolved in the same manner: businesslike and fair. The principle of utmost good faith in the reinsurance context is the cornerstone of the honourable engagement concept in the reinsurance market and it generally necessitates arbitrators to settle disputes based pursuant to fairness, custom, and the realities of the reinsurance market rather than strictly following the rule of law.[263] This allows arbitrators to follow a more pragmatic and commercial approach in resolving reinsurance disputes and also facilitates the submission of 'evidence and arguments that may have not seen the light of day in a courtroom.'[264]

It should be noted that, because arbitrators who are instructed by the honourable engagement are not required to strictly follow and apply the law, it is possible for them to interpret the contract differently from the settled ways of courts. This means that the case law concerning contract interpretation or some relevant precedents may completely be overlooked. Accordingly, it is possible for some inconsistency between decisions concerning the same or similar clauses to surface.

257 Section 46(1)(b) of the Arbitration Act 1996.

258 *Eagle Star Insurance Co Ltd v Yuval Insurance Co Ltd* [1978] 1 Lloyd's Rep 357; *Home Insurance Co and St Paul Fire and Marine Insurance Co v Administratia Asiguraricor de Stat* [1983] 2 Lloyd's Rep 674; *Overseas Union Inc v AA Mutual International Ltd* [1988] 2 Lloyd's Rep 63; and Court of Appeal's decision in *Home and Overseas Insurance Co Ltd v Mentor Insurance Co (UK) Ltd.* [1989] 1 Lloyd's Rep 473.

259 Larry Schiffer, The Honorable Engagement Clause (But I Thought I Had a Legal Contract!), *IRMI*, March 2007, available at www.irmi.com/articles/expert-commentary/the-honorable-engagement-clause (last visited August 17, 2022).

260 Ibid.

261 Noussia (n 13) 70.

262 Ibid.

263 Schiffer (n 259): For instance, where the arbitration clause requires parties to submit their case within 30 days, this may be interpreted by the arbitration panel as a requirement of the sole introduction of the facts and arguments within 30 days instead of a full-scope submission concerning the case to be made to the panel in 30 days.

264 Ibid.

3.9. Concluding Remarks

One of the initial issues that draws attention looking at the concepts of reinsurance and incorporation, is the scantiness of the relevant case law. This is due to two reasons: Reinsurance disputes are mainly referred to arbitration, and the strict legal principles that apply in shipping also find application in the reinsurance context. The courts that undertake the task of determining the aspects of incorporation in the reinsurance context have almost always turned to the case law on bills of lading incorporating charterparties. However, reinsurance contracts and shipping contracts are fundamentally different. Furthermore, reinsurance as a separate branch of law has its peculiarities and its own legal tools pertaining to arbitration.

Two significant aspects of reinsurance contracts have an undeniable impact on their incorporation. These are the nature of reinsurance contracts and their peculiarity of being perceived as back-to-back with the underlying insurance contract provided they are proportional. From a different perspective, bills of lading also have their own peculiarity as they are transferable. Implementation of this feature in the reinsurance context is not possible due to the structural formation of a reinsurance relationship. Hence, what would be the outcome if the case law on bills of lading as an authority is removed from the equation on the evaluation of incorporation in the reinsurance context?

Firstly, reinsurance should be categorized as liability insurance as reinsurance contracts do not form 'an extension to the original insurance,' and thus, they should not be categorized as further insurance on the subject matter originally insured. The legal relationship of the reinsurer is limited to the one the reinsurer has with the reinsured. In other words, unless otherwise provided, there would be no privity of contract between the originally insured and the reinsurer. Reinsurance contracts, fall under the two-contract scenario where A and B make a contract incorporating terms agreed between A (or B) and C or where A and B make a contract incorporating terms agreed between C and D. If a contractual structure falls under this category, the requirement concerning incorporation would be subject to some strict criteria. This is because, as in the context of bills of lading, the involvement of a third party in the contractual structure would be the case, and the protection of the oblivious third party would be promoted. If the reinsurance contract is considered a further insurance on the subject matter originally insured, then it would fall under the single-contract scenario, and it would be at least possible to discuss the potential of a generic full reinsurance clause to incorporate the insurance arbitration clause. This is because this type of scenario would hypothetically be formed of a situation where there is a privity of contract between the reinsurer and the original insured. Hence, it may be argued that no specific reference would be necessary between the familiar parties because the terms of the insurance contract would be open or accessible to all parties. In summary, adopting the approach indicated in *Wasa v Lexington* paves the way for a potential disorder concerning the implementation of incorporation.

Reinsurance contracts, by their nature, should be classified as liability insurances as they insure the liability of the reinsured for the original insured. Reinsurance contracts are no extensions of the original insurance. These contracts are indeed intertwined as reinsurance would not come into existence without there being an underlying insurance contract. However, this is a level of interconnection that would be observable at the time of contract formation. Hence, this intertwinement should not be perceived as affecting the assessment of the nature of reinsurance contracts. Reinsurance is a distinct liability insurance and by no means is an extension of the original insurance. An otherwise perception has the potential to impair the notion of incorporation in the reinsurance context and to allow the incorporation of arbitration clauses by means of a generic full reinsurance clause.

Reinsurance contracts falling under the category of the two-contract scenario would normally be subject to strict requirements concerning their incorporation of insurance arbitration clauses. There are two categorizations that reinsurance incorporation is concerned with. The first is pertaining to the contractual structure, and the second is concerning the nature of reinsurance contracts. As *Habas Sinai v Sometal*[265] establishes, the assessment of circumstances in different cases may create different results concerning contract categorization as such. The case provides a very clear guideline on how to assess the true contractual structure. On the other hand, *Wasa v Lexington* provides a quite controversial judgement that has the potential to alter the perception concerning the generally accepted classification of the nature of reinsurance contracts. Accordingly, considering both cases together, the latter is somewhat blurring the lucid categorization that is provided in the former.

Secondly, the validity of applying shipping principles concerning incorporation in the insurance context is debatable. Shipping contracts and reinsurance contracts have very little in common. They also both have their peculiarities. Bills of lading are negotiable, whereas proportional reinsurance contracts are presumed to be back-to-back with the underlying insurance contract. Accordingly, there are some fundamental differences between these contracts from the aspect of the implementation of incorporation. The first indicated branch of law adopts strict criteria for incorporation for the purposes of protecting the third-party holder of the bill of lading, whereas the latter adopts a method that may even be called 'a default perception of incorporation,' where the insurance and the reinsurance contracts are presumed back-to-back. Considering these essential dissimilarities of the said branches of law, the validity of applying the authority of bills of lading cases on reinsurance cases, should be open to examination.

Facultative reinsurance contracts consist simply of the slip to which the original policy is attached. This slip usually includes a full reinsurance clause that is providing 'terms and conditions as original' which should be perceived as an indicator of the back-to-back structure of these contracts and the presumed incorporation of the original policy terms into the reinsurance contract. The back-to-back assumption functions by virtue of the employment of the words 'as original' and constitutes a fundamental element of the reinsurance market. The wording facilitates the incorporation of the insuring clause of the underlying policy so that the coverage of both contracts overlaps. However, usually, these words are not held sufficient to incorporate an arbitration clause,[266] and the employment of specific words of incorporation is required to do so. Nevertheless, the alignment of these contracts and the overlapping of their coverage constitute elementary issues in reinsurance. Accordingly, even though at the end of the day, reinsurance cases mostly turn to the authority settled in bills of lading cases, the feasibility of holding this branch of law subject

265 [2010] 1 Lloyd's Rep 661.

266 These words normally incorporate only the obligations of the insured that are plausible at the reinsurance level. See Merkin (n 91).

to the same restrictions that apply in the shipping context is debatable. The assessment concerning the incorporation of insurance arbitration clauses should be done by taking the nature of the reinsurance contract and the facts of each individual case into account. Accordingly, if the particular facts of the case necessitate the implementation of strict rules concerning incorporation, this should essentially be derived from the characteristics and nature of reinsurance contracts and not from straightforwardly applying shipping principles in this substantially different branch of law.

Bibliography

The Arbitration Clause in Insurance & Reinsurance, *EMEA Legal Counsels*, Lexology, October 20, 2017.

Barlow, Lyde, *Reinsurance Practice and the Law*, Informa, 2009.

Birds, John, Lynch, Ben and Milnes, Simon, *MacGillivray on Insurance Law*, Sweet & Maxwell, 2012, 12th Edn.

Braithwaite, Christopher, Cut-Through Clauses, 1997, *BILA Journal*, 22.

Butler and Merkin's Reinsurance Law, 1999, Kluwer.

Cane, Peter, *Tort Law and Economic Interests*, Clarendon Press, 1991.

Carter, Robert, Ralph, Nigel and Lucas, Leslie, *Carter on Reinsurance*, Witherby, 2013, 5th Edn.

Chamberlain, Reynolds Porter, UK: In or Out, Incorporation of Direct Policy Terms in Reinsurance Contracts, *Mondaq*, January 8, 2002.

Dunn, Stephanie T., Corey, Todd and Quadrino, Leah M., A Gentlemen's Agreement: The Impact of Honorable Engagement Clauses in U.S. And English Reinsurance Agreements And Arbitration Today, April 6, 2006, *Mealey's Litigation Report: Reinsurance*, 16.

Edelman, Colin, *The Law of Reinsurance*, Oxford University Press, 2013, 2nd Edn.

Gilman, Jonathan, Merkin, Robert, Blanchard, Claire and Templeman, Mark, *Arnould: Law of Marine Inurance and Average*, Sweet & Maxwell, British Shipping Laws, 2013, 18th Edn.

Golding, Cecil Edward, *The Law and Practice of Reinsurance*, Witherby & Co. Ltd., 1987, 5th Edn.

Gürses, Özlem, The Construction of Terms of Facultative Reinsurance Contracts: Is Wasa v Lexington the Exception or the Rule?, January 2010, *The Modern Law Review*, 73(1), 119–140.

Gürses, Özlem, *Reinsuring Clauses*, Informa, 2014.

Gürses, Özlem, *Marine Insurance Law*, Routledge, 2015.

Gürses, Özlem, What Does 'Utmost Good Faith' Mean?, 2016, *Insurance Law Journal*, 27, 124–134.

Gürses, Özlem and Merkin, Robert, Facultative Reinsurance and the Full Reinsurance Clause, 2008, *Lloyd's Maritime and Commercial Law Quarterly*, 3, 366–388.

Jolly, Joanne and Anderson, Tracey, *UK: Wasa v Lexington – The Repercussions for Reinsurers*, Barlow Lyde & Gilbert LLP, August 5, 2009.

Kiln, Robert, *Reinsurance in Practice*, Witherby & Co., 1991.

Laeuchli, Urs Martin, Civil and Common Law: Contrast and Synthesis in International Arbitration, August 2007, *Dispute Resolution Journal*, 62.

Law Commission, *Review of the Arbitration Act 1996 A Consultation Paper*, Law Com No 257, 2022.

Lowry, John, Rawlings, Philip and Merkin, Robert, *Insurance Law: Doctrines and Principles*, Hart Publishing, 2011, 3rd Edn.

Matei, Dănilă Ştefan, Reinsurance from the Perspective of Property Insurance Contract, 2018, *Challenges of the Knowledge Society*, 12.

McDonald Jr., John J., Reinsurance Arbitration 2001: Will the New Ways Cripple the "Arbitration Clause"?, 2001, *Defense Counsel Journal*, 68, 328.

McGee, Andrew, *The Modern Law of Insurance*, LexisNexis Butterworths, 2018, 4th Edn.

Mendelowitz, Michael, Reinsurance, in *Insurance Handbook*, Barlow Lyde & Gilbert LLP, Tottel Publishing, 2007, 3rd Edn.

Merkin, Robert, *Colinvaux's Law of Insurance*, Sweet & Maxwell, 1997.

Merkin, Robert (ed.), *What Is Reinsurance*, LLP Professional Publishing, 1998, 77 (AIDA Reinsurance Working Party Report).

Merkin, Robert, Incorporation of Terms into Reinsurance Agreements, in Rhidian Thomas (ed.), *The Modern Law of Marine Insurance*, Informa, 2002, Vol. 2.

Merkin, Robert, *Recent Developments in Reinsurance Law*, Chartered Insurance Institute, May 17, 2016.

Merkin, Robert, Flannery, Louis, *Merkin and Flannery on the Arbitration Act 1996*, Informa law from Routledge, 2020.

Noussia, Kyriaki, *Confidentiality in International Commercial Arbitration: A Comparative Analysis of the Position Under English, US, German and French Law*, Springer, 2010.

Noussia, Kyriaki, *Reinsurance Arbitrations*, Springer, 2013.

Office for National Statistics, *United Kingdom Balance of Payments*, The Pink Book, 2008.

Office for National Statistics, *United Kingdom Balance of Payments*, The Pink Book, 2021.

O'Neill, Terry and Woloniecki, Jan, *The Law of Reinsurance in England and Bermuda*, Sweet & Maxwell, 2015, 4th Edn.

Patrik, Gary S., *Reinsurance in Foundations of Casualty Actuarial Science*, Casualty Actuarial Society, 2001, 4th Edn., 343–484.

Schiffer, Larry, *Expert Commentary: Reinsurance – Arbitration: A Primer*, IRMI, 2006.

Schiffer, Larry, *The Honorable Engagement Clause (But I Thought I Had a Legal Contract!)*, IRMI, March 2007.

Staring, G. S., *Law of Reinsurance*, CBC, 1993.

Sutton, David St. John, Gill, Judith and Gearing, Matthew, *Russel on Arbitration*, Sweet & Maxwell, 2015, 24th Edn.

Wilson, John F., *Carriage of Goods by Sea*, Pearson Education Limited, 2010, 7th Edn.

CHAPTER 4

Construction Contracts and the Incorporation of Arbitration Clauses

4. Construction Contracts and Arbitration

The construction market involves the construction and development of residential and non-residential buildings, construction work on civil engineering projects, and specialist construction activities.[1] In 2018, construction contributed £117 billion to the UK economy, 6% of the total.[2] A high proportion of people working in this sector are self-employed.[3] A great number of jobs pertaining to this sector are governed by contracts that are made specifically on the individual aspects of the overall construction project and these often include many small and independent construction firms. 'The construction industry is unusual because of the high proportion of self-employment in the sector – 36% in Q2 2019, compared to the average for the whole economy of 13%.'[4] The technically complex nature of most construction projects often necessitates the involvement of various contractors undertaking different parts of the overall project. Accordingly, different works concerning specific parts of the project are executed by different parties due to the technicality and specific expertise that even the simplest construction work may require. In other words, a construction project often involves multiple contracts, and the alignment of these, as it is in shipping and insurance contexts, constitutes a significant contractual goal to be achieved also in the construction context. Accordingly, the International Federation of Consulting Engineers (FIDIC), an international standards organization mainly providing contract templates, published some conditions pertaining to construction contracts in 1999 and 2011, and these rules generally facilitate contractual alignment.

One significant issue should perhaps be noted at this point. Indeed, one of the peculiarities of this sector is the high percentage of self-employment numbers it has. This illustrates that there are many professionals with different levels of experience who work on different aspects of construction projects, and accordingly, there are multiple contracts involved. Another notable distinctiveness of the sector is concerning the settlement of construction disputes. The construction industry has 'adjudication' as the essential dispute resolution

1 Standard Industrial Classification (UKSIC): Construction Is Section F, Made Up of Codes: 41–43, available at https://www.ons.gov.uk/file?uri=/methodology/classificationsandstandards/ukstandardindustrialclassificationofeconomicactivities/uksic2007/uksic2007web.pdf.

2 Chris Rhodes, *Construction Industry: Statistics and Policy*, House of Commons Library Briefing Paper 01432, December 16, 2019, 3, available at https://researchbriefings.files.parliament.uk/documents/SN01432/SN01432.pdf.

3 Ibid 8.

4 Ibid 3.

DOI: 10.4324/9781003268673-5

method in the UK because it is statutory and hence is a mandatory right.[5] Furthermore, parties may of course refer their disputes to adjudication by agreeing to do so in their contract. From the perspective of legislation, The Housing Grants, Construction, and Regeneration (Construction) Act 1996 (HGCR) confers adjudication as a statutory right for whoever party may wish to use it. This is the method of dispute resolution that is predominantly exercised in practice. To put it differently, due to the statutory place of adjudication in construction, only a limited number of construction disputes get to arbitration in the construction industry. A decision on adjudication is valid unless and until overturned in proceedings (i.e. litigation or arbitration) that finally determine the outcome of the dispute. However, although limited in number, there are construction cases concerned with the issue of the incorporation of the arbitration clause in the construction context.

4.1. Contractual Structure and Legal Relationship in Construction Law

Construction projects are predominantly composed of many intertwined agreements due to their complex nature. Because a large number of parties are usually involved in construction projects, the contractual structure often includes many subcontracts. Evidently, it would not be reasonable to expect a single contractor to have the expertise to undertake all individual work tasks concerning the main construction project since different aspects of the project require different types and levels of expertise. For the purposes of overcoming the demand regarding specific expertise and specialized materials, it has been a norm in the construction market for the contractor to employ subcontractors for specific parts of the overall construction project. Accordingly, contractors employ subcontractors for design services on the project, the procurement of materials, or the execution of specific parts of the construction works.[6]

Despite the fact that the term 'subcontractor' is a common term that is used in the construction industry, English law does not provide a definition for construction subcontracts.[7] Some fundamental reasons for this lack of definition are as follows: the uniqueness of each construction project that is requiring different expertise and craft, each project being planned and executed in various time frames, and the demand for a variety of equipment and material.[8] Subcontractors usually have expertise in exercising specific aspects of the construction project. Accordingly, their employment is generally beneficial because it increases the mutual understanding concerning the execution of the project as the parties share their expert knowledge.[9] The performance of the main contractor strongly depends on the performance of the subcontractors as the subcontractors mostly contribute more than 50%[10] and up to around 90%[11] of the total value of the construction project. The

5 Lawrence Davies, *Adjudication Versus Other Approaches to Construction Disputes,* Out-Law Guide, November 23, 2018, available at www.pinsentmasons.com/out-law/guides/adjudication-construction-disputes.

6 J. Florian Pulkowski, The Subcontractor's Direct Claim in International Business Law, 2004, *International Construction Law Review*, 21, 31.

7 Ibid 33.

8 Lew Yoke-Lian and S. Hassim, Review of Subcontracting Practice in Construction Industry, August 2012, *IACSIT International Journal of Engineering and Technology*, 4(4), 442–445, 442.

9 M. M. Kumaraswamy and J. Matthews, Improved Subcontractor Selection Employing Partnering Principles, 2000, *ASCE Journal of Management in Engineering*, 16, 47–57, 53.

10 V. Albino and A. C. Garavelli, A Neural Network Application to Subcontractor Rating in Construction Firms, 1998, *International Journal of Project Management*, 16, 9–14, 9.

11 Yoke-Lian and Hassim (n 8) 442.

main contractor is usually responsible for general issues regarding the management of the project, which involves contract administration with employers/owners, procurement of equipment and material, and monitoring the progress of the overall project.[12] In many situations, the main contractor does parts of the overall work, and the subcontractors do the others. In addition to these, the main contractor may have tasks that are executive in nature among the hands-on ones.

The general provisions of construction contracts do not always identify the subcontractor but rather contain broader definitions. This may result in the inclusion of even the simple providers of materials, which are however related to the contractor under another contract, (i.e. a sale contract) as subcontractors. In other words, the broad definition of a subcontractor may cause the provider of the goods for the execution of the construction project to possibly be categorized as a subcontractor, a legal status that is mostly affiliated with a contractor that is undertaking to execute a specific part of the construction project. Due to the broadness of the possible interpretation of the meaning of a subcontractor in the contractual layout and the large number of interrelated agreements a construction project may involve, a dispute that arises from the main construction contract may have reflections on the related subcontracts.[13] This is because construction contracts and construction subcontracts are intertwined, and the latter is a subsidiary of the former. Such reflections of the dispute may eventually produce parallel arbitration proceedings.[14]

Indeed, the construction subcontract is of a subsidiary nature to the main contract. Construction subcontract usually includes references to the main contract as well as definitions concerning the role of the subcontractor and the employer of the main contract.[15] This is because the subcontract comes into existence as somewhat of an extension of the main contract and constitutes a ring of the contractual chain. Despite being linked, these are concluded as separate contracts between different parties. The contractual structure concerned with a construction project includes different contracts pertaining to specific aspects or parts of the overall project as concluded between different parties. Furthermore, one of the parties to these different contracts being the same does not directly create the result of the liability arising from the construction contract to extend its scope to include the subcontract. There is generally no direct liability between the employer and the subcontractor provided that such liability has not been established by further contractual arrangements.

4.2. Contractual Chain and Subcontracts

Being interrelated contracts, the construction contract and a construction subcontract evidently have the potential of affecting each other. For instance, a delay in the execution of the subcontract may also cause a delay in the execution of the main contract. Similarly,

12 Vacharapoom Benjaoran, A Cost Control System Development: A Collaborative Approach for Small and Medium-Sized Contractors, 2009, *International Journal of Project Management*, 27, 270–277, 273.

13 Stavros Brekoulakis and Ahmed El Far, Subcontracts and Multiparty Arbitration in Construction Disputes, in Stavros Brekoulakis and David Brynmor Thomas (eds.), *Global Arbitration Review*, The Guide to Construction Arbitration, 2017, 87–99, 87.

14 Ibid.

15 Pulkowski (n 6) 1295–1297.

a modification pertaining to the scope of the construction contract may affect the scope of the construction subcontract. Nevertheless, the assessment of the level of such a contractual impact is usually subject to the evaluation of some legal issues concerning the contractual chain.

4.2.1. Contractual Chain

The contractual structure generally illustrates the layout and borders of the contractual relationship between the parties. This structure in the construction context includes a contractual chain that is including separate but intertwined contracts. Within the contractual chain, some legal elements, such as risks, liabilities, and rights, are transferred by virtue of waivers, exclusions, and limitations. Accordingly, the contractual chain enables the rights, liabilities, and risks to be transferred between the contracts pertaining to a construction project and, thus, between the subcontractor and the employer. However, for such a transfer to take place and for a clause of the main contract to apply in the sub-construction context, it needs to be inserted into the subcontract by virtue of a method aimed at achieving back-to-back alignment.

The robustness of the contractual chain is of prime importance for the main contractor taking their position in the middle in such a contractual structure. The chain is only as strong as its weakest link. If the contractual chain is not strong enough, then the transfer of any liabilities or risks to the subcontractor may be problematic.[16] Construction subcontracts do not remove the liability of the main contractor to the employer for the main construction contract because the main contractor delegating their responsibility and risks undertaken generally does not free the main contractor from such undertakings merely because the execution of specific parts of the overall work is outsourced to third-party subcontractors. The main contractor is liable to the employer for the main contract to be complied with, regardless of whether the main contractor undertakes the entirety of the work itself or delegates parts of it to subcontractors.[17] Therefore, the contractual chain functions as a mechanism enabling the transfer of rights, risks, and liabilities, and it does not impair the separate nature of the construction contracts and subcontracts.

Ordinarily, there is no direct contractual link between the employer and the subcontractor. The claim of the employer is directed toward the main contractor and the latter mirrors its claim towards the subcontractor if they are responsible for the delay or the defect. Accordingly, the employer may only be obliged to pay the main contractor because delegating parts of the overall work to several subcontractors may have been a decision given by the contractor. This decision may be considered an executive one that is perhaps given to enable to completion of the project more efficiently and quickly. It should be noted that some large construction contracts include provisions governing the extent and conditions under which the works may be subcontracted. These large contracts generally provide the employer with the right to approve or reject subcontractors proposed by the main contractor.

---

16 Luigi Di Paola, Back-to-Back Contracts, 2009, *International Construction Law Review*, 26, 489–490.

17 However, this issue would evidently be subject to the terms of the contract between the contractor and subcontractor and, also, may depend on the existence of a separate contract between the employer and the contractor.

Subcontractors may usually not sue the employer for the subcontract price even in the case where the main contractor defaults or becomes insolvent.[18] The employer is deemed to be liable for paying only to the contractor. This suggests that the contractual link only survives where the middle party, the contractor, remains in its legal position in the contractual chain. However, due to the convoluted nature of construction works, the contractual relationship is rarely this simple.[19] Because of the different characteristics they may consist of, construction subcontracts are often subject to different applications.

4.2.2. Types of Construction Subcontracts and Transferability of Liability

The extent of a contractual chain, thus, the transferability of legal elements such as rights, liabilities and risks are customarily subject to the characteristics of the contracts that they are transferred between. The complexity of the contractual relationships in the construction business may be said to be derived from the complexity of the construction projects themselves and the variety of different types of expertise they require.[20] Specifications, exclusions, and limitations are often determined in construction contracts and construction subcontracts because each project usually requires a different type of expertise or a specific type of equipment or material to be provided. Reflecting different concerns and considerations, a distinction between the subcontractors in the construction business is often made.

There are essentially two different types of construction subcontractors: domestic subcontractors and nominated subcontractors.[21] The straightforward distinction to be made is that domestic subcontractors are chosen by the main contractors, whereas nominated subcontractors are selected by (or agreed with) the employer.[22] Opting for a nominated subcontractor usually benefits both the employer and the contractor. From the aspect of the employer, nominating a subcontractor for the purposes of employment understandably enables the employer to have greater control over the execution of the work and procurement of the material that is used by the subcontractor. From the point of the contractor, the nomination of a subcontractor by the employer may be regarded as advantageous because the element of nomination may minimize the risk and liability from the work of the subcontractor concerning the position of the contractor.[23] Nonetheless, 'Whether this would be possible will depend on the factual circumstances surrounding the process of selection of the subcontractor and any direct contact that the employer may have had directly with the subcontractor.'[24] This does not provide a direct release from liabilities for the contractor because a nominated subcontractor may not be selected by the employer against the wishes of the contractor.[25] It simply indicates the existence of

18 Nicholas Gould, *Subcontracts*, Fenwick & Elliott, February 2012, 1. Nonetheless, it may be noted that some countries like France actually provide for direct payment by the employer to the subcontractors.

19 Ibid.

20 Yoke-Lian and Hassim (n 8) 442.

21 Brekoulakis and El Far (n 13) 89.

22 Clause 5.1 of The International Federation of Consulting Engineers (FIDIC) Conditions of Contracts for Construction definition of a Nominated Subcontractor 'In the Contract, "nominated Subcontractor" means a Subcontractor: (a) who is stated in the Contract as being a nominated Subcontractor, or (b) whom the Engineer, under Clause 13 [Variations and Adjustments], instructs the Contractor to employ as a Subcontractor.'

23 Brekoulakis and El Far (n 13) 89.

24 Ibid.

25 Ibid.

an approval mechanism concerning the employability of the subcontractor, and thus, the liability of the contractor remains to exist to some extent. The contractor normally assumes liability for defects, delays, and so on caused by the subcontractor, regardless of whether the latter is nominated or not. However, such a principle does not effectively work if the main contractor had objected to with grounds to the nomination of the subcontractor, if the employer overrode these grounds and ordered the main contractor to hire the nominated subcontractor anyway, and if the default of the subcontractor has a link with the particular ground of refusal of the main contractor.

4.3. Incorporation of Terms in Construction Contracts

Generally, there is no privity of contract between the employer and a subcontractor because the subcontract is often concluded between the main contractor of the employer and the subcontractor.[26] The distribution of work between the contractor and the subcontractor depends on the construction of the subcontract. These subcontracts establish separate contractual relationships and are usually subject to the general rules of contract formation. The alignment of the contracts involved in the construction project to ensure that the rights and obligations are corresponding does not primarily affect the established contractual chain.[27] In other words, the rights and obligations would still be concerning the separate nature of contracts and the contracts being aligned would not create direct liability between the employer and the subcontractor. The position of the contractor in the contractual chain remains the same, and thus, the contractor is responsible for the acts and defaults of the subcontractors, regardless of the division that subcontractors may be domestic or nominated.[28] Nevertheless, holding the contractor accountable for any breach of the subcontractor may not seem truly fair. Thus, indemnification as a protection mechanism is usually at the disposal of the contractor. By means of including an indemnification clause in the subcontract, the contractor may ensure that they would be indemnified by the subcontractor where the subcontractor is in breach of the contract.[29]

Subcontracts in the construction industry may be referring to many other contracts or documents and accordingly, it is considered a rare occasion for a single document to contain all the terms and conditions of the construction subcontract.[30] The main concerns about the formation of construction contracts are the establishment of the contractual chain and the alignment of contracts, the document being silent on some crucial aspects of the contractual relationship may be regarded worrying. It constitutes one of the main requirements in construction that the contracting parties have similar and corresponding provisions in their contracts related to the construction project. This is fundamentally because, although these contracts are essentially formed to govern different aspects of the overall work, they still constitute parts of one substantial project. Provided that the provisions of the subcontract mirror the terms of the main

26 I. N. Duncan Wallace, *Hudson's Building and Engineering Contracts*, Sweet & Maxwell, 1995, Vol.2., 11th Edn., 1314, 13–016.

27 Brekoulakis and El Far (n 13) 91.

28 Clause 4.4 of FIDIC Conditions of Contracts for Construction.

29 Brekoulakis and El Far (n 13) 91.

30 Gould (n 18).

contract, a chain of responsibility is established.[31] Having corresponding provisions for different aspects of the work sets up a well-structured and clear contractual relationship.

4.3.1. Corresponding Contracts Pertaining to a Construction Project

There are fundamentally two methods of aligning contracts: drafting them in a similar way or by means of incorporating parts of the main contract into the subcontract.[32] Accordingly, contracts may inherently be drafted alike, or they may be referring to each other or different documents for incorporation purposes. The alignment of contracts by virtue of having corresponding provisions in a subcontract indeed provides clarification concerning the scope and extent of the rights, liabilities, and risks in a contractual relationship.

The International Federation of Consulting Engineers (FIDIC) published some standard conditions concerning the structure of construction contracts and subcontracts, respectively, in 1999 and 2011. The FIDIC Conditions of Subcontract for Construction are being used in conjunction with the FIDIC Conditions of Contract for Construction, as they have the same number of clauses that are similar in content and structure, which enable parties to construct aligned contracts.[33] The FIDIC Conditions pertaining to both contracts and subcontracts are standard conditions that may be chosen and incorporated by the parties as the applicable clauses to their contracts. The incorporation of the FIDIC Conditions enables parties to align their contracts. It should be noted that this merely constitutes one of the methods of contract alignment and in practice, especially under circumstances involving small contractors, the subcontractor sends their terms and conditions to the main contractor who then negotiates terms so a harmonization with the main contract would be created.

A few issues concerning the content of the conditions should be addressed at this point. First, FIDIC subcontract conditions stipulate the same language and applicable law to govern both contracts.[34] This manifests the fundamental requirement for contracts to be aligned that they need to be in the same language and be subject to the rules of the same legal system. Ticking these two boxes evidently facilitates the establishment of the bare minimum required for the alignment of contracts as this minimizes the risk of contracts having substantial differences. Second, there is generally no privity of contract between the subcontractor and the employer.[35] Only the existence of some special or unusual circumstances,[36] illustrating that the employer expressly aiming to form a direct contractual link with the subcontractor would create such privity between the said parties. However, this occurs significantly rare because such a formation is generally 'contrary to the purpose of the main construction contract and the practice and expectation when negotiating contracts informally between parties in the construction industry.'[37] Third, it

31 Will Hughes, Ronan Champion and John Murdoch, *Construction Contracts: Law and Management*, Routledge, 2015, 5th Edn., 45, 3.3.10.

32 Di Paola (n 16) 490.

33 Brekoulakis and El Far (n 13) 90.

34 Sub-clause (1.8) of the FIDIC Conditions of Sub-contracts for Construction 2011.

35 Sub-clause (1.10) of the FIDIC Conditions of Sub-contracts for Construction 2011.

36 *Kirk & Kirk Ltd v Croydon Corporation* [1956] JPL 585, where it was held that since the delivery arrangements were part of the nomination of the subcontractor and the supply contract was a separate contract between the contractor and supplier and that since the main contractor was bound to provide bricks and the change in the work, being authorized to assist him in a matter which was primarily his liability, no variation was involved.

37 Wallace (n 26) 1314, 13–016. See *Hampton v Glamorgan C.C.* [1917] A.C. 13.

is provided that the subcontractor shall have the same rights and remedies that the main contractor has under the main construction contract.[38] This evidently signalizes the desire for the alignment of the contracts concerning the construction project. The contractual chain that connects the contractual structure in a construction project enables the transfer of legal elements such as risks and liabilities. This chain to have a solid structure constitutes one of the main concerns of the contractor for the purposes of transferring their potential liabilities that may arise due to a delay or defective work of the subcontractor. The parties having aligned rights and remedies facilitates such a transfer to go smoothly as the right and remedies of the contractor would have been reflected on the allocated rights and remedies of the subcontractor.

Indeed, structuring contracts in a similar manner – by means of applying FIDIC Rules or not – constitutes a method of alignment for the contracts pertaining to construction projects. Even though this method of harmonized drafting may be considered quite ideal for achieving alignment, it may not always be possible to be this precise in the drafting stage. Accordingly, it is common practice for these documents to refer to documents or contract terms that are available to the concerned parties for the purposes of incorporation.

4.3.2. Incorporation by Reference

It is frequent for construction subcontracts to contain words of incorporation, which are referring to some identifiable documents or set of terms that are applicable to the subcontract. The unclear expression of the intention to incorporate may constitute a problem in assessing whether incorporation takes place. The general rule in English law is that the incorporation by reference (especially in the context of incorporating arbitration agreements) necessitates the employment of express words that clearly identify the term to be incorporated into the subcontract.[39] In *Lafarge Redland Aggregate v Shephard Hill Civil Engineering*,[40] one of the essential issues to be addressed before the court was whether extensive references in the subcontract to the main contract, including an obligation for the subcontractor to read and note the provisions of the main contract, was sufficient to establish direct liability between the employer and the subcontractor. Although it was accepted that the provisions of the main contract had an important bearing on the contractual relationship between the subcontractor and the contractor, such extensive references were held insufficient to establish a contractual relationship between the employer and the subcontractor due to the lack of privity between the said parties. Consequently, it was held that the subcontractor was free to pursue a separate arbitration with the contractor due to the separate nature of the concerned contracts.

One issue to be noted is that the mere existence of clear and express references may not be sufficient for incorporation to be successful. Each case must be individually considered to determine the actual purpose and extent to which it is desired to incorporate the term of the main contract.[41] As a direct result of the privity of contract, the terms of the main contract generally do not have a binding effect on the subcontract unless the incorporation

38 Sub-clause (2.4) of the FIDIC Conditions of Sub-contracts for Construction 2011.

39 J. McGuinness, *The Law and Management of Building Subcontracts*, Blackwell Publishing, 2007, 2nd Edn., 54–55.

40 [2000] 1 WLR.

41 Wallace (n 26) 1357, 13–100.

is successfully achieved. In this regard, the possibility of the subcontractor being familiar with the terms of the main contract is immaterial.

The alignment of contracts in construction projects is a goal to be achieved. In order to achieve this, the subcontract, 'as one would expect, makes numerous references to the main contract and many of its provisions are expressed in terms of the main contract and its provisions.'[42] Alignment of the relevant contracts is crucial to create a contractual relationship pertaining to construction, of which legal aspects are foreseeable.

It should be noted that, where a subcontract provides that the terms of it are aligned with the main contract, this usually does not mean that literally all terms of the main contract (including those pertaining to the contract price)[43] are directly incorporated into the subcontract. Indeed, the provisions are usually construed in a manner that is fitting the purposes of the 'subcontractual relationship.' In *Geary, Walker & Co. Ltd v Lawrence*, the agreed provision of the contract indicated that 'terms of payment for the work . . . shall be exactly the same as those set forth in clause 30 of the main contract.'[44] The amount of retention under the main contract would exceed the sum payable to the subcontractor under the subcontract when the construction project is concluded. The words of incorporation were held effective, and it was indicated by the Court of Appeal that the terms of the main contract in respect of payments were applicable to the subcontract. On the other hand, the payments are held to be in the same proportion as the subcontract sum to the main contract sum.

Clearly, each case should be considered individually concerning the precise purpose and extent to which it is purported to incorporate the terms of the main construction contract. Ascertaining the objective intentions of the parties, often by interpreting the language used in the documentation,[45] should be the applicable method to decide whether incorporation was intended and, if so, to assess the allowed extent of it.

4.4. Dispute Resolution in Construction

Arbitration has long been a preferred method of dispute resolution in the construction industry. Its favourability hinges upon the realities of construction projects such as the often involvement of many large sub-projects and works being financed, supplied, and executed by companies frequently from countries other than the country where the construction of the project is taking place. This particular dispute resolution method enables the appointment of arbitrators with specialized expertise in construction since disputes with complex technical aspects necessitate their settlement to be handled by a tribunal that has the relevant technical background and understanding. Thus, the complexity of

---

42 Lord Hobhouse of Woodborough in *Lafarge Redland Aggregate Ltd v Shephard Hill Civil Engineering Ltd* [2000] UKHL 46; [2000] 1 WLR 1621.

43 *Geary, Walker & Co. Ltd v Lawrence & Son* [1906] Hudson's Building and Engineering Contracts, 4th Edn., Vol. 2.

44 Ibid.

45 'Doubtful or ambiguous references to main contract documents or terms are much more likely to be aimed at the technical descriptions of the subcontract work to be found in the drawings, specifications or bills of quantities of the main contract rather than at the contractual or legal provisions in the main contract documentation.' Wallace (n 26) 1357, 13–103.

such an international and technical structure makes arbitration an attractive method for the resolution of construction disputes.[46]

It should nevertheless be noted that this specific branch of law has its specific method of statutory dispute resolution: adjudication. This method being a statutory one, its incorporation is usually immaterial since construction disputes 'falling within the scope of the HGCR are subject to statutory adjudication.'[47] Nonetheless, there are still several cases being referred to arbitration, especially where one party is dissatisfied with a decision rendered in an adjudication proceeding and challenges it through arbitration. Accordingly, the way arbitration clauses are incorporated in the construction context constitutes an issue to be addressed. However, concerning the predominance of statutory adjudication in construction, we first turn to this specific dispute resolution method to understand its role in the construction industry.

4.4.1. Construction Adjudication and the Latham Report

The Arbitration Act 1996 and the HGCR went through the parliament at the same time. What made this situation in a way ironic from the aspect of construction arbitration was the fact that the HGCR suggested statutory adjudication, a dispute resolution method that may regarded to be emulating arbitration in some respects. Due to the said peculiarity of the concerned legislation, in practice, only a limited number of construction disputes get to arbitration.

The HGCR was born following the review of construction excellence by Sir Michael Latham which is called the Constructing the Team, or the Latham Report. The Report was created as a result of a joint review of Procurement and Contractual Arrangements in the United Kingdom Construction Industry, conducted by Sir Michael Latham.[48] The Report highlighted that to be able to avoid some disputes, it was a necessity to realistically admit that a certain number of disputes were unavoidable.[49] The Report went further to suggest that if a dispute arises 'despite everyone's best efforts to avoid them'[50] then, the inclusion of the contract of a clear route indicating how a dispute is to be referred to adjudication would be an essential element for the settlement of it in the construction industry.[51] The adoption of adjudication as the fundamental dispute resolution method in the Latham Report paved the way for its further legislative adoption in the HGCR. It is provided under section 108 of the HGCR that 'a party to a construction contract has the right to refer a dispute arising under the contract for adjudication.'[52]

Concerning the characteristics of this particular dispute resolution method, it may be argued that adjudication constitutes a peculiarity of construction law. Adjudication is a quick

46 David Kiefer and Adrian Cole, Suitability of Arbitration Rules for Construction Disputes, in Stavros Brekoulakis and David Brynmor Thomas (eds.), *Global Arbitration Review*, The Guide to Construction Arbitration, 2017, 81–86, 81. Furthermore, a number of standard contract forms providing for arising construction disputes to be referred to arbitration: Sylvie Cécile Cavaleri, *Concurrent Delay in Construction Disputes*, Werlauff Publishing, 2015, 39. See this example: Section 9.3. to 9.8. of the JCT 2005 Standard Building Contract with Quantities, Revision 2, 2009.

47 Cavaleri (n 46) 39.

48 Sir Peter Coulson, *Coulson on Construction Adjudication*, Oxford University Press, 2015, 3rd Edn., 5.

49 Ibid 6, 1.13.

50 See paragraph 9.4 of the Latham Report.

51 Ibid.

52 Section 108(1) of the Housing Grants, Construction, and Regeneration (Construction) Act 1996.

process as a decision has to be given within 28 days following the referral of the dispute to the adjudicator.[53] Hence, in a way, it provides somewhat of 'quick and dirty justice.'[54] The method aims to encourage the continuity of the cash flow in the construction project, and hence, it may be considered to accommodate the general desire of the industry to have a mechanism that produces a fast and impartial resolution allowing the contract to carry on.[55] The remedies in adjudication are usually of monetary and time-related nature. For that reason, it may not be considered the best choice for parties, who are 'seeking creative remedies for overly complex technical or factual disputes.'[56] Adjudication is a concept satisfying the need of the construction industry to have somewhat of a 'temporary finality.'[57] The decision on adjudication is binding between the parties and may be enforced unless it is overturned by a decision rendering finality to the resolution of the dispute in litigation or arbitration.

The result of the adjudication needs to be implemented at once essentially for the mere purpose of maintaining the continuity of the construction project. For instance, if the award of the adjudication involves payment, then this must be made at once.[58] However, the decision of the adjudicator may be overturned by the courts or an arbitrator.[59] Accordingly, adjudication is potentially a 'temporary' method of resolution. The robustness of the adjudication award is fundamentally derived from the desire of the parties to be subject to a decision or not, which was made in a short period of time on perhaps a very complex dispute about a very complex construction project. The credibility of this dispute resolution mechanism may be best questioned as Lord Berkeley put it:

> I do not believe that there is any situation in which the adjudication could be made binding on all contracts. If there is a serious problem, one cannot expect disputes worth tens or hundreds of millions of pounds to be resolved in four weeks.[60]

It is hard to disagree with this statement considering the possible multiplicity and complexity of contracts pertaining to diversified aspects of a major construction project.

Adjudication bears similarities with arbitration. As a matter of fact, adjudication may be regarded a type of arbitration, that is being conducted and finalized relatively faster.[61]

---

53 Section 108(2)(c) of the Housing Grants, Construction, and Regeneration (Construction) Act 1996.

54 *Quick and Dirty Dispute Resolution*, June 22, 2015, Association of Mediation Assessors, Trainers, and Instructors, available at www.amati.org.uk/uk-quick-and-dirty-dispute-resolution/. Also see Sylvie Cécile Cavaleri, Construction Adjudication in a Comparative Perspective: The Case of the Danish Speedy Resolution, 2022, *The International Construction Law Review*, 169–189 at 170 where the author considers the possible negative sides of this method that 'one may mention the inequality between the parties inherent to short proceedings, where the claimant has much more time to prepare their request than the respondent has to answer it, and as for as certain adjudication regimes are concerned, uncertainties as to how a decision on adjudication can be enforced if the losing party does not comply voluntarily.'

55 Nevertheless, the relevant bill did not receive great compliments initially. See Lord Berkeley, April 1, 1996, Housing Grants, Construction, and Regeneration Bill, Hansard, Vol. 571, column 13.

56 Davies (n 5).

57 Matt Molloy, *Arbitrating After Adjudication*, Practical Law Construction Blog, March 19, 2013, available at http://constructionblog.practicallaw.com/arbitrating-after-adjudication/.

58 See paragraph 9.7.2. of the Latham Report.

59 Section 108(3) of the Housing Grants, Construction, and Regeneration (Construction) Act 1996.

60 Lord Berkeley, March 28, 1996, Housing Grants, Construction, and Regeneration Bill, Hansard, Vol. 570, column 1911.

61 Rupert Choat, Arbitration and Adjudication: A Tale of Two Acts, *Building*, October 9, 2015, available at www.building.co.uk/communities/arbitration-and-adjudication-a-tale-of-two-acts/5078023.article.

'In practice adjudication has ended up far from the lawyer-free process envisaged by some of the parliamentarians who enacted it. In fact, it often looks and feels like arbitration.'[62] Nevertheless, because it requires a decision pertaining to the settlement of a dispute to be rendered within a definite period of time, adjudication is evidently distinguishable from arbitration.

Furthermore, one may argue that there is some level of obligatoriness for adjudication in the construction context. Nonetheless, one should carefully interpret the 'mandatory' nature of this concept as, in fact, it provides a right rather than an obligation for the contracting parties. It is fundamentally a market shortcut. The level of 'obligatoriness' of statutory adjudication in construction disputes was examined in *Cubitt Building and Interiors Ltd v Richardson Roofing (Industrial) Ltd.*[63] The question before the court was whether a specific form of a subcontract or the provisions of the HGCR obliged a party to adjudicate before it could arbitrate or issue court proceedings. The plaintiff sought a declaration that its terms and conditions were incorporated into the subcontract, and hence, the arbitration proceedings commenced by the defendant should be decided to stay pending adjudication. Defendant argued a specific form of the subcontract was incorporated and the application of the plaintiff should itself be stayed pursuant to Section 9 of the Arbitration Act 1996. Accordingly, one of the fundamental issues to be considered in this case was 'the clash' of the HGCR and the Arbitration Act 1996.

The words of Akenhead J in the concerned case are of great significance as they evaluate the level of 'obligatoriness' of the statutory adjudication process:

> [O]f course, it is open to any party to apply for relief to the requisite tribunal to enable it to exercise its right to adjudicate. I do not accept however that there must be a stay of any legitimately constituted proceedings, whether in arbitration or in court proceedings, where there is merely a discretionary right to adjudicate as opposed to a binding pre-conditional adjudication requirement . . . Thus, it may be appropriate in certain circumstances to build into the timetable in court or arbitration proceedings a 28-day period to enable one party to adjudicate if, for any good reason, it cannot sensibly pursue adjudication at the same time as its court or arbitration proceedings . . . if the Court believes, following representations, that there is a measurably good prospect that adjudication will finally resolve the disputes or some of them, the court may well build into its timetable for trial some time to enable a party to adjudicate. That, however, is different from a stay. A party who has started court or arbitration proceedings is entitled to have those proceedings resolved as reasonably expeditiously as the Court can achieve and justice demands; it should not be forced to have those proceedings delayed or stayed by it itself being forced to adjudicate when it does not want to exercise its right to do so.[64]

The statutory nature of adjudication has an undeniable impact on the number of construction disputes that are being referred to arbitration in the UK. In fact, this specific dispute resolution method pertaining to construction disputes may be argued to have 'killed domestic arbitration in the UK.'[65] On the other hand, the referral to arbitration in

---

62 Ibid.

63 [2008] EWHC 1020 (TCC) (Judgement May 9, 2008).

64 Akenhead J in *Cubitt Building and Interiors Ltd v Richardson Roofing (Industrial) Ltd* [2008] EWHC 1020 (TCC), 72.

65 Nicola Laver, Interview with Hamish Lal, The Evolving Role of Arbitration in Construction Disputes, June 15, 2017, *Hardwick Legal Solicitors*, available at www.hardwicklegal.com/the-evolving-role-of-arbitration-in-construction-disputes/ (last visited July 23, 2019).

international construction projects has increased significantly over the years.[66] Considering the complexity of construction projects, the relevant disputes to be referred to arbitration may be found quite reasonable especially when the element of internationality is added to the equation. An international project usually has a bigger scope than a national one, and accordingly, it is generally more likely for a project, which is international in nature, to give rise to a range of complex and technical disputes.

Indeed, the HGCR provides for statutory adjudication for the resolution of construction disputes. However, the 'quick and dirty justice'[67] it offers may not seem appropriate for every dispute as its 'superficiality' may be said to possibly hinder both its inclusiveness of technical aspects and details of the construction dispute to a certain degree and also its capability of producing comprehensive decisions. Very often, construction disputes include complex technical matters, market terminology, and issues that may be dependent on the specific resolutions that the implementation of specific principles of construction law provides. Therefore, the 'restricted' scope of adjudication may be argued to make it unreasonable to expect this method to produce truly well-rounded resolutions in a period that is less than a month.[68] One thing that should be noted is that parties to adjudication may also use technical expert witnesses. However, the assessment of the technical aspects of the disputes in adjudication is made much speedier than they are done in arbitration or in litigation. Accordingly, adjudication may perhaps work perfectly for some relatively uncomplicated disputes whereas may not be suitable for overly complex ones.

4.4.2. Incorporation of Adjudication

The HGCR provides that a party to a construction contract has the right to refer any dispute arising under the contract to adjudication. If the contract is lacking any provision concerning adjudication procedure – or if the procedure contained in the contract does not comply with Section 109 of the Act – before one can refer a dispute to adjudication, the following should be made sure: 'that a dispute exists; the dispute arises out of the relevant contract; the relevant contract includes an adjudication procedure or if not; 'the contract' is a construction contract as defined by the Act.'[69] Provided that the indicated criteria are not met, the contract is normally not governed by the HGCR, and thus, adjudication does not apply.

However, adjudication may still find its application under the contract and not particularly pursuant to the HGCR. In *RWE Npower v Alstom Power Ltd*[70] a contract for boiler maintenance was not considered a construction contract under the HGCR. On the other hand, adjudication was adopted as a method of dispute resolution and the Scheme for Construction Contracts (England and Wales) Regulations 1998 (1998 Scheme)[71] was

---

66 Ibid.

67 *Quick and Dirty Dispute Resolution* (n 54).

68 'Adjudication is a very quick process and the adjudicator has 28 days to decide the dispute once it has been referred to him. This period can also be extended to 42 days by the referring party or longer by the agreement of both parties' Davies (n 5).

69 *User's Guide to Adjudication*, Construction Industry Council, 2017, 8, available at www.architecture.com/-/media/gathercontent/work-with-us/additional-documents/usersguidetoadjudicationcicpdf.pdf (last visited July 13, 2022).

70 [2009] EWHC B40.

71 (SI 1998/649).

incorporated into the contract. The 1998 Scheme supplements the HGCR and applies to construction contracts in England, Wales, and Scotland entered into from May 1, 1998, up to the date. Part I of the 1998 Scheme 'provides a fall-back position where a construction contract does not include all the adjudication provisions'[72] contained in Section 108 of the HGCR. If that would be the case, the provisions of the 1998 Scheme that are pertaining to adjudication 'take effect as implied terms and replace completely any such provision in the contract.'[73]

It was emphasized by the court in *RWE Npower v Alstom Power Ltd* that the parties were aware of the potential results of their incorporation of the 1998 Scheme into their contract and by doing so, they also incorporated the statutory regime. To put it another way, the decision of the adjudicator was honoured on a 'pay now, argue later' basis.[74] What is worth mentioning about *RWE Npower v Alstom Power Ltd* is that the relevant contract in this case not even being an actual 'construction contract' that is falling into the scope of the HGCR, the ascertainable intention and knowledge of the parties were considered of great significance and their incorporation of a certain provision considered to have created a contractual result that would similarly be created in the construction context. Accordingly, even though adjudication is a peculiar method of dispute resolution in construction disputes, by upholding the incorporation of such a 'unique method' outside of its regular context, the court illustrated the significance of party autonomy concerning the notion of incorporation of dispute resolution clauses. Therefore, this case manifests that the right to go to adjudication arises not only as a statutory one in construction disputes, but it may also possibly arise due to contract drafting indicating the intention of the parties to be subject to this particular method of dispute resolution. Accordingly, adjudication may also be contractual and not only statutory. Dispute boards under the FIDIC contracts constitute examples of contractual adjudication. Furthermore, parties may agree to select adjudication as the dispute resolution method on a one-off basis.[75] Similarly, in such a case, the parties would be bound by this particular dispute resolution method not due to the applicability of the HGCR to their disputes but rather because of the way they drafted their contract to incorporate adjudication.

4.4.3. Construction Arbitration

Arbitration being confidential enables parties to keep the details of their dispute private and hence, constitutes a good dispute resolution method for the parties that are concerned about the confidentiality of their trade secrets. Furthermore, this method allows parties to appoint arbitrators with significant backgrounds in construction disputes and being experts in the field. International companies involved in a construction project understandably refrain from being subject to the jurisdiction of a different legal system, as they may have little or no knowledge of. Hence, international arbitration has long been a traditional

72 Guidance Note: The Scheme for Construction Contracts, *The Chartered Institute of Arbitrators & Adjudication Society*, 2020, 2, available at www.ciarb.org/media/4163/the-scheme-for-construction-contracts.pdf.

73 Ibid.

74 Michelle Rousell, *Contractual Adjudication Using the Scheme for Construction* Contracts, Thomson Reuters, Practical Law Construction Blog, January 15, 2010, available at http://constructionblog.practicallaw.com/contractual-adjudication-using-the-scheme-for-construction-contracts/ (last visited September 30, 2022).

75 Ibid.

method of dispute resolution in construction projects, and accordingly, construction disputes constitute one of the largest parts of commercial disputes before arbitral bodies.[76] Adjudication undeniably has a detrimental impact on construction arbitration in the UK. However, this effect is mainly limited to domestic arbitration. On the contrary, arbitration is still a highly preferred dispute resolution method in international construction contracts. The main reasons for this preference may be said to be

> a shared desire to have the dispute resolved on a final and binding basis by an experienced, specialist and partly party-nominated tribunal and; a perception that tribunals are more likely to make awards based on consistent and uniform understanding of how major construction contracts operate.[77]

Because the main construction contract and the construction subcontract constitute two different and separate contracts, they may contain provisions concerning different methods of dispute resolution. Nonetheless, the individual nature of these contracts does not impair the popularity of arbitration as a dispute resolution method in construction projects, and it may be considered quite usual to bring some of the third parties to the contractual relationship into the arbitration. Such possible involvement of third parties necessitates the evaluation of the contractual structure construction projects consist of. This particularly bears importance concerning the provisions of the contract pertaining to arbitration rules chosen by the parties and whether these allow the joinder of third parties into the proceedings.

The main contractor in a construction project, by virtue of their central position in the contractual chain, may wish to incorporate an arbitration clause into the subcontract in an attempt to make disputes that are arising from different aspects of the substantial construction project subject to the implementation of the same dispute resolution mechanism. Thus, it is usual for the contractor seeking to bring the subcontractor, who may be liable for the delay in the execution of the works, in the arbitration against the employer. Furthermore, in the case of a dispute, the employer may seek to bring a claim against the main contractor, with whom the employer has an arbitration agreement, and against the subcontractor, engineer, or architect with whom he may not have an arbitration agreement.[78] Also, in the case of insolvency of the main contractor, the employer may seek to arbitrate with the subcontractor.[79] Contrastingly, other than certain circumstances to occur, the employer does not have an interest in such a multi-party arbitration as the employer normally holds the contractor fully liable regardless of the possible inability of the contractor to transfer their liability to the actually responsible party, the subcontractor.[80] Transferability of liabilities from the aspect of the main contractor often

---

76 For instance, in 2015, disputes that arose from construction and engineering project constituted 25% of all cases before the International Chamber of Commerce, and that was the largest percentage of any subject matter by a significant margin. See 2015 ICC Dispute Resolution Statistics.

77 Laver (n 65).

78 There may be no arbitration agreement between the employer and the engineer or the architecture, or the case may be the existing arbitration agreement between the said parties to not be referring the possible or existing dispute to the same arbitrator. Under the circumstances that the similar or same dispute to be settled by different arbitrators, the result may be conflicting.

79 Dimitar Kondev, Do Recent Overhauls of Arbitration Rules Respond to the Need for Multi-party arbitration in the Construction Industry?, 2015, *International Construction Law Review*, 32, 63, 66.

80 Brekoulakis and El Far (n 13).

does not constitute a concern for the employer. The employer, fundamentally, has no interest in third-party joinder proceedings between the employer and the main contractor because the involvement of a joinder potentially complicates the matter and delays its final resolution.

The arbitration agreement in the main construction contract between the contractor and the employer does normally not expand to cover the subcontractor under the subcontract and likewise, the arbitration agreement in the construction subcontract between the contractor and the subcontractor does usually not extend to include the employer under the main contract.[81] The separate nature of construction contracts pertaining to the same project may cause the emergence of separate arbitrations that possibly create conflicting outcomes for similar matters. These contracts being interrelated in nature, a dispute that arises between two parties may be based on similar facts and thus may give rise to similar legal issues in a dispute between two other parties involved in the same construction project.[82] However, due to these contracts being separate, there would be two separate arbitrations on a similar subject matter. To put it differently, concerning disputes arising from similar subject matters, the subcontractor may potentially be successful in their claim and consequently obtain an arbitral award whereas the main contractor fails to get one.

'There is often a need for multi-party arbitration in the construction industry.'[83] However, multi-party arbitration proceedings between the employer, the main contractor, and the subcontractor do not take place by default due to the contractual and bilateral nature of arbitration, and therefore, a party may seek to include a third party in the arbitration under certain circumstances.[84]

> It will often be the main contractor who is interested in multi-party arbitration, as it would enable him to pursue his recourse claims against his contracting parties (e.g. subcontractors and suppliers) within the same arbitration. The main contractor can also be interested in such a complex arbitration in case of claims pursued by subcontractors or suppliers hired by him, which are based on defaults for which the employer is ultimately responsible under the terms of the main contract.[85]

Arbitration usually enables 'the claims arising out of multiple contracts to be brought forth and decided in a single arbitration and thus, multiple arbitrations to be consolidated into one.'[86] However, the combination of such arbitrations is generally not considered appropriate unless the consent of the concerned parties is provided or the dispute had arisen from the same legal relationship and the agreements to arbitrate are compatible.[87] If all of the parties who are involved in the construction project (employer, contractor, and

81 Andrea M. Steingruber, *Consent in International Arbitration*, Oxford University Press, 2012, 9.01.

82 Brekoulakis and El Far (n 13) 87–99, 93.

83 Dimitar Kondev, *Multi-Party and Multi-Contract Arbitration in the Construction Industry*, Wiley-Blackwell, 2017, 58.

84 Stavros Brekoulakis, *Third Parties in International Commercial Arbitration*, Oxford University Press, 2010, 1.09–1.13.

85 Kondev (n 83) 58.

86 Kiefer and Cole (n 46) 81; available at www.kslaw.com/attachments/000/005/444/original/Suitability_of_Arbitration_Rules_for_Construction_Disputes.pdf?1509633709 (last visited April 28, 2022). ICC Arbitration Rules, Article 9 allowing joinder of parties from multiple contracts; ICDR Rules Article 7; discussing joinder of parties to an arbitration; ICC Arbitration Rules, Article 10; providing for the consolidation of arbitrations.

87 Ibid 82.

subcontractor) seeking to settle their disputes subject to multiparty arbitration proceedings, then it would be safe to enter into two identical arbitration clauses, which clearly provide for multiparty arbitration and manifest the relevant party intention.

Generally speaking, for the disputes between the subcontractor and the contractor to be subject to the provisions of the arbitration clause in the main construction contract, the language of incorporation should be distinctly provided in a way indicating the true intention regarding multiparty arbitration. The contractual relationship that constitutes the fundamentals of the construction project comes into existence after long negotiations. The multiplicity of contracting parties and complexity of construction contracts may cause the significance of drafting and incorporation of the arbitration clause to possibly be overlooked.[88] However, especially in the construction context, the proper formation of the clause and its sufficient incorporation constitute crucial issues that require specific elaboration.

4.5. Incorporation of Arbitration Clauses and Construction Contracts

There may be some gaps or aspects of the contractual relationship that are not covered in the content of the documents constituting the subcontract. Accordingly, these usually contain incorporation clauses referring to distinct documents and rules, to fill the contractual gaps and align contracts. The references are usually made to a standard form of contract or subcontract[89] or to another contract, which is made between different parties concerned with the same construction project but possibly not in all respects appropriately applicable to the contract in hand.[90] Evidently, the reference may also be made to some other existing contracts between the same parties and the scope of such a reference would indeed be relatively easier to assess because the parties to the contractual relationship would be the same.[91]

Some modification may also be necessary where the subcontract is referring to a document that is not entirely applicable or operable without some manipulation of its words to the contractual relationship of the parties to the subcontract. For instance, if the document that is referred to contains an arbitration clause, indeed, the wording of such a clause would usually have been formed in a way involving the disputes between the parties of this distinct contract. For example, if the reference is made to the main contract, then the arbitration clause probably stipulates its application over the disputes between

88 Jagath C. Korale and Chitra Weddikkara, *The Impact of Inclusion of Arbitration Clause by Reference in Main Contract and Subcontract Documents in the Construction Industry and Its Negative Connotations*, World Construction Conference 2012 – Global Challenges in Construction Industry, Colombo, Sri Lanka, June 28–30, 2012, 202–208, 207.

89 *Geary Walker & Co. Ltd. v Lawrence & Son* (n 43) 382; *Modern Building Wales Ltd v Limmer & Trinidad Co Limited* [1975] 2 Lloyd's Rep 318; [1975] 1 WLR 1281; *Brightside Kilpatrick Engineering Services v Mitchell Construction [1973] Ltd.* [1975] 2 Lloyd's Rep 493.

90 The reference may be made to the terms of a superior main or subcontract – for instance, a sub-subcontract referring to a subcontract. Also see Wallace (n 26) 1584, 18–031.

91 Incorporation concerning the scenarios theory was evaluated in two significant cases: *Habas* and *Athena*. These cases and the scenarios theory are analyzed in various parts of the book and thus will not be mentioned here at this point. See *Habas Sinai ve Tibbi Gazlar Istihsal Endustri AS v Sometal SAL* [2010] 1 Lloyd's Rep 661; *Sea Trade Maritime Corp v Hellenic Mutual War Risks Association (Bermuda) Ltd (The Athena)* [2006] EWHC 2530 (Comm).

the employer and the main contractor. Hence, the incorporation of such an arbitration clause into the subcontract may necessitate the modification of the words pertaining to the identification of the parties to the contractual relationship.

In a 1973 case, *Sidney Kaye, Eric Firmin & Partners v Bronesky*[92] where a reference was made to the Royal Institute of British Architects (RIBA) Conditions of Engagement, which might well have been intended to regulate the amount of and entitlement of remuneration only, the Court of Appeal held that the reference was successful to incorporate the arbitration clause that was included in the RIBA Conditions into the architect's subcontract. *Sidney Kaye v Bronesky* was a case in which the document (the set of rules) was appropriately identified, and hence, the words of incorporation were held extensive enough to incorporate the arbitration clause. The defendants obtained a stay of action, but the plaintiffs argued that the dispute was not falling within the scope of the arbitration agreement. The Court of Appeal upheld the decision to stay. It should be noted that the provisions of the standard agreements generally are neither incorporated by default nor implied 'unless the client is familiar with the usual relationship between client and architect and has engaged similar professionals before on similar terms.'[93]

In *Modern Building Wales Ltd v Limmer & Trinidad Co Limited*,[94] the incorporation of arbitration clauses into construction contracts was considered by the Court of Appeal and it was examined whether the words 'fully in accordance with the appropriate form for nominated subcontractor (RIBA 1965 edition)' were sufficient for incorporation. The words of incorporation were referring to 'the Form' of RIBA that would be appropriate in the context of the subcontract. It was held by relying on expert evidence that such words of incorporation would indicate the reference to the 'Green Form' of the nominated subcontract. The 'Green Form' included an arbitration clause, and thus, the main question before the Court of Appeal was whether the arbitration clause was incorporated. It was held that the words of incorporation were sufficient to incorporate the arbitration clause, and accordingly, the stay was granted. It was indicated that there would be no doubt that anyone in the industry would understand the words 'in full accordance with the appropriate form for nominated subcontractors (RIBA 1965 edition)' to refer to what is known as the 'Green Form.'[95] Hence, no further clarification is considered necessary in assessing the document purported to be incorporated into the subcontract. The Court of Appeal relied on the inference that anyone in the industry would have understood a reference being made to the 'Green Form' of subcontract would also be aware of the fact that 'the Form' contains an arbitration clause and the contracts administrator of the subcontractor having 41 years of experience of subcontracting, was not excluded from the scope of such presumption. Furthermore, the concerned contractual structure was considered one of a single contract, and accordingly, general words were found sufficient for the incorporation of the arbitration agreement.[96]

The next issue to be addressed by the Court of Appeal was concerning the scope of the incorporation clause. It was argued that the language of the incorporation clause was

92 [1973] 4 BLR 1, C.A. (*Sidney Kaye v Bronesky*).

93 Hughes, Champion and Murdoch (n 31) 22, 2.4.

94 [1975] 2 Lloyd's Rep 318; [1975] 1 WLR 1281. (*Modern Building*).

95 [1975] 2 Lloyd's Rep 318, 320.

96 Robert Merkin and Louis Flannery, *Merkin and Flannery on the Arbitration Act 1996*, Informa Law from Routledge, 2020, 127, 6.2.2. (xii). See Chapter 1, 'The Foundations of Incorporation and Arbitration Clauses.'

only appropriate to incorporate the clauses of the 'Green Form' pertaining to the supply of labour, plant, and machinery. It was indicated by Buckley LJ that

> the words were fully wide enough to introduce into the contract between the parties all the terms of the 'Green Form' which relate to the supply of labour, and so forth carrying out the works, including the arbitration clause, which is itself a clause relating to those matters.[97]

That is to say, *Modern Building*, although predating the Arbitration Act 1996, reveals significant principles concerning the scope of the words of incorporation. Where the document that is to be incorporated is clearly ascertained, then the question should be 'to what extent this contract will be incorporated?' Regarding the assessment of such an extent, it was indicated that the mere incorporation of the terms regarding the execution of the construction work (labour and machinery) by means of excluding the arbitration clause would be unfair since arbitration was selected as a resolution method for disputes arising from the execution of the construction work. In other words, the execution of the works and the related dispute resolution mechanism were held interrelated. Hence, with regard to *Modern Building*, it may not be necessary to make a specific reference to the arbitration clause if the arbitration clause is included within a set of standard terms in the construction context. This is because, if it is clearly manifested by the parties that the governance of a certain set of rules to their contractual relationship is their preferred option, then the exclusion of the arbitration clause from that 'set' may potentially violate party autonomy. Therefore, where the set of terms to be incorporated is clearly defined, a specific reference to an arbitration clause in such a set may not be a necessity in the construction context.

Sidney Kaye v Bronesky[98] and *Modern Building*[99] although being cases that predated the Arbitration Act 1996, establish that if a clear reference is made to a set of terms including an arbitration clause, a specific reference to such arbitration clause may not be necessary. Accordingly, these cases do not follow the rule established by the House of Lords in *Thomas v Portsea*.[100] This particular case, being concerned with shipping contracts, sets a strict requirement pertaining to the incorporation of arbitration clauses and establishes that these may only be incorporated by express and specific reference made to them. Hence, the incorporation of an arbitration clause contained in a set of rules that are referred to by means of employing general words of incorporation, is not possible according to the approach adopted in *Thomas v Portsea*. This particular marine case provides a basis for the built-up of substantial case law (also non-marine cases) on the matter of incorporation of arbitration clauses and accordingly, for the development of some strict rules concerning the incorporation of arbitration clauses. However, the fairness of applying rules fundamentally derived from shipping principles in the construction context seems quite unsatisfying. For one thing, it is clear that construction has its own peculiarities. Nevertheless, construction law, like other branches of law dealing with the issue of incorporation in chain contracts, has also been exposed to the implementation of the strict rule of incorporation as adopted in the shipping context. The approach of the courts concerning incorporation in the

97 [1975] 2 Lloyd's Rep 318, 323.
98 [1973] 4 BLR 1, C.A.
99 [1975] 2 Lloyd's Rep 318.
100 [1912] A.C. 1.

construction context has not always been consistent. This is because courts, over time, had different perceptions regarding the implementation of the strict 'shipping' rule on other 'non-marine' branches of law concerned with incorporation.

Up to this point, *Modern Building*[101] and *Sidney Kaye v Bronesky*[102] fundamentally established that the incorporation of arbitration clauses that are contained in a set of rules, which are clearly referred to by the parties to a construction dispute in a way manifesting the compatible party autonomy, may not particularly necessitate a specific reference to be made to them. Another important construction case predating the Arbitration Act 1996 dealing with the incorporation of arbitration clauses is *Aughton Ltd v M F Kent.*[103] The significance of this case derives from the clear division of opinions of the judges on the matter of incorporation. In *Aughton Ltd v M F Kent*, Ralph Gibson LJ and Sir John Megaw, reaching the same conclusion that the incorporation was not successful, followed fundamentally different routes. These routes were found so irreconcilable[104] by some judges subsequently that some considered this 'decision as not binding upon them at all.'[105] Evidently, *Aughton Ltd v M F Kent* provides us with different perspectives concerning the issue of incorporation and, accordingly, is specifically discussed in the following section, along with some other relevant construction cases that predated the Arbitration Act 1996.[106]

4.6. Case Law Concerning Incorporation of Arbitration Clauses in Construction Context and the Arbitration Act 1996

i. *Aughton Ltd v M F Kent Services Ltd* and Afterwards

Aughton Ltd v M F Kent[107] may be regarded as the fundamental case concerned with the incorporation of arbitration clauses in the construction context prior to the Arbitration Act 1996. The Court of Appeal in this case considered whether the employment of general words of incorporation was sufficient to incorporate the terms, including an arbitration provision from a construction subcontract into a sub-subcontract in the context of a stay application.

Proceedings took place between Aughton and Kent with reference to work done by Aughton. The contractual layout was as follows: There was a main contract between the Ministry of Defence and Press, under which the latter was the main contractor for the work. Press then engaged Kent as a subcontractor, and subsequently Kent engaged Aughton to carry out work connected with the electrical installation. Aughton accepted the offer made by Kent in their letter. The letter stated in paragraph (7) that 'you (Aughton) will enter into a sub-subcontract with us (Kent) based on GC Works 1 as discussed at our meeting.' Furthermore, the letter also included the words 'our previous correspondence and the documentation encompassed in our enquiry forms part of our agreement.' It was argued

101 [1975] 2 Lloyd's Rep 318.

102 [1973] 4 BLR 1, C.A.

103 *Aughton Ltd v M F Kent Services Ltd* [1991] 57 BLR 1. (*Aughton Ltd v M F Kent*).

104 Merkin and Flannery (n 96) 6.2.2. (xx).

105 Ibid. HHJ Gilliland QC in *Cooperative Wholesale Society v Saunders & Taylor* [1995] 11 Con LJ 118.

106 It should be noted that *Extrudakerb v White Mountain Quarries* [1996] NI 567, a Northern Ireland case examined here, is dated July 1996 and the Arbitration Act 1996 is passed on June 17, 1996. However, most of the act's provisions came into force on January 31, 1997.

107 (1991) 57 BLR 1.

that the arbitration clause was incorporated into the sub-subcontract by virtue of the words in paragraph (7) and not from GC Works 1. To put it differently, the arbitration clause argued to be incorporated in accordance with the conditions of the Press/Kent subcontract requiring the examination of what had been discussed at the meeting and the previous correspondence and documentation and not from GC Works 1. Actually, the latter was the standard form, which was used for establishing the main contract and included an arbitration clause, which was not relied on by the subcontractors (Kent) when sued by sub-subcontractors (Aughton) for sums allegedly due.

The words 'previous correspondence and documentation' referred to in the sub-subcontract, argued to contain main contractor/subcontractor documentation, by Clause 61 of which all disputes between the parties to the subcontract and relating to the subcontract, other than certain matters in which the decision of the main contractor was to be conclusive, were to be referred to arbitration. It was argued that, by virtue of the said clause, subcontractors were entitled to apply for a stay against the sub-subcontractor's claim. The fundamental issue before the Court of Appeal to determine was whether general words were sufficient to incorporate terms including the arbitration clause from a subcontract into a sub-subcontract. Consequently, the stay was refused.

Although reaching the same decision, the two judges in *Aughton Ltd v M F Kent* followed fundamentally different routes. Sir John Megaw adopted the strict approach of incorporation that is fundamentally derived from shipping cases (particularly the *Thomas v Portsea* principle) and indicated the lack of precise reference to the arbitration clause formed a basis for his decision of non-incorporation and, therefore, the refusal of stay. This particular approach seems to be inconsistent with the one applied in *Modern Building*.[108]

On the other hand, Ralph Gibson LJ rejected the suggestion that there was any special rule of construction pertaining to the incorporation of arbitration clauses and emphasized that the main issue to be assessed was whether the parties had, by their words, clearly expressed an intention to incorporate the arbitration clause.[109] Ralph Gibson LJ consequently put forth that an express reference to an arbitration clause was not a necessity for its incorporation, and accordingly, the employment of general words may be considered sufficient to incorporate the arbitration clause, depending on its terms.[110]

Even though Ralph Gibson LJ too refused the stay to be granted, he followed a different approach than Sir John Megaw. The path followed by Ralph Gibson LJ paves the way to distinguish construction contracts and shipping contracts[111] as his judgement fundamentally highlights that there is no 'one size fits all' but rather a party autonomy should prevail. Accordingly, his judgement distinguishes the principle applied in *Thomas v Portsea*.

One may find the approach adopted by Ralph Gibson LJ in *Aughton Ltd v M F Kent* more consistent with the one adopted in *Modern Building* as, in the view of the learned judge, no specific reference was needed for the incorporation of an arbitration clause.

108 [1975] 2 Lloyd's Rep 318.
109 [1991] 57 BLR 1, 25 and 81, respectively.
110 Ibid 23 and 79, respectively.
111 See *Rena K* [1979] 1 All ER 397; in a shipping case, on the other hand, under similar circumstances, it was held that the arbitration clause was incorporated. However, concerning the general application with shipping cases, indeed, a restrictive approach is adopted when it comes to the incorporation of arbitration clauses, and accordingly, the employment of specific words of incorporation is generally required.

However, Ralph Gibson LJ considered the issue from the aspect of the admissibility of a potential arbitration agreement. He indicated that *Modern Building* was a case dealing with persons in trade who were regularly exchanging the document, and accordingly, they would understand that the reference was made to the 'Green Form.' *Modern Building* further included a written arbitration agreement, which was referred to for the purposes of incorporation. Contrary to this, the sub-subcontract in *Aughton* included the words 'based on . . . discussed at our meeting.' Thus, such an indication referring to an oral discussion held to be precluding the agreement from falling into the scope of the statutory requirements for an arbitration agreement to be 'in writing.' In other words, even though more flexible approaches concerning the incorporation of arbitration clauses were considered both in *Modern Building* and *Aughton Ltd v M F Kent* (at least from the side of Ralph Gibson LJ), the point of divergence between these cases was created by the formality requirement of arbitration agreements to be 'in writing' as the concerned contractual structure in *Aughton Ltd v M F Kent* was not meeting this criterion.

Sir John Megaw, on the other hand, regarded *Thomas v Portsea* principles applicable in *Aughton Ltd v M F Kent* and rejected the employment of general words of incorporation to sufficiently incorporate arbitration clauses. 'Three important interrelated factors peculiar to arbitration agreements'[112] were introduced by Sir John Megaw: (1) an arbitration agreement may preclude the parties from bringing a dispute before the court, (2) an arbitration agreement has to be a written agreement, and (3) an arbitration agreement is of a different nature from other clauses, and constitutes a self-contained contract. Sir John Megaw accepted that these factors were equally applicable to arbitration clauses in construction contracts as they are to arbitration clauses in charterparties.[113] He accordingly concluded that, like shipping contracts, specific reference clearly manifesting the intention of the parties to incorporate an arbitration agreement is also sought in the construction context.[114] He went further to suggest that general words of incorporation never suffice.[115]

The substance and applicability of the posed factors may be examined. First, indeed an arbitration agreement precludes parties from being heard by the court. However, at the same time, it facilitates the promotion of party autonomy concerning the method of dispute resolution that the parties wish to be applicable to their dispute. Therefore, provided that party selection concerning the dispute resolution method is clearly manifested, the preclusion of court jurisdiction would not constitute a complication as it perhaps could do some 30 years ago when *Aughton Ltd v M F Kent* was decided at a time when courts were perhaps more jealous of their jurisdiction than they are now.[116] Second, it should be kept in mind that *Aughton Ltd v M F Kent* being a case predating the Arbitration Act 1996 was subject to the provisions of its predecessors. It was then laid down by legislation (Section 32 of the Arbitration Act 1950 as re-enacted in section 7(1)(e) of the Arbitration Act 1979) that an arbitration agreement had strictly to 'be written.' However, the Arbitration

112 [1991] 57 BLR 1, 30.

113 *T. W. Thomas & Co. Ltd. v Portsea Steamship Co Ltd, The Portsmouth* [1912] A.C. 1.

114 [1991] 57 BLR 1, 31.

115 Ibid 32.

116 Adrian Baron, The International Arbitration Act, the Fiction of Severability and Claims for Restitution – Part Two, 2000, *Arbitration International*, 16(2), 159–188, 183. See Peter Sallman, The Impact of Caseflow Managemenet in the Judicial System, 1995, *University of New South Wales Law Journal*, 18, 193.

Act 1996 clarified issues concerning the interpretation of relevant concepts such as 'being in writing' and 'evidenced in writing.' Third, the self-contained nature of an arbitration agreement introduced as a factor necessitates the employment of an express reference to such agreement for its incorporation. Nevertheless, provided it is vivid that the parties are truly familiar with the content and scope of a contract, which happens to include an arbitration clause, then why such a clause should be treated differently from the rest of the contract terms? Construction contracts are frequently formed between experienced players in the market, who are usually familiar with standard and ordinary rules that often contain an arbitration clause.

Another issue is the clearly inappropriate categorization of construction contracts. Construction contracts essentially have very little in common with contracts of shipping. However, despite the contracts before the Court of Appeal in *Aughton Ltd v M F Kent* being construction contracts and subcontracts (also sub-subcontracts), Sir John Megaw preferred implementing some principles that are fundamentally adopted in the shipping context of the case at hand.[117] Nonetheless, very different principles apply to shipping contracts. The main reason that it is relatively harder to incorporate arbitration clauses into bills of lading is the negotiable nature of these documents, and as they change hands very often, it may not always be very convenient or practical (or even possible) to inform every new holder of them concerning the existence of the charterparty arbitration clause and of its potential incorporation. Furthermore, it may clearly not be justifiable to bring an oblivious third-party holder into arbitration provided they are not familiar with the charterparty arbitration clause. Essentially, the negotiable nature of bills of lading necessitates the adoption of stricter rules in the shipping context. Thus, the mere chain structure of construction contracts and shipping contracts does not possibly justify the application of the same rules of incorporation to construction subcontracts and bills of lading. Hence, it may be considered unreasonable to expect an approach applicable in the shipping context to appropriately fulfil the needs of a substantially different area of law. *Aughton Ltd v M F Kent* is of great significance as it provides us with the opportunity to question and evaluate some different aspects of the concept of incorporation of arbitration clauses in different branches of law.

Accordingly, even though the incorporation was not allowed, and thus, the stay was not granted in *Aughton Ltd v M F Kent* (and accordingly, it may not actually be categorized as a 'pro-arbitration case'), it should be kept in mind that the stay in this case was refused not on the grounds of arbitration clauses requiring special treatment (at least from the aspect of Ralph Gibson LJ). Once the intention to adopt a particular set of contract rules as a whole is properly manifested, the intention to incorporate an arbitration clause included in this particular set is usually considered to have been ascertained as well.[118] In *Aughton Ltd v M F Kent*, the stay was not granted merely because the reference was made to oral discussions,[119] which were unable to constitute an arbitration agreement by virtue of provisions of the Arbitration Act 1950 in the first place.[120] The approaches of Sir John Megaw and Ralph Gibson LJ have received both support and criticism.

117 *Thomas v Portsea* [1912] A.C. 1.
118 Wallace (n 26) 1585, 18–033.
119 [1991] 57 BLR 1, 29.
120 As re-enacted in section 7(1)(e) of the Arbitration Act 1979.

ii. *Lexair v Edgar Taylor* – Support for Sir John Megaw

Similar to *Aughton*, the court in *Lexair Ltd v Edgar W Taylor Ltd*[121] was also concerned with an application of stay. The essential issue to be decided by the court was whether an arbitration clause contained in the main contract was incorporated into a subcontract for electrical works so that the court proceedings had to stay in favour of arbitration. The judge particularly referred to the judgement of Sir John Megaw in *Aughton*, and based on the facts of the case in hand, it was held that the arbitration clause was not incorporated, and hence, the stay was not granted.

iii. *Ben Barrett v Henry Boot* – Incorporation Was Not Allowed

In *Ben Barrett & Sons v Henry Boot Management Ltd*[122] a reference to another document including an arbitration clause was held insufficient for purposes of incorporation. Henry Boot, the defendant, was a contractor for the work at the University of Manchester, and Ben Barrett & Sons, the plaintiffs, were subcontractors for brickwork. The letter of intent indicated that the works could be carried out in accordance with the 'Works Contract/2 JCT Form,' and this document was found to amount to a contract. Taking the points made by the two judges in *Aughton Ltd v M F Kent*,[123] it was indicated by Judge John Lloyd QC that these different approaches were irreconcilable. The emphasis was placed on *Thomas v Portsea*[124] and also on the concern that 'arbitration clause being a self-contained contract and thus separate from the main contract between the parties.'[125] Accordingly, the general words of incorporation were held insufficient to incorporate the arbitration clause even though the rest of the terms were incorporated. To put it differently, the strict *Thomas v Portsea* approach found application in *Ben Barrett v Henry Boot* too. Due to the fact that the very significant approaches of Ralph Gibson LJ and Sir John Megaw were merely considered 'irreconcilable' and no further analysis on the matter was provided, *Ben Barrett* may be regarded a missed opportunity on the way to shaping a more comprehensive case law concerning incorporation in the construction context.

iv. *Extrudakerb v White Mountain Quarries* and the Officious Bystander Test

The views of Ralph Gibson LJ in *Aughton Ltd v M F Kent* found support later in a Northern Ireland case. *Extrudakerb v White Mountain Quarries*[126] was essentially concerned with the assessment of whether an express reference to an arbitration clause was needed for its incorporation. The defendant main contractor was carrying out resurfacing works and the plaintiff subcontractor provided their quotation to lay surface water channels. The defendant main contractor accepted the plaintiff subcontractor's offer subject to certain amendments, including that the subcontract would be in the Federation of Civil

---

121 (1993) 65 BLR 90.

122 [1995] CILL 1026. (*Ben Barrett*).

123 (1991) 57 BLR 1.

124 [1912] A.C. 1.

125 Which is also consistent with the inter-related factors pertaining to arbitration clauses, which were indicated by Sir John Megaw in *Aughton*. The factors were provided: the potential of the arbitration clauses to preclude parties to bring a dispute before a court of law, the requirement for an arbitration agreement to be a 'written agreement,' and arbitration clauses to constitute a self-contained contract collateral or ancillary to the substantive contract. [1991] 57 BLR 1, 30.

126 [1996] NI 567. (*Extrudakerb v White Mountain*).

Engineering Contractors (FCEC) form of subcontract. A dispute arose and following the plaintiff's issuing a writ, the defendant applied for a stay based upon an arbitration clause contained in the 'FCEC Form.'

It was held that while arbitration agreements had to be in writing, it did not follow that they had to be specifically referred to in the contractual documents. In the case before the court, the parties had agreed that the work would be done on the terms of the 'FCEC Form' of the subcontract, which were familiar to the parties, who both knew that these terms contained an arbitration clause. Consequently, there was scarcely doubt that it had been the intention of the parties that the arbitration clause should apply in the event of a dispute. Accordingly, the employment of general words of incorporation were held sufficient to incorporate the arbitration clause.

The part of primary importance in *Extrudakerb v White Mountain* is that the construction contracts were distinguished from shipping contracts, and it was provided by the High Court that

> while there were compelling reasons of commercial convenience for the perpetuation of the rule that, in relation to bills of lading, an arbitration clause could not be incorporated into the bill by reference to the terms of the charterparty without expressly referring to the bill, those reasons did not apply with the same degree of force in relation to construction of sub-contracts, where arbitration agreements were commonly found. It was open to the court to adopt an approach to the construction of such contracts which would put into effect the intention of the parties while demanding that the intention to incorporate the arbitration clause be established with sufficient clarity.[127]

Compatible with the analysis provided by Ralph Gibson LJ in *Aughton Ltd v M F Kent*,[128] it was reiterated that the contractual relationship in the context of construction shows great differences from one established in the shipping context.[129] Accordingly, the court was of the view that it is unfair to adopt the same strict rules of incorporation in these fundamentally different branches of law.

Another significant aspect of *Extrudakerb v White Mountain* was Carswell LJ giving weight to the assessment of the objective intention of the parties and applying the 'officious bystander test.'[130] The test fundamentally suggests for the purpose of inference of a term, 'to ask whether the term in question is so obvious that it goes without saying; so that if an officious bystander were to have suggested it at the time of the contract the parties would have replied "Oh, of course!" '[131] The learned judge, by applying this particular test, indicated that the parties agreed that the work would be done on the terms of the FCEC form of subcontract, in which the scope and context of it were known to them. Thus, the

127 [1996] NI 567 at [579].

128 [1991] 57 BLR 1.

129 Carswell LJ in *Extrudakerb (Maltby Engineering) Ltd v White Mountain Quarries* [1996] NI 567 at [579].

130 *Shirlaw v Southern Foundries [1926] Ltd* [1939] 2 KB 206 at 227, [1939] 2 All ER 113 at 124, CA, per MacKinnon LJ (affd [1940] AC 701, [1940] 2 All ER 445, HL). See also *Reigate v Union Manufacturing Co (Ramsbottom) Ltd* [1918] 1 KB 592, CA; *Re Comptoir Commercial Anversois and Power, Son & Co* [1920] 1 KB 868 at 899–900, CA; *McClelland v Northern Ireland General Health Services Board* [1957] 2 All ER 129; *Bronester Ltd v Priddle* [1961] 3 All ER 471; [1961] 1 WLR 1294 CA; *Liverpool City Council v Irwin* [1977] AC 239, 254; [1975] 2 All ER 39, 44, HL; *Lymington Marina Ltd v Macnamara* [2007] EWCA Civ 151; [2007] 2 All ER Comm 285.

131 Halsbury's Laws of England – officious bystander test.

parties were aware of the fact that the selected form of subcontract included an arbitration clause. Consequently, it was stated by the learned judge that 'if the officious bystander had been importunate enough to ask them if they considered that the arbitration clause should apply in the event of a dispute, I feel little doubt that the answer would have been clear that it would.'[132] As the parties were aware of the contents of the contract and thus, of the arbitration clause, they presumed to have clearly intended to incorporate the arbitration clause by means of referring to the FCEC form of subcontract. The officious bystander test is a significant tool at disposal to provide accurate assessments of contract interpretation and of what is truly known (or should be known) to the contracting parties involved in their ordinary course of business. Carswell LJ agreed because arbitration potentially precludes court jurisdiction, the clear manifestation of parties concerning the selection of this dispute resolution method over court litigation is generally a necessity. Nevertheless, he was not satisfied with such a 'mere potential' to overbalance party autonomy where the factual intention of the parties to refer their disputes to arbitration is vivid.

It may be noted that *Extrudakerb v White Mountain*, being a decision of the High Court of Northern Ireland, does not have a binding effect on the courts of England. However, it still constitutes persuasive authority and the judgement is of significance since the approach adopted by Ralph Gibson LJ in *Aughton* and the implementation of the officious bystander test as a method of assessing the true and expected knowledge of the contracting parties are the focal issues given weight to by the Irish court.

v. The Arbitration Act 1996 and the Departmental Advisory Committee (DAC) Report

The cases analyzed above predate the Arbitration Act 1996.[133] The Arbitration Act 1950 required arbitration agreements to be 'in writing' whereas at the same time lacked the definition of what constitutes being 'in writing.' The Arbitration Act 1996, on the other hand, elucidates some legal issues concerned with the formation of arbitration agreements. The requirement of arbitration agreements to be 'in writing' is retained in the Arbitration Act 1996 as well. Nevertheless, the Arbitration Act 1996 attempts to resolve the problems pertaining to the scope and definition of 'being in writing.' Section 5 of the Arbitration Act 1996 indicates that there is an agreement in writing if it is (1) made in writing, (2) made in exchange of communications, or (3) evidenced in writing. Hence, the definition of being in writing is expanded and somewhat explained in the Arbitration Act 1996.[134]

Furthermore, because the Arbitration Act 1996 expressly regulates the concept of incorporation under Section 6(2), the adoption of a blindfolded strict approach concerning the incorporation of arbitration clauses has perhaps turned into something inappropriate in light of this provision. The relevant section is as follows: 'The reference in an agreement to a written form of the arbitration clause or to a document containing an arbitration clause constitutes an arbitration agreement if the reference is such as to make that clause part of the agreement.' It is clear that no specific employment of words is needed for the incorporation of an arbitration clause as the relevant provision of the Arbitration Act 1996 is silent regarding such a requirement. On the other hand, the DAC Report emphasizes

132 [1996] NI 567 at [578].

133 Except *Extrudakerb v White Mountain Quarries* [1996] NI 567 being decided a month later than the passing of the Arbitration Act 1996. However, the act's provisions did not come into force until January 1997.

134 See Chapter 1, 'Foundations of Incorporation and Arbitration Clauses.'

that this is a matter to be left for the courts to decide. It was taken into consideration by the DAC that there have been inconsistent comments, particularly in *Aughton Ltd v M F Kent*, as to whether an arbitration clause could be regarded as incorporated only if it was specifically referred to, as this was the view of Sir John Megaw, or if the test was the lesser one of whether the intention to incorporate could be gleaned from the words used, as this was the view of Ralph Gibson LJ.[135] It may not be wrong to say that DAC, by means of refraining from supporting the strict approach adopted by Sir John Megaw in *Aughton*, favoured the view of Ralph Gibson LJ, indicating,

> It seemed to us . . . that although we are of the view that the approach of Ralph Gibson L.J. should prevail in all cases, this was really a matter for the court to decide. The wording we have used certainly leaves room for the adoption of the charterparty rules in all cases since it refers to references to a document containing an arbitration clause as well as a reference to the arbitration clause itself. Thus the wording is not confined to cases where there is a specific reference to the arbitration clause, which Sir John Megaw (but not Ralph Gibson L.J.) considered was a requirement for effective incorporation by reference.[136]

4.7. Concluding Remarks

Given the large number of parties and intertwined agreements in construction projects, disputes that possibly arise regarding the main construction contract or the subcontracts may have repercussions on each other. Because generally there is no contract between the employer and the subcontractor, there is of course no privity of contract between them. However, the complex and technical nature of construction projects may give rise to similar disputes and parallel arbitration proceedings. Alignment of the relevant construction contracts is usually of prime importance in dealing with these projects. This is because the alignment of corresponding provisions enables the establishment of well-structured contractual chains. The alignment may be achieved by means of drafting the contracts in a similar manner or by virtue of incorporation, and it is usually considered crucial in dealing with construction disputes.

Indeed, adjudication as a dispute resolution method plays a dominant role in construction disputes in the UK. This is because a construction dispute to be referred to this method is provided as a statutory right by the HGCR. However, arbitration has always been a favourable method of dispute resolution in this particular branch of law, and the narrow-scoped nature of adjudication does not go any further than spiking the guns of international arbitration. Indeed, many disputes are referred to adjudication because this is a quick and relatively cheaper method. Thinking about the realities of the construction business, speed and cost efficiency evidently attract the interests of the parties. The decisions being 'quick and dirty' are mostly considered less important than the cash flow to continue. Therefore, adjudication may indeed be argued to have 'killed domestic construction arbitration in the UK.'[137] On the other hand, for the resolution of construction disputes of international character, arbitration has always been regarded as a 'safe harbour.' Therefore, arbitration in

135 Merkin and Flannery (n 96) 139.
136 DAC Report para 42.
137 Laver (n 65).

construction disputes, and hence, the incorporation of arbitration clauses in the construction context, constitute significant concepts to be evaluated.

Shipping cases that are concerned with the incorporation of arbitration clauses by reference have more or less dominated many branches of law concerned with the same matter. In the shipping context, the usual litigious attitude of the courts is the implementation of restricted rules in assessing whether a charterparty arbitration clause is incorporated into bills of lading.[138] The employment of specific indications and express words of reference has almost always been the general requirement pertaining to incorporation in this particular branch of law. Furthermore, this general requirement has also found application in different branches of law, including construction.

Aughton Ltd v M F Kent[139] is of great significance in the sense that two judges in this case, Ralph Gibson LJ and Sir John Megaw, reaching the same conclusion, followed completely different routes. The judgement of Ralph Gibson LJ is particularly crucial as the learned judge, by distinguishing construction contracts from shipping contracts, emphasized that the strict principle in the shipping context is not directly applicable to construction contracts. It was stated by the learned judge that a specific reference to an arbitration clause in the construction context may not always be necessary, and the general words of incorporation may be deemed sufficient for the incorporation of an arbitration clause. The different approach of Sir John Megaw in *Aughton Ltd v M F Kent* concerning the incorporation of arbitration clauses is also evaluated in a relatively briefer way in this chapter. Even though the incorporation of the arbitration clause in *Aughton Ltd v M F Kent* was ultimately not allowed and the stay was eventually not granted, this was not due to arbitration clauses requiring specific treatment.

Furthermore, in *Extrudakerb v White Mountain*,[140] the approach of Ralph Gibson LJ was given specific weight to. An important aspect of this case is that the ascertainment of the objective intention of the parties was particularly considered by Carswell LJ and the officious bystander test was applied. The test suggests, for the purpose of inference of a term, 'to ask whether the term in question is so obvious that it goes without saying; so that if an officious bystander were to have suggested it at the time of the contract the parties would have replied "Oh, of course!"'[141] Considering the realities of the construction market, the application of this particular test seems more than convenient. At the end of the day, the actual knowledge concerning the potential incorporation of an arbitration clause is of great significance. Construction business may be regarded a bit differently from any other. This is because for the formation of an initial construction contract, almost all of the infrastructure planning and work must have been done in the first place. A construction project usually has many aspects that are foreseeably not possible to be executed by a single party. The actors of this market are usually involved in multi-layered contractual structures. Especially in international construction projects, arbitration is often the preferred dispute resolution method. Therefore, the following two aspects looking over this branch of law regarding the incorporation of arbitration clauses essentially draw attention: (1) the substantial differences between construction contracts with shipping documents and hence the different criteria

138 *T. W. Thomas & Co. Ltd. v Portsea Steamship Co Ltd, The Portsmouth* [1912] A.C. 1.

139 [1991] 57 BLR 1.

140 [1996] NI 567.

141 Halsbury's Laws of England – officious bystander test.

that they should be subject to when it comes to the incorporation of arbitration clauses and (2) the necessity of implementing the officious bystander test and assessing the actual knowledge of the parties regarding the potential incorporation of an arbitration clause.

Bibliography

Albino, V., and Garavelli, A. C., A Neural Network Application to Subcontractor Rating in Construction Firms, 1998, *International Journal of Project Management*, 16.

Baron, Adrian, The International Arbitration Act, the Fiction of Severability and Claims for Restitution – Part Two, 2000, *Arbitration International*, 16(2), 159–188.

Benjoran, Vacharapoom, A Cost Control System Development: A Collaborative Approach for Small and Medium-Sized Contractors, 2009, *International Journal of Project Management*, 27, 270–277.

Brekoulakis, Stavros, *Third Parties in International Commercial Arbitration*, Oxford University Press, 2010.

Brekoulakis, Stavros and El Far, Ahmed, Subcontracts and Multiparty Arbitration in Construction Disputes, in Stavros Brekoulakis and David Brynmor Thomas (eds.) *Global Arbitration Review*, The Guide to Construction Arbitration, 2017, 87–99.

Cavaleri, Sylvie Cécile, *Concurrent Delay in Construction Disputes*, Werlauff Publishing, 2015.

Cavaleri, Sylvie Cécile, Construction Adjudication in a Comparative Perspective: The Case of the Danish Speedy Resolution, 2022, *The International Construction Law Review*, 169–189.

Choat, Rupert, Arbitration and Adjudication: A Tale of Two Acts, *Building*, October 9, 2015, available at www.building.co.uk/communities/arbitration-and-adjudication-a-tale-of-two-acts/5078023.article.

Coulson, Peter, *Coulson on Construction Adjudication*, Oxford University Press, 2015, 3rd Edn.

Davies, Lawrence, *Adjudication Versus Other Approaches to Construction Disputes*, Out-Law Guide, November 23, 2018, available at www.pinsentmasons.com/out-law/guides/adjudication-construction-disputes.

Geary Walker & Co. Ltd. v Lawrence & Son, *Hudson Building Contracts*, Geary Walker & Co. Ltd., 1906, 4th Edn., Vol. 2.

Gould, Nicholas, *Subcontracts*, Fenwick & Elliott, February 2012.

Guidance Note: The Scheme for Construction Contracts, *The Chartered Institute of Arbitrators & Adjudication Society*, 2020, 2, available at www.ciarb.org/media/4163/the-scheme-for-construction-contracts.pdf.

Hughes, Will, Champion, Ronan and Murdoch, John, *Construction Contracts: Law and Management*, Routledge, 2015, 5th Edn.

Kiefer, David and Cole, Adrian, Suitability of Arbitration Rules for Construction Disputes, in Stavros Brekoulakis and David Brynmor Thomas (eds.) *Global Arbitration Review*, The Guide to Construction Arbitration, 2017, 81–86.

Kondev, Dimitar, Do Recent Overhauls of Arbitration Rules Respond to the Need for Multi-Party Arbitration in the Construction Industry?, 2015, *International Construction Law Review*, 32.

Kondev, Dimitar, *Multi-Party and Multi-Contract Arbitration in the Construction Industry*, Wiley-Blackwell, 2017.

Korale, Jagath C. and Weddikkara, Chitra, *The Impact of Inclusion of Arbitration Clause by Reference in Main Contract and Subcontract Documents in the Construction Industry and Its Negative Connotations*, World Construction Conference 2012 – Global Challenges in Construction Industry, Colombo, Sri Lanka, June 28–30, 2012.

Kumaraswamy, M. M. and Matthews, J., Improved Subcontractor Selection Employing Partnering Principles, 2000, *ASCE Journal of Management in Engineering*, 16.

Laver, Nicola, Interview with Hamish Lal, *The Evolving Role of Arbitration in Construction Disputes*, Hardwick Legal Solicitors, June 15, 2017.

McGuinness, J., *The Law and Management of Building Subcontracts*, Blackwell Publishing, 2007, 2nd Edn.

Merkin, Robert and Flannery, Louis, *Merkin and Flannery on the Arbitration Act 1996*, Informa Law from Routledge, 2020.

Molloy, Matt, *Arbitrating After Adjudication*, Practical Law Construction Blog, March 19, 2013.

Paola, Luigi Di, Back-to-Back Contracts, 2009, *International Construction Law Review*, 26, 489.

Pulkowski, J. Florian, The Subcontractor's Direct Claim in International Business Law, 2004, *International Construction Law Review*, 21, 31.

Quick and Dirty Dispute Resolution, June 22, 2015, Association of Mediation Assessors, Trainers and Instructors.

Rhodes, Chris, *Construction Industry: Statistics and Policy*, House of Commons Library Briefing Paper 01432, December 27, 2018.

Rousell, Michelle, *Contractual Adjudication Using the Scheme for Construction Contracts*, Thomson Reuters, Practical Law Construction Blog, January 15, 2010.

Sallman, Peter, The Impact of Caseflow Managemenet in the Judicial System, 1995, *University of New South Wales Law Journal*, 18, 193.

Standard Industrial Classification (UKSIC): Construction Is Section F, Made Up of Codes: 41–43, available at https://www.ons.gov.uk/file?uri=/methodology/classificationsandstandards/ukstandardindustrialclassificationofeconomicactivities/uksic2007/uksic2007web.pdf.

Steingruber, Andrea M., *Consent in International Arbitration*, Oxford University Press, 2012.

User's Guide to Adjudication, Construction Industry Council, 2017, available at www.architecture.com/-/media/gathercontent/work-with-us/additional-documents/usersguidetoadjudicationcicpdf.pdf (last visited July 13, 2022).

Wallace, I. N. Duncan, *Hudson's Building and Engineering Contracts*, Sweet & Maxwell, 1995, Vol. 2., 11th Edn.

Yoke-Lian, Lew and Hassim, S., Review of Subcontracting Practice in Construction Industry, August 2012, *IACSIT International Journal of Engineering and Technology*, 4(4), 442–445.

CHAPTER 5

Singapore Law and Incorporation of Arbitration Clauses

5. Singapore Law and Arbitration

In an attempt to explore the legal concept of incorporating arbitration clauses, specific weight is given to Singapore arbitration in this chapter. The particular reason for this is that Singapore, being a common law jurisdiction, has been under the large influence of the decisions of English courts and English contract law. Correspondingly, some well-settled English principles, such as the 'restricted rule' that generally necessitates the employment of specific words of incorporation, have dominated the practice in relevant areas of law in this specific jurisdiction. Some English contract law principles had an undeniable impact on the 'shaping process' of the relevant law of Singapore. It is true that the decisions of English courts are not binding in the legal system of Singapore, but they may indeed be used for interpretative purposes. Accordingly, the implementation of some of these principles has shown parallels with some of the decisions of the English courts, in which they find application, even after the Republic of Singapore officially became independent on August 9, 1965, subsequent to some 140 years of British rule on the territory.

Nevertheless, some of these principles do not seem to find wide application in Singapore law anymore as this particular jurisprudence has been showing signs of deviation from its somewhat of a parallel application with English law over recent decades. What we are fundamentally witnessing now is the evolution of Singapore law in accordance with the desire of the country to become an internationally leading arbitration hub and create its own autochthonous jurisprudence. 'The Singaporean deviation' may particularly be found observable in the abstinence of Singaporean courts from straightforwardly applying the English 'restricted rule of incorporation' and in the general implementation of contextual interpretation in this jurisdiction.

According to the Report of the Chartered Institute of Arbitrators (CIArb) titled 'Securing the UK's position as a global disputes hub: Best practice lessons between Singapore and the UK,'

> [The Singapore] government provides invaluable holistic and long-term strategic thinking that enables the sector to transcend more transitory short-term concerns. Linked to this is the significance of government funding for the sector, and the readiness of the government to back-up its aspirations for the sector – both domestically and internationally – with concrete political action.[1]

1 *Securing the UK's Position as a Global Disputes Hub: Best Practice Lessons Between Singapore and the UK*, 2020, The Chartered Institute of Arbitrators (CIArb) Report of the All-Party Parliamentary Group for Alternative Dispute Resolution (researched and funded by Chartered Institute of Arbitrators), available at www.ciarb.org/media/14995/appg-report_digital-new.pdf.

DOI: 10.4324/9781003268673-6

Consequently, the government proactively promotes the international dispute resolution market.[2] To put it differently, Singapore does not abstain from allocating necessary resources and time in the battle for the throne.

This chapter analyzes the Singaporean approach concerning the incorporation of arbitration clauses before and after the indicated deviation took place. It does so by means of examining relevant Singaporean cases in light of reasons that may have led courts to seek alternative applications other than some English law principles.

5.1. Singapore Arbitration at a Glance

In recent years, Singapore has made remarkable strides in fulfilling its ambition of becoming a preferred international arbitration hub,[3] and it is the most popular seat for international arbitration in Asia.[4] Singapore, as a global arbitration hub, has been challenging the position of well-established arbitration centeres, such as London, Paris, and Hong Kong, and just recently it took 'top arbitration slot along with London for first time.'[5] The year 2021 was the fifth consecutive year that SIAC's caseload has exceeded 400 and the total sum in dispute was $6.54 billion (the highest sum in dispute for a single administrated case was $1.95 billion, which is more than twice the highest sum in dispute in 2020).[6] Furthermore, 86% of the cases handled by SIAC in 2021 were international in nature.[7]

The statistics illustrate that the submission rate to Singapore arbitration has increased vigorously over the years and there is no doubt the trend will be an upward one for the foreseeable future. 'An unequivocal judicial policy of facilitating arbitration has firmly taken root in Singapore'[8] in compliance with its aspiration of becoming the preferred hub for international arbitration. Furthermore, generally, the approach of 'minimal intervention' is adopted in Singapore arbitration due to 'the need to respect party autonomy (manifested by their contractual bargain) in deciding both the method of dispute resolution and the procedural rules to be applied.'[9] The statistics may be considered to indicate that the global arbitration market generally responded positively to the adoption of this non-interventionist approach and 'Singapore's progressive and pro-arbitration judicial policy.'[10]

---

2 Anastasia Medvedskaya, London vs Singapore: A (False) Struggle for the Title of World's Leading Seat of Arbitration, *Jus Mundi*, September 24, 2021, available at https://blog.jusmundi.com/london-vs-singapore-a-false-struggle-for-the-title-of-worlds-leading-seat-of-arbitration/ (last visited August 10, 2022).

3 Singapore Parliamentary Debates, Official Report, October 31, 1994, Vol. 63, Cols. 625–627. See also Harisankar K. Sathyapalan, International Commercial Arbitration in Asia and the Choice of Law Determination, 2013, *Journal of Integrative Agriculture*, 30, 621–636, 625.

4 John Choong, Mark Mangan, and Nicholas Lingard, *A Guide to the SIAC Arbitration Rules*, Oxford University Press, 2018, 1–18, 1.

5 Jane Croft, Singapore Takes Top Arbitration Slot Along with London for First Time, *Financial Times*, May 6, 2021, available at www.ft.com/content/7942f589-8b73-4e51-aad9-7780e9fab2c0 (last visited August 10, 2022).

6 *SIAC Annual Report 2021*, available at www.SIAC-AR2021-FinalFA.pdf.

7 Ibid.

8 *Tjong Very Sumito v Antig Investments* [2009] SGCA 41 at [28].

9 Ibid.

10 Nicholas Poon, Reconsidering the Enforceability of Bare Intention to Arbitrate – *KVC Rice Intertrade Co Ltd v Asian Mineral Resources Pte Ltd* [2017] SGHC 32, 2017, *Singapore Academy of Law Journal*, 29, 540–551, 540.

5.2. Singapore Law and English Law

This part fundamentally investigates the similarities and differences of Singapore law and English law concerning the applications of both these legal systems dealing with the incorporation of arbitration clauses between chain contracts. Singapore law is specifically chosen as one of the subjects of such an investigation because it represents an immigrant society and accordingly, it finds its roots in the laws of different nations.[11] Some elements that created the foundations of Singapore's legal system are predominantly derived from English law.[12] Even after Singapore's independence in 1965, English law remained to be the dominant influence, and its principles are still undeniably reflected in the legal system of Singapore.[13] Thus, the connection between English law and Singapore law goes back decades and continues to exist even up to the present time. By virtue of their long-standing correlation, the well-established overall effect of English law on this legal system is irrefragable. Consequently, it is unsurprising that some principles of English law on arbitration are also echoed in Singapore law.[14]

The relevant examples reflecting the bountifulness of English law are illustrated in the chapters analyzing the incorporation of arbitration clauses in chain contracts in this jurisdiction.[15] The English Arbitration Act 1996 is designed in compliance with Model Law, which is drafted by the United Nations Commission on International Trade Law (UNCITRAL) and sets standards for harmonizing national arbitration laws.[16] Therefore, it would not be wrong to say that most of the main problems arising under Model Law had their way through English litigation.[17] Nevertheless, it should be noted that although the English Arbitration Act 1996 contains many provisions derived from the Model Law, the English law has not adopted it in its entirety. The Model Law principles promote the prevalence of party intention and autonomy. This is manifested in the relevant part of Model Law remarking 'in fulfilling the requirements of international commercial arbitration . . . the parties should be free to agree on how their arbitration should be conducted.'[18] The

---

11 Yihan Goh and Paul Tan, An Empirical Study on the Development of Singapore Law, 2011, *Singapore Academy of Law Journal*, 177. Predominantly influenced by English law, Singapore's legislative and common law origins also find inspiration from other jurisdictions, such as Australia (land law and company law) and India (from which Singapore Penal Code and Evidence Act were imported).

12 Andrew Phang, Reception of English Law in Singapore: Problems and Proposed Solutions, 1990, *Singapore Academy of Law Journal*, 2, 20.

13 Goh and Tan (n 12) 177.

14 Robert Merkin and Johanna Hjalmarsson, *Singapore Arbitration Legislation*, Informa Law from Routledge, 2016, Annoted, 3.

15 The main bills of lading authorities are *T. W. Thomas & Co. Ltd. v Portsea Steamship Co Ltd, The Portsmouth* [1912] A.C. 1 (*Thomas v Portsea*); *The Elizabeth H* [1962] 1 Lloyd's Rep 172; *The Merak* [1964] 2 Lloyd's Rep 527; *The Annefield* [1971] 1 Lloyd's Rep 1; *The Rena K* [1978] 1 Lloyd's Rep 545; *The Varenna* [1983] 1 Lloyd's Rep 416; *Federal Bulk Carriers Inc v C Itoh & Co Ltd (The Federal Bulker)* [1989] 1 Lloyd's Rep 103; *The Nerano* [1994] 2 Lloyd's Rep 50; and *The Heidberg* [1994] 2 Lloyd's Rep 287; *The Delos* [2001] 1 Lloyd's Rep 703. Leading reinsurance cases are *Pine Top Insurance Co v Unione Italiana Anglo Saxon Reinsurance Co Ltd* [1987] 1 Lloyd's Rep 476; *Excess Insurance v Mander* [1997] 2 Lloyd's Rep 119; and *Trygg Hansa Insurance Co Ltd v Equitas* [1998] 2 Lloyd's Rep 439. The leading construction decisions are *Modern Building Wales Ltd v Limmer & Trinidad Co Limited* [1975] 2 Lloyd's Rep 318; *Aughton Ltd v M.F. Kent Services Ltd* [1991] 57 BLR 1; and *Extrudakerb (Maltby Engineering) Ltd v White Mountain Quarries* [1996] NI 567.

16 Merkin and Hjalmarsson (n 15) 2.

17 Ibid 5.

18 UNCITRAL Model Law on International Commercial Arbitration Explanatory Documentation Prepared for Commonwealth Jurisdictions, 1.11(1), 1991, available at www.uncitral.org/pdf/english/texts/arbitration/ml-arb/Model-Law-Arbitration-Commonwealth.pdf.

manifestation suggests that Model Law adopts a non-interventionist approach, which may also be considered to promote the adoption of more liberal methods regarding the incorporation of arbitration clauses in chain contracts. It is true that the parties are free to choose the principles that are applicable to their arbitration and have a certain freedom to bend the rules governing the arbitration process as a whole. This inevitably raises the question of whether the incorporation of an arbitration clause should be excluded from the entirety of this structure and, if so, why. Provided that the incorporation of an arbitration clause is clearly reflecting the vivid and ascertainable intention of the parties to incorporate it so, a non-interventionist approach may be found appropriately applicable to all aspects of the arbitration process, in a way possibly including the incorporation of the arbitration agreement, which initially gave birth to the process, too.

Containing many provisions based upon the Model Law, the English Arbitration Act 1996 clearly allows the incorporation of arbitration clauses by reference and regulates this matter. Nevertheless, it may be considered to be a silent piece of legislation concerning the level of court intervention in the arbitration process allowed, and as the DAC Report frankly admits, it leaves this issue to the discretion of the courts. It is true that English law has not adopted the entirety of the Model Law. However, it is also true that the English Arbitration Act 1996 widely reflects the provisions of the Model Law. Accordingly, a couple of deductions may be made. First, it may be argued that the incorporation of arbitration clauses as a notion may be deemed to constitute a part of the overall arbitration as it establishes the foundation of the whole process. Second, being one of its principal features, Model Law promotes the prevalence of party autonomy over the 'arbitration process.' Accordingly, it may be possible to expand the scope of the 'arbitration process' in a way to include the 'process of incorporation' and, hence, the latter to be subject to less strict criteria of implementation. Nonetheless, there are indeed numerous examples in English law in which the strict approach concerning the incorporation of arbitration clauses prevailed to enable the promotion of commercial certainty and jurisdictional foreseeability (especially in the shipping context)[19] even sometimes at the cost of party autonomy.

5.3. Background of Singapore Arbitration Legislation

5.3.1. Duality: International Arbitration and Domestic Arbitration

Singapore has two parallel arbitration systems: a domestic one, which is legislated under the Arbitration Act 2001,[20] and an international one, enshrined in the International Arbitration Act 1994.[21] One of the essential reasons for establishing such a dual system may be argued to have derived from the desire to make Singapore appealing as an international arbitration hub.[22] In order to achieve such a goal, the compatibility with internationally accepted rules had to be clearly demonstrated and accordingly, Singapore International Arbitration Act 1994 implemented the Model Law 1985 into Singapore law. The Act is based on the Model Law and aims to give effect to the New York Convention on the Recognition and

19 *T. W. Thomas & Co. Ltd. v Portsea Steamship Co Ltd, The Portsmouth* [1912] A.C. 1. (*Thomas v Portsea*).

20 Singapore Arbitration Act 2001, published in revised form in 2002.

21 Singapore International Arbitration Act 1994. The act was significantly amended by the International Arbitration (Amendment) Act 2012 (No.12 of 2012).

22 Merkin and Hjalmarsson (n 15) 4.

Enforcement of Foreign Arbitral Awards (New York Arbitration Convention) 1958 and for matters connected therewith.

The structure and wording of the arbitration clause would manifest the selection of the parties concerning the applicability of one of these pieces of legislation (national or international) to their existing and future disputes. If the parties to the arbitration agreement have their places of business outside of Singapore and wish to conduct the arbitration under Singaporean rules, then the legislation applicable would be the International Arbitration Act 1994. However, the parties may choose for the Arbitration Act 2001, which in fact has a national character, to be applicable to their dispute instead,[23] and thus 'opt out' of the governance of the International Arbitration Act 1994. The selection of the Arbitration Act 2001 would facilitate the conduct of a greater degree of court supervision over the dispute and hence, may be considered preferable instead of the application of the International Arbitration Act 1994. On the other hand, if the parties have their place of business in Singapore, they would normally be subject to the application of the Arbitration Act 2001. Likewise, they may prefer to 'opt in' and prefer International Arbitration Act 1994 to be applicable and, therefore, choose to be subject to the supervision of the court to a lesser extent than they would be subject to under the application of the Arbitration Act 2001.

The provided options of opting in and out concerning the governance of the indicated pieces of legislation that would normally apply by default depending on the domestic or international character of the dispute, seem to be in line with the non-interventionist character of the Model Law. These options provide freedom to parties concerning the selection of the rules applicable to the resolution of their dispute and the determination of the level of potential court intervention they may wish their dispute to be subject to. Accordingly, this legal system provides a scale concerning the amount of court intervention that may take place and the freedom to select the weight of such possible intervention. Singapore arbitration legislation provides a dual system that is enabling parties to choose between the application of two different pieces of legislation and select the one, which they consider more suitable to their dispute.

5.3.2. Stay of Judicial Proceedings

The freedom of parties to opt in and out of domestic and international arbitration systems in Singapore law enables them to determine the level of potential court intervention that may be applicable to their dispute. The term 'court intervention' here may be interpreted as the assessment of the bare minimum that would lead the court to grant a stay of its proceedings. Singapore Arbitration Act 2001 and Singapore International Arbitration Act 1994 have specific provisions governing the implementation of a stay.

Concerning domestic arbitrations, the intervention of the court would usually extensively be possible, and a party may appeal to the court as long as such an application meets certain criteria of the law. This is because the application of the non-interventionist approach is usually found unsuitable for domestic disputes between small businesses and consumers[24]

23 Section 15(1) of the International Arbitration Act 1994 (Singapore).
24 Merkin and Hjalmarsson (n 15) 3.

as such parties may lack awareness concerning the arbitration process, and this may necessitate the procurement of a greater degree of legal protection for them.

Another reason for allowing the involvement of the court in disputes of national character is because there is no specific legislation in Singapore that protects small businesses and consumers from the possibly 'unreasonable' contract terms.[25] The courts have a discretionary right to grant a stay under Section 6 of the Singapore Arbitration Act 2001 for disputes of national character and they may decide not to grant one if they assess that the circumstances do not necessitate this. A party may apply for a stay if the following conditions are met: (1) the applicant is a party to the arbitration agreement, (2) the agreement covers the matter in dispute before the court, (3) the applicant has not delivered any pleading or taken any step in the proceedings other than the entry of an appearance, and (4) the applicant remains ready and willing to arbitrate.[26] Following the application, the courts would apply a test and consider whether there is 'no sufficient reason why the matter should not be referred to arbitration,' according to Section 6(2)(a) of the Singapore Arbitration Act 2001. Nevertheless, it should perhaps be noted that in accordance with the discretionary nature of the courts' right to grant a stay and perhaps to provide some room for wider interpretation, this particular piece of legislation does not clarify 'what circumstances would constitute a sufficient reason for not referring the matter to arbitration.'[27] However, even though granting a stay is a discretionary right, it may be argued that the courts of Singapore would usually be inclined to grant a stay if the aforementioned conditions are met.[28] This may be considered to be showing compatibility with the general pro-arbitration climate in Singapore.

On the other hand, the International Arbitration Act 1994 (Art 8 of the Model Law) makes it mandatory for the court to grant a stay provided the legislative conditions are met. Section 6 of the Singapore International Arbitration Act 1994 stipulates that 'stay of the judicial proceedings, which are brought in respect of any matter which the parties have agreed to refer to arbitration'[29] would be mandatory. Accordingly, courts would grant a stay unless satisfied that no arbitration agreement exists or the existing one is 'null and void, inoperative or incapable of being performed.'[30] It is similarly clear from the language of Section 9(4) of the English Arbitration Act 1996 that a stay to be granted is also mandatory in England as the section stipulates that 'the court shall grant a stay unless satisfied that the arbitration agreement is null and void, inoperative, or incapable of being performed.'[31]

5.3.3. Where Does This Leave Us?

Singapore, being a former British colony and now a republic that forms a part of the common law system, adopted several principles in its arbitration law that are enshrined in the English Arbitration Act 1996. One of the fundamental reasons for this is that England

25 Ibid. Unlike the UK Unfair Contract Terms Act 1977, which is applicable in English law context.

26 Michael Moser and John Choong, *Asia Arbitration Handbook*, Oxford University Press, 2011, 690, 15.115.

27 Ibid 15.116.

28 Ibid.

29 Merkin and Hjalmarsson (n 15) 27.

30 Section 6(2) of the Singapore International Arbitration Act 1994.

31 Section 9(4) of the English Arbitration Act 1996. Also see *Halki Shipping Corporation v Sopex Oils Ltd* [1998] 1 Lloyd's Rep 465 (CA).

is the most prosperous source of case law on arbitration legislation[32] and, therefore, has an undeniable impact on the global market of international arbitration.

As it is in the rest of the common law jurisdictions, it is also well-settled in Singapore that courts will prioritize an arbitration agreement provided the substantial constructive elements of such an agreement are manifested. The jealousy of arbitration of the courts may no longer be presumed to widely exist as indicated in an English decision, *Eagle Star Insurance Co v Yuval Insurance*, 'at one time the Courts used to be very jealous of arbitrations. They used to find all sorts of reasons for interfering with arbitrators and their awards. But the approach to arbitration has changed in modern days.'[33] This particular case, being decided over some 40 years ago, clearly reveals that even back then the tables were turning.

It was emphasized in *Tjong Very Sumito v Antig Investments Pte Ltd*[34] that, provided the intention of the parties to arbitrate is ascertainable, Singapore courts will be in favour of this method of dispute resolution in the interests of expediency and party autonomy. It is stated by V K Rajah JA that

> [t]here was a time when arbitration was viewed disdainfully as an inferior process of justice. Those days are now well behind us. An unequivocal judicial policy of facilitating and promoting arbitration has firmly taken root in Singapore. It is now openly acknowledged that arbitration . . . help(s) to effectively unclog the arteries of judicial administration as well as offer(s) parties realistic choices on how they want to resolve their disputes at a pace they are comfortable with. More fundamentally, the need to respect party autonomy in deciding both the method of dispute resolution as well as the substantive law to govern the contract, has been accepted as the cornerstone element underlying judicial non-intervention in arbitration. In essence, a court ought to give effect to parties' contractual choice as to the manner of dispute resolution unless it offends the law.[35]

Furthermore, Singapore courts will be inclined to promote arbitration provided the intention of the parties to arbitrate is ascertainable even under circumstances where the scope of such an intention is perhaps questionable, as this was the case in *KVC Rice Intertrade Co Ltd v Asian Mineral Resources Pte Ltd.*[36]

It is evident that where the selection concerning the dispute resolution method is clearly manifested, courts will respect the wishes of the parties. Nonetheless, such manifestation may be difficult to assess especially dealing with chain contracts involving multiple parties. The issue gets even more complex where the possibility of incorporating an arbitration clause by reference is added to the equation.

Courts of different jurisdictions may require different obligations to be fulfilled to allow the incorporation of arbitration agreements. Furthermore, there may be different methods of contract interpretation, and therefore, courts of different legal systems may decide differently on the nature of the contractual relationship before them. Making the relevant assessments would clearly affect the outcome. Thus, the comparison of English law and Singapore law on the matter provides an interesting analysis. The

32 Merkin and Hjalmarsson (n 15) 5.
33 [1978] 1 Lloyd's Rep 357 (CA) at [360].
34 [2009] SGCA 41.
35 [2009] SGCA 41 at [28].
36 [2017] SGHC 32 (*KVC Rice v Asian Mineral*). The case is concerned with a 'bare' arbitration agreement.

relevant developments in the said jurisdictions have shown quite a parallel emergence until the point when Singaporean case law eventually started to show signs of deviation. Nevertheless, the relevant English legal principles have undeniably affected the approach adopted by Singaporean courts concerning the incorporation of arbitration clauses.

Accordingly, to shed light on how the incorporation of arbitration clauses works in the Singaporean context, one must initially evaluate some crucial cases concerned with this matter, taking the impact of the relevant English law principles on Singapore arbitration law into account. This would further elicit at what point the English impact had begun to fade away, and Singapore law made a deviation from the parallel pathways that the implementations of the said jurisdictions created.

5.4. Incorporation of Arbitration Clauses in Singapore Law

5.4.1. The Strict Rule of Incorporation

Determining whether an arbitration clause is incorporated is rather crucial as it designates whether parties will be subject to arbitration proceedings rather than court proceedings. Therefore, the applicable principles concerning the assessment of the methods of incorporation of arbitration clauses are equally important.

With regard to the incorporation of arbitration clauses, there are well-established principles fundamentally stemming from English law. The relevant English jurisprudence, which is derived from the implementation of these principles, provides a non-binding guideline for other courts of common law that is generally used for interpretative purposes.

English law predominantly applies the test of the strict rule of incorporation that fundamentally requires specific and express words of incorporation to be employed for the purposes of incorporating arbitration clauses by reference in chain contracts. Some recent examples of English case law further implement the 'scenarios theory' that promotes the examination of the essence of contractual relationships in a multi-layered contractual structure. To be able to assess how these principles have influenced Singapore courts over the years, first, the fundamentals of them and, second, their implementation in the Singaporean context are evaluated.

Where a party seeks to incorporate the terms of one contract between different parties into another contract, general words of incorporation will normally not be sufficient to incorporate the dispute resolution provision. Being analyzed under the chapters concerning bills of lading incorporating charterparties, reinsurance contracts incorporating insurance contracts, and construction subcontracts incorporating construction contracts, English law predominantly adopts a strict rule/restricted approach in dealing with the incorporation of arbitration clauses. Accordingly, the employment of clear and express words of incorporation constitutes a general requirement to be able to incorporate an arbitration clause. Such a requirement appears to be projecting a formalistic attitude and prioritization of legal certainty. Nonetheless, the justification of the required level of strictness may be found debatable in occasions where such a restricted approach possibly trivializes the promotion of party autonomy for the sake of promoting legal/commercial certainty.

The implementation of the strict rule of incorporation is highlighted in the shipping context in a landmark House of Lord decision *T W Thomas & Co Ltd v Portsea Steamship*

Co Ltd, The Portsmouth.[37] The decision fundamentally found its grounds in the fact that bills of lading are negotiable instruments and this generally necessitates the employment of specific words of incorporation to enable the protection of the possibly oblivious third party. The negotiable nature of bills of lading was noted by Lord Robson, and it was indicated that if it were to seek to deprive either party of their 'ordinary legal remedies,' then the wording 'cannot be too explicit and precise.'[38]

The strict rule of incorporation is indeed a well-settled one in English law, especially in the shipping context dealing with charterparties and negotiable bills of lading. The third-party holder of a bill of lading may have no knowledge of the charterparty terms that contain an arbitration clause, which potentially may deprive such oblivious third party of their 'ordinary legal remedy' of being heard before a court. The general invisibility and inaccessibility of charterparty terms usually necessitate a substantial level of protection to be extended to third parties.

Even though the application of this may not be found justifiable under all circumstances,[39] it still provides a solid starting point for cases particularly concerned with bills of lading incorporating charterparty arbitration clauses. The promotion of commercial certainty has usually been asserted to necessitate the implementation of the strict rule of incorporation.[40] This is because the strict rule fundamentally targets the protection of the oblivious holder of the bill of lading, who is not required to have knowledge of the terms of the underlying charterparty or may not be in a position to discover these. In other words, the strict rule of incorporation finds its roots in the shipping context. However, the restricted approach of incorporation is usually not confined to bills of lading and it also applies in different contexts involving multi-layered contracts and multiple parties despite its appropriateness may often be found problematic. The realm of its application frequently extends widely that it even applies in the contexts of reinsurance[41] and construction[42] despite these branches of law being concerned with contractual relationships of fundamentally different natures. As a general rule, an arbitration clause in a contract between A and B would not be incorporated into a contract between B and C unless express words of incorporation to do this so are employed.[43]

In *Star-Trans Far East Pte Ltd v Norske-Tech Ltd and Others*,[44] by following the English Court of Appeal decision in *Aughton Ltd v MF Kent Services Ltd*,[45] the Singapore Court of

---

37 [1912] AC 1. (*Thomas v Portsea*).

38 Ibid 10.

39 *Sea Trade Maritime Corp v Hellenic Mutual War Risks Association (Bermuda) Ltd (The Athena)* [2006] EWHC 2530 (Comm); see *Habas Sinai Ve Tibbi Gazlar Isthisal Endustri AS v Sometal SAL* [2010] EWHC 29 (Comm) at [13] (*Habas Sinai v Sometal*).

40 Joseph David explains in his treatise, *Jurisdiction and Arbitration Agreements and their Enforcement*, Sweet & Maxwell, 2010, 2nd Edn., 5.15.

41 An English law that is concerned with incorporation of arbitration clause: *Pine Top Insurance Co v Unione Italiana Anglo Saxon Reinsurance Co Ltd* [1987] 1 Lloyd's Rep 476.

42 In respect of construction subcontracts incorporating the arbitration clause contained in the underlying construction contract, the main case can be regarded as *Aughton Ltd v MF Kent Services Ltd* [1991] 57 BLR 1. (*Aughton*).

43 See *L&M Concrete Specialists Pte Ltd v United Eng Contractors Pte Ltd* [2000] 2 SLR(R) 852 at 18 where it was held by the court that for an arbitration agreement in one contract to be incorporated into another, it must be brought to the attention of the other contracting party with a 'red hand pointing to it.'

44 [1996] 2 SLR(R) 196 (*Star-Trans*).

45 [1991] 57 BLR 1.

Appeal ruled that clear and express reference to an arbitration clause in a distinct contract was required to allow the incorporation of such a clause into a separate contract. The principle further remained applicable for many years. However, some recent Singapore cases are indicating a clear deviation from the straightforward adoption of the strict rule of incorporation. The foundations of the deviation also seem to bare some similarities with the principles of the English 'scenarios theory' that finds its roots in *Sea Trade Maritime Corp v Hellenic Mutual War Risks Association (Bermuda)Ltd*[46] that later further developed in *Habas Sinai v Sometal.*[47] The scenarios theory simply suggests that the material distinction between 'one-contract' and 'two-contract' cases depends on whether the contracts in question were concluded between the same or different parties. It suggests that the involvement of a third party in the contractual structure would necessitate the adoption of a more restrictive approach concerning incorporation, and this would create the situation of multiple contracts falling into the scope of the two-contact category. The multi-layered structure of the contractual relationship would be deemed to be obscuring the intention of the parties to the main contract to incorporate the dispute resolution clause of the incorporated contract among other provisions of it. In other words, the intention would be presumed not as clear as it would be under a one-contract scenario. Keeping in mind that Singapore law finds its merits in English law, English principles such as 'the strict rule of incorporation' and 'the scenarios theory' have evidently been effective in Singaporean case law.

I. Star-Trans – Adopting the Strict English Rule

The strict rule of incorporation found application in Singapore jurisprudence in 1996[48] and was applied by the Singapore Court of Appeal in *Star-Trans.*[49] Star-Trans, a freight forwarder, had entered into a contract with Norske-Tech and Speditor. The purpose of this contract was for Star-Trans and Speditor to organize ocean carriage of goods to a construction site in Indonesia for Norske-Tech, who had undertaken the construction project and the said contract included an arbitration clause. Another company, PT Riau, had provided a performance guarantee to secure the performance of Norske-Tech of its contractual obligations. The performance guarantee included the signatures of Star-Trans, Norske-Tech, and PT Ritau. After disputes arose between Star-Trans, Norske-Tech, and PT Ritau, Star-Trans commenced court proceedings. Norske-Tech and PT Ritau applied for a stay on the ground that Star-Trans, in fact, had agreed to refer disputes that may arise between the said parties to the arbitration.

One of the primary issues before the court was to determine whether PT Ritau was a party to the contract before the court, due to providing the performance guarantee for Norske-Tech concerning the fulfilment of their contractual obligations. Clause 3 of the performance guarantee stated that 'all the rights of Norske-Tech under the contract may

46 [2006] EWHC 2530 (Comm).
47 [2010] EWHC 29 (Comm).
48 Subramanian Pillai, Singapore: Case Update – 'International Research Corp PLC v Lufthansa Systems Asia Pacific Pte Ltd and Another [2013] SGCA 55,' *Mondaq*, January 31, 2014, available at www.mondaq.com/x/289470/Arbitration+Dispute+Resolution/Case+Update+International+Research+Corp+PLC+v+Lufthansa+Systems+Asia+Pacific+Pte+Ltd+and+another+2013+SGCA+55 (last visited August 10, 2022).
49 [1996] 2 SLR(R) 196, [28].

be exercised by PT Ritau.' It was held by the Court of Appeal that Clause 3 was not sufficient to bring PT Ritau into the contract as an additional party on the ground that Clause 3 did not oblige PT Ritau to assume all of Norse-Tech's liabilities. Thus, PT Ritau was held to be free to choose the obligation they wished to discharge.[50] Furthermore, it was indicated by the court that the performance guarantee was neither agreed upon nor signed by the Speditor and therefore they had not agreed for PT Ritau to be added as a party to the contract. In the simplest term, PT Ritau needed to be a party to the contract to be able to invoke the arbitration agreement. On the other hand, considering the argument raised by Norske-Tech and PT Riau concerning the incorporation of the arbitration agreement into the performance guarantee pursuant to Clause 3, the Court of Appeal needed to assess whether such incorporation was successfully achieved, resulting in PT Ritau to be able to invoke the agreement to arbitrate. It was held by the Court of Appeal that although the boundaries between the contract and the performance guarantee were not entirely clear, the performance guarantee was still a separate and distinct contractual undertaking in relation to the contract.[51] Hence, general words such as 'all rights' were held insufficient for the incorporation of the arbitration clause into the performance guarantee by reference.

Star-Trans is a significant case in the sense that it clearly illustrates the influence of English law on Singapore. The Singapore Court of Appeal in *Star-Trans* has taken notice of the strict English approach pertaining to the incorporation of arbitration clauses and adopted the strict approach. It was indicated that in the cases that are concerned with the incorporation of a charterparty arbitration clause into bills of lading, courts will construe words of incorporation narrowly.[52] It was ruled by the Court of Appeal that express and clear reference to an arbitration clause contained in a distinct contract would be required for a court to be able to find that the clause had been incorporated into a separate contract.

Star-Trans was the initial Singaporean case importing the strict English rule of incorporation. Thus, the judgement established essential jurisprudence on the matter. The Singapore Court of Appeal adopting the approach manifested in an English construction case, *Aughton*, ruled that clear and express reference to an arbitration clause was required for incorporation. Furthermore, the fact that a reference was made to a construction case, even though the case in hand was one of shipping, in a way verifies that the strict rule of incorporation was also deemed applicable in other branches of law, provided that the contractual structure concerned with would meet the necessary criteria to apply this particular approach.

That being said, it should be noted that *Star-Trans* predated the Singapore Arbitration Act 2001 and was instead decided under the now-repealed Arbitration Act (Cap 10, 2002 Rev Ed), which was based on English law.[53] Accordingly, the Court of Appeal in a later case, *International Research v Lufthansa Systems*,[54] considering the up-to-datedness and applicability of *Star-Trans* to the case in hand 'observed that the analysis developed in

50 Ibid [21–22].
51 [1996] 2 SLR(R) 196 (*Star-Trans*) at [34–35].
52 Ibid [28].
53 Lawrence Boo, Arbitration, 2013, *Singapore Academy of Law, Annual Review*, 14, 81, 4.36.
54 [2013] SGCA 55.

English law is no longer helpful and that is time to put the authorities aside in construing the provisions'[55] of Singapore arbitration legislation.

The contractual structure in *Star-Trans* was considered to be a two-contract form, and this led to the implementation of the strict rule of incorporation. There were fundamentally two contracts indeed: (1) a main contract between A and B and (2) a performance guarantee to secure the performance of obligations of A, secured by C that bore the signature of A, B, and C. However, the actual quantity of the contracts may not bear significance from a contract law perspective because depending on the realities of the contractual structure, the existence of two contracts may possibly not always constitute a two-contract scenario. The issue in *Star-Trans* was whether C was a party to the main contract due to the performance guarantee indicating 'all rights of A . . . may be exercised by C and rights of A may at any time be assigned to C.' Thus, what needed to be assessed was whether the contractual structure was forming a one-contract scenario due to the cohesive structure of the contractual relationships. The indication in the performance guarantee to 'all rights' held not to be specific enough to incorporate the arbitration clause. It was indicated that due to contractual scopes not being entirely clear, C's contractual status was also not clear. Therefore, the performance guarantee was held to be a distinct and separate contractual undertaking.[56] Thus, the situation was held to constitute a two-contract case that is subject to the application of the strict rule of incorporation. Consequently, the absence of clear words was held to be precluding the incorporation of the arbitration clause into the performance guarantee.

It should be reiterated that *Star-Trans* predates the current Singapore arbitration legislation and, therefore, perhaps does not reflect the modern ambitious approach of Singapore to become a preferred hub for international arbitration. Furthermore, evidently, the realities of the market have changed, and thus, the legal and commercial concerns have also changed. Modern examples of disputes concerned with multiple parties and contractual layers signalize the adoption of a less strict approach concerning incorporation. The interpretation of one-contract and two-contract cases has evolved to cover more complex contractual relationships over the years. The modern realities of commerce necessitate the 'contracts scenario' to be interpreted in a way more comprehensive than the mere black-and-white categorization of contractual relations and instead, to shed light on the grey areas in a way to appropriately assess the scope of party autonomy. A fundamental issue to be concerned with in dealing with a multi-layered and multi-partied contractual layout is the assessment of which specific resolution method the parties choose to refer their dispute to. Singapore jurisdiction has been producing progressive decisions that fundamentally prioritize the ascertainment of the core intention of the parties regarding such. The strict rule of incorporation concerning arbitration clauses does not seem to apply 'by default' in this particular jurisdiction anymore and the adoption of a more flexible trend manifests itself in the recent decisions of the Singapore courts on the matter. The aforementioned *International Research v Lufthansa Systems*,[57]

55 Boo (n 54) 81, 4.36. Furthermore 'Singapore arbitration legislation' referred to the legislative structure that consists of the Singapore Arbitration Act 2001 and the Singapore International Arbitration Act 1994 in the context of this chapter.

56 [1996] 2 SLR(R) 196 (*Star-Trans*) at [34–35].

57 [2012] SGHC 226.

being the most striking example of the departure of Singapore law from the strict English rule, is particularly analyzed later in this chapter.

II. *L&M CONCRETE SPECIALISTS V UNITED ENG. CONTRACTORS* – THE EMPHASIS OF THE STRICT RULE

The strict rule of incorporation established itself a solid position in Singapore after the decision of the Singapore Court of Appeal in *Star-Trans*.[58] The court in *L&M Concrete Specialists Pte Ltd v United Eng. Contractors Pte Ltd*[59] subsequently stated that for an arbitration agreement in one contract to be incorporated into another, it must be brought to the attention of the party with a 'red hand pointing to it.' The indicated statement may seem familiar as the Singapore court was borrowing the phrase, which was used by Lord Denning in an English case, *Thornton v Shoe Lane Parking Ltd*.[60]

Indeed, under the influence of English law, Singapore adopted the strict rule of incorporation concerning arbitration clauses. The application of this restricted approach may be seen vividly in *Star-Trans* and *L&M Concrete v United Eng. Contractors*. Furthermore, the commentaries on the Singapore arbitration law appear to have accepted that there has been a clear implementation of the strict rule in Singapore jurisprudence. It was suggested that

> as an arbitration clause in a contract is considered a separate and independent agreement, words of its incorporation must be specific. While general words of inclusion may be sufficient to incorporate terms referred to in another document and which are germane to the underlying contract as part of the contract, an arbitration clause being a collateral agreement cannot be so incorporated. Courts have therefore tended to construe words of incorporation restrictively.[61]

The words 'courts have a tendency to construe words of incorporation strictly' may be regarded to be referring to *Star-Trans*. However, there is a clear departure from the strict rule of incorporation in Singapore. To be able to illustrate this departure clearly, some more recent examples of Singapore case law are examined below. Particular weight is given to the aforementioned *International Research v Lufthansa Systems*[62] as it constitutes one of the most striking examples of the departure of Singapore law from the strict English rule to date.

5.4.2. Departure from English Law in Singapore: The Search for an Autochthonous Jurisprudence

Since Singapore has been searching for a national identity that reflects the diversity of its people, the desire to produce an autochthonous jurisprudence[63] 'has been one that has

58 [1996] 2 SLR(R) 196 (*Star-Trans*) at [28].
59 [2000] 2 SLR(R) 852 at [18].
60 [1971] 1 All ER 686 at [691]; [1971] 2 QB 163.
61 *Halsbury's Laws of Singapore*, Vol. 1(2), LexisNexis, 2011 Reissue, 20.021.
62 [2012] SGHC 226.
63 It was emphasized back in 1985 by Professor Geoffrey Wilson Bartholomew, one of the very first advocates of the development of an autochthonous legal system for Singapore, that it was only a question of time before Singapore could have an autochthonous legal system: In Conversation: Prof G W Bartholomew, 1985, *Singapore Law Review*, 6, 56.

captured the imagination for some time now.'[64] Singapore law, even though still under the influence of some English principles to a certain degree, has been evolving significantly to accommodate the realities of the international arbitration market that often prioritize the promotion of party autonomy. Accordingly, this sometimes leads to some well-established rules being undermined for the sake of promoting the true wishes of the parties.[65]

Some core principles that reflect the desire to provide originality and internality have been adopted by the courts of Singapore in accordance with their aspiration to produce autochthonous jurisprudence.[66] First, Singapore courts are citing local decisions in preference to foreign decisions. The effect of the Practice Direction[67] of the Singapore Supreme Court, which mandates lawyers to cite Singapore cases whenever possible prior to referring to foreign cases, is a significant one if not ground-breaking. The underlying reason for this can be regarded as the desire of Singapore courts to create a jurisprudence that is 'self-sufficient' rather than having one that is 'foreign-dependent.' Such a compulsion indeed facilitates the development of autochthonous jurisprudence. This implementation suggests that there is now a rather large body of Singapore case law from which to cite and also that Singapore case law fundamentally draws away from the wide impact of English jurisprudence.[68] Nevertheless, this does not suggest that Singapore is a confined jurisdiction. When it comes to questions where the local position remains unclear or undefined, referring to foreign decisions is not only needed but also advisable.[69] Singapore courts citing local decisions in preference to foreign decisions purely suggests that there is an ongoing and passionate aspiration for Singapore to become a 'self-sufficient hub' for international arbitration. Furthermore, the mandatory reflection of the domestic character of the jurisdiction and the advice regarding the inclusion of the 'international element' where deemed necessary seem to have struck a balance between the scope of the desired self-sufficiency and the permitted level of the impact of external factors on this jurisprudence.

Second, the courts of Singapore are generally willing not to follow the traditionally strong position of English law and its principles if they considered such an adoption inappropriate. Indeed, being the predominant source of case law on arbitration,[70] English law has an undeniably substantial effect on the decisions given by the courts of Singapore since this legal system is overwhelmingly influenced by English arbitration legislation. It is evident that its strong position enables English law to create some harmonization. However, the desire of Singapore courts to produce autochthonous jurisprudence has recently been prevailing. It was stated by the Singapore Court of Appeal in *Man Financial (S) Pte Ltd v Wong Bark Chuan David* that

---

64 Goh and Tan (n 12) 177.

65 *International Research Corporation Plc. v Lufthansa Systems Asia Pacific Pte* [2012] SGHC 226.

66 Goh and Paul (n 12) 177.

67 Singapore Supreme Court Practice Direction No 1 of 2008 (June 13, 2008). Paragraph 4 of the Practice Direction No 1 of 2008 states, 'Judgments from other jurisdictions can, if judiciously used, provide valuable assistance to the Court. However, where there are in existence local judgments which are directly relevant to the issue, such judgments should be cited in precedence to foreign judgments. Relevant local judgments will be accorded greater weight than judgments from foreign jurisdictions. This will ensure that the Courts are not unnecessarily burdened with judgments made in jurisdictions with differing legal, social or economic contexts.'

68 Goh and Tan (n 12) 193.

69 Ibid 194.

70 Merkin and Hjalmarsson (n 15) 5.

> local courts most simultaneously recognize that the days of a uniform common law are no longer a given. It is true that in the commercial context, there is more likelihood of (and desirability for) uniformity. However, even in the commercial setting, uniformity should not be taken too far.[71]

Furthermore, concerning incorporation, the need for abiding by such harmonization was particularly rejected in favour of the implementation of a more liberal interpretation of the contract based on its commercial purpose and context in *Man Financial v Wong Bark*. The provided analysis of the Singapore Court of Appeal was potentially undermining the strict English rule that expresses words to be employed for the incorporation of an arbitration clause.[72] The decision of the Court of Appeal indicates that Singaporean judges are drastically independent and would have no hesitation in not following English authority if they regard it as wrong.

Third, the judgements of Singaporean courts tend to be very detailed and constantly refer to international principles of arbitration law. Therefore, the sources of judgements have become more globalized and diversified. Indeed, it was indicated above that Singapore courts are citing local decisions in preference to foreign decisions and there is a Practice Direction enforcing this. However, this does not suggest international principles are ignored. On the contrary, it may be argued that by means of prioritizing the citation of Singapore cases and, evidently, taking international principles of arbitration law into consideration, an advanced level of arbitration law that also has an autochthonous character is intended to be created. Therefore, anything that comes out of Singapore is significant in terms of legal principles.

I. *Mancon (BVI) Investment Holding Co Ltd v Heng Holdings SEA (Pte) Ltd*[73]

The main issue to be addressed in *Mancon* was the assessment of the legal principle that was applicable to the situation where the arbitration clause is only found in the main agreement and not in the supplement agreement. Accordingly, the court was in the position to assess whether the contractual structure was constituted of a single contract so that the principal and supplemental agreements could be considered to be falling under the single-contract division.

In *Mancon* the arbitration clause in a joint venture agreement was held to be validly incorporated into a subsequent supplemental agreement despite the latter did not make any specific references to the arbitration clause. This case indicates the adoption of a relatively flexible approach concerning the interpretation of the 'scenarios theory' that would eventually affect the level of specificity that may be required of the words to be employed for incorporation purposes. Furthermore, *Mancon* was referred to in *International Research v Lutfhansa Systems*[74] with the suggestion that it might be the time for Singapore law to depart from the notion that there is a continuing place for the strict English rule of incorporation in Singapore law.

---

71 [2008] 1 SLR(R) 663 at [133]. (*Man Financial v Wong Bark*).

72 *International Research Corporation Plc. v Lufthansa Systems Asia Pacific Pte* [2013] SGCA 55.

73 [2000] 3 SLR 220 (*Mancon*).

74 [2013] SGCA 55 at [29].

II. *International Research v Lufthansa Systems* – Rejection of Star-Trans and the Application of the Strict Rule of Incorporation in Singapore

In the landmark decision of *International Research v Lutfhansa Systems*, the strict rule concerning the incorporation of arbitration clauses by reference is abandoned. The Singapore Court of Appeal, by means of departing from the strict rule of incorporation, rejected to approach adopted in *Star-Trans*[75] on this matter. Accordingly, the strict rule of incorporation does not apply in Singapore following this particular case.[76]

International Research v Lufthansa Systems[77] is momentous due to two reasons: the case questions both the justification of the strict rule of incorporation and its applicability in the Singapore context. The court in this case provided a painstaking analysis of the implementation and development of the strict rule of incorporation in England and Singapore. Especially two fairly recent English cases, *Sea Trade Maritime Corp v Hellenic Mutual War Risks Association (Bermuda) Ltd, (Athena)*[78] and *Habas Sinai v Sometal,*[79] were taken into account from the aspect of the 'scenarios theory' that categorizes the structural layout of contract formation. The fundamental reason for this is because these cases provide a fresh perspective and significantly refine the interpretation of the 'strict rule of incorporation,' and what this concept means from the aspect of party autonomy. Furthermore, a relevant view expressed by the High Court of Hong Kong in *Astel-Peiniger Joint Venture v Argos Engineering & Heavy Industries Co Ltd*[80] on the matter was also endorsed in *International Research v Lufthansa Systems*. One may argue that such an endorsement also played an important role in the High Court of Singapore, making the decision to deviate from the parallel implementation of the concept of incorporation in Singapore law and English law. The fact that a Hong Kong decision is endorsed also suggests that Singapore courts have no reservation in putting different views adopted in various jurisdictions in a melting pot for the purposes of producing the best possible legal principle applicable to a dispute.

International Research v Lufthansa Systems was essentially concerned with three two-party commercial agreements. Lufthansa, a company that was in the business of providing information technology services to companies in the aviation industry, entered into a Cooperation Agreement with Datamat Public Company Ltd, which provides information and computer technology services including the distribution of hardware and software maintenance services. Under the Cooperation Agreement, Lufthansa agreed to supply, deliver, and commission a new Maintenance, Repair and Overhaul System (MRO System), which is a component of the Electronic Data Protection System (EDP System). Datamat had agreed to provide the EDP System to Thai Airways under an agreement that was entered into earlier. Datamat later entered into a Sales and Purchase Agreement with International Research Corporation Public Company Ltd (IRCP), a company engaged primarily in the business of providing information and communication technology products and services. IRCP had three main obligations: to provide a bankers' guarantee in the name of Datamat

75 [1996] 2 SLR(R) 196 (*Star-Trans*) at [28].
76 Merkin and Hjalmarsson (n 15) 19. Also see *The Titan Unity* [2013] SGHCR 28.
77 [2012] SGHC 226; overruled by the Singapore Court of Appeal [2013] SGCA 55.
78 [2006] EWHC 2530 (Comm). (*The Athena*).
79 [2010] EWHC 29 (Comm).
80 [1994] 3 HKC 328 (a Hong Kong case, *Astel-Peiniger*).

in order for Datamat to comply with its obligations under the EDP System Agreement, to supply and deliver various hardware and software products to EDP System, and to pay Lufthansa for the goods and services provided by Lufthansa under the Cooperation Agreement. Following the failure of Datamat to meet its payment obligations, Datamat, Lufthansa and IRCP entered into Supplemental Agreement No. 1. Under this agreement, Datamat was obliged to transfer to IRCP monies received from Thai Airways, and upon receiving these monies, IRCP would pay Lufthansa for the works and services rendered by Lufthansa. Later, Supplemental Agreement No. 2. was entered into by the said three parties and under this agreement, IRCP would pay Lufthansa for the sums payable by Datamat under the Cooperation Agreement directly from IRCP's bank account. The Cooperation Agreement contained a multi-tiered dispute resolution mechanism including Clause 37.3, indicating, 'All disputes arising out of this Cooperation Agreement, which cannot be settled by mediation . . . shall be finally settled by arbitration to be held in Singapore in the English language under Singapore International Arbitration Centre Rules (SIAC Rules).' Payment disputes arose and several meetings were held between the parties. Lufthansa sent letters demanding payment of outstanding sums from IRCP. IRCP refused payment. Lufthansa initiated arbitral proceedings pursuant to Clause 37.3. of the Cooperation Agreement. IRCP argued that they were not a party to the arbitration agreement, which was contained in the Cooperation Agreement, and even if they were a party, Lufthansa had failed to comply with the preconditions for the commencement of arbitration proceedings contained in Clause 37.2. of the Cooperation Agreement. The arbitral tribunal rejected IRCP's challenge. IRCP applied to the High Court pursuant to Section 10 of the Singapore International Arbitration Act 1994 read with Art 16(3) of the Model Law 1985 to set aside the arbitral tribunal's preliminary ruling on jurisdiction.

A. *Contractual Relationship: One Contract or Two Contracts?*

Considering whether IRCP was bound by the arbitration agreement, the court emphasized that this was an issue that depends predominantly on the objectively ascertainable intentions of the parties.[81] *International Research v Lufthansa Systems*, sets a good example of how party autonomy is evaluated in the Singapore context. The perceptions of the parties regarding the nature of supplemental agreements are considered to be indicating what they actually intended to do with the agreement in question. Lufthansa contended that the supplemental agreements should be construed as 'extensions' of the Cooperation Agreement, and they all constitute 'one composite agreement.' On the other hand, IRCP's position was that the supplemental agreements were 'separate and distinct' from the Cooperation Agreement. It should be noted that both parties were accepting that if the agreements decided to be distinct in nature, then clear and express words were required to incorporate the Dispute Resolution Mechanism into the Supplemental Agreements. Thus, the assessment of the nature of the supplemental agreements constitutes a significant aspect of this case as such an assessment would pave the way to determine under which category the relevant contract falls and accordingly, whether the incorporation of the arbitration agreement was successful.

81 [2012] SGHC 226 at [22].

To reiterate, the scenarios theory of English law facilitates the assessment of the contract's nature and, accordingly, whether the relevant incorporation was successful. The most comprehensible distinction concerning contracts under the 'scenarios theory' was provided by Christophe Clarke J in *Habas Sinai v Sometal.*[82] The existing two categories, single-contract and two-contract, were extended to four different situations in *Habas Sinai v Sometal*. The single-contract cases are indicated to be (1) A and B make a contract in which they incorporate standard terms and (2) A and B make a contract incorporating terms previously agreed between A and B in another contract or contracts in which they were both parties. Concerning the single-contract scenario, usually the adoption of a flexible approach towards incorporation would be considered applicable. This is simply because the contracts would involve the same parties and therefore, may be perceived to constitute one composite contractual structure. As to the two-contract cases: (3) A and B make a contract incorporating terms agreed between A (or B) and C and (4) A and B make a contract incorporating terms agreed between C and D. Concerning, two-contract cases, generally a more restrictive approach concerning incorporation would be applicable due to the involvement of third parties in these formations. What is contended by the IRCP in *International Research v Lufthansa Systems*, compatible with the decision in *Star-Trans*, was that a clear and express reference was required for the incorporation of the arbitration clause due to the contract before the court falling under the two-contract category. The strict English principle was adopted in *Star-Trans*. However, more recent cases dealing with the issue seem to be indicating the adoption of more liberal approaches concerning the assessment of the boundaries of the possible scenarios and how far they may stretch.

In an English marine insurance case, *Athena*,[83] the question was whether an arbitration agreement included in the rules of the defendant association was incorporated into an agreement for war risks insurance. The insurance is made by the agents of the association 'in accordance with the rules and by-laws of the Association' and the vessel *Athena* entered into the defendant war risks association. Following this, Sea Trade completed its application for membership in the association and agreed to conform with the rules and by-laws of the Association. A dispute arose as to whether the arbitration clause, included in the rules of the Association, was incorporated into Sea Trade's insurance contract.

The shipowners rejected the incorporation of the arbitration agreement into the insurance contract and that the general words of incorporation were insufficient to include the arbitration agreement that was included in the general conditions, which were referred to. The association argued that the arbitration clause had been incorporated into the insurance. The fundamental necessity concerning *The Athena* was to fairly assess the contractual structure and relationship to be able to categorize it either under the single-contract scenario or the two-contract scenario. There were two contracts quantity-wise: an insurance contract for Athena and a separate contract granting Sea Trade a membership status of the association. Nonetheless, the actual structure could be forming a composite structure, which would eventually lead the contracts to be considered to form a single contract. It was indicated by Langley J that, despite there being quantitatively two contracts from which

82 [2010] EWHC 29 (Comm). It should be noted that the first basic distinction regarding this issue was created by Langley J in *The Athena* [2006] EWHC 2530 (Comm). Clarke J in *Habas Sinai v Sometal* took this division to a further level by creating further contractual categories.

83 [2006] EWHC 2530 (Comm).

the dispute before the court arose, the case before him was what is called a single-contract case. The structure was held to constitute a single-contract case so that the incorporation was subject to flexible rules. Therefore, the rest of the terms of the association's rules that include an arbitration clause were held to be incorporated into Sea Trade's insurance contract. Furthermore, the plaintiff's argument contending specific reference was needed to incorporate the arbitration clause in the Association's rules was considered 'hopeless.'[84] Moreover, it was also noted by Langley J that there were several English authorities neither citing nor applying the approach applied in *Thomas v Portsea*, which imposes narrow rules concerning incorporation.[85]

After *Athena*, the scenarios theory was evaluated in detail in *Habas Sinai v Sometal*.[86] One of the most significant aspects of *Habas Sinai v Sometal* is that the categorization of the scenario where 'A and B make a contract incorporating terms previously agreed between A and B in another contract or contracts which they were both parties' was classified as a single-contract situation[87] and distinguished to not require the strict rule to be applicable. One may regard this as an effort to reshape and redefine the existing categories to make them more meaningful and applicable to multi-layered contractual relationships. Moreover, it was indicated by Clarke J in *Habas Sinai v Sometal* that the retention of the strict rule was partly attributable to the desirability of not changing an approach established for better or for worse and that the rule was not easily congruent with ordinary principles of construction.[88] It may be argued that the fact that the strict rule was accepted as a principle that may be applicable 'for better or for worse' is in a way suggesting that there is a clear excess of power that would lead to the normalization of the implementation of the strict rule when it is not actually applicable or fair to use it.

Both *Athena* and *Habas Sinai v Sometal* seem to have refined the implementation of the strict rule of incorporation by means of promoting the assessment of the true construction of the contractual formation before the court. In light of these English decisions, it may be argued that a 'single-contract scenario' may include multiple and closely-related agreements of the same parties even though the situation would evidently include more than one agreement. In such as case, falling under the single-contract category, contracts would be subject to flexible rules and accordingly, general words may be used to incorporate an arbitration clause that is contained in a referred document. A two-contract scenario, on the other hand, would include different contracting parties to multiple and closely related agreements. In contrast to the single-contract scenario, parties to a two-contract formation would be subject to the implementation of a stricter rule of incorporation. In plain sight, under the second category, an arbitration clause contained in a separate document may ordinarily only be incorporated if express and specific words of incorporation are effectively provided.

---

84 Ibid [68].

85 Ibid [69].

86 [2010] EWHC 29 (Comm).

87 *Habas Sinai v Sometal*, from this aspect, overruled *Aughton Ltd v MF Kent Services Ltd* [1991] 57 BLR 1. In *Aughton*, the strict rule held to be applicable to the circumstance where the contracts in question fall under the second category: same parties contracting but there are more than one contract that they are parties to. This was a purely quantitative reasoning suggesting that if there are multiple contracts, then the situation constitutes a two-contract scenario and thus requires strict approach to be applicable.

88 [2010] EWHC 29 (Comm) at [52].

Following the recap on the relevant English case law, we now turn back to *International Research v Lufthansa Systems*.[89] As indicated, one of the main issues to be assessed by the court was the perception of the concerned parties of the supplemental agreements and their fundamental intentions regarding the applicability of these. The assessment of such is considered to provide clarification concerning the incorporation and applicability of the arbitration agreement. Accordingly, one of the main questions to be asked was 'what were the common intentions of the parties, if any, when objectively ascertained, as to the applicability of the Dispute Resolution Mechanism to resolve their disputes at the time when all of them entered into the supplemental agreements?'[90] Examining the possible incorporation of the Dispute Resolution Mechanism clause in *International Research v Lufthansa Systems*, it was stated by the court that

> an assertion that the Dispute Resolution Mechanism was incorporated into the Supplemental Agreements or the various agreements between the parties were, in essence, one Composite Agreement, are two ways saying the same thing *viz* that the three parties, from an objective perspective, intended to be bound by the Dispute Resolution Mechanism.[91]

To put it differently, where the contracts are clearly perceived by the parties to constitute one composite contract, there would be no need for the incorporation of a specific part as this part would already be deemed to form a part of the composite block of contracts anyway. Accordingly, the courts of Singapore would have no hesitation to bypass 'the fictional need' to incorporate provisions in the case where contracts are considered to constitute one composite structure. Therefore, the Singapore High Court found in *International Research v Lufthansa Systems* that the arbitration clause contained in the main contract would bind a third party, which subsequently entered into a supplement agreement.

However, the decision of the High Court that the parties had intended that the Dispute Resolution Mechanism in the Cooperation Agreement was to be incorporated as part of the Supplemental Agreements was overturned by the Singapore Court of Appeal.[92] Nevertheless, the emphasis should be laid on the fact that the decision of the High Court was on the 'concept of incorporation' indicating if the contracts, as a result of contextual interpretation, were to be read as one composite contract, then the fictional need to incorporate the provisions from one contract to another could be bypassed. On the other hand, the decision of the Court of Appeal was directly on the nature of supplemental contracts and the contractual relationship, and eventually, it was decided by the court that the Cooperation Agreement and the supplemental contracts were separate. In other words, the Court of Appeal did not agree with the findings of the High Court on the object and purposes of the Supplemental Agreements. This was merely a rejection of the findings concerning the nature of the Supplemental Agreements. Therefore, the ruling of the High Court, with regard to 'the concept of incorporation,' preserves its value and relevancy as the judgement prioritizes contextual interpretation even though the

89 [2012] SGHC 226.
90 Ibid [48].
91 Ibid.
92 [2013] SGCA 55.

assessment of the contractual relationship that is made by the High Court has not been approved by the Court of Appeal.[93]

B. An Evaluation of the Strict Rule and Singapore Jurisprudence

The High Court in *International Research v Lufthansa Systems* was presented with the opportunity to analyze the development and implementation of 'the traditional English narrow approach'[94] of incorporation in Singapore. The Court revisited an earlier case, *Star-Trans Far East Pte Ltd v Norske-Tech Ltd*,[95] and accordingly, its analysis extended to an earlier English decision, *Thomas v Portsea*,[96] which constituted the fundamental reference point of the court's decision in *Star-Trans*.

At this point, it would be useful to remember the underlying reasons that are provided to justify the application of the strict rule of incorporation in *Thomas v Portsea*.[97] First, *Thomas v Portsea* was a case concerned with bills of lading and their possible incorporation of a charterparty arbitration clause. Therefore, the subject matter of the case was appertaining to a specific branch of law that was concerned with negotiable documents such as bills of lading. It was set forth that 'if the obligations of those who are parties to such a contract are to be enlarged beyond the matters which ordinarily concern them, or if it is sought to deprive either party of his ordinary legal remedies, the contract cannot be explicit and precise.'[98] The reservation of the court may be said to be purely based on the negotiable nature of the bills of lading and the protection of third parties such negotiable nature necessitates. It should also be noted that the plaintiffs relied on Bingham LJ's suggestion in *The Federal Bulker*[99] that the strict rule should apply for the sake of clearance and certainty of the law and the law being well-understood is more important than the law being perfect. This particular suggestion of Bingham LJ in *The Federal Bulker*, alongside being purely formalistic and almost readily sacrificing the pursuit of creating good law for the sake of certainty of law, also pertained to a bill of lading case. It was emphasized by the court in *International Research v Lufthansa Systems* that

> *The Federal Bulker* and many of the cases cited by the International Research Corp. were cases involving bills of lading and other specific species of contracts and in those contracts there may be a merit for the sake of certainty in applying the strict rule but with regard to *International Research v Lufthansa Systems*, this could not be the inflexible position.[100]

Second, the court was of the view that the arbitration clause, due to the way it was structured, was falling short to include claims of a different nature that may arise under the

93 Furthermore, it should be noted that one of the main reasons provided by the Court of Appeal for overruling the decision of the High Court in *International Research v Lufthansa Systems* was that the requirement of complying with the preconditions to commence arbitration was not fulfilled. Therefore, it may be argued that a completely different aspect of the subject matter of the case led the court to decide that the appellant was not bound by the arbitration agreement. Also see *HSBC Institutional Trust Services (Singapore) Ltd (Trustee of Starhill Global Real Estate Investment Trust) v Toshin Development Singapore Pte Ltd* [2012] 4 SLR 738.

94 Merkin and Hjalmarsson (n 15) 81.

95 [1996] 2 SLR(R) 196 (*Star-Trans*).

96 [1912] A.C. 1.

97 The reasons of justification that provided in *Thomas v Portsea* were also summarized in *The Athena* [2006] EWHC 2530 (Comm) at [72–73].

98 [1912] A.C. 1. at [11].

99 [1989] 1 Lloyd's Rep 103 at [105].

100 [2013] SGCA 55 at [28].

bill of lading and a degree of manipulation to be done would be essential for it to include these so. This, again, reflects the negotiable character of the bills of lading and the desire of courts to provide protection for the third-party holders of these. Such a general concern of the courts does not seem to find equitable application in other branches of law dealing with non-negotiable contracts. Third, one of the concerns of the court was the potential of an arbitration clause to oust the jurisdiction of the court. Thus, to avoid such an outcome, the court in *Thomas v Portsea* required very clear words of incorporation to be employed to incorporate an arbitration agreement.

These three main concerns that were fundamentally provided to justify the adoption of the strict approach in *Thomas v Portsea* were also adopted in many subsequent English cases, including *Aughton*.[101] The Court in *International Research v Lufthansa Systems* also considered this English decision. It should be noted that *Aughton*, a construction case dealing with the incorporation of a construction subcontract arbitration clause into a sub-subcontract and, hence, pertaining to a completely different branch of law, evidently, had a different contractual nature than what *Thomas v Portsea* had. However, the reasons given for the application of the strict rule were referred to in *Aughton*,[102] and they were held to be sufficient for the application of the same principle in this branch of law as well. *Aughton* depended on the same concerns in adopting the application of the strict rule of incorporation in the construction context.[103] An essential one of these was the possible preclusion of the parties from bringing a dispute before the court of law without them being evidently intended to refer their dispute to arbitration. If the parties were indeed intended to refer their dispute to arbitration, this had to be made in writing to undoubtedly illustrate the relevant intention in a written form. Furthermore, the self-contained nature of the arbitration agreement was considered an important peculiarity that was precluding the court from perceiving the arbitration agreement as merely another term of the substantive contract.

As indicated, there are roughly three concerns regarding the incorporation of arbitration clauses: They may potentially oust the jurisdiction of the courts; if parties intended to arbitrate, they must clearly manifest this in a written form and the proper way to do this so may be complicated; and also, because arbitration agreements are separate, their incorporation should also be specifically made. However, it would be unrealistic to argue that the same principles that influenced courts over some 100 years ago when *Thomas v Porstea* was decided to find equal application in modern arbitration practice particularly considering the wide use of arbitration as a dispute resolution method and the general awareness of commercial parties of its common implementation in commerce. Nonetheless, some fundamental issues that were taken into account by the court in *Thomas v Porstea* also constituted reference points for *Star-Trans* in Singapore after some 80 years. However, the courts of Singapore generally tend to promote arbitration in the interests of expediency and party autonomy, provided that the intention of the parties to refer their dispute to arbitration is objectively ascertainable, particularly in light of *International Research v Lufthansa Systems*.[104] The decision has now effectively reversed *Star-Trans*.

101 [1991] 57 BLR 1.
102 Ibid [20].
103 Ibid.
104 Also see *Tjong Very Sumito v Antig Investments Pte Ltd* [2009] SGCA 41.

Furthermore, the reservation pertaining to the incorporation of arbitration clauses due to the separate nature of arbitration agreements was criticized in *Habas Sinai v Sometal*[105] and the criticism found support later in the Singaporean *International Research v Lufthansa Systems.*[106] Indeed, an arbitration agreement would constitute a separate and self-contained contract referring a potential or existing dispute to arbitration and, by doing this so, would oust the jurisdiction of the courts. Therefore, arbitration clauses may be considered to have a different character than the rest of the contract provisions. Nevertheless, this would constitute 'a mere legal technicality'[107] for contracting parties. The intention of the parties to arbitrate would be the predominant element to be assessed in allowing the incorporation of an arbitration clause, even though there may be some formal requirements that are not completely met. To put it differently, the ascertainable and clear intention to arbitrate prevails over a technicality. Therefore, the concern with regard to arbitration agreements being separate in nature and their incorporation, therefore necessitating very formal requirements to meet, may not be completely founded. This issue was explicitly clarified in *Habas Sinai v Sometal* and emphasized in *International Research v Lufthansa Systems.*[108] A businessperson to a commercial contract (not a commercial lawyer) would not attribute a different level of importance to different contract terms, and therefore, the businessperson would not discriminate between the regular terms of the contract and the arbitration clause. The businessperson 'would have no difficulty regarding an arbitration clause . . . as part of the contract and as capable of incorporation, by appropriate wording, as any other term of . . . a contract.'[109] Furthermore, it was also emphasized by Clarke J in *Habas Sinai v Sometal* that, on the contrary, the businessperson to the commercial contract would actually be surprised to be told that 'all the terms of the contract' to be interpreted so as to mean 'all but the arbitration clause.'[110] Party autonomy and its manifestation to arbitrate constitute the fundamentals of commercial arbitration. Accordingly, the way parties interpret their very own contract, which contains an arbitration provision, is an element of equal importance in assessing the incorporation of an arbitration agreement.

It was highlighted in *International Research v Lufthansa Systems* that no references were made in *Star-Trans* to the judgement of Ralph Gibson LJ in *Aughton*. Sundaresh Menon CJ in *International Research v Lufthansa Systems* stated that the fundamental reason for this was perhaps even though Ralph Gibson LJ made distinctive comments on incorporation, he still reached the same result with Sir John Megaw, refusing the stay of proceedings in favour of arbitration. Nonetheless, the learned judge in *International Research v Lufthansa Systems* clarifies that Ralph Gibson LJ in *Aughton*, undertaking a contextual analysis, considered the practices and realities of the market. He indicated that the arbitration clause was eligible for a modification to make it applicable to the sub-subcontract. The words of incorporation were held to be manifesting the intention of the parties to incorporate all terms of the subcontract, including the arbitration provision, into the sub-subcontract. *Star-Trans* being the first case adopting the strict English approach in the Singapore context in

105 [2010] EWHC 29 (Comm) 51.
106 [2013] SGCA 55.
107 *International Research Corporation Plc. v Lufthansa Systems Asia Pacific Pte* [2013] SGCA 55 at [27].
108 [2013] SGCA 55 at [27].
109 *Habas Sinai v Sometal* [2010] EWHC 29 (Comm) 51.
110 Ibid.

an evident way, one may perhaps consider that the judgement excluding the evaluation of Ralph Gibson LJ's comments was a missing opportunity to produce a 'better law.' This was criticized in *International Research v Lufthansa Systems*[111] and the comments that were made by Ralph Gibson LJ were found more similar[112] to contextual interpretation that found application in a recent Singapore case *Zurich Insurance (Singapore) Pte Ltd v B-Gold Interior Design & Construction Pte Ltd.*[113] The court took the view that the task concerning *International Research v Lufthansa Systems* was to consider the contextual approach and the parties' objective intentions. Accordingly, in light of *Zurich Insurance*, it was held that express words were not needed for the incorporation of the arbitration agreement. The party autonomy concerning the applicability of the Dispute Resolution Mechanism (arbitration clause) was deemed to be manifested sufficiently.

Another issue is that the court in *International Research v Lufthansa Systems* further considered the bindingness of *Aughton* as an authority imposing the application of the strict rule of incorporation outside the shipping context. This was fundamentally because *Aughton* was a judgement of the English Court of Appeal, whereas the judgement of *Habas Sinai v Sometal* was produced by a lower court of England. The decision of the Court of Appeal in *Aughton* was that the strict rule of incorporation was applicable in contexts other than shipping. On the other hand, the judgement of the lower court on a similar matter was manifesting a rejection of this former decision. The inconsistent structure was found to blur the implementation of the incorporation of arbitration clauses. Accordingly, the Singapore Court of Appeal in *International Research v Lufthansa Systems* considered the authority of *Aughton* imposing the application of the strict rule principle (even on the lower courts of England) as 'unclear.'[114] To put it differently, it was not clear to the Singapore Court of Appeal whether the restricted approach/strict rule of incorporation was applicable outside the bills of lading context.

5.4.3. Does the Strict Rule of Incorporation Still Have a Place in Singapore?

Singapore arbitration law, as indicated, has a dual character. Parties may prefer to choose between the International Arbitration Act 1994 or the Arbitration Act 2001 to apply to their dispute if they wish to 're-arrange the level of court intervention.' The possible options of 'opting in' and 'opting out' that Singapore arbitration legislation provides derive from the non-interventionist character of the Model Law 1985 since Singapore arbitration legislation is essentially based on the Model Law 1985.[115] As indicated, *Star-Trans* in 1996, imported the strict English rule that imposes the adoption of a restricted approach concerning incorporation.

However, when this case was decided, the governing legislation was the old Arbitration Act (Cap 10, 1985 Rev Ed), which was enacted in 1953 and based on the older English arbitration legislation. The old Arbitration Act was repealed and replaced with the Singapore Arbitration Act 2001 (Act 37 of 2001, the new Arbitration Act). Arbitration Act

111 [2013] SGCA 55.
112 Ibid [26].
113 [2008] SGCA 27.
114 [2013] SGCA 55 at [28].
115 *International Research Corporation Plc. v Lufthansa Systems Asia Pacific Pte* [2013] SGCA 55 at [31].

2001 followed the International Arbitration Act 1994,[116] which implements and adopts the principles of the Model Law. Furthermore, it went through significant amendments in 2012 to keep this particular legislation in line with the modern international practices of arbitration. Singapore law is generally a progressive one.

The legislative aspect of incorporation in the Singapore context should also be mentioned at this point. Adopting the key principles of the Model Law 1985, Singapore arbitration legislation reflects the characteristics of the Model Law. Art 7(2) of the Model Law indicates that 'the reference in a contract to a document containing an arbitration clause constitutes an arbitration agreement provided that the contract is in writing and the reference is such as to make that clause part of the contract.' Furthermore, Section 4(1) of the International Arbitration Act 1994 on interpretation indicates that reference may be made to the documents of the United Nations relating to the Model Law.[117] Reading both provisions together, it may be argued that it would be sufficient for the reference to be made solely to the document and not specifically to the arbitration clause that is contained in the document.[118] Art 7(2) of the Model Law 1985, seems to be promoting the adoption of a less strict approach in assessing incorporation than what is generally adopted in English contract law.[119]

I. Astel-Peiniger: A Hong Kong Example

A decision of the Hong Kong High Court, *Astel-Peiniger Joint Venture v Argos Engineering & Heavy Industries Ltd*,[120] regarding the law on the incorporation of arbitration clauses by reference was also taken into consideration in *International Research v Lufthansa Systems*.[121] Hong Kong arbitration legislation, like Singapore legislation, also adopts and reflects the principles of the Model Law and, accordingly, provides fruitful examples for Singapore courts.

Astel-Peiniger shows similarities to *International Research v Lufthansa Systems* in the sense that it also deals with the effectiveness and applicability of some English principles concerned with the incorporation of arbitration clauses. The plaintiff in *Astel-Peiniger* was a sub-subcontractor to an assembly subcontract, and the defendant was a subcontractor in a construction dispute. The fundamental matter before the court was to assess which one of them was responsible under the sub-subcontract for the supply and construction of mobile paint sheds. The sub-subcontract was on a back-to-back basis and proportional to the subcontract. Also, the plaintiff was given a copy of the subcontract prior to the conclusion of the sub-subcontract, and they did not raise any objections when they were given it. The defendant sought a stay of proceedings and argued that due to the incorporation of a

116 Significantly amended by the International Arbitration (Amendment) Act 2012 (No.12 of 2012).

117 Section 4(1) of the Singapore International Arbitration Act 1994: 'For the purposes of interpreting the Model Law, reference may be made to the documents of a) the United Nations Commission on International Trade Law and b) its working group for the preparation of the Model Law, relating to the Model Law.'

118 Peter Binder, *International Commercial Arbitration and Conciliation in UNCITRAL Model Law Jurisdictions*, Sweet & Maxwell, 2010, 3rd Edn., 2–032 (referring to *Report of the Working Group on International Contract Practices on the work of its seventh session* Doc A/CN.9/246 at para 19).

119 It should perhaps be noted that general principles of English contract law usually promote the adoption of some strict rules concerning incorporation. On the other hand, English arbitration legislation (the Arbitration Act 1996) regulates the matter in a more extensible manner.

120 [1994] 3 HKC 328 (a Hong Kong case, *Astel-Peiniger*).

121 [2013] SGCA 55 at [33].

subcontract arbitration clause into the sub-subcontract by reference, the dispute had to be referred to arbitration.

The decision of the Hong Kong High Court in *Astel-Peiniger* is significant essentially because of two reasons. First, it provides a clear illustration of the interpretation of Article 7(2) of the Model Law and, therefore, sets an example for the Singapore Court of Appeal in *International Research v Lufthansa Systems*. Second, by means of evaluating the effectiveness and applicability of some English law principles on the matter – and deciding that they are not effective anymore – in a way, paves the way for Singapore courts to depart from the strict English rule concerning the incorporation of arbitration clauses.

First, the High Court in *Astel-Peiniger*, by means of referring to *travaux préparatoires* of the Model Law 1985, held that under Article 7(2) of the Model Law, the document containing an arbitration clause does not have to be between the same parties to the contract, into which the arbitration clause is intended to be incorporated. By allowing the incorporation of the arbitration clause into the sub-subcontract, the High Court granted a stay and referred the matter to arbitration. It was indicated that the provision in the sub-subcontract indicating that it would be back-to-back with the subcontract sufficiently demonstrated the intention of the parties to incorporate the arbitration clause into the sub-subcontract. Furthermore, considering the proportional nature of the sub-subcontract to the subcontract, the High Court was convinced that some modifications would be allowed to facilitate the implementation of the arbitration clause in the subcontract context.

Second, Kaplan J, sitting in the Hong Kong High Court, questioned the applicability of *Thomas v Portsea*:[122] an English decision that created the basis for the decision in Singaporean *Star-Trans*[123] and also was taken into account in *International Research v Lufthansa Systems.*[124] In light of the interpretation of Article 7(2) of the Model Law, *Thomas v Portsea* held to have no application in Hong Kong.[125] The case was distinguished as it dealt with a negotiable instrument, a bill of lading, and accordingly, different considerations applied in that context. Regarding the concern about arbitration to oust the jurisdiction of the courts, which was voiced in this English case, Kaplan J made the following statement:

> The expressions of reservations about ousting the jurisdiction of the court in that case fall on infertile ground in Hong Kong at the end of the twentieth century, *a fortiori*, when the legislature has enacted the Model Law which relegates the role of the court to basically one of support for the arbitral process and gives full effect to the principle of full party autonomy. In the light of my construction of art 7(2) of the Model Law discussed above, I am therefore quite satisfied that in so far as *Thomas v Portsea* default is authority for the proposition that the arbitration clause must be specifically referred to before it can be satisfactorily incorporated, it has no application in Hong Kong. The task before the court in determining whether or not there

122 [1912] A.C. 1.

123 [1996] 2 SLR(R) 196 (*Star-Trans*). The case imported the strict rule of incorporation into Singaporean jurisprudence by following an English case: *Aughton Ltd v MF Kent Services Ltd* [1991] 57 BLR 1, which fundamentally adopts the principles laid out in *Thomas v Portsea* [1912] A.C. 1.

124 [2013] SGCA 55.

125 *Astel-Peiniger Joint Venture v Argos Engineering & Heavy Industries Co Ltd* [1994] 3 HKC 328 at [340].

> has been incorporation by reference is one of construction, namely, to ascertain the parties' intentions when they entered into the contract by reference to the words that they used.[126]

The test to assess whether incorporation was achieved is considered to have relevance with contract construction and the manifestation of the intention of the parties to incorporate. It was stated by Kaplan J,

> I have to concentrate solely on the parties' intention, which must be gleaned from the words they have used. If I am satisfied that this arbitration clause has been incorporated, it is irrelevant to me that the parties may have thereby created some problems for themselves. It frequently happens that parties enter into arbitration clauses which are poorly drafted and which give rise to problems . . . if I am satisfied that the parties clearly intended to incorporate the subcontract arbitration clause, they are problems which will have to be dealt with by the parties themselves as and when they arise.[127]

In *Astel-Peiniger*, the intentions of the parties regarding the incorporation of the subcontract arbitration clause into the sub-subcontract are held to be clearly manifested due to the meaning of the words, which were employed by them. Moreover, the plaintiff was given the opportunity to consider the terms of the subcontract as the plaintiff was given a copy before the conclusion of the sub-subcontract and they did not specifically object to the incorporation of the arbitration clause. *Astel-Peiniger* may be regarded to be illustrating the opinion difference between Hong Kong courts and English courts concerning the incorporation of an arbitration clause by general reference to the document that the clause is included in. The Hong Kong High Court, since the adoption of Model Law 1985,[128] has been demonstrating a more liberal approach towards the incorporation by reference. With regard to the fact that it was referred to without any reservations in *International Research v Lufthansa Systems*,[129] *Astel-Peiniger* has paved the way for the unfaltering departure of Singapore law from English principles on the matter.

Evidently, there are some justifiable concerns manifested in *Thomas v Portsea* that may be argued to rightfully apply in the shipping context. However, the adoption of the strict rule of incorporation has been overextended impermissibly from its original application in the context of bills of lading incorporating charterparties. The rule has been considered applicable in different branches of law, such as reinsurance and construction regardless of these specific branches of law deal with different types of contractual relationships that necessitate the application of different principles. This issue was emphasized in *International Research v Lufthansa Systems*,[130] and it was indicated that the strict rule may not be regarded as a general rule to apply. The fundamental element for a court to assess dealing with the issue of incorporation should be the intention of parties to refer existing or future disputes to arbitration at the time contract is being concluded. Furthermore, the English scenarios theory,[131] which is developed to categorize contractual structure would indeed provide a great deal of convenience in assessing the realities of the contractual

126 Ibid.
127 Ibid [343].
128 Hong Kong implemented the Model Law 1985 into its legal system in 1990.
129 [2013] SGCA 55.
130 [2013] SGCA 55 at [34].
131 Perhaps in the more detailed way (four divisions) as it is developed in *Habas Sinai v Sometal* rather than the relatively more restricted contractual categorization (two divisions) provided in *The Athena*. This is because

relationship. The theory should be implemented purely as a supplement to assess party autonomy and some room should be provided for its accurate interpretation. The desire to abide by the technical categorization the theory provides should never prevail over the promotion of party autonomy.

In *International Research v Lufthansa Systems*, the matter before the court to assess was the true interpretation of the contractual relationship. Treating the existing contractual relationship as one of two-contract because merely it meets the quantitative criteria, held not to be justifiable in this case. It was held that the matter was of contractual interpretation and in undertaking this exercise, the task was one which must be done having regard to the context and the objective circumstances attending the entry into the contract. As stated in *International Research v Lufthansa Systems*, 'Be it incorporation or construction, the court is always seeking to ascertain the parties' objective intentions.'[132] Therefore, avoiding the blindfolded application of one-contract and two-contract arrangements, the court in *International Research v Lufthansa Systems* preferred to consider the matter as one of contextual interpretation and endorsed the approach adopted in *Zurich Insurance*,[133] which is looked into in the following parts of this chapter.

5.4.4. The Ascertainable Objective Intention of the Parties and Contextual Interpretation

What necessitates contract interpretation? This straightforward question has a quite straightforward answer. Contract interpretation facilitates the promotion of the actual meaning of the contract in the way that the contracting parties attach meaning to it. Then an inevitable follow-up question would be, where the intention of the parties and the meaning of the contract that is ascertainable from the wording of it clash, then which of these elements would prevail? If the answer given is 'the true intention of the parties,' then another question needs to be asked: how far would the pursuit to ascertain such an intention should go? If the true intention of the parties is deemed to be objectively ascertained from the contractual wording, then another assessment to be made would be the extent to which the formal construction of the contract prevails over party intention. It is a slippery slope. Furthermore, the addition of the element of arbitration into the equation necessitates the assessment of the parties' true intention to arbitrate.

Evidently, if the intention to arbitrate is clear, then, the dispute arising from the contractual relationship would be referred to arbitration. However, this may not be easy to determine as the method of interpretation of the contract may vary in different jurisdictions. English law mostly employs an objective approach that emphasizes a literal or textual interpretation of a contractual document.[134] On the other hand, Singapore, despite being a common law jurisdiction as well, generally implements contextual interpretation. Accordingly, different legal systems may possibly provide different answers to the same questions. For instance,

---

the court found the latter English distinction between single-contract and two-contracts unhelpful in resolving this issue.

132 *International Research Corporation Plc. v Lufthansa Systems Asia Pacific Pte* [2012] SGHC 226 at [48]; [2013] SGCA 55 at [34]: The Singapore Court of Appeal agrees with the Singapore High Court: 'As the Judge rightly noted, "[b]e it incorporation or construction, the court is always seeking to ascertain the parties' objective intentions."

133 [2008] SGCA 27. (The Zurich Criteria).

134 Jonas Rosengren, Contract Interpretation in International Arbitration, 2013, *Journal of International Arbitration*, 30(1), 1–16, 2.

the answer given to the question 'What would be the status of an arbitration clause that is contained in a draft document prepared during the pre-contractual negotiations?' may be different. Would that be possible to discuss the incorporation of such an arbitration clause or would it not even be possible to purport that a valid arbitration agreement exists? Due to the extent and style of contract interpretation showing dissimilarities in various jurisdictions, different legal systems may possibly provide different answers to the same question. Accordingly, the concept of contract interpretation may significantly alter the contractual outcome.

English law, to a greater extent in comparison with other legal systems, takes a literal approach to interpreting contracts.[135] On the other hand, one should be careful in analyzing the meaning of the 'literal approach.' Defining the literal approach adopted in English law as a method in that the words and phrases are separated from their context in an adamant way would not provide a fair illustration of modern English law on contractual interpretation.[136] The scope of contemporary English law on contract interpretation shows a tendency to go beyond the wording to give room for considerations of business common sense. It was indicated in *Mannai Investments Ltd v Eagle Star Assurance*[137] that in determining the meaning of the language of a commercial contract, English law generally favours a commercially sensible construction as such a construction would be more likely to give effect to the intention of the parties. Therefore, in English law, the interpretation of the words of the contract would be done in a way that a reasonable commercial person would construe them.[138] Thus, it would not be wrong to say that the interpretation of the contract in this jurisdiction would be conducted in a manner that oversees the considerations of business common sense but would still be subject to the limitation of literal interpretation.[139]

It may be considered reasonable to expect that a legal system adopting a literal approach concerning contract interpretation to disallow the admission of any pre-contractual element of negotiation as evidence. Being subject to various exceptions,[140] the general rule in English law, especially concerning international arbitrations, is that the extrinsic evidence[141] that

135 Ibid 4.

136 Ibid 4.

137 [1997] AC 749.

138 Ibid [770]. See also Gerard McMeel, The Rise of Commercial Construction in Contract Law, 1998, *Lloyd's Maritime and Commercial Law Quarterly*, 382.

139 On the other hand, see *Emirates Trading Agency LLC v Prime Mineral Exports Private Limited* [2014] EWHC 2014 (Comm) where the judge, by taking recent Singapore cases into consideration, decided that negotiation provisions agreed by commercial parties were likely to be upheld and given effect by English courts rather than being dismissed on the basis of uncertainty as this would follow the original intention of the parties. *Emirates Trading* may considered to be illustrating the contemporary and soften approach of English contract law concerning contract interpretation.

140 There are a limited number of exceptions to the contractual interpretation rule that holding pre-contractual negotiations inadmissible for the interpretation of the contract. For example, the 'private dictionary' scenario would mean the parties to the contract alleged to have attached particularly special meanings to their words, in a way that the used words would not be understood in the clear and straightforward way in the ordinary sense. Another situation is, where pre-contractual negotiations are relevant, for instance where rectification is sought, or fraud is alleged. See *Pre-Contractual Negotiations: Strategic Use in International Arbitration* July 21, 2017, Allen & Overy, available at www.allenovery.com/publications/en-gb/Pages/pre-contractual-negotiations-strategic-use-in-international-arbitration.aspx (last visited August 11, 2022).

141 *Black's Law Dictionary*, 638, 9th Edn., 2009: Extrinsic evidence can be defined as 'evidence relating to a contract but not appearing on the face of the contract because it comes from other sources, such as statements between the parties or the circumstances surrounding the agreement.'

particularly including pre-contractual negotiations that may reveal the objective intention of the parties – for example, former drafts of contracts – to be inadmissible to interpret a contract.[142] It was restated by Lord Hoffman in *Investors Compensation Scheme Ltd v West Bromwich Building Society* that the extrinsic material would be admissible as long as '(a) it is relevant – ie, it would affect the way in which the language of the document would have been understood by a reasonable man; and (b) it was reasonably available to all contracting parties.'[143]

Singapore courts, showing parallel implementations with the applications of English law, were predominantly interpreting contracts objectively, meaning that recourse had to be made to the parties' expressed intentions in the contractual language rather than their actual intention.[144] In other words, as a general rule, the evidence of the subjective declarations of the intention of the parties was not considered admissible in Singapore.[145] However, the examples of recent Singaporean case law signal a departure from this general rule. It may be argued that the position of the courts of Singapore concerning the applicability of an arbitration clause, which is found in one of the contracts that is constituting a part of a group of contracts, tends to be manifesting the adoption of the 'contextual approach' that requires the examination of the objective circumstances that applied at the stage of contract conclusion, including the objectively ascertained intentions of the parties.[146] 'At a substantive level, Singapore adopts the contextual approach with regard to the interpretation of contracts and this is accepted as settled law.'[147] In other words, the courts of Singapore usually tend to interpret contracts broadly rather than narrowly.

Zurich Insurance may be regarded to have refined the implementation concerning the admissibility of extrinsic evidence that may potentially affect the interpretation of the meaning of the contractual words and expressions. The case predominantly establishes that courts should adopt a contextual approach to interpreting contracts. In *Zurich Insurance* and later in *Sembcorp Marine Ltd v PPL Holding Pte Ltd*,[148] it was emphasized that extrinsic evidence may be admitted to cure latent ambiguity.[149] It was indicated by the Court of Appeal in *Sandar Aung v Parkway Hospitals Singapore Pte Ltd*[150] that the parol evidence

142 *Chartbrook Ltd v Persimmon Homes Ltd* [2009] UKHL 38.

143 [1998] 1 WLR 896, at 912–913 (*ICS*). Words of Lord Hoffmann in *ICS* were referred to in *International Research Corporation Plc. v Lufthansa Systems Asia Pacific Pte* [2012] SGHC 226, [52], and this approach was considered by the Singapore Court of Appeal in *Zurich Insurance (Singapore) Pte Ltd v B-Gold Interior Design & Construction Pte Ltd* [2008] SGCA 27, [125].

144 Jihan Goh, The New Contractual Interpretation in Singapore: From 'Zurich Insurance' to 'Sembcorp Marine,' December 2013, *Singapore Journal of Legal Studies*, 301–330, 318.

145 *Zurich Insurance (Singapore) Pte Ltd v B-Gold Interior Design & Construction Pte Ltd* [2008] SGCA 27, 125.

146 David Joseph and David Foxton, *Singapore International Arbitration Law & Practice*, 2018, LexisNexis, 62, 13.1. The said shift becomes more vivid in light of *Star-Trans Far East Pte Ltd v Norske-Tech Ltd and Others* [1996] 2 SLR(R) 196 (*Star-Trans*); *Sembcorp Marine Ltd v PPL Holding Pte Ltd* [2013] SGCA 43; *Zurich Insurance (Singapore) Pte Ltd v B-Gold Interior Design & Construction Pte Ltd* [2008] SGCA 2; *International Research Corporation Plc. v Lufthansa Systems Asia Pacific Pte* [2013] SGCA 55 at [29].

147 *BQP v BQQ* [2018] SGHC 55 at [123].

148 [2013] SGCA 43, (*Sembcorp Marine*).

149 *Zurich Insurance (Singapore) Pte Ltd v B-Gold Interior Design & Construction Pte Ltd* [2008] SGCA 27 at [50]; *Sembcorp Marine Ltd v PPL Holding Pte Ltd* [2013] SGCA 43 at [59].

150 [2007] 2 SLR 891.

rule[151] operates as a restriction on the use of extrinsic material to affect a contract,[152] and that the contextual interpretation approach rather than contractual interpretation[153] is adopted in Singapore. In *Sandar Aung*, the Court of Appeal acknowledged the admissibility of the extrinsic material even if no ambiguity is detected in the contractual language.

In *Zurich Insurance*, the Singapore Court of Appeal held that extrinsic evidence including pre-contractual negotiations to interpret a contract would be admissible if it is 'relevant, reasonably available to all the contracting parties and relates to a clear or obvious context.'[154] These elements may be considered to establish the 'Zurich criteria' and to constitute restrictions on admissibility adopting the contextual approach. Under the traditional approach, the prerequisite for the courts to resort to extrinsic evidence would be strictly limited.[155] However, *Zurich Insurance* sets forth a simple but significant framework that is not exhaustive but rather inclusive, provided that the requirements to allow the admittance of extrinsic evidence are met; these would be considered in the scope of interpretation that is conducted in a contextual manner. To put it differently, *Zurich Insurance*, instead of setting forth restrictions for extrinsic evidence to be admissible, instead, provides an approach adopting general admissibility, unless there is ambiguity in the contract.[156] In other words, the 'Zurich criteria' provide boxes to tick for the 'extrinsic evidence admissibility checklist.'

Subsequently, the Court of Appeal in *Sembcorp Marine* formulated specific requirements to ensure that the 'Zurich criteria' are met and, by doing so, refined the criteria.[157] Furthermore, it was emphasized that the law governing the admissibility of extrinsic evidence in Singapore was statutory and since jurisdictions such as the United Kingdom, Hong Kong, and New Zealand do not have equivalent provisions, their cases pertaining to contract interpretation 'must be treated with a degree of caution.'[158] It was observed by Lord Hoffmann in *Chartbrook Ltd v Persimmon Homes Ltd* that 'courts should be careful about transposing rules formulated by and for a particular legal system

151 Section 94 of the Singapore Evidence Act (Cap 97, 1997 Rev Ed).

152 *Sandar Aung v Parkway Hospitals Singapore Pte Ltd* [2007] 2 SLR 891.

153 Contextual interpretation was also endorsed in a former Singapore case: *Singapore Telecommunications Ltd v Starhub Cable Vision Ltd* [2006] 2 SLR 195.

154 [2008] SGCA 27.

155 There are limited number of exceptions to the contractual interpretation rule that holding pre-contractual negotiations inadmissible for the interpretation of the contract. For example, a 'private dictionary' scenario would mean the parties to the contract alleged to have attached a special meaning to their words in a way that the used words would not be understood in the clear and straightforward way in the ordinary sense. Another situation is where pre-contractual negotiations are relevant – for instance, where rectification is sought or fraud is alleged. See *Pre-Contractual Negotiations: Strategic Use in International Arbitration* (n 141).

156 Goh (n 145) 305.

157 Sundaresh Menon CJ, delivering the judgement of the Court of Appeal in *Sembcorp Marine* [2013] SGCA 43 at [73], stated, 'Indeed, it is trite that the court must have regard to the context at the time of contracting when considering the issue of implication. Therefore, to buttress the evidentiary qualifications to the contextual approach to the construction of a contract, the imposition of four requirements of civil procedure are, in our view, timely and essential: (a) first, parties who contend that the factual matrix is relevant to the construction of the contract must plead with specificity each fact of the factual matrix that they wish to rely on in support of their construction of the contract; (b) second, the factual circumstances in which the facts in (a) were known to both or all the relevant parties must also be pleaded with sufficient particularity; (c) third, parties should in their pleadings specify the effect which such facts will have on their contended construction; and (d) fourth, the obligation of parties to disclose evidence would be limited by the extent to which the evidence are relevant to the facts pleaded in (a) and (b).'

158 [2013] SGCA 43 at [39].

operating under a particular philosophy into another legal system premised on another philosophy.'[159] With regard to the words of Lord Hoffmann in *Chartbrook*, the concepts of contextual interpretation of contracts and the admissibility of extrinsic evidence (and thus, the admissibility of pre-contractual negotiations) require specific evaluation. Accordingly, these concepts are merely analyzed in the Singapore context, and a comparative analysis is not provided. Nonetheless, solely some relevant English decisions are taken into account to better illustrate the implementation of these legal concepts.

We observe a striking shift in the modern approach to contract interpretation in Singapore. *Zurich Insurance*, being a landmark decision, represents the state of the law concerning party autonomy and contextual approach. Singapore Court of Appeal in *Zurich Insurance* goes the extra mile and extends the limit of the ascertainment of the parties' intentions to include the realm of the pre-contractual period. The deviation of Singapore law from the parallel implementation of the relevant English principles on contract interpretation[160] was considered to be in accordance with 'common sense and logic.'[161] Indeed, *Zurich Insurance* redefines what is 'objectively ascertainable' in a contractual structure and seeks to find what is actually known to the parties.

In a number of 'other common law jurisdictions such as Australia, New Zealand, and Hong Kong, the contextual approach now prevails over the traditional approach'[162] perhaps due to the necessity to be able to accord with ordinary commerce where the traditional contractual approach fails to do so. The law in Singapore regarding the admissibility of extrinsic evidence for contract interpretation purposes further illustrates the adoption of the contextual approach over formal contractual interpretation.[163] Accordingly, the Singapore Court of Appeal in *Zurich Insurance* took the opportunity to emphasize that the contextual approach is 'here to stay in Singapore.'[164]

Singapore courts adopt the contextual interpretation, and thus, they usually tend to go beyond the wording and pursue to assess the objectively ascertainable intentions of the parties while interpreting a contract. As they adopt the contextual interpretation approach, Singapore courts show some flexibility concerning the admissibility of extrinsic evidence, which includes pre-contractual negotiations. Singapore courts consider such evidence to constitute dependable aid to assess the actual intention of the parties while interpreting the contract. This raises the question of whether an arbitration agreement that is contained in the pre-contractual negotiations of a contract which has not been concluded would still be binding. *Zurich Insurance* and *Sembcorp Marine* have essentially established ground rules that are applicable in contract interpretation to be able to provide an answer to this.

In *BCY v BCZ*,[165] the Singapore High Court refined the matter of enforceability of arbitration clauses included in the contracts that have not been concluded. It was emphasized

159 [2009] UKHL 38 at [39]. (*Chartbrook*)

160 Embodied in *Investors and Full Metal Jacket Ltd v Gowlain Building Group* [2005] EWCA Civ 1809.

161 [2008] SGCA 27 at [133].

162 *Zurich Insurance (Singapore) Pte Ltd v B-Gold Interior Design & Construction Pte Ltd* [2008] SGCA 27 at [133].

163 *Singapore Telecommunications Ltd v Starhub Cable Vision Ltd* [2006] 2 SLR 195; *Sandar Aung v Parkway Hospitals Singapore Pte Ltd* [2007] 2 SLR 891.; *Sembcorp Marine Ltd v PPL Holding Pte Ltd* [2013] SGCA 43; *Zurich Insurance (Singapore) Pte Ltd v B-Gold Interior Design & Construction Pte Ltd* [2008] SGCA 27.

164 [2008] SGCA 27 at [133].

165 [2016] SGHC 249.

that for an arbitration agreement in an unsigned document to be effective, the intention of the parties at the pre-contractual stage to arbitrate must be clearly ascertainable.[166] It was stated by Steven Chong J in *BCY v BCZ*, 'When the jurisdiction of an arbitral tribunal is challenged on the basis that there is no binding arbitration agreement, the usual ground for such a challenge is that the contract which incorporates the arbitration clause was itself never concluded.' In this familiar situation, it has been held that 'the validity of the arbitration agreement and the existence of a binding contract would "stand or fall together" and the court would usually determine both issues collectively.'[167]

It should be noted that an arbitration agreement to be freestanding in nature is technically possible. Generally, arbitration agreements would constitute a part of the substantive contract. Nonetheless, an arbitration agreement may evidently be concluded in a separate nature pertaining to disputes relating to a number of contracts or to an overall project.[168] This issue was considered in the shipping context in an English case, *Viscous Global Investments Ltd v Palladium Navigation.*[169] The parties contracted to transport rice under bills of lading that contained several arbitration clauses. A dispute arose concerning alleged damage to the cargo. The arbitration clause that is included in a provided letter of undertaking was found to be 'perfectly capable of operating as a new and free-standing agreement.'[170] This was fundamentally because the letter was containing everything that was needed for the establishment of an arbitration clause: It was comprehensive and included the applicable procedure, the constitution of the tribunal, the time for the defendant to appoint the arbitrator, and the substantive law to be applied.[171] Accordingly, the English Commercial Court was of the view that given such a comprehensive set of provisions, there was no apparent reason that the parties should not have intended to letter of understanding to replace the charterparty arbitration clauses in their entirety.[172] Indeed, under the provided circumstances, the intention to construct a freestanding arbitration agreement would be ascertainable.

More recently in *BQP v BQQ*,[173] the question before the High Court of Singapore was whether pre-contractual negotiations were admissible in evidence to construe written agreements. The High Court, dismissing the challenge to the jurisdictional ruling of the arbitral tribunal, held that the admissibility of pre-contractual negotiations was a procedural issue to be determined by the tribunal. There were two dispute resolution clauses of two different contracts that were entered into, establishing jurisdiction for two

166 [2016] SGHC 249. The court at this point relied on an English Court of Appeal decision *Sulamérica Cia Nacional de Seguros SA and others v Enesa Engelharia SA and others* [2013] 1 WLR 102 [9] and [25] and stated that the governing law of the arbitration agreement had to be determined by a three-step test: (1) the express choice of the parties, (2) the implied choice of the parties that can be ascertained from their intentions at the time of contracting, or (3) the system of law which the arbitration agreement has the closest and most real connection. As there was no express choice of law to govern the arbitration, the court had to determine the implied choice of law: [2016] SGHC 249, [40].

167 Steven Chong J in *BCY v BCZ* [2016] SGHC 249, [1]. See also *Hyundai Merchant Marine Company Ltd v Americas Bulk Transport Ltd* [2013] EWHC 470 (Comm) at [35–36], cited in *Jiangsu Overseas Group Co Ltd v Concord Energy Pte Ltd and another matter* [2016] 4 SLR 1336 at [48].

168 Gary Born, *International Commercial Arbitration*, Wolters Kluwer, 2014, Vol. 1, 2nd Edn., 491.

169 [2014] EWHC 2654. (*Viscous Global v Palladium Navigation*).

170 Ibid 22.

171 Ibid.

172 Ibid 23.

173 [2018] SGHC 55.

different arbitration institutions. The main issue before the court was to determine whether the jurisdiction of the tribunal had been superseded by a subsequent agreement, which provides jurisdiction for a different arbitration institution.

If the arbitration clause in the first agreement was superseded by the arbitration clause in the second agreement, then this situation was going to amount to the Singapore International Arbitration Centre (SIAC)[174] Tribunal lacking jurisdiction over the claims submitted to it pursuant to the arbitration clause in the first agreement. In such a case, the arbitration clause in the subsequent agreement would be deemed to prevail and provide for arbitration in Indonesia. The parties had different arguments regarding the nature of the second agreement. The plaintiff indicated that the second agreement was a definite legal agreement and, therefore, when it was signed the first agreement, ceased to be in force, and hence, the first agreement was no longer valid. The defendant contended that the phrase 'definite legal agreement' was referring only to a subsequent offshore agreement, and because the second agreement was an onshore agreement, it did not constitute a definite legal agreement, and thus, the first agreement remained in force. The wording of the second agreement, providing that 'the second agreement will be implemented by way of an onshore wood supply agreement to be finalized between parties,' was interpreted by the court as 'the first agreement to be performed by or carried into effect or given effect by an onshore agreement.'[175] It was emphasized by the Singapore High Court in *BQP v BQQ* that the drafters of the contract did not use the word 'supersede' as they did elsewhere.[176] The parties were aware of the concepts of 'supersession' and 'implementation.' By means of interpreting the contractual relationship in a contextual way,[177] and thus, taking the pre-contractual negotiations into consideration, the High Court evaluated the scope of the pre-contractual emails and drafts between the parties as evidencing the intention of the parties to construct an onshore contract 'given that the parties were exchanging emails almost daily and expressly discussing draft onshore agreement language.'[178]

The contractual language was considered in this case and the High Court particularly evaluated the meaning and use of the word 'supersede.' The parties were aware of the concept of an agreement to possibly be 'superseded,' and indeed, they could employ this specific word for the purposes of repudiation of the initial contract. They did not. Furthermore, the language that the parties were using in their email correspondence was considered to be constituting 'onshore agreement language' that suggests the nature of the electronic communication to reflect an 'onshore legal relationship.' Accordingly, one may argue that the literal aspect of the contract was evaluated in a contextual manner to ascertain the objective intentions of the contracting parties. Furthermore, the way that the

174 Singapore International Arbitration Centre (SIAC) was founded in 1991 and issued its Arbitration Rules. The most recent version of the Rules is 2013. The Rules of the SIAC are regularly adopted in international arbitrations that are governed by IAA. See Merkin and Hjalmarsson (n 15) 5.

175 [2018] SGHC 55 at [82].

176 First draft of the clause referred to 'the date of execution of definitive legal agreements superseding this Memorandum of Understanding (MOU).' This illustrates that the drafters of the contract had not reservation using a strong word, such as 'supersede' when needed. Drafters of the contract were aware of the concepts of 'supersession' and 'implementation'; *BQP v BQQ* [2018] SGHC 55, 82.

177 [2018] SGHC 55 at [123]: 'At a substantive level Singapore adopts the contextual approach to the construction of contracts. This is settled law.'

178 [2018] SGHC 55, 90, see [16] and [29].

contracting parties used certain words and styles was also considered to be indicating how they perceived their legal relationship.

5.4.5. Sky Is the Limit: The Assessment of Singapore Courts of the Validity of Arbitration Agreements and Their Incorporation – the Meanings of 'Silence' and 'Bare Minimum'

It is evident that 'Singapore's progressive and pro-arbitration judicial policy'[179] encourages the promotion of arbitration agreements to the highest degree possible, provided that party autonomy concerning the selection of arbitration as the preferred dispute resolution method is manifested. Nevertheless, there are some examples in this jurisprudence in which the impacts of adopting such a progressive policy may be argued to have blurred the meaning and scope of such manifestation. It is indeed true that the adoption of the contextual method concerning contract interpretation necessitates a wide evaluation of the circumstances at the time parties conclude the contract. However, some examples of such interpretation in the Singaporean context may be argued to have produced some 'far-fetched legal results' that must be approached with a certain degree of caution.

I. *R1 International Pte Ltd v Lonstroff AG* – Incorporation of an Arbitration Clause due to Silence and Timing of Incorporation and Contract Formation

To reiterate, the courts of Singapore usually adopt an objective approach and interpret contracts in a contextual manner. This fundamentally necessitates the examination of the actual circumstances including the objectively ascertainable intentions of the parties at the time the contract is entered into.[180] *R1 International Pte Ltd v Lonstroff AG*[181] essentially takes this evaluation a step further.

R1 International (R1) was a rubber supplier and Lonstroff (L) was a company that processed rubber. The dispute between the appellant R1, a Singapore company, and respondent L, a Swiss company, concerned a certain order of rubber that was allegedly delivered defective. After taking delivery of the second shipment of rubber, the respondent notified the appellant that the rubber emitted a foul smell. Due to allegations regarding defects in the product, L initiated proceedings against R1 in Switzerland on the basis that R1 had breached the second contract by supplying defective rubber. Not disputing the presence of smell, the appellant R1 indicated that 'smell' was not a contractually specific parameter of rubber, and accordingly, they were not in breach of contract regarding this matter. The R1 sought an anti-suit injunction in Singapore to restrain the Swiss proceedings. The basis for R1 seeking an anti-suit injunction was that L was in breach of the terms of the contract note including an agreement to arbitrate any disputes in Singapore, which was sent shortly after the deal had apparently been agreed upon. The contract note was neither countersigned nor returned. L argued that there was in fact no arbitration agreement, and thus, they were entitled to commence proceedings in Switzerland, and the Singapore High Court agreed with that. The court emphasized that the arbitration agreement was not incorporated since the contract had been concluded and performed between both

179 Poon (11) 540.

180 Joseph and Foxton (n 147) 62, 13.1.

181 [2014] SGHC 69; [2014] SGCA 56 (*R1 International*). The Singapore Court of Appeal reversed the decision of the Singapore High Court.

parties before L was notified of the arbitration agreement, and also, no discussion took place pertaining to the incorporation of the arbitration agreement during the negotiations between the parties.[182]

Nevertheless, this was perhaps too straightforward of an evaluation from the perspective of the Singapore Court of Appeal, and consequently, the appeal was allowed.

The essential issue before the Court of Appeal to assess was whether the arbitration agreement stipulating disputes to be settled by arbitration in Singapore was incorporated into the contract subsequent to the contract's formation. To put it differently, the Court of Appeal was in the position to consider the timing of incorporation and whether 'subsequent incorporation' as a concept was possible to implement by assessing the 'substance of silence.'

It is stated by the court that

> although silence by one party may not by itself constitute acceptance of the terms sent by the other party, it does not follow from this that silence is fatal to a finding that the terms sent have been accepted. The effect of silence is context-dependent. In many cases, while there may not be actual communication of acceptance, the parties' positive, negative or even neutral conduct can still evince acceptance.[183]

The court also referred to *Midlink Development Pte Ltd v The Stansfield Group Pte Ltd*,[184] where it is clarified that the meaning of silence essentially depends on the context and for it to be presumed acceptance, the objectively assessed conduct of the parties should support the existence of the contract. The Court of Appeal was of the view that 'a failure to object might in the circumstances be found to constitute assent to the incorporation of the other party's terms'[185] and accordingly that L's 'silence in the circumstances amounted to assent.'[186] Thus, the 'subsequent incorporation' of the arbitration agreement in the contract note was allowed because the timing of it was not actually considered 'subsequent' in accordance with the pattern of the parties' transactions.

The decision of the Court of Appeal may seem controversial and perhaps too ambitious. On the other hand, it may also be considered to be indicating an important judicial recognition that supports the notion that if the true conduct and relevant intention of the parties are clear, this would obviate the necessity for seeking further conduct for validation. Whichever the approach may be, *R1 International* is momentous as it truly evaluates the concept of timing and implementation of incorporation in Singapore jurisprudence.

The Singapore Court of Appeal in *R1 International* was fundamentally concerned with two issues: whether standard terms that include an arbitration clause may be incorporated subsequent to the deal and, if so, when such an incorporation would take place. Accordingly, the Court of Appeal had the task to assess whether the Singapore arbitration clause was incorporated into the second contract, even though it was sent by the appellant R1 after the deal had been concluded.[187] *R1 International* is of significance in the sense that it remarks the importance of the incorporation of arbitration agreements: If an arbitration

182 [2014] SGHC 69 at [34].
183 [2014] SGCA 56, [53].
184 [2004] 4 SLR(R) 258, [50] and [52].
185 [2014] SGCA 56, [54].
186 [2014] SGCA 56, [54]. [67].
187 [2014] SGCA 56, [2].

clause is incorporated, then the seat of arbitration and the scope of matters arising under the agreement to arbitrate will directly be determined due to such incorporation.[188] It is also important as the court assesses the meaning of 'silence' and finds the attributed meaning of the concept in the context of *R1 International* sufficient to effectuate the incorporation of the Singapore arbitration clause.

There were five transactions, which were negotiated and concluded in a very similar manner and the dispute arose out of the second of these transactions, in which the Contract Note included a rider specifying that arbitration would be conducted in Singapore. The Court of Appeal explored 'the salient details surrounding each of the transactions.'[189] The method of dealing for each transaction was, more or less, as follows: (1) The negotiations concerning the sale and purchase of rubber would be carried out via email or telephone and the basic terms would be agreed upon. (2) R1 would send an email to L setting out the agreed terms and the parties would refer to these emails of R1 as 'Email Confirmations.' Then L would also send R1 a 'Purchase Order.' (3) Subsequently, R1 would send L a 'Contract Note' that specifies the sale and request L to countersign and return a copy of the Note. Subsequently, the delivery would take place and R1 would issue an invoice. On its part, L would accept delivery and pay the invoice.

Concerning the first contract, L had made payment without protest despite seeing the Contract Note was referring to terms of the International Rubber Association Contract (IRAC) for 'Technically Specified Rubber.' Under the IRAC terms, disputes are resolved by arbitration in London but parties are permitted to agree otherwise. The Contract Note for the second transaction was referring to IRAC terms but was also containing a rider which specified that arbitration would be conducted in Singapore. For the Second Contract, at no point did the L ever demur from the applicability of the Contract Note[190] and made the payment knowing that the Note referred to IRAC terms and the Singapore Arbitration Clause.

The fundamental issue before the Court of Appeal to assess was whether the Singapore Arbitration Clause had been incorporated into the second contract. The arguments of R1 at the Singapore Court of Appeal were found reasonable and compatible with business common sense. It was argued by R1 that it was typical in commodity trading transactions for parties to first negotiate key commercial terms with the understanding that a later set of terms would follow. Because L was an experienced buyer in the rubber commodities market, it would be reasonable to expect the standard terms of R1 (contained in the Contract Note) to follow.[191] It was held by the Court of Appeal, in compliance with business common sense, that there was indeed a mutual understanding between R1 and L, and it was found that IRAC terms had been incorporated.

Some important points may be extracted from the decision of the Singapore Court of Appeal in *R1 International*. First, the judgement may be regarded as a pure restatement of the adoption of the contextual approach in Singapore. The Court of Appeal, by means

188 Jonathan Chen Yeen Muk, The Sound of Silence – An Analysis of the Incorporation of Arbitration Terms after Contract Formation, 2015, *Asian International Arbitration Journal*, 11(1), 93–104, 93.
189 [2014] SGCA 56, [13–32].
190 [2014] SGCA 56, [71].
191 [2014] SGCA 56, [41].

of adhering to its former decision in *International Research v Lufthansa Systems*,[192] reaffirmed the applicability of the contextual approach also in determining whether a contract was concluded in *R1 International*. This was one of the most crucial issues to be assessed by the court. To be able to do so, the Court of Appeal implemented the contextual approach and evaluated the following: The realities of the industry of which the parties were members, the character of the documents containing the relevant terms, and the essentials of the transactions between the parties. The assessment of these issues provided insight of the characteristics of the contractual relationship of the parties. Regarding the realities of the industry, the Court of Appeal was of the opinion that the parties were both well-experienced players in the commodities market. The court made the assessment that it would be unlikely for L to lack expectation concerning the terms of the R1 to follow their agreement of sale and purchase of rubber as this constitutes the usual practice in this market. Moreover, the character of the document incorporated (the IRAC Terms) was observed to be known to L, and the document was accepted to have created a part of the transactions, which were again familiar to L. Even though the dispute arose regarding the provisions of the Contract Note that was provided subsequent to the 'completion of the deal,' the Court of Appeal approached the matter from a purely contextual standpoint and evaluated the 'bigger picture.' Considering all the relevant components of the case in a contextual framework, the court allowed the incorporation of the Singapore Arbitration Clause. The evaluation of these components is considered to indicate a mutual understanding of the parties of the practical aspects of their contractual relationship and the realities of the rubber commodities market.

Second, the strict requirements of offer and acceptance were held not to be necessarily appropriate.[193] The Court of Appeal, in that regard, cited an English High Court case, *Statoil ASA v Louis Dreyfus Energy Services LP*, in which Aikens J accepted that

> [i]f the principal terms have been agreed and the parties are . . . 'sorting out details against the background of a concluded contract,' then the strict requirements of positive offer and positive acceptance are not necessarily appropriate. If one party makes a proposal for terms and the other does not object to it when asked if it has objections, that can, in appropriate circumstances, be taken as acceptance of that term.[194]

It was observed by the Court of Appeal that the rubber commodities market was one where the concerned parties were experienced players, and it was the regular practice in this particular market for the parties to merely agree on the essential terms of each transaction, with the rest of the terms to be followed up and specified subsequently.[195] Observing that the realities of the market were clearly acknowledged by the parties, the Court of Appeal appeared to be of the view that the implementation of the strict requirements of offer and acceptance was not necessarily appropriate in this case. The decision reflects the reluctance of Singapore courts to be restricted by some rigid rules concerning contract formation,

192 Consistent with a previous decision of its own; *International Research Corporation Plc. v Lufthansa Systems Asia Pacific Pte* [2013] SGCA 55, 53.

193 [2014] SGCA 56, [55].

194 [2009] 1 All ER (Comm) 1035, [70]. Aikens J uses the phrase 'sorting out details against the background of a concluded contract,' as stated by Bingham J in *Pagnan SpA v Feed Products Ltd* [1987] 2 Lloyd's Rep 601 at 619.

195 [2014] SGCA 56, [60].

and the general tendency is to both consider the way contracts are concluded in specific markets and also the overall market realities.

Third, the Court of Appeal indicated that the terms sent over by R1 were accepted by L due to the silence of the latter. For the first contract, L made a payment without a protest even after seeing that the contract note included a reference to IRAC terms that R1 intended to incorporate. Concerning the second contract, the Court of Appeal found that R1 did not demur from the application of R1's Contract Note and made a payment again without protest even after it knew that the contract note referred to the IRAC terms and contained a rider which specified that arbitration would be conducted in Singapore.[196]

The silence to pave the way for incorporation may be considered controversial, and indeed, a 'pure silence' would usually not be sufficient for incorporation to take place. However, what was considered in *R1 International* by the Court of Appeal was the combination of the characteristic elements of the case, and the final assessment of the court was that the incorporation was allowed. *R1 International*, indeed, included parties that were familiar with the realities of the commodities market, in which they were doing business. L concluded the initial transaction without any protest despite being aware of the fact that IRAC Terms are intended to be incorporated. Concerning the second agreement, L, again, concluded the relevant transaction with a payment despite being aware of the IRAC Terms and the rider specifying the Singapore Arbitration Clause. The conduct of L is held to be reflecting a clear understanding of the way in which the transactions within this particular market are made and the impact of such a manner on the implementation of the contractual relationship between R1 and L. Accordingly, it would perhaps not do the justice to say that the Singapore Court of Appeal allowed the incorporation merely due to L's silence but the decision actually pertained to the realities of the case and the 'bigger picture' they reflected. The concept of 'silence' should be interpreted as the lack of conduct of L, even though they had the opportunity to protest.[197] Therefore, it would be felicitous to argue that the reasoning of the Court of Appeal for allowing the incorporation of the arbitration clause in question is based on 'lack of conduct' rather than 'pure silence.' The distinction seems to have conceptual significance and therefore needs to be highlighted for clarification purposes even though it does not alter the meaning substantially.

II. *KVC Rice v Asian Mineral* – To What Extent of Singaporean Courts Uphold Arbitration?

KVC Rice v Asian Mineral is the first Singaporean case evaluating the issue of the enforceability of a bare arbitration clause specifying neither the seat of arbitration nor the method for establishing the tribunal. Allowing the enforceability of such a clause, the case is indeed ground-breaking but also some aspects of it should be considered carefully.[198]

In compliance with the pro-arbitration policy adopted in Singapore, it is not inapprehensible, especially in dealing with arbitration agreements of international character that the courts of Singapore would be inclined to stay their proceedings to effectuate the

196 Ibid [71].
197 For a detailed analysis of the case, see Muk (n 189).
198 Poon (n 11) 540.

intention of the parties to arbitrate and for the sake of promoting the arbitration agreement. In *KVC Rice v Asian Mineral*,[199] a mere intention of the parties to arbitrate was enforced; nonetheless, the relevant arbitration agreement was devoid of details.[200] The essential issues before the Singapore High Court to assess were whether the bare arbitration clause included in the parties' contract was incapable of being performed and subsequently, whether the proceedings before the court need not stay in line with Section 6(2) of the International Arbitration Act 1994. It was indicated by the court that 'a bare arbitration clause which merely provides for submission of disputes to arbitration . . . remains a valid and binding agreement'[201] provided that 'parties have evinced in clear intention to settle any dispute by arbitration.'[202] Furthermore, the court was of the view that the place of arbitration[203] and method for establishing the tribunal[204] not being specified was not an issue detrimentally affecting the application of arbitration as the selected dispute resolution method.

Two fundamental aspects of this decision that are particularly concerned with the practicalities of contract drafting and the applicability of legal principles should be noted. Concerning the former, the decision in *KVC Rice v Asian Mineral* highlights the cruciality of drafting arbitration clauses in a way that clearly sets forth that it is the undisputable wish of the parties to refer any existing or future disputes to arbitration. The clear construction of an arbitration clause would fairly minimise, if not eliminate, the potential disputes that may arise pertaining to intent, ambit, and application of an arbitration clause. A clearly structured arbitration clause would facilitate the speedy resolution of the dispute because the issues concerning the implementation of the arbitration process would be easily ascertainable as plainly reflected in the clause. From the aspect of the applicability of legal principles, *R1 International* vividly illustrates that it would be a highly undesirable outcome that a clear agreement to arbitrate that is manifesting the wishes of the parties being frustrated merely due to the failure of the parties to designate a seat of arbitration.[205]

KVC Rice v Asian Mineral is of significance as it is concerned with a 'deficient' arbitration clause in the conventional sense, which is lacking the specification of the place of arbitration and stipulations concerning the methods of establishing an arbitral tribunal. The Singapore High Court was of the view that such deficiencies were not adequate to allay the validity and enforceability of the clause.[206] One may argue that the court exceeded

199 [2017] SGHC 32.

200 [2017] SGHC 32 at [23]. See also: Rachel Chiu Li Hsien, *Clothing the Bare: The Enforcement of Arbitration Clauses in Singapore*, New York University School of Law, Centre for Transnational Litigation, Arbitration and Commercial Law Blogs, March 2, 2018, available at https://blogs.law.nyu.edu/transnational/2018/03/clothing-the-bare-the-enforcement-of-arbitration-clauses-in-singapore/?fbclid=IwAR0afIXy_t6VEa3HfTptnfqy3uKunagGv7tZTtgFEomyci6XnSH-c061yF0#_ftn8 (last visited August 9, 2022).

201 [2017] SGHC 32, [29]. This finding is in line with the Singapore Court of Appeal's holding in *Insigma Technology Co Ltd v Alstom Technology Ltd* [2009] 3 SLR(R) 936 (*Insigma*) at [31].

202 [2017] SGHC 32, [29].

203 Similar with the English decision in *Chalbury McCouat International Ltd v PG Foils Ltd* [2010] EWHC 2050 (TCC), where the parties had agreed upon 'arbitration as per prevailing laws of European Union in the Europe' without specifying a seat or any governing law, the court still gave effect to the clause.

204 Hsien (n 201).

205 Alastair Henderson, Emmanuel Chua, and Yosuke Homma, *'Bare' Arbitration Clauses and the Extent to Which the Singapore Court May Assist*, Herbert Smith Freehills, Arbitration Notes, March 9, 2017, available at https://hsfnotes.com/arbitration/2017/03/09/bare-arbitration-clauses-and-the-extent-to-which-the-singapore-court-may-assist/ (last visited January 14, 2019).

206 Hsien (n 201).

its limits of effective interpretation and in a way retrospectively intervened in the phase of contract negotiations even though this was indeed not the business of the courts. As it is rightfully stated in *TMT Co Ltd v The Royal Bank of Scotland*,

> Certainly, whether under English or Singapore law, party autonomy in selecting arbitration or other dispute resolution mechanisms would be encouraged and supported, but additionally, neither English nor Singapore courts would readily rewrite the agreements entered into between parties, especially in a commercial agreement between commercial entities, which presumably would have been scrutinised by legal advisors. If there were any slips despite such scrutiny, the parties would have to live with the consequences.[207]

Indeed, a rewritten bargain is not the parties' bargain.[208]

A bare intention to arbitrate to be enforced by means of the 'excessive' intervention of the court to dispel the deficiencies in the arbitration clause may seem to contradict party autonomy that affords primacy to the parties' right to choose how they wish to resolve their disputes.[209] Accordingly, one may consider the appositeness of the decision debatable. However, whatever the legal approach concerning *KVC Rice v Asian Mineral* would be, the judgement is significant in the sense that it illustrates how far the courts of Singapore may go in an attempt to prioritize an arbitration agreement even where the validity of such an agreement is in question. The case is concerned with a bare intention to arbitrate and that does not specify some essential aspects of the arbitration process that are normally required to be specified. *KVC Rice v Asian Mineral* provides a striking illustration that the Singapore courts will endeavour to do their best to facilitate and promote arbitration between commercial parties provided they are convinced this is the fair thing to do,[210] even when the necessity of making such effort sometimes may seem contradictive. Thus, answering the question that to what extent Singapore courts would uphold arbitration, we can, in the simplest terms, say that when it comes to arbitration there are no rigid boundaries restricting courts provided the intention to arbitrate can objectively be ascertained.

5.5. *Concluding Remarks*

Singapore, being a common law jurisdiction, has always been under the strong influence of English law. Such influence is also reflected in the matter of incorporation of arbitration clauses by reference. Singapore courts, for decades, had no hesitation to apply the strict rule of incorporation, which is predominantly a rule of English contract law concerning the incorporation of arbitration clauses. The strict rule of incorporation was imported into Singapore jurisprudence in 1996 as this principle was first applied in *Star-Trans*. It

207 *TMT Co. Ltd v The Royal Bank of Scotland plc* [2017] SGHC 21 at [68].

208 Poon (n 11). Also see *Sembcorp Marine Ltd v PPL Holding Pte Ltd* [2013] SGCA 43.

209 Stavros Brekoulakis, The Notion of the Superiority of Arbitration Agreements Over Jurisdiction Agreements: Time to Abandon It?, 2007, *Journal of Integrative Agriculture*, 24(4), 341, 358.

210 As this is the general approach adopted in common law jurisdictions. However, in this sense, it would not be wrong to say that Singapore courts are going the extra mile. See Mahdev Mohan and Eu-Yen Tay, The New International Arbitration (Amendment) – A Broader Framework for Interim Relief or Just a Tune-Up?, 2010, *2008 Asian Business & Rule of Law Initiative*, available at https://ink.library.smu.edu.sg/cgi/viewcontent.cgi?article=1001&context=sol_aprl&fbclid=IwAR2lI4-ucJEw7GTkC-eHif0Ma11MyO9F-PzZxdNWpyQYIyrMkYPJDGXIhR0 (last visited August 11, 2022).

is an important decision as it illustrated, by means of referring to an English construction case, *Aughton*, the potential of the strict English approach to potentially apply in different branches of law in Singapore. In other words, *Star-Trans* reflected that the strict English rule of incorporation had a similar scope of application in Singapore law. Like English law, also in Singapore law, the application of the strict approach was allowed in branches of law other than shipping, which deals with negotiable documents. For instance, *L&M Concrete Specialists*, despite being a construction case, further implemented the strict rule of incorporation in Singapore.

However, the implementation of such a strict and also foreign approach was harshly criticized later in *International Research v Lufthansa Systems*. The criticism was not unfounded. First, Singapore is willing to fulfil its ambition of becoming a preferred international arbitration hub by means of removing the obstacles in the way to becoming one. Providing flexibility for international commercial parties rather than subjecting them to some strict and formal rules is definitely the preferred pathway in Singapore. Second, the establishment of autochthonous jurisprudence is desired in Singapore so that self-sufficiency and independency from the influence of foreign jurisdictions are indeed desired goals to be achieved. However, this should not be read as Singapore being a confined jurisdiction. It simply means that the courts of Singapore are willing to depart from the 'traditionally impactful' English position and establish a self-sufficient and national jurisprudence. Singaporean judges are significantly independent and would not hesitate to reject an English authority if they regard such abandonment as a necessity. Third, in light of some fairly recent English cases, such as *The Athena* and *Habas Sinai v Sometal*, it was emphasized in *International Research v Lufthansa Systems* that 'the strict rule is one that has been over extended from its roots, which are to be found in a particular and specific context and it is appropriate to identify those roots clearly so that the rule can be situated in its proper place.'[211] Similarly, Singapore courts would examine the true structure of the contractual chain rather than accepting a strict, straightforward, and foreign rule that may fail to aid the court in assessing the actual contractual structure. It is accepted in this jurisdiction that the background and the facts of the case, and in particular, the actual ascertainable intention of the parties would prevail over the application of some foreign strict rule that may potentially fail to provide a fair guideline. This brings us to another significant aspect of Singapore jurisdiction: contextual interpretation. English law, to a greater extent, in comparison with different legal systems, adopts a literal approach to interpreting contracts. This issue is significant for the purposes of this chapter as the general rule in English law, specifically applicable to international arbitrations, is that the extrinsic evidence would be inadmissible in interpreting a contract. Due to wide English influence, Singapore courts have been interpreting contracts in a similar manner. However, *Zurich Insurance* in 2008 reflected a departure from this approach and a contextual approach, which predominantly requires the assessment of the objective circumstances surrounding the entering into the contracts in question, was adopted instead. In this particular case, the extrinsic evidence including pre-contractual negotiations to interpret contracts held admissible. The developed principle is often called 'Zurich criteria.' Furthermore, *R1 International* and *KVC Rice v Asian Mineral* indicate the contemporary approach of

211 *International Research Corporation Plc. v Lufthansa Systems Asia Pacific Pte* [2013] SGCA 55 at [23].

Singapore courts concerning contract interpretation and the concept of incorporation. In the former, incorporation of an arbitration clause as a result of one party's silence, and in the latter a bare intention to arbitrate, lacking specifications concerning the place of arbitration and methods for establishing the tribunal, were held enforceable. These cases give us an idea regarding the scope of the limits that Singaporean courts would have in assessing the incorporation of arbitration clauses by means of conducting contextual interpretation. It is visible that Singaporean courts are willing to promote arbitration agreements where the intention of parties to implement this dispute resolution method is clear. It may even be suggested that, when the intention to arbitrate is not fully apparent, Singapore courts may potentially not hesitate to go the extra mile and endeavour to find a crumb of such an intention if convinced that this would be the way to reflect the actual direction of party autonomy.

Bibliography

Binder, Peter, *International Commercial Arbitration and Conciliation in UNCITRAL Model Law Jurisdictions*, Sweet & Maxwell, 2010.

Boo, Lawrence, Arbitration, 2013, *Singapore Academy of Law, Annual Review*, 14, 81.

Born, Gary, *International Commercial Arbitration*, Wolters Kluwer, 2014, Vol. 1.

Brekoulakis, Stavros, The Notion of the Superiority of Arbitration Agreements Over Jurisdiction Agreements: Time to Abandon It?, 2007, *Journal of Integrative Agriculture*, 24(4), 341.

Choong, John, Mangan, Mark and Lingard, Nicholas, *A Guide to the SIAC Arbitration Rules*, Oxford University Press, 2018, 1–18.

Croft, Jane, Singapore Takes Top Arbitration Slot Along with London for First Time, *Financial Times*, May 6, 2021.

Goh, Yihan, The New Contractual Interpretation in Singapore: From 'Zurich Insurance' to 'Sembcorp Marine,' December 2013, *Singapore Journal of Legal Studies*, 301–330.

Goh, Yihan and Tan, Paul, An Emprical Study on the Development of Singapore Law, 2011, *Singapore Academy of Law Journal*, 540.

Halsbury's Laws of Singapore, LexisNexis, 2011 Reissue, Vol. 1(2).

Henderson, Alastair, Chua, Emmanuel and Homma, Yosuke, *'Bare' Arbitration Clauses and the Extent to Which the Singapore Court May Assist*, Herbert Smith Freehills, Arbitration Notes, March 9, 2017.

Hsien, Rachel Chiu Li, *Clothing the Bare: The Enforcement of Arbitration Clauses in Singapore*, New York University School of Law, Centre for Transnational Litigation, Arbitration and Commercial Law Blogs, March 2, 2018.

In Conversation: Prof G W Bartholomew, 1985, *Singapore Law Review*, 6, 56.

Joseph, David, *Jurisdiction and Arbitration Agreements and Their Enforcement*, Sweet & Maxwell, 2010.

Joseph, David and Foxton, David, *Singapore International Arbitration Law & Practice*, LexisNexis, 2018.

McMeel, Gerard, The Rise of Commercial Construction in Contract Law, 1998, *Lloyd's Maritime and Commercial Law Quarterly*, 382.

Medvedskaya, Anastasia, London vs Singapore: A (False) Struggle for the Title of World's Leading Seat of Arbitration, *Jus Mundi*, September 24, 2021, available at https://blog.jusmundi.com/london-vs-singapore-a-false-struggle-for-the-title-of-worlds-leading-seat-of-arbitration/ (last visited August 10, 2022).

Merkin, Robert and Hjalmarsson, Johanna, *Singapore Arbitration Legislation*, Informa Law from Routledge, 2016, Annoted.

Mohan, Mahdev and Tay, Eu-Yen, The New International Arbitration (Amendment) – A Broader Framework for Interim Relief or Just a Tune-Up?, 2010, *Asian Business & Rule of Law Initiative*, available at https://ink.library.smu.edu.sg/cgi/viewcontent.cgi?article=1001&context=sol_aprl.

Moser, Michael and Choong, John, *Asia Arbitration Handbook*, Oxford University Press, 2011.

Muk, Jonathan Chen Yeen, The Sound of Silence – An Analysis of the Incorporation of Arbitration Terms After Contract Formation, 2015, *Asian International Arbitration Journal*, 11(1), 93–104.

Phang, Andrew, Reception of English Law in Singapore: Problems and Proposed Solutions, 1990, *Singapore Academy of Law Journal*, 2, 20.

Pillai, Subramanian, Singapore: Case Update – 'International Research Corp PLC v Lufthansa Systems Asia Pacific Pte Ltd and Another [2013] SGCA 55,' *Mondaq*, January 31, 2014, available at www.mondaq.com/x/289470/Arbitration+Dispute+Resolution/Case+Update+International+Research+Corp+PLC+v+Lufthansa+Systems+Asia+Pacific+Pte+Ltd+and+another+2013+SGCA+55 (last visited August 10, 2022).

Poon, Nicholas, Reconsidering the Enforceability of Bare Intention to Arbitrate – KVC Rice Intertrade Co Ltd v Asian Mineral Resources Pte Ltd [2017] SGHC 32, 2017, *Singapore Academy of Law Journal*, 29, 540–551, 540.

Pre-Contractual Negotiations: Strategic Use in International Arbitration, July 21, 2017, Allen & Overy, available at www.allenovery.com/publications/en-gb/Pages/pre-contractual-negotiations-strategic-use-in-international-arbitration.aspx (last visited August 11, 2022).

Rosengren, Jonas, Contract Interpretation in International Arbitration, 2013, *Journal of International Arbitration*, 30(1).

Sathyapalan, Harisankar K., International Commercial Arbitration in Asia and the Choice of Law Determination, 2013, *Journal of Integrative Agriculture*, 30, 621–636.

Securing the UK's Position as a Global Disputes Hub: Best Practice Lessons Between Singapore and the UK, 2020, The Chartered Institute of Arbitrators (CIArb) Report of the All-Party Parliamentary Group for Alternative Dispute Resolution (researched and funded by Chartered Institute of Arbitrators), available at www.ciarb.org/media/14995/appg-report_digital-new.pdf.

SIAC Annual Report 2021, available at www.SIAC-AR2021-FinalFA.pdf.

Singapore Parliamentary Debates, Official Report, October 31, 1994, Vol. 63, Cols. 625–627.

UNCITRAL Model Law on International Commercial Arbitration Explanatory Documentation Prepared for Commonwealth Jurisdictions, 1.11(1), 1991, available at www.uncitral.org/pdf/english/texts/arbitration/ml-arb/Model-Law-Arbitration-Commonwealth.pdf.

PART II

NOT INCORPORATION – BUT A CLOSE ANALOGY

Arbitration Clauses Binding Third Parties

CHAPTER 6

Arbitration Agreements and Third Parties

The requirements concerning the involvement in litigation and arbitration show differences: Where legal or financial interests constitute the fundamental necessities to initiate court proceedings, it is usually the agreement setting up the basis for the involvement of the parties in arbitration.[1] Accordingly, arbitration is inherently consensual. 'The concept of private arbitrations derives simply from the fact that the parties have agreed to submit to arbitration particular disputes arising between them and only between them.'[2] The arbitrator's powers have a consensual basis, and accordingly, they have no authority to make orders that are binding to third parties.[3] The consensual nature of arbitration may be argued to be a direct reflection of the doctrine of privity of contracts. According to the well-known statement of Lord Haldane, 'In the law of England, certain principles are fundamental. One is that only a person who is a party to a contract can sue upon it.'[4]

Nevertheless, it may be perceived common for the 'traditional role and bilateral nature of arbitration' to fail to accommodate the necessities of contemporary and sophisticated transactions of commerce that possibly 'require the participation of several parties for the delivery of large-scale projects.'[5] Brekoulakis argues that there are two shortcomings of the 'strict adherence of the requirement of consent': first, such necessitates the prevalence of formalistic exercise in identifying parties to arbitration where the manifestation of consent matters more than the actual interest of a party, and second, 'it converts the jurisdictional task into a rather cumbersome quest for evidence of consent, which often proves elusive.'[6] Multi-party arbitration is extremely common in the modern contexts of maritime, insurance, construction, assignment, subrogation, and generally concerning the implementation of the Contracts (Right of Third Parties) Act 1999. Accordingly, the involvement of third parties in arbitration is barely a rare occasion and the doctrine of

1 Stavros Brekoulakis, *Third Parties in International Commercial Arbitration*, Oxford University Press, 2010, 1.08–1.09. 'Thus, any legal or financial interest that a third party might have in the dispute between the parties bound by an arbitration agreement is, in principle, irrelevant.': Ibid 1.10.

2 *Oxford Shipping Co Ltd v Nippon Yusen Kaisha, The Easter Saga* [1984] 2 Lloyd's Rep 373 (Comm) 379.

3 Clare Ambrose, Karen Maxwell and Michael Collett, *London Maritime Arbitration*, Informa, 2017, 4th Edn., 244.

4 *Dunlop Pneumatic Tyre Co Ltd v Selfridge & Co Ltd* [1915] UKHL 1 (April 26, 1915); [1915] AC 847, 853. For a similar statement by Lord Macnaghten, see *Keighley Maxsted & Co v Durant* [1901] AC 240, 245; [1900–03] All ER 40, 45: 'As a general rule, only persons who are parties to a contract acting either by themselves or by an authorised agent can sue or be sued on the contract. A stranger cannot enforce the contract, nor can it be enforced against a stranger.'

5 Brekoulakis (n 1) 1.12.

6 Ibid 1.17.

DOI: 10.4324/9781003268673-8

privity of contract, at least in this regard, may be considered to have been 'outgrown' by the contemporary realities of commerce.[7]

Following this, it is highly likely for multi-party/multi-layered contracts to contain an arbitration clause for the purposes of bringing the third party into arbitration. Accordingly, an essential issue to be addressed is the efficiency of a 'collective reference'[8] to provisions of a distinct and separate contract or document containing an arbitration agreement to binding a third party.

It follows from the doctrine of privity of contract, one of the issues to be addressed in exploring the correlation between the concept of incorporation and arbitration, is the exceptions to the rule stipulating that arbitration agreements are not effective on third parties. Indeed, fundamentally, an arbitration agreement is private and only affects the parties to it. In other words, as a general rule, third parties are not bound by the arbitration agreement or able to invoke it. Furthermore, an arbitration award pertaining to a specific issue arising between A and B is not binding where the same issue arises between B and C. In *Sun Life Assurance Company of Canada v Lincoln National Life Insurance Co*[9] it was the view of Mance LJ that a third party may not solely rely on the favourable parts of a previous award and avoid being bound by its non-favourable parts. Accordingly, the court decided that an issue of estoppel is effective merely between parties to the original proceedings and their privies, and therefore, it is not fair for a third party to gain any benefit from an award to which they are not a party.

The doctrine of privity, which imposes that agreements are only enforceable by or against parties to them, comes with some exceptions to it.[10] Section 1 of the Contracts (Rights of Third Parties Act) 1999 stipulates that a third party may, in their own right, enforce a term of the contract if the contract expressly provides that they may, or the term in question purports to confer them a specific benefit.[11] Furthermore, Section 8 of the Act specifically indicates that the arbitration agreements are included in the scope of this particular piece of legislation. Hence, Section 8 facilitates a third party who wishes to enforce their rights under a contract containing an arbitration clause to become a party to that arbitration agreement.[12] The main precondition for this is the dispute in question to have arisen 'between this third party and the promisor relating to the enforcement of the substantive term by the third party.'[13]

This is not an issue of incorporation. However, there is such a close analogy that the English courts are hardly reluctant to consider this as somewhat of a method that creates 'incorporation-like results.' From the arbitration perspective, English courts have taken the view that a third party commencing proceedings on an insurance policy which contains an arbitration clause has consequently agreed in writing to the dispute to be referred to arbitration by doing this so.

7 Ibid 1.16.

8 Ibid 2.187.

9 [2004] EWCA Civ 1660; [2005] 1 Lloyd's Rep 606 (*Sun Life Assurance v Lincoln National Life Assurance*).

10 Ambrose, Maxwell, and Collett (n 3) 259.

11 Section 1(1) of the Contracts (Rights of Third Parties) Act 1999.

12 Masood Ahmed, Loosening the Grip of the Contracts (Rights of Third Parties) Act 1999 on Arbitration Agreements, 2014, *Journal of International Arbitration*, 31(5), 515–540, 515.

13 Andrew Tweeddale, Arbitration Under the Contracts (Rights of Third Parties) Act 1999 and Enforcement of an Award, 2011, *LCIA, Arbitration International*, 27(4), 653–662, 656.

There are also concepts of assignment and subrogation of rights, and the establishment of these constitutes a contractual matter to be considered.[14] In English law, party A to a contract may assign their rights to third-party C, and by doing so, the assignor A transfers these rights to the assignee C. The right of subrogation, on the other hand, suggests that the insurance company, subsequent to indemnifying the insured (or the reinsured), brings an action against a third party, in the name of the insured (or the reinsured). In the following section, Section 8 of the Contracts (Rights of Third Parties) Act 1999 and the legal concepts that create 'incorporation-like' results are evaluated for the purpose of bringing clarity to what incorporation is and is not. Furthermore, the devices that 'bypass' the doctrine of privity such as the Himalaya clause, the concept of implied contracts, and the relevant aspects of the London Court of International Arbitration (LCIA) Rules and the recent case law concerning 'quasi-contractual' injunctions are also investigated. The chapter finally provides a brief evaluation of the 2022 Review of the Arbitration Act 1996 by the Law Commission from the perspective of the position of third parties.

6.1. The Contracts (Rights of Third Parties) Act 1999

The doctrine of privity fundamentally entails as a rule that a third party, who is not a party to a contract shall neither be liable in respect of that particular contract nor able to enforce it.[15] However, the doctrine undoubtedly has its exceptions, and the Contracts (Rights of Third Parties) Act 1999 regulates some of the 'broad situations' giving rise to these. The provisions of the Act may be considered to be creating 'a very wide-ranging exception to the benefit side of the privity of contract doctrine.'[16] The Act fundamentally enables the entitlement of a third party, who need not be named or did not exist at the time contract was being concluded, to enforce a term that purports to confer a benefit on them.[17] To put it differently, English law facilitates a non-signatory party to be bound by an arbitration agreement.

Concerning the scope of its application,

> it was foreseen that with proper drafting, the Rights of Third Parties Act may be used by a developer to enforce rights against subcontractors so that numerous and complex collateral warranties would no longer be required. It might also be used by subcontractors to take advantage of clauses in a main contract restricting their potential liability for negligence. Again, the subcontractors may be able to rely on a main contract in order to take advantage of indemnity provisions. One can also foresee that there may be situations where a subcontractor

14 Edwin Peel, *Treitel on the Law of Contract*, Sweet & Maxwell, 2015, 14th Edn., Ch. 15.

15 Robert Merkin and Johanna Hjalmarsson, *Singapore Arbitration Legislation*, Informa, 2016, 267. See *Tweddle v Atkinson* [1861] 1 B & S 393; 121 ER 762.

16 At least in the way these were considered by one of the former members of the Law Commission, Andrew Burrows, who was involved with the drafting of the Act: Andrew Burrows, The Contracts (Rights of Third Parties) Act 1999 and Its Implications for Commercial Contracts, 2000, *Lloyd's Maritime and Commercial Law Quarterly*, 540. Also see Tweeddale (n 13) 655. It should also be noted that there were some attempts (such as the use of collateral warranties in the 1990s by the players of the construction market) to tackle the inconvenience that the doctrine of privity of contract may have created before the passing of the Contract (Rights of Third Parties) Act 1999: Robert Merkin and Séverine Saintier, Privity of Contract: Statutory Developments, in Robert Merkin and James Devenny (eds.) *Essays in Memory of Professor Jill Poole – Coherence, Modernisation and Integration in Contract, Commercial and Corporate Laws*, Informa Law from Routledge, 2018, 137.

17 Tweeddale (n 13) 655.

claims monies directly from an employer if the employer fails to pay the main contractor for works done by the subcontractor.[18]

It may be safe to say that it created somewhat of an 'elbow room' for third parties to enforce originally distinct agreements provided that the statutory conditions are met. The Act may be argued to have predominantly revolutionized contract drafting in various areas of law that deal with typical contracts that are concerned with third parties in the UK.[19]

6.1.1. The Concerns Regarding the Scope of the Contracts (Rights of Third Parties) Act 1999 and Arbitration Agreements

It is true that under certain circumstances, it is possible for a third party to be included in an originally distinct contractual relationship, and the Contracts (Rights of Third Parties) Act 1999 provides a general scope for the extension of such circumstances.

Nevertheless, the issue gets somewhat complex when such a scope includes arbitration agreements and possibly brings the third party to the realms of an arbitration agreement. There is fundamentally 'nothing in the 1999 Act that allows a contract between the promisor and the promise to impose a burden on a third party, and an obligation to arbitrate might generally be thought as burdensome.'[20] The aptitude of including arbitration agreements into the scope of the Act has therefore raised concerns particularly, because these argued to impose a duty to arbitrate, and the main philosophy of the reform of privity of contract was 'to confer rights and not impose duties.'[21] The philosophy may also be considered in line with the well-accepted rule that solely rights and benefits may be assigned and not obligations, burdens, and liabilities.[22]

Despite the raised concerns, arbitration agreements were considered to fall into the scope of the Contracts (Rights of Third Parties) Act 1999, and Section 8 of the Act lays out the circumstances in which a third party shall be treated as a party to an arbitration agreement.

The Contracts (Rights of Third Parties) Act 1999 provides that a third party who is not a party to a particular contract would have the right to enforce the terms of the contract in question either if the contract includes an express provision which purports to confer a benefit on the third party or if it allows such enforcement of the third party.[23] On the other hand, the inclusion of the concept of arbitration into the scope of this specific legislation evidently creates some legal challenges due to the private nature of this dispute resolution mechanism.[24] One obvious issue is the apparent elusiveness of the extent to which the interpretation of this section stretches to bind the third parties with the arbitration.

Accordingly, this was considered to be 'one of the most difficult issues'[25] faced by the Law Commission in proposing the reform of the privity of contract in 1996. The

18 Ibid.

19 Multi-layered contractual structures, distribution contracts, software licences, etc.

20 Merkin and Saintier (n 16) 154.

21 Law Commission, *Privity of Contract: Contracts for the Benefit of Third Parties*, Law Commission No. 242, July 1996, 14.18.

22 *Davies v Collins* [1945] 1 All ER 247, 249; House of Lords in *Linden Gardens Trust Ltd v Lenesta Sludge Disposals Ltd* [1994] 3 All ER 417, 427.

23 Ambrose, Maxwell, and Collett (n 3) 259.

24 Mance LJ in *Sun Life Assurance v Lincoln National Life Assurance* [2005] 1 Lloyd's Rep 606 emphasized that arbitration is a consensual and private affair between specific parties to a specific arbitration agreement.

25 Law Commission (n 21) 14.14.

recommendation of the Commission was to exclude the arbitration agreements from the scope of this particular reform, as it was suggested that these agreements do not operate sufficiently unless any entitlement of the third party to submit to arbitration also entails the duty of the third party to submit to arbitration.[26] In other words, it was emphasized that the reform was solely concerned with conferring rights and benefits to third parties. Imposing a duty to arbitrate, on the other hand, is considered to be falling outside the scope of the intended reform due to its stipulating nature. With one of the main philosophies of the reform being the conferring of rights and not the imposition of duties on third parties,[27] the inclusion of arbitration agreements in the relevant scope is considered to be contradicting such a central philosophy. The Law Commission was further of the view that it was a necessity to keep the resolution process intact, and therefore, the draft bill conferred 'no rights on a third party in the case of . . . an agreement to submit to arbitration present or future disputes'[28] as 'that in some cases this could lead to some claims being advanced in arbitration and other claims being advanced in courts.'[29]

The recommendation of the Law Commission concerning the exclusion of arbitration agreements from the legislative scope was disregarded by the Parliament and the application of the Rights of Third Parties Act was extended to include arbitration.[30]

It is indeed debatable whether it is truly possible to categorize arbitration agreements as 'burdens' that are imposed as duties.[31] In *AES Ust-Kamenogorsk Hydropower Plant LLP v Ust-Kamenogorsk Hydropower Plant JSC*,[32] it was considered that a right conferred upon a third party to bring arbitration proceedings against a promisor amounts to a benefit (and not a burden) provided that the third party chooses to exercise that right.[33] Section 1(4) particularly states that the third party's right to enforce a contract term is always 'subject to and in accordance with any other relevant terms of the contract.' Accordingly, this particular section establishes the framework for this discussion: 'if a positive benefit is conferred upon the third party, but there is an arbitration clause relating to all disputes, it is arguable that the benefit is conditional only and subject to enforcement only in arbitration.'[34] It is indeed debatable whether an arbitration agreement creates a conditional benefit in such a legislative context.

6.1.2. Decoding Section 8 of the Contracts (Rights of Third Parties) Act 1999 and the Doctrine of Conditional Benefit

The introduction of Section 8 lays out the circumstances in which a third party should be treated as a party to arbitration included in a contract to which that third party is

26 Ibid 14.14–14.16.

27 Ibid 14.18.

28 Section 6(2)(d) of the Draft Bill annexed to the report.

29 Tweeddale (n 13) 654.

30 Ibid 653.

31 May arbitration agreements truly be categorized as 'burdens' that are imposed as duties? See Ying Khai Liew, Explaining Assignments of Arbitration Agreements, March 2021, *Cambridge Law Journal*, 80(1), 101–129, 104–107. Also see Brekoulakis (n 1) 2.23–2.29.

32 [2010] EWHC 772 (Comm).

33 The case went to the Supreme Court concerning other issues and not on this ruling *Ust-Kamenogorsk Hydropower Plant JSC v AES Ust-Kamenogorsk Hydropower Plant LLP* [2013] UKSC 35. Appeal dismissed.

34 Merkin and Saintier (n 16) 154.

not originally a party. Section 8(1) of the Contracts (Rights of Third Parties) Act 1999 provides that

> where (a) a right under section 1 to enforce a term (the substantive term) is subject to a term providing for the submission of dispute to arbitration (the arbitration agreement) and; (b) the arbitration agreement is an agreement in writing for the purposes of Part I of the Arbitration Act 1996, the third party shall be treated for the purposes of that Act as a party to the arbitration agreement as regards disputes between himself and the promisor relating to the enforcement of the substantive term by the third party.[35]

In other words, this particular section stipulates the conditions under which a third party may enforce rights pertaining to a contract that they are not a party to, however, may become bound by the arbitration agreement in the contract in question. Tweeddale finds the logic behind this section 'straightforward' as he goes further and explains that

> if a party wants to take the benefit of a right under a contract, then it will be bound by the arbitration clause within the contract. Therefore, if a third party brings court proceedings claiming a benefit under a contract to which the Rights of Third Parties Act applies, the promisor can insist that the litigation be stayed to arbitration.[36]

The concerns of the Law Commission that led to the exclusion of the arbitration agreements from the scope of the proposed reform were not unfounded. The substantial obstacle to overcome was to figure out how to strike a justified balance between 'enabling a third party to enforce a benefit conferred by a contract in accordance with its terms yet also respecting the principle that a person should not be bound by an arbitration agreement unless he has agreed to arbitrate.'[37] The sought balance may be said to have been established by adopting 'the conditional benefit approach,'[38] which stipulates if the contracting parties agree that 'enforcement of a benefit conferred on a third party is to be subject to arbitration then the third party will be bound by the arbitration clause in the sense that he cannot enforce that benefit without also accepting the obligation to arbitrate.'[39] In other words, according to this doctrine, the conferment of the benefit may not be separated from the acceptance of a certain obligation for the purpose of actually being able to enjoy such a particular benefit. They go hand in hand. The conditional benefit doctrine stipulates the party who is taking a certain contractual benefit should also be subject to potentially imposed conditions.[40]

35 Section 8(1) of the Contracts (Rights of Third Parties) Act 1999.

36 Tweeddale (n 13) 656.

37 Ambrose, Maxwell, and Collett (n 3) 259.

38 *Schiffahrtsgesellschaft Detlef von Appen GmbH v Wiener Allianz Versichrungs AG and Voest Alpine Intergrading GmbH* [1997] 2 Lloyd's Rep 279 (Comm) 285–286 *(The Jay Bola)*; [1997] EWCA Civ 1420; *Charterers Mutual Assurance Association Limited v British & Foreign* [1998] I L Pr 838 (Comm); *Montedipe SpA v JTP-RO Jugotanker, The Jordon Nicolov* [1990] 2 Lloyd's Rep 11 (Comm) 15.

39 Ambrose, Maxwell, and Collett (n 3) 260. Thus, the obligation to arbitrate arises as a legal incident of the asserted right: *QBE Europe SA/NV and another v Generali Espana de Seguros Y Reaseguros* [2022] EWHC 2062 (Comm), 6, [17].

40 Paul Todd, Arbitration, Privity of Contract and Carriage of Goods by Sea, in Jason Chuah (ed.) *Research Handbook on Maritime Law and Regulation (Research Handbooks in Private and Commercial Law)*, Edward Elgar, 2019, 375–410.

The Jay Bola[41] may be argued to clearly illustrate the implementation of the conditional benefit doctrine. The vessel *Jay Bola* was time-chartered by its owners and subsequently voyage-chartered by its time charterer. The voyage charter in this case included a London arbitration clause, where the time charter was governed by English law and the bills of lading were produced in Brazil. The voyage charterer insured the cargo of steel bars with an insurer, but the insurance policy contained no arbitration clause. The cargo was damaged in a fire onboard the vessel *Jay Bola* and considerable losses were suffered by cargo owners. The insurer indemnified the voyage charterer and took an assignment of rights against the time charterer. The essential issue to assess was whether the London arbitration clause contained in the voyage charter was binding upon the insurer as insurers commenced proceedings in Brazil. The gist of the case was as follows: The shipowners admitted liability and they commenced a limitation action in the Admiralty Court in London seeking a decree of limitation of liability under the UK legislation, which gives effect to the London Convention. They paid the amount of the limit into Court and a decree of limitation was pronounced. Under the London Convention, this decree limits the liability of both the time charterers and the shipowners, and the insurers, in the name of the cargo owners, are entitles to a pro rata share of that fund. The insurance company had an interest in suing in Brazil, because Brazil was not a party to the London Convention, and accordingly, if the insurers could obtain a judgement against time charterers in Brazil, that judgement was not going to be subject to the limitation that the London Convention provides. It was decided by the English court that the insurers had started proceedings as the assignee of the voyage charterers pursuant to the voyage charterers' rights under the voyage charterparty, and thus, the insurers were bound by the arbitration clause contained in the voyage charter. To put it differently, the right to make claims under the voyage charter was assigned from the voyage charterer to the insurers, but the provisions governing such claims were of the terms of the voyage charter, including the arbitration clause. The rights could not be exercised inconsistently with the terms of the voyage charter. Accordingly, the insurers were held to be bound by the arbitration agreement because the rights of the voyage charterer under the sub-charterparty (voyage charter) was the benefit that the insurers gained by virtue of subrogation, and such a benefit was subject to the arbitration agreement.[42] The insurers were bound by the arbitration clause[43] because they were not able to assert the assigned right without also accepting the obligation to arbitrate.[44]

Consequently, two substantial legal arguments can be extracted from *The Jay Bola*; first, the conditional benefit that derives from an underlying arbitration agreement may trigger the stay of proceedings for the assignee, and second, consistency of the acts with the characteristics of the underlying agreement is a matter to be considered by the courts as this was done so in disallowing the insurers to initiate 'inconsistent' foreign proceedings.

Another issue to be considered is the assessment of the intention regarding the conferment of a benefit to a third party. Accordingly, courts fundamentally seek and assess whether parties intended to confer a benefit or a right to a third party. This issue was considered

41 *The Jay Bola* [1997] 2 Lloyd's Rep 279 (Comm).

42 Ibid 291. Same confirmed later in *CMA CGM SA v Hyundai MIPO Dockyard Co Ltd* [2008] EWHC 2791 (Comm); [2008] 2 CLC 687.

43 [1997] 2 Lloyd's Rep 279.

44 See *Montedipe SpA v JTP-TO Jugotanker (The Jordan Nicolov)* [1990] 2 Lloyd's Rep 11 (Comm).

in *Fortress Value Recovery I LLC v Blue Skye Opportunities Fund LP and others*[45] and the initial decision of the Commercial Court that the third-party appellants were not to be treated as parties to an arbitration agreement under Section 8(1) of the Contracts (Rights of Third Parties) Act 1999 was upheld by the Court of Appeal since the intention to confer such a right on the appellants held not to be apparent.[46] Fundamentally the relationship between the Contracts (Rights of Third Parties) Act 1999 and Arbitration Act 1996 was evaluated in order to assess the extent of the applicability of arbitration agreements to third parties in *Fortress Value v Blue Skye*.

The claimants brought proceedings against defendant managers of an investment structure that was based around an English limited partnership holding underlying assets under the Blue Skye Fund, which was regulated by a Deed. The case was essentially concerned with the partnership agreement pertaining to the establishment and management of an investment fund. The claimants alleged that the defendants designed and implemented a dishonest scheme to restructure the fund and its assets, to diminish or eliminate the rights and interests of the fund's partners concerning the assets. The third-party fund managers were given immunity from suit under the Deed. The fund managers were subject to judicial proceedings and they applied to have the action stayed pursuant to Section 9 of the Arbitration Act 1996 on the basis that the dispute was subject to arbitration. The fundamental issue before the court was whether third-party fund managers were entitled to a stay in favour of arbitration as they argued that under Section 8 of the Rights of the Third Parties Act 1999, they should be treated as parties to the arbitration agreement.

Accordingly, *Fortress Value v Blue Skye* was mainly concerned with Section 8(2). This particular section stipulates that

> where (a) a third party has a right under section 1 to enforce a term providing for one or more descriptions of dispute between the third party and the promisor to be submitted to arbitration (the arbitration agreement), (b) the arbitration agreement is an agreement in writing for the purposes of Part I of the Arbitration Act 1996, and (c) the third party does not fall to be treated under subsection (1) as a party to arbitration agreement, the third party shall, if he exercises the right, be treated for the purposes of that Act as a party to the arbitration agreement in relation to the matter with respect to which the right is exercised, and be treated as having been so immediately before the exercise of the right.[47]

The section clearly indicates that a third party will be considered a party to the arbitration agreement provided they choose a particular matter to be resolved by arbitration, and the status of the third party will be established as a party to the arbitration just before exercising the right to arbitrate.[48]

With regard to *Fortress Value v Blue Skye*, especially concerning the construction of the contract, it was concluded that the managers did not have the right to arbitrate[49]

45 [2012] EWHC 1486 (Comm); [2013] EWCA Civ 367. (*Fortress Value v Blue Skye*).

46 'It is however to impute to the parties a really very far-reaching intention if it is to be inferred that they positively intended to bring about the result that third parties would be bound by the outcome of arbitration proceedings which they had not themselves initiated in order to secure a benefit apparently conferred upon them by the Agreement.' [2013] EWCA Civ 367, [36].

47 Section 8(2) of the Contracts (Rights of Third Parties) Act 1999.

48 Ahmed (n 12) 522.

49 *Fortress Value v Blue Skye* [2013] EWCA Civ 367, [31], [45]–[47].

because Section 8(2) would not operate in the absence of precise wording of conferment of the benefit to arbitrate to the third party.[50] The lacking of such expression led the court to consider the underlying intentions of the parties. At first instance, Blair J refused to grant a stay as he was of the opinion that any claim against the third party that arose was not itself subject to arbitration and thus, immunity had to be pleaded as a defence to the judicial proceedings. The learned judge stated that 'the exclusions are by their nature defensive and do not confer a positive right of action. It makes no real sense to say that a contractual defence, as opposed to a contractual right of action, is "subject to arbitration." '[51]

Furthermore, Tomlinson LJ sitting at the Court of Appeal, concluded that there was

> [n]o express language in the agreement to the effect that either the indemnity or the exclusion is subject to arbitration clause. In each case that result can only be achieved by way of inference. It is however to impute to the parties a really far reaching intention if it is to be inferred that they positively intended to bring about the result that third parties would be bound by the outcome of arbitration proceedings which they had not themselves initiated in order to secure a benefit apparently conferred upon them by the agreement.[52]

The intention to confer the right to arbitrate to a third party was held not to be sufficiently and clearly manifested on the face of the agreement. *Fortress Value v Blue Skye* sets forth that if the benefit consists of a defence or limitation of liability, an agreement concerning Section 8(2) of the Contracts (Rights of Third Parties) Act 1999 is necessary 'to oust the presumption that arbitration clause does not apply to the defence.'[53]

The case may also be argued to be concerned with the issue of choice. It provides different interpretations of Section 8(1) of the Contracts (Rights of Third Parties) Act 1999 as various reasons provided for rejecting the application of this particular section in this case.[54] The fundamental discussion was pertaining to the assessment of arbitration to be subject to choice. Tomlinson LJ, looking into the wording of it, stated,

> Section 8(1) of the 1999 Act provides that the third party shall be treated as a party to the arbitration agreement as regards disputes between himself and the promisor relating to the enforcement of the substantive term by the third party. It is thus not in respect of all disputes arising out of or in connection with the agreement that the third party is to be treated as a party to the arbitration clause, but only disputes relating to the enforcement of the particular substantive term of which the third party has the benefit.[55]

To put it differently, the learned judge distinguished 'substantive terms' and indicated that a third party is not treated as a party to arbitration unless the relevant dispute is relating to the enforcement of a specific substantive term of which the third party has the benefit.[56]

---

50 Todd (n 40) 402.
51 [2012] EWHC 1486, [89].
52 [2013] EWCA Civ 367, Tomlinson LJ at [36].
53 Merkin and Saintier (n 16) 154.
54 Todd (n 40) 402.
55 *Fortress Value v Blue Skye* [2013] EWCA Civ 367, Tomlinson LJ at [30].
56 [2013] EWCA Civ 367 (Tomlinson LJ), [30].

Another concern of Tomlinson LJ was the potential creation of a burden, which the managers are not willing to undertake, should their status be considered to be falling within the scope of Section 8(1). Therefore, the learned judge indicated if this is accepted,

> then by reason of section 8(1) of the 1999 Act the third party has not only had conferred upon him a right or benefit but has also had imposed upon him a burden which he did not agree to undertake, viz, a positive obligation to submit to arbitration a dispute concerning his entitlement to rely upon the exclusion clause.[57]

A conferred right or benefit to come with a certain obligation to be imposed on the beneficiary must come with a very clear expression of the choice to do so.

The learned judge went further to evaluate which party, in fact, had the choice to arbitrate with regard to the interpretation of Section 8(1). The learned judge indicated that

> the third party has a choice whether to seek indemnity, knowing that if he does so he must pursue in arbitration. The third party has by contrast on this hypothesis no choice whether to be bound by an arbitration initiated by a partner.[58]

Accordingly one may argue that this particular section in fact does not provide third parties with the choice to arbitrate but instead leaves this choice to the contracting party and they may choose to apply for a stay or not.[59] Indeed, the application for a stay is the event facilitating arbitration and merely a contracting party is able to apply for it so. In other words, the choice to arbitrate lies with the contracting party. It is Section 8(2) and not Section 8(1) that is pertaining to the choice of the third party and this was an issue within Section 8(1), and therefore, under the circumstances, the third party would only be able to exercise the substantive right in question if they wish to do so and would not have the right to choose to arbitrate.[60]

The judgement illustrates the distinction between the objectives of Section 8(1) and Section 8(2) and establishes that if the intention of the parties is to confer a procedural right to a third party regarding the referral of disputes to arbitration, they should be doing this so by means of Section 8(2).[61] Another issue to be noted is that the judgement is also considered to be 'consistent with a very strong party autonomy approach'[62] and illustrates that whether the third party has the option to arbitrate under the Contracts (Rights of Third Parties) Act 1999 will be subject to very profound evaluation within the considerably restrictive scope of this particular Act. Since Section 8 is not very 'user-friendly,' unlike the Arbitration Act 1996,[63] the decision provides some clarity by somewhat decoding the meaning of Section 8. *Fortress Value v Blue Skye* establishes an in-depth analysis of one of the circumstances under which a third party may or may not become bound by an arbitration agreement and highlights that drafting transactional documents that potentially may confer a right on a third party should be done with care

57 Ibid [29].
58 Ibid.
59 Todd (n 40) 402.
60 Ibid.
61 *Fortress Value v Blue Skye* [2013] EWCA Civ 367, Toulson LJ at [56].
62 Todd (n 40) 402.
63 Anthony Diamond, The Third Man: The 1999 Act Sets Back Separability?, 2001, *Arbitration International*, 17(2), 211–219, 212.

and in a way capturing the true intentions of the parties regarding the resolution of disputes that involve third parties. Accordingly, one may argue that the Contracts (Rights of Third Parties) Act 1999 does not seem to be undermining the law of contract but rather promotes 'the bargain between the original parties by honouring the intentions therein (to benefit the third party).'[64] Nonetheless, it may necessitate some level of decoding to be conducted from time to time concerning the way this legislation is implemented since it is less user-friendly than the Arbitration Act 1996.

One particular issue to be noted at this point for the sake of establishing integrality among the chapters is that despite following the common law doctrine, the Contracts (Rights of Third Parties) Act 1999 has no direct relevance to Singapore law.[65] However, Yeo provides three valid points of relevance illustrating how this specific piece of legislation indirectly affects Singapore:

> First, many international contracts are governed by English law, and the modified privity doctrine is now part of domestic English contract law. Secondly, in view of the fact that several other significant common law jurisdictions have already made legislative reforms of the common law privity doctrine, the English model is one possible model for Singapore to follow if it is considering reform in this area. It provides an interesting study of how the problem of privity can be approached, and how realistically it can be expected to solve the various problems raised by the privity doctrine. Thirdly, the extent to which the statutory reform may affect common law developments related to the privity doctrine is of relevance to Singapore, because the English common law is still at least highly persuasive in Singapore.[66]

6.2. Assignment

There are some legal concepts that establish a sensitive balance such as the one between the privity of contract and the assignment of contractual rights. In a straightforward way, the doctrine of privity of contract establishes that a third party may not enforce a benefit or be liable for any obligation under a contract to which they are not a party, whereas the assignment of contractual rights suggests quite contrarily that, upon agreement, the rights of a contracting party are transferable to an assignee. Even though it is widely accepted in many legal systems that the parties are allowed to assign their contractual rights partially or completely to a non-contracting third party,[67] the transferability of an arbitration agreement that may be contained in the assigned contracts constitutes an issue to be addressed due to the private and separate nature of such agreements. However, it may be noted as established in *The Jay Bola* that, provided the contractual rights or causes of action are originally subject to the arbitration agreement, it may also be binding for the third party.[68]

64 Andrew Phang, On Justification and Method in Law Reform – The Contracts (Rights of Third Parties) Act 1999, June 2002, *Journal of Contract Law*, 18, 42.

65 Andrew Phang (ed.), *Cheshire, Fifoot and Furmston's Law of Contract*, Butterworths, 1998, 2nd Singapore and Malaysian Edn., 782–793.

66 Tiong Min Yeo, When Do Third Party Rights Arise under the Contracts (Rights of Third Parties) Act 1999 (UK)?, 2001, *Singapore Academy of Law Journal*, 13(1), 34–53, 35, Research Collection School of Law.

67 Mertcan Ipek, *Assignment of Contractual Rights and İts Impact on Aritration Agreements*, MUHF-HAD C.22, S.1, 521–550, 523, available at https://dergipark.org.tr/tr/download/article-file/274363. See *Butler v Capel* [1823] 107 ER 377.

68 *The Jay Bola* [1997] 2 Lloyd's Rep 279, 285–286; [1997] EWCA Civ 1420.

It should be noted at this point that the Contracts (Rights of Third Parties) Act 1999 does not particularly deal with the concept of assignment. In the realm of application of the Act, the rights of the third party would be in addition to the originally contracting party rather than instead of the rights of the contracting parties.[69] Opposite to the transferal of the rights to the assignee, concerning the application of the Act, 'the original contracting parties retain their rights, one consequence of which is that there could be more than one operative arbitration clause, in relation to what is essentially the same dispute.'[70] However, in the context of assignment, the rights are transferred to the assignee, and therefore, the assignor does not have these transferred rights anymore. Those belong to the assignee following their transfer.

6.2.1. Nature of Assignment

The legal concept of assignment is established where the assignor assigns their contractual rights to a third-party assignee and, consequently, where these particular rights are transferred to the assignee. To put it differently, assignment is a concept of contract law[71] that involves 'the immediate transfer of an existing proprietary right, vested or contingent, from assignor to the assignee.'[72] This concept is particularly concerned with the transfer of rights and the intention to do so.[73]

> Anything that in the eye of law can be regarded as an existing subject of ownership, whether it can be a chose in possession or a chose in action, can to-day be assigned, unless it be expected from the general rule on some ground of public policy or by statue.[74]

To illustrate, A purchases goods from B on deferred payment credit and B needs finance. Accordingly, B assigns A's debt to C and receives payment from C. This means A now owes the funds to C and not to B. When A's payment falls due, A pays to C and not to B as now C is entitled to the payment due to assignment instead of B. In this very straightforward layout, A is the debtor, B the assignor, and C the assignee. As a concept and a practice, assignment is commonly seen in the insurance context and maritime context where a shipowner assigns their rights to freight and demurrage under a charterparty or perhaps, where the seller of the goods assigns the benefit of the marine insurance policy pertaining to the goods in question.[75]

Another issue that should be evaluated is the position of this legal concept concerning the doctrine of privity of contract. Some relevant deductions may be made. It is clear

69 Todd (n 40) 397.

70 Ibid 397.

71 Peel (n 14) Ch 15.

72 Windeyer J in *Norman v Federal Commissioner of Taxation* [1963] 109 CLR 9, 26: a decision of the High Court of Australia. Also see William Blackstone, *Commentaries on the Laws of England*, Clarendon Press, 1766, ii, 326. For different considerations of meaning of the word 'assignment,' see *Siemens Schweix AG v Thorn Security Ltd* [2008] EWCA Civ 1161, [88].

73 As argued in Greg Tolhurst, *The Assignment of Contractual Rights*, Hart Publishing, 2016, 30.

74 Windeyer J in *Norman v Federal Commissioner of Taxation* [1963] 109 CLR 9, 26. See also Blackstone (n 72) 326. See further for different considerations of the meaning of the word 'assignment,' *Siemens Schweix AG v Thorn Security Ltd* [2008] EWCA Civ 1161, [88].

75 Ambrose, Maxwell, and Collett (n 3) 256.

that 'assignment does not create privity of contract between the assignee and obligor.'[76] If it did, 'it would not be possible to maintain the distinction that is drawn between the assignment of contractual rights and contractual duties.'[77] Because of that, the assignee depends upon the continued existence both of the contract and of the parties to the contract as considered in the Australian case of *Re Kenneth Wright Distributors Pty Ltd v Hall*.[78] Furthermore, as illustrated in *Coulls v Bagot's Executor & Trustee Co Ltd*,[79] a contract for the benefit of a third party does not create an assignment. Moreover, as Jacobs JA refined in *International Leasing Corp (Vic) Ltd v Aiken*,[80] 'the assignment does not substitute the assignee for the assignor as a matter of contract.'[81] Concerning the privity of contract, the assignee replaces the assignor and, accordingly, is perceived as a replacement instead and not as a third party anymore.[82]

6.2.2. The Correlation of Assignment and Arbitration Agreements

Concerning the correlation between assignment and arbitration agreements the following issues are examined. First, the meaning of involving an assignee in arbitration and the way of doing this so is evaluated. This is done so through the lens of issues such as consent, notice, and separability of agreements. Second, various issues concerning assignment such as the position of the assignee and the scope of the assignment are addressed.

6.2.2.1. The Involvement of the Assignee in Arbitration

It is now settled[83] that the third-party assignee C may initiate arbitration proceedings against the debtor/obligor A and also continue arbitration proceedings that are previously initiated by assignor B.[84] Nonetheless, not every aspect concerning the implementation of assignment as a legal concept is equally refined.

The transfer of contractual rights to an assignee third party may have a meaning from the aspect of arbitration if the underlying contract contains an arbitration clause. One of the essential issues to assess is whether the transferee is bound by the arbitration clause contained in the main contract provided 'the original party to the contract transfers their substantive claims, rights, and/or obligations'[85] to this third-party transferee and, if so, under which circumstances. This particularly bears importance as the determination of

76 Tolhurst (n 73) 3.27. Also see *Bexhill UK Ltd v Razzaq* [2012] EWCA Civ 1376, [44].

77 Ibid 3.27.

78 [1973] VR 161.

79 [1967] 119 CLR 460 (an Australian case).

80 [1967] 2 NSWR 427, 438 (and another Australian case).

81 Tolhurst (n 73) 3.27.

82 Ipek (n 67) 532; Juan Carlos Landrove, *Assignment and Arbitration – A Comparative Study*, Schulthess Verlag, 2009, 163.

83 *Rumput (Panama) S.A. v Islamic Republic of Iran Shipping Lines* [1984] 2 Lloyd's Rep 259 (*The Leage*); *Court Line v Aktiebolaget Gotaverken AB* [1984] 2 Lloyd's Rep 283 (*The Halcyon the Great*); *Kaukomarkkinat O/Y v Elbe Transport-Union GmbH* [1985] 2 Lloyd's Rep 85; *Montedipe SpA v JTP-TO Jugotanker* [1990] 2 Lloyd's Rep 11, 15 (Comm) (*The Jordan Nicolov*); *The London Steamship Owners Mutual Insurance Association Ltd v Bombay Trading Co Ltd* [1990] 2 Lloyd's Rep 21, 25.

84 Liew (n 31) 102. See *Court Line v Aktiebolaget Gotaverken AB* [1984] 2 Lloyd's Rep 283, 289 (*The Halcyon the Great*); *Montedipe SpA v JTP-TO Jugotanker* [1990] 2 Lloyd's Rep 11, 19 (Comm) (*The Jordan Nicolov*).

85 Brekoulakis (n 1) 2.03.

such would indicate whether a relevant arbitration claim may be brought against or by the assignee C irrelevant of their 'inherently external' position to the arbitration that originally takes place between the assignor B and the debtor/obligor A.

Although 'it is universally accepted that arbitration agreements are as assignable as any other contract,'[86] there are fundamentally two issues to be evaluated concerning the implementation of this legal concept. These are the role of notice, consent, and acceptance pertaining to the transfer and the legal status of the arbitration agreement from the aspects of separability and integrality of these to the main contract. This is because, even though the assignment of contractual rights and obligations 'plays an increasingly vital role in modern-day efficient commercial life'[87] and profoundly applies in different jurisdictions, regulations and guidance concerning the implementation of the assignment are generally lacking. For instance, there is uncertainty in English law 'whether the assignee must join the assignor to initiate arbitration proceedings, whether an assignor can remain in arbitration proceedings already commenced, and whether the obligor may initiate arbitration proceedings against the assignee.'[88] Furthermore, Liew argues that the rules of international arbitration also lack clarification of profound matters concerning the assignment of arbitration agreements[89] 'leaves parties to international arbitration in a state of uncertainty as to whether they are better off arguing for or against English law as the applicable law.'[90] Accordingly, the evaluation of notice, consent, and acceptance in the context of the assignment of arbitration agreements, as well as of the legal status of these agreements, would shed some light on some relevant aspects of the implementation of assignment as a legal concept.

6.2.2.1.1. Notice, Consent, and Acceptance

The assignment as a legal concept is predominantly subject to the freedom of contract.[91] Accordingly, whether there is a need for assessing both if the assignee C is required to expressly consent to the arbitration agreement contained in the assigned contract, and also if the debtor/obligor A is required to consent to the assignment of such agreements, is an important issue to be considered pertaining to the assignment of arbitration agreements.[92]

The issue about the consent of the assignee C pertaining to the assignment essentially stems from the necessity to assess whether they need to be aware of the arbitration agreement, of which notice is properly given to them, and have consented to the assignment of this specific agreement alongside the assigned contract or if their general consent would be sufficient.[93]

---

86 Ibid 2.06; Liew (n 31) 101; Andrea Vincze, Arbitration Clause – Is it Transferred to the Assignee?, 2003, *Nordic Journal of Commercial Law*, 1, 3–4.

87 Liew (n 31) 101.

88 Ibid 102.

89 Stephen Jagusch and Anthony C. Sinclair, The Impact of Third Parties in International Arbitration: Issues of Assignment, in Loukas A. Mistelis and Julian D.M. Lew (eds.) *Pervasive Problems in International Arbitration*, Kluwer Law International, 2006, 15–16.

90 Liew (n 31) 102. Also see Anita Garnuszek, The Law Applicable to the Contractual Assignment of an Arbitration Agreement, 2016, *Arbitration: The International Journal of Arbitration, Mediation and Dispute Management*, 82(4), 348–355.

91 *Shayler v Woolf* [1946] 1 Ch. 320, 322.

92 Brekoulakis (n 1) 2.06.

93 Ibid 2.08.

Parties to assignments are fundamentally affected by the concept of notice,[94] and it may serve different purposes concerning assignment:

> After an assignment, a debtor may pay the assignor rather than the assignee. The debtor's position may be determined by whether the debtor has received valid notice of assignment. Next, an assignor may assign the one chose in action more than once. As between rival assignees each of whom claims the benefit of the assignment, notice will be determinative. Further, after an assignment the debtor may acquire a claim against the assignor which the debtor wishes to press against the assignee. To a large extent, notice determines whether the debtor may do so.[95]

The issue of notice concerning assignment is not evaluated in depth under this part. Nevertheless, a couple of deductions concerning its construction and form may be made. First, the construction of notice from the aspect of its clarity must be made in its context as established in *Colonial Mutual General Insurance Co Ltd v ANZ Banking Group (New Zealand) Ltd.*[96] In this case, the Privy Council was of the view that 'in the context of a notice to an insurance company by a mortgagee of the insured property, the language of the notice was plain and unambiguous'[97] and, therefore, was sufficient to notify the insurer about the assignment of the transfer of the policy from the mortgagor to the mortgagee. Second, essentially no certain form of notice is required for it to be validly given. Nonetheless, Hirst J in *Herkules Piling Ltd v Tilbury Construction Ltd*[98] states 'that there must be some kind of formal notification by the assignee, or by the assignor on his behalf, to the debtor'[99] for the purposes of notice to be considered effective. In this case, it was held that

> the debtor did not receive notice of assignment when he received a copy of the contract of assignment from assignor on discovery in arbitration proceedings, and rejected as wrong a submission that the debtor must or may pay the assignee where he learns by some other credible means that the money does not or may not belong to the assignor but to the assignee.[100]

Accordingly, the notice should be given in a way expressing the intention of its giver for it to be valid for the assignment to take place and thus, an accidental discovery of the assignment would not be sufficient.[101]

Furthermore, concerning assignment, the issue of consent is predominantly a twofold one: It deals with the consent of both the assignee C and the debtor/obligor A[102] specifically from the aspect of freedom of contract. Regarding the assignee, the essential issue to be determined is whether the awareness or the express consent of the assignee for the application of an arbitration agreement contained in the assigned contract is required or if general consent of the assignee to the main contract would be sufficient.[103]

94 David Fox, Roderick Munday, Barış Soyer, Andrew Tettenborn and Peter Turner (eds.), *Sealy & Hooley's Commercial Law*, Oxford University Press, 2020, 6th Edn., 828.

95 Ibid 828.

96 [1995] 1 WLR 1140. Also see *Mannai Investment Ltd v Eagle Star Life Assurance Co Ltd* [1997] AC 749.

97 [1995] 1 WLR 1140, 1145.

98 [1992] 32 Con LR 112.

99 Ibid 121.

100 Fox et al. (n 94) 831.

101 Ibid.

102 Brekoulakis (n 1) 2.07.

103 Ibid 2.08.

In many jurisdictions, the assignment of the underlying contract is perceived to entail the assignment of the associated arbitration agreement, and thus, the transfer of such an agreement is considered to be an automatic one together with the underlying contract.[104] To put it differently, general consent usually qualifies the automatic transfer of the arbitration agreement alongside the main contract.[105] The arbitration agreement is usually considered an ancillary right to the assigned principal rights and thus, it follows the assigned rights.[106] Concerning the position of the debtor/obligor it is important to also evaluate whether their previous consent is required to make such a party bound by a contract and an arbitration agreement with a party different than the originally contracted with.[107] The general position is that 'in the absence of any indication to the contrary, there is a presumption . . . that the signatory of an arbitration agreements accepts that the agreement may be assigned.'[108] In other words, usually no previous consent of the debtor/obligor is sought for the assignment of the arbitration agreement to take place.[109]

6.2.2.1.2. Separability and Integrality

Although the assignability of arbitration agreements is widely accepted, the separability of these agreements has been argued to preclude their straightforward transfer without the consent of the parties. The separable character of arbitration agreements has contended to preclude the automatic transfer of these agreements because the separability and autonomy of these otherwise argued to be undermined by such a transfer.[110] Arbitration agreements are indeed separate by nature from the contract they are contained in. The concept of separability provides some immunity to these agreements. Therefore, their separability, which creates the result that the invalidity of the principal contract to not impair the validity of the arbitration agreement, is an interesting issue to be addressed in the context of assignment. Nonetheless, it should be emphasized at this point that separability usually has little relevance with transferability[111] and, therefore, should not stand in the way of assignability. Girsberger rightfully argues that it is confusion associated with the principle of autonomy that, because arbitration agreements are separate in nature from the main contract, the transfer of a right to an assignee would not automatically include the arbitration

104 Particularly, see Chapter 10, 'Parties to International Arbitration Agreements,' in Gary B. Born, *International Commercial Arbitration*, Wolters Kluwer Law International, 2020, 3rd Edn. The transferability of these agreements was previously challenged on the grounds of these are personal obligations and especially binding upon the original parties to them. In *Cottage Club Estates Ltd v Woodside Estates Co. (Amersham) Ltd* [1928] 2 KB 463 (KB), because arbitration agreement considered to be a personal one, assignment did not transfer the assignee any right in such an agreement. This is now largely 'superseded,' and it is internationally accepted that parties may assign arbitration agreements as they have the autonomy to do it so similar to the autonomy they have for the assignment of other contracts: Ibid Chapter 10, 'Parties to International Arbitration Agreements.'

105 Brekoulakis (n 1) 2.09.

106 Grigera Naón, Choice-of-Law Problems in International Commercial Arbitration, 2001, *Recueil des Cours*, 289, 9, 147.

107 Brekoulakis (n 1) 2.30.

108 Philippe Fouchard, Emmanel Gaillard, and John Savage, *Fouchard, Gaillard, Goldman on International Commercial Arbitration*, Kluwer Law International, 1999, 431, [717].

109 Unless the assignment of an arbitration agreement is excluded by the original parties: *Bawejem Ltd v MC Fabrications* [1999] 1 All ER (Comm) 377.

110 Brekoulakis (n 1) 2.19.

111 Ibid.

agreement.[112] On the contrary, extending the impact of separability to the implementation of assignment 'would undermine the essence and purpose of assignment.'[113]

An issue to be considered is whether the independent nature of these agreements imposes the need to obtain a clear expression of intent pertaining to their transfer.[114] To be able to address this issue, the underlying reason these agreements are perceived as separate should be considered. The separate character of these agreements is fundamentally derived from the motivation 'to prevent *mala fide* parties from escaping the arbitration process originally agreed upon by invoking the nullity of the contract of which it is part.'[115] Accordingly, the separate nature of arbitration agreements should not be impairing their facility to be transferred with the underlying contract as these are accessories of the latter.[116]

This, accordingly, brings us to the evaluation of another concept: the integrality of the arbitration agreement (at least from the aspect of assignment) to the main contract. The word 'integrality' is chosen to differentiate the impacts of certain characteristics of arbitration agreements pertaining to different aspects of the law. The concept of separability essentially has something to do with the issue of validity, whereas the integrality of the arbitration agreement to the main contract may be evaluated through the lens of assignability. These are fundamentally different. In the words of Brekoulakis, 'the transferee substitutes the transferor and assumes its legal position all together and in exactly the same terms.'[117] Thus, the arbitration agreement moves intact with the main contract in the context of the assignment. The transferred benefits and obligations that may arise from the underlying contract go hand in hand. In other words, where there is an arbitration clause that the original party would be bound by, the assignee would also usually be bound by that arbitration clause. Therefore, the third-party assignee, in the absence of a contrary contractual provision, would presumably be bound by the underlying arbitration clause since it would not be possible otherwise 'to assert the assigned contractual right in question without also accepting the obligation to arbitrate.'[118]

The lawful assignee usually enjoys all the benefits of the assigned right that were to be enjoyed by the original party. Accordingly, the assignee would be able to commence arbitration proceedings against the assignor's contractual counterparty[119] and to continue arbitration proceedings initiated by the assignor.[120] In accordance with the statement made by Hobhouse J in *Jordan Nicolov*,[121] they would have 'the right to invoke the arbitration clause, take arbitration proceedings, and if successful on the merits, obtain an award.'[122] This

112 Daniel Girsberger, The Law Applicable to the Assignment of Claims Subject to an Arbitration Agreement, in Franco Ferrari and Stefan Kröll (eds.) *Conflict of Laws in International Arbitration*, Otto Schmidt/De Gruyter European Law Publishers, 2010, 390.

113 Brekoulakis (n 1) 2.19.

114 Landrove (n 82) 152.

115 P.A. Gélinas, Arbitration Clauses: Achieving Effectiveness, in A.J. van den Berg (ed.) *Improving the Efficiency of Arbitration Agreements and Awards: 40 Years of Application of the New York Convention*, ICCA Congress Series, 1999, ICCA, Vol. 9, 62.

116 Ipek (n 67) 527.

117 Brekoulakis (n 1) 2.19.

118 *Montedipe SpA v JTP-TO Jugotanker (The Jordan Nicolov)* [1990] 2 Lloyd's Rep 11 (Comm).

119 Liew (n 31) 102.

120 *The Halcyon the Great* [1984] 2 Lloyd's Rep 283, 289; *Montedipe SpA v JTP-TO Jugotanker* [1990] 2 Lloyd's Rep 11 (Comm) (*The Jordan Nicolov*) 19.

121 *Montedipe SpA v JTP-RO Jugotanker* [1990] 2 Lloyds Rep 11 (*The Jordan Nicolov*).

122 Hobhouse J in *The Jordan Nicolov* [1990] 2 Lloyd's Rep 11, 17.

further suggests that the assignee may be subject to a stay of proceedings fundamentally because they replace the assignor and are considered to be 'claiming under or through a party to the agreement' pursuant to section 82(2) of the Arbitration Act 1996.

6.2.2.2. Various Issues Concerning the Involvement of the Assignee in Arbitration

The legal correlation of assignment and arbitration being briefly evaluated, we now turn to the examination of some legal issues that may arise in the process of transferring the arbitration agreement by means of assignment.

One of the first issues to be addressed is the assessment of the title to sue as some clarification might be needed regarding the position of the assignee as a party to the arbitration.[123] The essential issue that may arise regarding the practical application of the assignment is to determine the party who is actually entitled to sue.[124] Would the assignee or the assignor have the title to sue? Ambrose et al. suggest that it would be safer for both the assignee and the assignor to initiate the arbitration, particularly if there is some unclarity pertaining to the time bar.[125] Indeed, it is common for the assignee to join the assignor as a party to any proceedings, and in the case of an equitable assignment to be made, the same would also apply in arbitration.[126]

Another issue is pertaining to the subsequent assignment of the arbitration agreement to the commencement of the arbitration.[127] The subsequent assignment rises three questions: First, what would be the position of the assignee pertaining to the arbitrators that are already appointed? Second, how the assignment would actually facilitate the actual involvement of the assignee in arbitration? And third, what would be the actual scope of the assigned rights?

The first question is an interesting one since the appointment of arbitrators might already have taken place prior to the joining of the assignee. As a fundamental principle of arbitration, the parties have the freedom to choose the arbitrators who will determine their dispute, and hence, the lack of involvement of the assignee in the selection process may rise questions regarding the fairness of it from the aspect of the assignee.[128] The partial or complete replacement of assignee C with assignor B usually indicates the acceptance of assignee C of the appointed tribunal as if assignee C had contributed to the selection and appointment processes of the arbitrators. Accordingly, this usually does not give the right to the assignee to appoint a new tribunal as indicated in *The Jordan Nicholov.*[129]

The second question is concerning the actual facilitation of the involvement of the assignee in the already commenced arbitration process. Indeed, assignment creates a legal transformation on the position of the assignee and enables the assignee to Act as replacing the assignor. Nonetheless, the assignee does not become a party to a subsequently commenced arbitration just by means of assignment since the assignee 'must perfect the assignment by giving notice to the other side and must intervene in arbitration by giving notice to the arbitrator(s).'[130] The legal effect of the absence of notice of the assignor

123 Ambrose, Maxwell, and Collett (n 3) 257.
124 Ibid.
125 Ibid. Also see *Sim Swee Joo Shipping v Shirlstar Container Transport* [1994] CLC 188 (Comm).
126 Ambrose, Maxwell, and Collett (n 3) 257.
127 Jagusch and Sinclair (n 89) 312.
128 Ibid.
129 Hobhouse J in *Montedipe SpA v JTP-RO Jugotanker (The Jordan Nicolov)* [1990] 2 Lloyd's Rep 11, 16.
130 Ambrose, Maxwell, and Collett (n 3) 257.

regarding an arbitration, which already started was considered by the English Court of Appeal in *Baytur SA v Finagro Holding SA*.[131] The dispute in this case arose out of a sales contract which referred to arbitration. Unknown to the tribunal, at the pending stage of the claims, the claimant got dissolved and their assets and liabilities were transferred to other companies. After an award was given in the claimant's favour, the respondent challenged this award. What the court focused on was whether there was a need for notice of the equitable assignment. Reference was made to the decision of Phillips J (as he then was) in *The Felicie*[132] and to *The Jordan Nicolov*[133] where Hobhouse J (as he then was) clarified that an assignee that is succeeding to the rights of the assignor in a pending arbitration must give notice both to the arbitrators in order to pursue the matter in arbitration and also, to the other party to perfect the assignment. Accordingly, the submission to the jurisdiction of the arbitrators had to be effective. The Court of Appeal decided that the arbitration lapsed when buyers were dissolved as it cannot take place when one of the two parties ceases to exist. The Court of Appeal held the assignee did not automatically become a party to a pending arbitration because they failed both to give notice to the sellers and also to submit to the jurisdiction of the tribunal. However, the assignees could successfully become parties to the arbitration 'if they have given notice of the assignment to the respondent and submitted to the jurisdiction of the tribunal before the assignor ceased to exist.'[134] It is worth noting that the assignor would still be liable for the costs incurred prior to the involvement of the assignee.[135] The legal basis for the liability of the assignee for the costs, which arise subsequent to the involvement of the assignee, is the rightful assumption that the assignee submitted to the overall jurisdiction of the tribunal also pertaining to award costs.[136] Nevertheless, the indication of Lloyd LJ in *Baytur SA v Finagro Holding SA* should be noted as it suggests that the assignee must bear the risk in the case that an insolvent assignor is subsequently liquidated and held liable for all the costs of an unsuccessful arbitration if that would be the outcome.[137]

The third question to be posed is concerning the legal scope of the assignment. This was an issue considered in *The Jordan Nicolov*, and it was indicated by Hobhouse LJ that

> where the assignment is the assignment of the cause of action, it will, in the absence of some agreement to the contrary, include . . . all the remedies in respect of that cause of action. The relevant remedy is the right to arbitrate and obtain an arbitration award in respect of the cause of action. The assignee is bound by the arbitration clause in the sense that he cannot assert the assigned right without also accepting the obligation to arbitrate. Accordingly, it is clear both from the statute and from a consideration of the position of the assignee that the assignee has the benefit of the arbitration clause as well as of the other provisions of the contract.[138]

Integrality appears to reflect the true intention of the parties selecting assignment, which allows them to enjoy the full benefit of the original contract subsequent to its stretching

131 *Baytur SA v Finagro Holding SA* [1992] QB 610 (CA).
132 [1990] 2 Lloyd's Rep 21.
133 Ibid 11.
134 Jagusch and Sinclair (n 89) 313.
135 Ambrose, Maxwell, and Collett (n 3) 257.
136 Ibid.
137 *Baytur SA v Finagro Holding SA* [1992] QB 610 (CA); Jagusch and Sinclair (n 89) 313.
138 *Montedipe SpA v JTP-TO Jugotanker (The Jordan Nicolov)* [1990] 2 Lloyd's Rep 11, Hobhouse LJ at 15, 16.

to include the assignee. In other words, the contract that is subject to assignment stays intact where a precise reflection of it is created to include the assignee instead of the assignor. It should be noted that such a reflection also creates similar procedural liabilities and outcomes for the assignee. For instance, the assignee may become subject to the stay of proceedings pursuant to Section 9 of the Arbitration Act 1996, and they may also be subject to injunctions precluding them from pursuing foreign proceedings in breach of arbitration agreements.[139] Accordingly, they are usually treated similarly to the original party to the arbitration agreement concerning the implementation of the stay. This also applies in Singapore where it is established that a third party has the right to arbitrate, then they will have the choice to apply for a stay if an action pertaining to the subject matter of the relevant arbitration is brought against them in the courts of Singapore.[140]

6.3. Subrogation

Subrogation essentially means substituting one party for another.[141] To put it differently, in the context of subrogation, one stands in another's shoes in a legal setting for the purposes of collecting a debt or damages on behalf of another party. In the insurance context, subrogation functions as follows: subsequent to indemnifying the loss of the insured, the insurer steps into the shoes of the insured and brings 'action against the responsible third-party to recoup what he has paid to the assured and prevent the latter from "double-dipping" or getting paid twice; once by the insurer and then by the perpetrator of the loss.'[142] Subrogation differs from assignment in both the method of creation and the results produced. This part fundamentally investigates the nature of subrogation as a legal concept and explores its correlation with arbitration agreements.

6.3.1. Nature of Subrogation as a Substitution Mechanism: Standing in One's Shoes

Subrogation, a legal concept that has attracted almost no criticism in English law[143] in the last two centuries,[144] is a double-option substitution mechanism that establishes a 'party-specific remedy.'[145] This particular legal concept entitles the assured to direct their claim either to the insurer or to the third party, who has caused the relevant loss to occur and, therefore, creates the indicated duality concerning the 'source of recovery' that may be

139 Ambrose, Maxwell, and Collett (n 3) 256, 15, 37.

140 Merkin and Hjalmarsson (n 15) 268.

141 Robert Merkin and Jenny Steele, *Insurance and the Law of Obligations*, Oxford University Press, 2013, 97.

142 Proshanto K. Mukherjee, Windfall in the Law of Subrogation: Marine Insurance in Motion, in Proshanto K. Mukherjee et al. (eds.) *Maritime Law in Motion*, WMU Studies in Maritime Affairs 8, Springer, 2020, 563–579, 563.

143 But see Kyriaki Noussia, *The Principle of Indemnity in Marine Insurance Contracts – A Comparative Approach*, Springer, 2007, 215–216 for the disagreements pertaining to the origins of the rights of subrogation in English law; one view suggests that subrogation has a close link with equity and is imposed by the courts to prevent unjust enrichment, where the other propounds that it is implied in the insurance contract that the assured lends their name to an action against a third party wrongdoer.

144 Reuben Hasson, Subrogation in Insurance Law – A Critical Evaluation, Winter 1985, *Oxford Journal of Legal Studies*, 5(3), 416–438, 416.

145 See Merkin and Steele (n 141) 97; Stephen Watterson, Subrogation, in Graham Virgo and Sarah Worthington (eds.) *Commercial Remedies: Resolving Controversies*, Cambridge University Press, 2017, 437.

preferred. On the other hand, it further imposes a non-avoidable duty of indemnification on the preferred 'source.' If the claim of the assured is directed to the insurer, the insurer would not be able to avoid remedying the assured, and similarly, if the claim is directed to the third-party wrongdoer, it would not be possible for the third party to argue that the claim should have been directed to the insurer initially.[146] In other words, where the concept provides the assured with the selective option for the 'remedying source,' it meanwhile imposes an initial liability on the preferred source of remedy to compensate for the loss without any alternative options. It is a mechanism of substitution where the 'insurer acquires all rights, claims and defenses of the assured, in other words, just about anything.'[147]

The extensiveness of this substitution is expressed in *North of England Iron S.S. Insurance Association v Armstrong*[148] as the subrogation is the right of the insurance company to collect literally anything that the assured could have recovered. However, in this case, the value of the ship, *Hetton*, actually being £9,000, was assessed as £6,000 for insurance purposes, and the insurance was effected for the latter amount. *Hetton* ran down by another ship and sunk. The underwriters paid the assured owners the full amount of £6,000 as a total loss. Subsequently, the amount of £5,000 was recovered at the Court of Admiralty. The fundamental question regarding the payment recovered at the Court of Admiralty was 'who gets to keep the surplus?'[149] *North of England Iron S.S. Insurance Association v Armstrong*, regarding the extensiveness of the scope of subrogation, provides a valuable illustration that the agreed value would be conclusive.[150] It was held that, due to the conclusive nature of the agreed policy and therefore the agreed value for all purposes and intents, any damages recovered pertaining to salvage belonged to the underwriters. It was stated by Cockburn CJ that 'where the value of a thing insured is stated in the policy in a manner to be conclusive between two parties . . . as regards to value, . . . the parties are estopped between one another from disputing the value of the thing insured as stated in the policy' and 'if parties will enter into such policies they must take the consequences.' What should be noted regarding this particular case is that the value was a fixed one due to the nature of the policy, and hence, the parties had to take the consequences of the policy they got into. Nonetheless, as Noussia rightfully argues, 'an assured failing to disclose to the insurer that the agreed valuation in a single policy or the total sum of the agreed valuations of more than one policy is excessive, is guilty of a breach of a duty of disclosure.'[151] This constitutes another aspect of insurance law to be taken into account. Bearing in mind that, disclosure is not constituting a focal point of this part, this is the sole mention of the concept.

What is essential regarding the scope of subrogation may be argued to be the full satisfaction of the agreed value of the occurred loss. The subrogation is extrinsic. The insurer, taking over the right to sue the assured, would be doing this so in the name of the assured, with the assistance of the assured, and the implementation of this would be implied in the insurance contract as stated in *Yorkshire v Nisbet*.[152] The subrogation would only be possible where

146 Özlem Gürses, *Marine Insurance Law*, Routledge, 2017, 274.
147 Mukherjee (n 142) 565.
148 [1870] L.R. 5 Q.B. 244.
149 See Mukherjee (n 142) 564.
150 Noussia (n 143) 131.
151 Ibid. See *Ionides v Pender* [1874] LR 9 QB 531 where the non-disclosure of an excessive over-valuation was considered for the first time.
152 *Yorkshire Insurance v Nisbet Shipping* [1962] 2 QB 330, 341.

the assured is fully indemnified for the underlying claim. Only after the full indemnification of the assured, it would be possible for the insurer to seek assistance from the assured, and the insurer would even be able to compel the assured to initiate the proceedings by their own name and join the assured as this was the case in *The Esso Bernicia.*[153] Indemnification constitutes a precondition of subrogation. Where the indemnification does not take place, any attempt of the insurer to subrogate to a third party would be deemed to fail in accordance with the words of Section 79 of the Marine Insurance Act 1906:

> where the insurer pays for a partial loss, he acquires no title to the subject-matter insured, or such part of it as may remain, but he is thereupon subrogated to all rights and remedies of the assured in and in respect of the subject-matter insured as from the time of the casualty causing the loss, in so far as the assured has been indemnified, . . . by such payment for the loss.[154]

Another issue is that subrogation is a concept where the interplay of insurance law and tort law becomes apparent. In a case before the Canadian Court of Appeal – namely, *Castellain v Preston* –[155] it was stated that

> as between the underwriter and the assured the underwriter is entitled to the advantage of every right of the assured, whether such right consists in contract, fulfilled, or unfulfilled or in remedy for tort . . . or in any other right, whether by way of condition or otherwise, legal or equitable.[156]

Because this particular concept constitutes an indispensable part of insurance, it is possible to make connections between tort, subrogation, and insurance. Insurance, from the aspect of tort, works in two ways. First, it functions as 'an alternative device to tort for procuring compensation for harm,'[157] and second, from the aspect of the defendant, it facilitates the avoidance of paying for their torts.[158] Furthermore, as indicated, the concepts of insurance and indemnity being closely intertwined, subrogation also has a close connection with the concept of indemnity as the former, in a way, restricts the scope of the latter. This issue was also illustrated in *Castellain v Preston* as it was stated that 'the assured, in the case of a loss against which the policy has been made, shall be fully indemnified, but shall never be more than fully indemnified.'[159]

6.3.2. The Correlation of Subrogation and Arbitration Agreements

Indeed, this legal concept works as a substitution mechanism and enables the transfer of the rights to a non-contracting party. Its function in insurance being straightforward and almost inarguably logical, as indicated, subrogation has been subject to little or no criticism. However, what may interestingly be evaluated is how this concept functions where an arbitration agreement is present. The correlation between subrogation and arbitration constitutes an intriguing issue to be addressed. One of the curious issues to be investigated is the assessment of the applicable law when subrogation comes into play and where the

153 *Esso Petroleum v Hall Russell (The Esso Bernicia)* [1989] AC 643.
154 Section 79(2) of the Marine Insurance Act 1906.
155 [1883]11 QBD 380.
156 Ibid 388.
157 Tony Weir, Subrogation and Indemnity, March 2012, *Cambridge Law Journal*, 71, Part 1, 1–7, 2.
158 Ibid.
159 [1883] 11 QBD 380, 386.

concerned contract includes an arbitration clause. Another major issue is the determination of the right to subrogate when arbitration is the selected method of dispute resolution.

The first issue to be examined regarding the interplay of arbitration agreements and subrogation is the law applicable where a relevant express choice is lacking. This issue was considered in a 2020 case, *Enka v Chubb*.[160] The contract that the dispute arose from was one pertaining to the construction of a power plant in Russia and contained a London arbitration clause. The parties to the contract were the contractor Enka and the employer. After an event of fire, an insurer, Chubb, initiated proceedings against Enka and other defendants in Russian courts to recover damages pursuant to the alleged right to subrogate. The governing law of the contract was Russian law. However, there was no express choice of law for the arbitration agreement. Enka applied to the English court for an anti-suit injunction to be able to prevent the Russian proceedings. Insurer Chubb argued the arbitration agreement was governed by Russian law because the contract that included the arbitration clause was governed by Russian law, and under Russian law, the nature of subrogated claims fell outside the scope of the arbitration agreement, and accordingly, they were properly brought before the Russian courts. The express choice of law was lacking, and the issue before the court was to determine the applicable law.

The court referred to *Sulamerica Cia Nacional de Seguros SA v Enesa Engelharia SA* [2013] 1 WLR 2012, where the three-stage test was applied as required by the English law conflict of laws, which rules as follows: 'namely; (i) is there an express choice of law? (ii) if not, is there an implied choice of law? (iii) if not, with what system of law does the arbitration agreement have its closest and most real connection?'[161] The main problem regarding this particular test is that the courts applying it sometimes have inconsistent results as the difference between the implied intention of the parties concerning the choice of law (ii) and the system of law that has the closest connection with the arbitration agreement (iii) is a 'fine one which has frequently been blurred in English jurisprudence.'[162] The decision of the Supreme Court in *Enka v Chubb*[163] provides clarity regarding the determination of the applicable law when an express choice regarding this issue is lacking. The decision establishes

> a strong presumption that in the absence of an express choice the parties impliedly chose the law of the seat of arbitration as being the law governing the arbitration agreement. While only a presumption, 'powerful countervailing factors' would need to be demonstrated to reach a different conclusion.[164]

Hence, English law was found to be the applicable law to the arbitration agreement in *Enka v Chubb*, and the Russian proceedings were restrained due to the granted anti-suit injunction. It is settled that where the choice pertaining to the selection of the law

160 [2020] UKSC 38. For a commentary of the case, see Anoushka Nehra, *Recent Developments in English Law Relevant to Arbitration*, Stewarts, June 19, 2020, available at www.stewartslaw.com/news/arbitration-relevant-recent-developments-in-English-law/ (last visited September 20, 2022).

161 *Enka Insaat ve Sanayi AS v OOO Insurance Company Chubb* [2020] EWCA Civ 574, [70]; [2020] UKSC 38; [2020] 1 WLR 4117.

162 See A. V. Dicey, John Humphrey Carlile Morris and Lawrence Collins, *Dicey, Morris & Collins on the Conflict of Laws*, Sweet & Maxwell, 2012, 15th Edn., 32–007.

163 [2020] UKSC 38.

164 Nehra (n 160).

applicable to the main agreement is absent, the arbitration agreement would be governed by the law of the seat.

The second crucial issue for the purposes of this part is to assess the existence of the right to arbitrate where subrogation is in question. The Court of Appeal in *The Jay Bola*[165] was concerned with whether the right to have an injunction to prevent the insurers of the sub-charterers from initiating court proceedings pertaining to the subrogated claim in the Brazilian courts, existed on the part of the time charterers, who were claiming to enforce an English arbitration clause. Insurers argued that they are not affected by the arbitration agreement as being the subrogated party since they were not parties to the arbitration agreement, which was included in the time charter. Hobhouse LJ rejected this argument on the grounds that the assessment of the exact rights that are actually transferred was essential. It was indicated that

> the rights which the insurance company has acquired are rights which are subject to the arbitration clause. The insurance company has the right to refer the claim to arbitration, obtain if it can an award in its favour from the arbitrators, and enforce the obligation of the time charterers to pay that award. Likewise, the insurance company is not entitled to assert its claim inconsistently with the terms of the contract. One of the terms of the contract is that, in the event of dispute, the claim must be referred to arbitration. The insurance company is not entitled to enforce its right without also recognizing the obligation to arbitrate.[166]

It may be argued that similar to the concept of assignment, issues such as the integrality of the transferred rights and the inseparability of these with the characteristics of the contract, play a fundamental role in assessing the scope of the subrogated rights. Arbitration, as being the expressly selected dispute resolution method in this particular case, is held to have a close connection with the overall terms of the contract and hence, with its characteristics.

This issue was of concern in *West Tankers Inc v Ras Riunione Adriatica Di Sicurta SpA & Anor.*[167] One of the fundamental issues was 'identifying the ambit of the subject-matter of the transfer'[168] to be able to assess whether the subrogated insurers were bound by the arbitration agreement. It was indicated by referring to *The Jay Bola* that the defendant insurers, by means of subrogation, were entitled to enforce the right of action of the insured charterer against the owners under Italian law. However, the referral of their claim to arbitration by means of referring it to English law constituted an inseparable component of the subject matter, which was transferred to the insurers altogether.

The encapsulated formulation provided in *The Jay Bola* received further approval in *Shipowners' Mutual Protection and Indemnity Association (Luxembourg) v Containerships Denizcilik Nakliyat ve Ticaret A.S. (The Yusuf Cepnioglu)*,[169] where it was stated that

> the arbitration agreement becomes binding on the claimant because it forms an integral part of the contract giving rise to the obligation, a circumstance which is not affected by the manner

165 [1997] 2 Lloyd's Rep 279.
166 Ibid 286.
167 [2005] EWHC 454.
168 Ibid [31].
169 [2015] EWHC 258 (Comm); [2016] 1 Lloyd's 641; [2016] EWCA Civ 386.

> in which the claimant obtained the right to enforce it. Accordingly, if it becomes necessary to enforce the obligation by proceedings, that must be done by arbitration.[170]

The integrality of arbitration as the selected dispute resolution method with the substantial parts of the contract, as well its own substantial character itself within the contract, is also observable in this case.

Both *The Jay Bola* and *The Yusuf Cepnioglu* were approved in a recent case *Aspen Underwriting v Credit Europe Bank*.[171] The possibility of 'a potential-inconsistency to be a deal-breaker' was also considered in *Aspen v Credit Europe*. Accordingly, it was indicated that where the application of an arbitration clause is in question, the well-established formulation of *The Jay Bola*, which suggests 'avoiding inconsistency,'[172] usually applies.

6.4. Some Devices that Bypass the Doctrine of Privity

There are also some gap-filling tools at the disposal of the contracting parties serving the purpose of bypassing the doctrine of privity.

6.4.1. Himalaya Clauses

The doctrine of privity may generally be considered to stand in the way of the straightforward application of naming a third party as a beneficiary person under English law.[173] Accordingly, this legal system developed its own tool to extend a level of protection to persons who are not parties to the bills of lading.[174]

In June 1952, Mrs Adler decided to go on a cruise, purchased a first-class ticket, and joined the ship *Himalaya* in Southampton, UK. She went ashore on July 16, when the ship reached Trieste, Italy. While boarding back the ship, the gangway came adrift and fell down against the side of the ship, throwing Mrs Adler onto the wharf below from a height of around five meters, consequently causing severe injuries including a broken leg, broken pelvis, and broken ribs. It was alleged by Mrs Adler that the gangway was not sufficiently secured by the crew. Due to her ticket containing a non-responsibility clause exempting the carrier from liability pertaining to her injuries, she sued the master, Mr Dickson, and the dispute, which is considered in *Adler v Dickson*,[175] eventually went to the English Court of Appeal. Denning LJ made an important evaluation regarding the roles of the third-party agents of the carrier in the cases of carriage of goods and concluded that

> in the carriage of passengers as well as of goods, the law permits a carrier to stipulate for exemption from liability not only for himself but also for those whom he engages to carry out

170 [2016] 1 Lloyd's 641, 652–653.

171 *Aspen Underwriting Ltd and Others v Credit Europe Bank NV* [2020] UKSC 11; [2020] Lloyd's Rep 520, 527, [27]. (*Aspen v Credit Europe*).

172 [2020] Lloyd's Rep 520, 527, [27].

173 Sir Guenter Treitel, The Battle Over Privity, in Sir Guenter Treitel, *Some Landmarks of Twentieth Century Contract Law*, Oxford University Press, 2002, 66.

174 See comments made by Lord Reid in *Midland Silicones* [1962] AC 446, 474.

175 *Adler v Dickson* [1955] 1 QB 158; [1954] 2 Lloyd's Rep 267 (C.A.).

> the contract; and this can be done by necessary implication as well as by express words. When such a stipulation is made, it is effective to protect those who render services under the contract, although they were not parties to it.[176]

It is true that the carrier may stipulate the exemption from liability not only for themselves but also for whom they have engaged to carry out the contract. However, in this particular case, there was neither an express nor an implied stipulation regarding the stretching of exemption for the servants or agents of the carrier company. In other words, even though such stretching was permitted, the contract of carriage in question did not contain any implied or clear expression regarding such an intention.[177] Accordingly, it was indicated that Mr Dickson was not covered by any exception because Mrs Adler's ticket did neither impliedly nor expressly extend the benefits of the carrier to their servants or agents, and thus, Mr Dickson was personally liable in tort.

Subsequent to *Adler v Dickson*, explicitly drafted Himalaya clauses, which benefit stevedores and others who are engaged by the carrier pertaining to the execution of different parts of the contract started to be inserted in bills of lading.[178] Himalaya clauses since then have been successfully facilitating the extension of benefits to employees, servants, agents, and subcontractors.[179]

Himalaya clauses are commonly found in contracts of carriage by sea serving the purpose of extending some of the exonerations of the carrier to create an implied new contract, under which a third party becomes a party.[180] In this regard, the clause confers only benefits on the offeree, who is originally a third party and, hence, is of unilateral nature.[181] Whereas the Himalaya clause works somewhat as a stretching mechanism for an existing contract of carriage, it does not create itself a carriage contract but merely extends the contractual benefits of an existing one.[182] The extent of the stretch is usually the rights, exemptions, defences, and immunities, which are applicable to the carrier to also cover the third parties, such as stevedores, terminal operators, and even dry dock companies.[183] Concerning the legal effect of these clauses, it may be argued that a Himalaya clause does not

> treat the third party as a beneficiary of a contract between two others; it is, on the contrary, to provide a framework for creating a separate collateral contract directly between one of the

---

176 *Adler v Dickson* [1954] 2 Lloyd's Rep 267, 272. However, the fundamental stipulation for such extension to apply was indicated to be the assent of the injured party to be obtained (either given expressly or by necessary implication), regarding the exemption of those persons.

177 *Adler v Dickson* [1954] 2 Lloyd's Rep 267, 272. It should also be noted that even if there would be such extension, the ticket did not contain any affirmation suggesting Mrs Adler was assenting to such extension. In other words, there was no indication suggesting she approved that any exemption that the company has to also cover the servants of the company.

178 William Tetley, Himalaya Clause – Heresy or Genius?, October 1977, *Journal of Maritime Law and Commerce*, 9(1), 111–130, 111.

179 Mr. Justice Harrington of the Federal Court of Canada, referring to *Adler v Dickson* in his decision in *Timberwest Forest Corp v Pacific Link Ocean Services Corp* [2009] 2 F.C.R. 496 at para [54] (a Canadian case).

180 See William Tetley, The Himalaya Clause Revisited, 2003, 9 *Journal of International Maritime Law*, 9, 40.

181 Todd (n 40) 407.

182 Ibid 407–408.

183 Tetley (n 178) 111.

> parties to main contract of carriage and the person who, though not a party to that contract, sought to rely on one of its terms.[184]

The evaluation concerning the position of third parties to bills of lading made by Lord Reid in *Midland Silicones*[185] does worth mentioning at this point. The case is essentially concerned with goods damaged due to the negligence of the appellant stevedores. Before the damage occurs, the property in the goods had passed to the respondents, and they sue in tort for the amount of the loss to them caused by that damage. The appellant stevedores seek to take advantage of provisions (also the one limiting liability to $500) in the bill of lading made between the sellers of the goods and the carrier. These provisions are expressed to be in favour of the carrier, but the appellant stevedores maintain on a number of grounds that they can rely on these with the result that, despite the damage of the goods of the respondents exceeding $500, respondents cannot recover more than the equivalent of that sum from them as damages.

The learned judge initially finds it 'impossible to deny the existence of a general rule that a stranger to a contract cannot in a question with either of the contracting parties take advantage of provisions of the contract' and observes that the appellant stevedores 'seek to get round this rule.'[186] He accepts the existence of the exceptions to the rule and evaluates, among others, the argument of the appellants that through the agency of the carrier they were brought into a contractual relationship with the shipper and that they can now found on that against the respondent consignees. He establishes four essential requirements to be satisfied for such a relationship to be created.[187] Eventually deciding that the agency argument must fail in this case, Lord Reid generally accepts the agency argument may be successful if some criteria are met:

> (first) the bill of lading makes it clear that the stevedore is intended to be protected by the provisions in it which limit liability, (secondly) the bill of lading makes it clear that the carrier, in addition to contracting for these provisions on his own behalf, should apply to the stevedore, (thirdly) the carrier has authority from the stevedore to do that, or perhaps later ratification by the stevedore would suffice, and (fourthly) that any difficulties about consideration moving from the stevedore were overcome.[188]

Even if it may be possible to extend the scope of the 'carrier' in the bill of lading to include stevedores for purposes of stretching the scope of the limitation of liability to include stevedores too, for its actual implementation, such an extension may not be done in an implied way. As Lord Reid states, 'even if one could spell out of the bill of lading an intention to benefit the stevedore, there is certainly nothing to indicate that the carrier was contracting as agent for the stevedore in addition to contracting on his own behalf.' Accordingly, he was of the view that the agency argument had failed.

Undoubtedly, the predominant aim of Himalaya clauses is to exempt the servants, agents, and subcontractors of the carrier from liability so that the rights that are at the disposal of

---

184 Treitel (n 173) 66. Also see *New Zealand Shipping Co Ltd v AM Satterthwaite & Co Ltd* (*The Eurymedon*) [1975] AC 154.

185 *Midland Silicones* [1962] AC 446 (On appeal from *Midland Silicones Ltd v Scruttons Ltd.*).

186 [1962] AC 446, 473.

187 Ibid 474.

188 *Midland Silicones* [1962] AC 446, 474.

the carrier may also be enjoyed by the indicated parties who are not originally parties to the contract of carriage. However, a question may be posed is that 'how far such stretching would go?' The evaluation of such a question should also include the position of arbitration clauses and Himalaya clauses. One of the underlying reasons for inserting a Himalaya clause into the bill of lading, for the sake of convenience and predictability, maybe to ensure that the claimants are bound by the bill of lading arbitration clause disregarding whether they sue the contractual carrier or the actual sub-carrier of the goods.[189] Nevertheless, the ability of a Himalaya clause to extend a bill of lading arbitration clause to a subcontractor will fundamentally depend on its construction.[190] The clauses

> are not entirely uniform in their wording; but their essential feature (so far as bill of lading contracts are concerned) is that they declare the carrier to have acted as agent for his servants, agents, and subcontractors for the purpose of securing to such persons the benefit of the carrier's exemptions from and limitations of liability.[191]

The inclusiveness of the Himalaya clause was further considered in *The Mahkutai*.[192] The Privy Council, in this case, was concerned with the assessment of whether the shipowner, who was not a party to the relevant bill of lading, could benefit from the exclusive jurisdiction clause of the bill of lading and invoke it against the cargo owners by means of triggering the Himalaya clause. Considering that one of the functions of Himalaya clauses is the prevention of cargo owners from avoiding the effect of contractual defences made available to persons who perform contractual services on behalf of the carrier, the Privy Council concluded that the Himalaya clause could not be interpreted wide enough to include the exclusive jurisdiction clause since the latter was not an exception, limitation, provision, condition, and liberty of the bill of lading.[193] The concerned Himalaya clause did not cover a jurisdiction clause suggesting the case to be referred to Indonesian courts. Moving from this, a general incorporation language may also not suffice[194] for imposing arbitration on the third party as 'arbitration,' as a dispute resolution method does not constitute one of the contractual defences, which are aimed to be made available to the employees, servers, agents, and subcontractors of the carrier.

A more recent Dutch case also touches upon the inclusiveness of Himalaya clauses from the aspect of arbitration. The events leading to the dispute in *Rio Taku*[195] were as follows: W received the bill of lading as consignee of a shipment of avocados onboard *Rio Taku*. L was the contractual carrier, who issued the bill of lading whereas M was the subcontractor who actually carried the avocados as the sub-carrier of L. W proceeded to sue L and M before the Court of Rotterdam. The arbitration clause in the bill of lading was referring to London arbitration and English law. M, accordingly,

189 Sebastiaan Barten, *Drafting Himalaya Clauses Covering Arbitration Clauses*, Van Steenderen Mainport Lawyers, Lexology, April 21, 2015, available at www.lexology.com/library/detail.aspx?g=510fc646-ace3-4992-b957-b91b69d6b3a7 (last visited September 20, 2022).

190 Ibid.

191 Treitel (n 173) 67.

192 [1996] AC 650.

193 Melis Özdel, *Bills of Lading Incorporating Charterparties*, Bloomsbury, 2015, 115.

194 See *OK Petroleum AB v Vitol Energy SA* [1995] CLC 850; [1995] 2 Lloyd's Rep 160 where the contract of sale was found insufficient to describe the time bar of the demurrage clause of the charterparty.

195 Court of Rotterdam, March 18, 2015, *Rio Taku*. Rechtbank Rotterdam, March 18, 2015 (ECLI:NL:RBROT:2015:2617) (a Dutch case).

challenged the jurisdiction of the Court of Rotterdam. M also argued that W was bound by the bill of lading arbitration clause since the bill included a Himalaya clause, stipulating that

> every employee, agent, sub-contractor and independent contractor of the carrier . . . shall be a beneficiary of this bill of lading and shall be entitled to all defences, liberties, exemptions and immunities from and limitations of liability which the carrier has under the provisions of this bill of lading and under any other applicable national law and as such may protect themselves against any liability whether or not arising out of negligence on the part of such persons, companies or other entities, and in entering into this contract, the carrier, to the extent of these provisions, does so not only on its own behalf but also as agent and trustee for each of the persons, companies or other entities described above, all of whom shall be deemed parties to the contract evidenced by this bill of lading.

The Himalaya clause was evidently not referring to arbitration. Nonetheless what needed to be assessed was whether the arbitration clause may be included in 'all defences, liberties, exemptions and immunities form and limitations of liability' that are made available to the sub-carrier M. The Court of Rotterdam ruled that the bill of lading arbitration clause did not apply to the dispute between the consignee W and the sub-carrier M since arbitration was a mutual agreement, and fundamentally, the Himalaya clause would only confer the right to invoke substantive defences. Arbitration was not considered to be one of them. *Rio Taku* highlights the significance of clarifying the issue of whether the right to arbitrate is conferred to third parties by means of appropriately drafting the Himalaya clause to reflect such intention.

6.4.2. *Implied Contracts – Through the Lens of* SEA2011 Inc v ICT Ltd *[2018] EWHC 520 (Comm)*

Implied contracts, being another device of bypass of the doctrine of privity, function where a *Brandt v Liverpool*[196] contract arises concerning consignees or indorsees falling outside of the scope of the application of the Carriage of Goods by Sea Act 1992.[197] Nonetheless, it should be noted that the use of the word 'bypass' in the context of implied contracts may be found debatable as circumstances concerned with an 'implied contract' involve 'the implication of a new contract, to which the third party to the original contract is party.'[198] Accordingly, even though the use of the word 'bypass' is preferred for the purposes of creating harmonization throughout this part, implied contracts inherently establish and imply a new contract, although the end result has similarities with the doctrine of privity being bypassed.

The concept of implied contracts is essentially concerned with the manifestation of a choice by virtue of exercising relevant conduct. Taking delivery of the cargo is usually perceived to constitute such manifestation.[199] This is also mentioned in the Report of the

196 *Brandt v Liverpool, Brazil and River Plate Steam Navigation Co Ltd* [1924] 1 KB 575 (CA).

197 Todd (n 40) 405. It should be noted that this particular case was concerned with whether the plaintiff was falling into the scope of application of the Bills of Lading Act 1855, which was repealed by the Carriage of Goods by Sea Act 1992. The answer was no.

198 Ibid.

199 Ibid.

Law Commission pertaining to the privity of contract as follows: 'Where a pledgee takes delivery of the goods and pays any carriage charges such as freight or demurrage, there may come into existence an implied contract between the pledgee and the carrier on the terms of the bill of lading.'[200]

The plaintiff in *Brandt v Liverpool* claimed for damages from the shipowner for negligence in the carriage of goods. The plaintiff was essentially precluded from relying upon the protection of the relevant legislation[201] because, although being an indorsee of the bill, they were a mere pledgee.[202] The plaintiff in the said case succeeded on the contract to be inferred from the presentation of the bill of lading because they exercised a choice by means of accepting the delivery of the goods against the presentation of the relevant bill of lading. The inferred contract's scope was held to be extended by the acceptance of goods under the bill of lading as fully encompassing the rights and obligations of the carrier on the terms of the bill of lading. The Court of Appeal was of the view that the conduct exercised by the plaintiff manifested a choice as they paid freight and took delivery of the cargo on presentation of the bill. This is considered to have established a contract under which the plaintiff could sue.

Accordingly, the fundamental principles regarding implied contracts may be argued to be the consent and the conduct of the third party. The consent of the third party pertaining to the creation of an implied contract is simply assessed by looking at the legal concepts of offer and acceptance. Where the third party takes the delivery of the cargo, this may potentially mean an exercise of choice.[203]

Concerning arbitration, if the new contract is on carriage contract terms, an arbitration clause may apply where consent is obtained both for the imposition of procedural burdens of arbitration and also for the substantive obligations of the contract.[204] Whether an arbitration clause is implied would depend on the legal assessment made based on the facts of each case, and *Brandt v Liverpool* establishes that 'the implication of the contract itself, and also its terms, arise not from operation of law, but from inferences from the third party's conduct.'[205] Accordingly, from the aspect of an implied arbitration agreement, the conduct made by the third party should be evaluated in light of the facts of the case to establish whether they consent to the imposition of procedural burdens of this method of dispute resolution.

The position of arbitration agreements pertaining to implied contracts is considered by the English Commercial Court in *SEA2011 Inc v ICT Ltd*.[206] The claim in this case was concerning an arbitration, which was brought against the claimant by the defendant pursuant to an arbitration clause in a sales agency agreement. One of the challenges of the claimant was that the defendant was not a party to the relevant sales agency agreement (dated January 28, 2011) that contained an arbitration agreement because there was no English company of that name in existence when an agreement

200 Law Commission (n 21) 2.59.

201 Section 1 of the Bills of Lading Act 1855 that repealed by the Carriage of Goods by Sea Act 1992.

202 Michael Thompson, Title to Sue on Overseas Contracts of Sea Carriage: The Need for Reform in Australia, 1994, *MLAANZ Journal*, 10, 17–34, 26.

203 Todd (n 40) 405.

204 Ibid.

205 Ibid 405–406.

206 [2018] EWHC 520 (Comm).

is made. At the time, the registered name of the company had been different, and they had only changed to their current name 12 months after the agreement had been entered, such that the arbitrator's jurisdiction as defined by the notice of arbitration, had not extended to assessing the disputes that were raised by the defendant. The court rejected the challenges pertaining to the jurisdiction of the arbitrator based on the identification of the parties to the arbitration agreement and on the nature of the contract.

The concerned parties to the sale agreement containing an arbitration clause were 'SEA Inc' and 'ICT Ltd.' SEA2011 INC's first jurisdictional challenge was that ICT Ltd was not a party to the agreement because at the time the agreement was concluded, ICT Ltd's registered name was IN Ltd and there was no UK company by the name ICT Ltd. It only changed its name to ICT Ltd 12 months after the agreement was entered. They also rejected ICT Ltd's contention that the doctrine of misnomer could be invoked for the purposes of correcting ICT Ltd to IN Ltd. The court was of the view that there had been a clear mistake regarding the meaning that could be readily corrected, which the sales agency agreement would convey to a reasonable person with all the relevant background knowledge.[207] Furthermore, based on the fact that their dealings continued for a number of years and referred to the terms of the Agreement as if they continued to apply, the judge held that an implied contract existed. It was held that the parties impliedly agreed to be in a contractual relationship, which is governed by the provisions of the Agreement.

It was decided that an implied contract existed. However, another issue considered by the court was whether the arbitration clause was part of that implied contract. Sir Ross Cranston in making such an assessment considered[208] Christopher Clarke J's evaluation in *Habas Sinai Ve Tibbi Gazlar Isthisal Endustri AS v Sometal SAL*[209] concerning the incorporation of arbitration clauses:

> Where parties are in dispute as to what they have agreed the task of the Court is to determine from the communications that passed between them in the context in which those communications were made what reasonable persons in their position would regard them as having intended to agree. Where those parties agree the essential terms of a contract and also that their contract shall include the terms of a previous contract or contracts between them the Court may have to determine which provisions of which contract(s) they meant to incorporate. If the Court is able to decide what those provisions were, it should not, in my judgment, be astute to impose any special rules which limit the ability of the parties validly to agree what, on ordinary principles of construction, they would be taken to have agreed.[210]

In light of this evaluation, the learned judge was of the view that under English law, there are no specific rules that apply in deciding on the incorporation of an arbitration clause in a contract, and thus, there was 'no reason that the position should be any different with the doctrine of implied terms.'[211] Sir Ross Cranston, again in light of *Habas Sinai v Sometal*, indicated that the parties may be presumed not to have consented to the governance of the

207 Ibid [32].
208 Ibid [43].
209 [2010] EWHC 29 (Comm) (*Habas Sinai v Sometal*).
210 Ibid [46].
211 [2018] EWHC 520 (Comm), [43].

arbitration clause if such a clause 'needs modification or would place an unduly onerous obligation on one of them, or if one party did not have proper notice of it.'[212] Nevertheless, he emphasized that none of these situations applied to the case at hand. With both parties having knowledge of the agreement and its arbitration clause, their dealings continued as usual so that there were no onerous obligations imposed on them, and the application of the provision did not necessitate a modification to be made for its proper implementation between the parties.[213] Accordingly, the consent of the parties was established in a 'normal, commercially realistic manner from the perspective of reasonable business people in the position of the parties.'[214]

6.4.3. London Court of International Arbitration (LCIA) Rules and CJD v CJE and Another *[2021] SGHC 61 – Circumstances for Joinder*

The scope and interpretation of Article 22.1(viii)[215] of the London Court of International Arbitration (LCIA) Rules 2014 is evaluated by the Singapore High Court in the 2021 case of *CJD v CJE*. The article in question predominantly governs the joinder of third parties to arbitrations, and thus, its evaluation provides us with answers concerning the circumstances under which written consent of parties may be considered to have been established, the cost of resolving the dispute, and how to avoid multiple proceedings.[216] This is essentially important because parties joining arbitration facilitate all matters and claims to be resolved in a sole arbitration and by the same tribunal and this evidently saves time and cost.[217]

CJD, CJE, and CJF entered into Joint Venture Agreement (JVA) that contains an arbitration agreement providing for disputes to be resolved in Singapore subject to LCIA Rules. Disputes had arisen between CJD and CJE on the grounds that the former had breached the contract by delaying its obligations, incurring liabilities and costs without the approval of the joint venture company, terminating the JVA wrongfully, and failing to act in good faith. Subsequently, CJE commenced an arbitration against CJD under the arbitration agreement included in the joint venture agreement. Following this, CJD applied to the arbitral tribunal to join CJF as a party to the arbitration. The tribunal rejected this application on the basis that the tribunal did not have jurisdiction to join the CJF in the arbitration as the CJF did not consent to be joined to arbitration pursuant to Article 22.1(viii) of the LCIA Rules 2014. The CJD then applied to the Singapore High Court to set aside the decision of the tribunal.

212 Ibid. In reference to *Habas Sinai v Sometal* [2010] EWHC 29 (Comm), [20–21], [47].

213 Sadie Buls and Stephen Lacey, English Commercial Court Considers Arbitration Clause in Implied Contract in s.67 Challenge, *Linklaters*, May 9, 2018, available at www.linklaters.com/en/insights/blogs/arbitrationlinks/2018/may/english-commercial-court-considers-arbitration-clause-in-implied-contract-in-s-67-challenge (last visited September 13, 2022).

214 [2018] EWHC 520 (Comm), [43].

215 It should be noted that LCIA Rules are updated and as of September 2022 (effective October 1, 2020) LCIA Arbitration Rules 2020 are in place. Accordingly, the matter governed by Article 22.1(viii) under the 2014 Rules now falls into the scope of Article 22.1(x) of the 2020 Rules.

216 Cameron S. E. Ford and Christopher Bloch, Joining Parties to Arbitration: CJD v CJE [2021] SGHC 61, *Squire Patton Boggs*, March 2021, available at www.squirepattonboggs.com/-/media/files/insights/publications/2021/03/joining-parties-to-arbitration/joining-parties-to-arbitration.pdf.

217 Ibid.

With the focal point of the litigation being the assessment of the ambit of Article 22.1(viii) of the LCIA Rules 2014, this particular provision was evaluated by the High Court. The Article essentially empowers tribunals

> to allow one or more third persons to be joined in the arbitration as a party provided any such third person and the applicant party have consented to such joinder in writing following the Commencement Date or (if earlier) in the Arbitration Agreement

even if another party to the arbitration objects to such joinder. The Singapore High Court dismissed the application and refused to join the CJF in the arbitration even though the CJF had signed the joint venture agreement containing an arbitration agreement.

The court particularly hinged on Article 22.1(viii) of the LCIA Rules 2014 and the meaning of this provision in the context of party autonomy. S Mohan JC stated that

> [p]arty autonomy allows parties a wide latitude to agree on almost all aspects of how a dispute is to be arbitrated. In the context of a multi-party contract, that autonomy may include the ability to agree on who may be party to an arbitration reference in the event a dispute arises.[218]

The learned judge went further to express his views concerning forced joinder to 'appear somewhat out of place' and perhaps 'anathema to the very definition of consent' in an area where party autonomy and consent play a key role.[219]

The reasoning of the court in dismissing the application was the lack of establishment of the required level of consent in this case. The learned judge provided three situations under which the 'consent' concerning Article 22.1(viii) of the LCIA Rules 2014 may be established: (1) where the third person and applying party have consented to such joinder in writing after the Commencement Date, (2) where the third person and applying party have consented to such joinder in writing earlier in the arbitration agreement, or (3) where the written consent of the third person and the applying party to such joinder involves applying a combination of (1) and (2).[220] The judge was of the view that the relevant arbitration agreement had to contain an express reference to the joinder, and thus, simply being a signatory and party to the JVA, which includes an LCIA arbitration agreement, would not establish sufficient consent to the joinder.[221] The learned judge provided two essential reasons for this. The first was concerning the literal interpretation of the wording of Article 22.1(viii), and the second was regarding the required threshold for allowing the joinder of parties and the consequences of setting a lower threshold than the provision actually necessitates. Accordingly, S Mohan JC assessed that the plain language of Article 22.1(viii) requires parties to consent to the joinder in writing because if it was the intention of the drafters of the LCIA Rules 2014 to allow such consent to be evidenced by signing, then they would reflect this in the way they draft this relevant provision.[222] The next issue considered by the learned judge was the effects of setting a lower threshold than the provision essentially allows. The court was of the view that

218 *CJD v CJE* and another [2021] SGHC 61, [1].
219 [2021] SGHC 61, [2].
220 Ibid [46].
221 Ibid [48].
222 Ibid [49].

> reading a lower threshold requirement into Article 22.1(viii) created uncertainty for third parties as to whether they would be called to defend against, or advance, claims in an ongoing arbitration. They would also be unable to nominate arbitrator(s) or participate in arbitrator selection, which derogated from the principle of party autonomy.[223]

In the context of LCIA Rules 2014, the court was of the view that the arbitration agreement had to allow the joinder specifically and, therefore, refused to join the CJF in arbitration despite them being signatories of the JVA containing an arbitration agreement.

One issue that should be noted is that if the arbitration was governed by the rules of the Singapore International Arbitration Centre (SIAC), the result would be different since these

> allow joinder where either the party to be joined is bound by the arbitration agreement, or all parties have consented. There is no requirement in those rules that the arbitration agreement include consent to being joined to arbitrations under that agreement.[224]

Furthermore, the current ICC Rules of Arbitration bestow the tribunal with wide discretion to join the third party. Another issue to be noted is that the LCIA Rules 2014 are updated and as of September 2022 (effective October 1, 2020) the LCIA Arbitration Rules 2020 are in place. Article 22.1(x) provides the tribunal with the power to decide

> to allow one or more third persons to be joined in the arbitration as a party provided any such third person and the applicant party have consented expressly to such joinder in writing following the Commencement Date or (if earlier) in the Arbitration Agreement; and thereafter to make a single final award, or separate awards, in respect of all parties so implicated in the arbitration.

Accordingly, the current LCIA Rules 2020 allow joinder with the express written consent of the third party and the applicant. What bears importance concerning multi-party contracts is that the parties to include express permissions for joinder provided arbitration is governed by LCIA Rules. Nevertheless, concerning the governance of SIAC Rules and ICC Rules, unless the arbitration agreement provides otherwise, all parties bound by the agreement may be joined to an arbitration.[225]

6.4.4. 'Quasi-contractual' Anti-Suit Injunctions – QBE Europe SA/NV v Generali Espana de Seguros Y Reaseguros *[2022] EWHC 2062 (Comm)*

Anti-suit injunctions essentially restrain parties from commencing or pursuing foreign proceedings.[226] Provided A and B enter a contract containing an arbitration agreement referring certain disputes to London arbitration, then in principle, these disputes would be resolved by London arbitration. If B initiates foreign court proceedings in defiance of the existing arbitration agreement or threatens to initiate such, then A may seek to obtain an anti-suit injunction from English courts.

223 Kohe Hasab, Kyri Evagora and Jemma A. Collins, *Joinder of Third Parties to LCIA Arbitrations: The Case of CJD v CJE and CJF [2021] SGHC 61*, April 1, 2021, Reed Smith, available at www.reedsmith.com/en/perspectives/2021/04/joinder-of-third-parties-to-lcia-arbitrations-the-case-of-cjd-v-cje-and (last visited September 9, 2022).

224 Ford and Bloch (n 216).

225 Ibid.

226 Ambrose, Maxwell, and Collett (n 3) 121.

This particular legal concept indeed functions in a restraining way. Nonetheless, one should interpret the word 'restrain' carefully. Evidently, English courts may stay their proceedings for the sake of the prevalence of an arbitration agreement instead, provided the dispute in question had agreed to be referred to arbitration by the parties. In fact, they usually 'give deference to an arbitration agreement.'[227] However, 'An English court is not competent to stay foreign proceedings, but it can restrain a party from commencing or pursuing foreign proceedings.'[228] If B persists with foreign proceedings regardless of an anti-suit injunction, 'then any resulting judgement of the foreign court is unlikely to be recognized or enforceable in England.'[229]

The implementation of the legal concept of anti-suit injunction showed nuances that were particularly vivid pre-Brexit. Brussels Regime[230] effectively prohibits anti-suit injunctions between contracting states. Although, until 2009, English courts continued to grant anti-suit injunctions regardless of the European rules[231] as this perhaps was not considered to constitute an incompatibility. The nuances concerning the application of this legal concept fundamentally existed due to this. Following the decision of the Court of Justice of the European Union (CJEU) in *The Front Comor*,[232] such practice of English courts ceased to exist because the CJEU assessed the incompatibility of 'restraining a party from pursuing proceedings before the courts of another EU or Lugano Convention state'[233] (to not to breach an arbitration agreement) with the Brussels I Regulation. However, since December 31, 2020, anti-suit injunctions 'are on the rise' following the end of the Brexit transition period.[234] The fundamental reason for this is because, following its withdrawal from the European Union, the UK is subject neither to the European Rules nor to the Brussels Regime enshrined in Brussels I Regulation that prohibits anti-suit injunctions between contracting states. Now parties may decide to seek anti-suit injunctions in English courts pertaining to foreign proceedings that are asserted to have been initiated in breach of an arbitration agreement regardless of whether these taking place in an EU or a Lugano Convention state.[235]

An interesting aspect of the implementation of anti-suit injunctions is concerning 'quasi-contractual' injunctions. Anti-suit injunctions, speaking from a contract law perspective, have different applications in the contractual context. It is very recently re-established

227 Marie Berard, Robert Shu, and Benjamin Barrat, High Court Grants "Quasi-Contractual" Anti-Suit Injunction in Support of Arbitration Agreement, *Clifford Chance*, September 15, 2022, available at www.cliffordchance.com/content/dam/cliffordchance/briefings/2022/09/high-court-grants-quasi-contractual-anti-suit-injunction-in-support-of-arbitration-agreement.pdf (last visited September 27, 2022).

228 Ambrose, Maxwell, and Collett (n 3) 121–122.

229 Anthony Menzies and Franc Gozalves, Anti-Suit Injunctions in the Post-Brexit World, *DAC Beachcroft*, September 26, 2022, available at www.dacbeachcroft.com/en/gb/articles/2022/september/anti-suit-injunctions-in-the-post-brexit-world/ (last visited September 27, 2022).

230 The Brussels Regime includes Regulation (EU) No 1215/2012 of December 12, 2012 (Brussels Recast), and the Convention on jurisdiction and the recognition and enforcement of judgements in civil and commercial matters of December 21, 2007, (Lugano Convention).

231 Ambrose, Maxwell, and Collett (n 3) 122.

232 *Allianz SpA v West Tankers Inc* Case C-185/07, [2009] 1 Lloyd's Rep 413 (*The Front Comor*).

233 Ambrose, Maxwell, and Collett (n 3) 122.

234 Jamie Curle, Dan Jewell, and Siona Spillett, *Why Anti-Suit Injunctions May Be on the Rise After Brexit?*, DLA Piper, October 27, 2021, available at www.dlapiper.com/de/austria/insights/publications/2021/10/why-antisuit-injunctions-may-be-on-the-rise-after-brexit/ (last visited September 27, 2022).

235 Ibid. For a meticulous analysis of the issue, see Ambrose, Maxwell, and Collett (n 3) 121–134.

in *QBE Europe SA/NV and another v Generali Espana de Seguros Y Reaseguros*[236] that although most applications for anti-suit injunctions are from parties to an arbitration or jurisdiction agreement,[237] there are also applications in which 'the claimant denies that it is party to the contractual choice of jurisdiction in issue, or does not assert (and perhaps positively denies) that the defendant is party to that contractual choice of jurisdiction, or . . . both.'[238] Following this, an application for an anti-suit injunction may be sought on 'quasi-contractual' grounds meaning against respondents that pursue claims derived from an agreement providing for arbitration, regardless of whether they are not being a party to that agreement.

The decision in *QBE v Generali Espana* is significant as it is the first decision pertaining to quasi-contractual anti-suit injunctions given post-Brexit. Accordingly, the judgement clarifies the position of English courts concerning the applicable principles and considerations pertaining to applications for such injunctions.

The case is related to an incident leading to hydrocarbon pollution due to the alleged damage to an undersea power cable that is given by the yacht *Angara* in 2016. The owner of the damaged cable was REE and their insurer was Generali Espana, which indemnified the owners in respect of the loss of approximately €7.7 million. Upon payment, Generali Espana became subrogated to the rights, which its insured REE could potentially have against the owners of the Angara. The insurance policy in favour of the owners of the Angara had been issued by QBE UK, and it provided for the resolution of any disputes through London arbitration. In November 2020, QBE Europe took over QBE UK's rights and obligations under the policy. In February 2022, Generali Espana initiated proceedings in the Spanish courts seeking to recover from QBE UK the sum it had paid to REE. Generali Espana asserted that the REE had a direct claim against QBE UK pursuant to the Spanish Maritime Navigation Act 2014, and it became subrogated to REE's rights pursuant to the Spanish Insurance Contracts Act 1980. Generali Espana further argued that the arbitration agreement providing for London arbitration, did not apply as its claim against the QBE UK was tortious in nature, and did not base on the insurance contract. If that would be approved, the QBE UK would not be allowed to resort to any contractual defences that they may have in the insurance context because the right of action would be considered independent of the underlying policy. QBE applied to the English court for an injunction. A crucial issue to be assessed by the English court was whether General Espana's claim was contractual in nature as General Espana argued that the claim was in tort under Spanish law. Accordingly, the substance of the claim had to be established.

The assessment to be made was similar to the one made in *Through Transport Mutual Insurance Association (Eurasia) Ltd v New India Assurance Co Ltd*,[239] which was later referred to in *The Prestige*.[240] In the former, the issue to be assessed was whether the defendant was bound by an arbitration agreement 'which in turn depends on whether it

236 [2022] EWHC 2062 (Comm) (*QBE v Generali Espana*).
237 Ibid 4, [9].
238 Ibid 5, [12].
239 [2003] EWHC 3158 (Comm); [2004] 1 Lloyd's Rep 206. (*Through Transport v New India*).
240 *The London Steamship Onwers' Mutual Insurance Association Ltd v The Kingdom of Spain, The French State* [2015] EWCA Civ 333 (*The Prestige*) by the same judge.

is seeking to enforce a contractual obligation derived from the contract of insurance or an independent right of recovery arising under'[241] the relevant legislation. Lord Justice Moore-Bick, referring to his judgement in *Through Transport v New India*, stated in *The Prestige* that

> [i]f in substance the claim is independent of the contract of insurance and arises under the Finnish legislation simply as a result of its having a right of action against an insolvent insured, the issue would have to be characterised as one of statutory entitlement to which there may be no direct equivalent in English law. In that case the issue would in my view have to be determined in accordance with Finnish law. If, on the other hand, the claim is in substance one to enforce against the insurer the contract made by the insolvent insured, the issue is to be characterised as one of obligation. In that case the court will resolve it by applying English law because the proper law of the contract creating the obligation is English law.[242]

Evaluating the substance of the insurer's claim, the learned judge further considered the applicable conflicts of law principle in light of *The Yusuf Cepnioglu*, in which the assessment was concerning

> whether the intention and effect of the foreign statute is to enable the victim to enforce against the insurer essentially the same obligations as those that could have been enforced by the insured or whether the statue has created a new and independent right which is not intended to mirror the insurer's liability under the contract of insurance.[243]

This is supported by the fact that both the High Court and the Court of Appeal in *The Prestige* found a direct right to enforce contractual rights arising under an insurance policy in considering the effect of such a foreign statute (Spanish Insurance Contract Act 1980). Accordingly, the learned judge was of the view that the foreign direct action right, and thus, the insurer's claims were contractual in substance and conditioned by the arbitration clause contained in the policy. To put it differently, *QBE v Generali Espana* established the promotion of arbitration agreements that are contained in underlying policies to possibly produce the result of third parties being restrained from pursuing a direct action claim against the liability insurer of the alleged wrongdoer in the foreign proceedings taking place in an EU or a Lugano Convention state. Quasi-contractual anti-suit injunctions are in the power of English courts, and this position is reaffirmed in light of *QBE v Generali Espana* post-Brexit.[244]

6.5. The Review of the Arbitration Act 1996 by the Law Commission and Third Parties

The Law Commission of England and Wales published a review of the Arbitration Act 1996 in September 2022.[245] The Consultation Paper essentially lays out some provisional

241 Lord Justice Moore-Bick was referring to his judgement: [2004] 1 Lloyd's Rep 206, [16] in *The Prestige* [2015] EWCA Civ 333, [13].

242 *The Prestige* [2015] EWCA Civ 333, [13].

243 *The Yusuf Cepnioglu* [2016] EWCA Civ 386, [1] by Longmore LJ.

244 Berrard, Shu, and Barrat (n 227).

245 Law Commission, *Review of the Arbitration Act 1996 – A Consultation Paper*, Law Com No 257, September 2022.

proposals on potential areas of reform concerning the implementation and interpretation of the Arbitration Act 1996. It should initially be noted that the incorporation of arbitration agreements as a legal concept is not included in the review of the Law Commission. In this regard, it may be said that the Law Commission's opinion pertaining to the implementation of this legal concept is in line with what was provided in the DAC Report some 25 years ago: This is essentially a matter to be left to the determination of courts in each individual case.

One of the overall deductions of the Review was that a root reform is neither needed nor wanted[246] as the Arbitration Act 1996 has stood the test of time.[247] However, some key points of possible reform, among others that were raised by the Law Commission, are pertaining to the position of third parties and arbitration. Accordingly, only the considerations of the Commission concerning third parties are mentioned in this part.

One area of possible uncertainty has been considered to be the powers of the court to order interim measures in support of arbitral proceedings and emergency arbitration. Section 44 of the Arbitration Act 1996 provides that the court has the power to make orders in support of arbitral proceedings. These supportive orders are (1) on the taking of witness evidence, (2) on the preservation of evidence, (3) relating to property, (4) pertaining to the sale of any goods the subject of the proceedings, and (5) granting an interim injunction or appointing a receiver.[248] The main uncertainty concerning the application of Section 44 is 'whether those powers are exercisable in the same way as in English civil litigation, specifically in relation to the power to make orders impacting third parties.'[249]

It is stated in the Review that 'our provisional view is that orders under section 44 can be made against third parties.'[250] This is also reflected in case law.[251] However, there also have been some nuances concerning the interpretation of Section 44. It may be argued that, as the Law Commission highlighted, Section 44 does not truly allow these orders to be made against third parties if considered from a linguistic perspective.[252] However, the decision of the Court of Appeal in *A v C* establishes that courts may 'at least sometimes' apply their powers against third parties.[253] Accordingly, 'section 44 injunctions made by the court may, when appropriate, extend to third parties.'[254]

---

246 Ibid 11.1.

247 Peter R. Morton, Louise Bond, and Eklavya M. Sharma, *The Law Commission Review of the Arbitration Act 1996*, K&L Gates, International Arbitration Alert, October 4, 2022, available at www.klgates.com/The-Law-Commission-Review-of-the-Arbitration-Act-1996-10-4-2022 (last visited October 15, 2022).

248 Section 44(2)(a) to (e) of the Arbitration Act 1996.

249 Elinor Thomas, Barry Fletcher, James Carter, and Philip Chong, *The Law Commission's Review of the Arbitration Act 1996 – Polishing a Gold Standard?*, DLA Piper, September 27, 2022, available at www.dlapiper.com/fr/france/insights/publications/2022/09/the-law-commissions-review-of-the-arbitration-act-1996/ (last visited October 15, 2022).

250 Law Commission (n 245), 7.3.

251 Blair J in *Public Joint Stock Co Bank v Maksimov* [2013] EWHC 3203 (Comm), [2013] All ER (D), [76–81].

252 Law Commission (n 245), 7.16. Also see *DTEK Trading SA v Morozov* [2017] EWHC 94 (Comm), [2017] 1 Lloyd's Rep 126.

253 Ibid. Also see *A v C* [2020] EWCA Civ 409, [2020] 1 WLR 3504.

254 Robert Merkin and Louis Flannery, *Merkin and Flannery on the Arbitration Act 1996*, Informa Law from Routledge, 2020, 6th Edn., 457, 44.7.5.

The orders that are within the power of the courts to make are different and each has its own body of rules.[255] Furthermore, although the exercise of the power of the courts raises the possibility of orders to be made against third parties, 'the precise extent will vary across the different matters.'[256] It is further clarified that involving third parties in the scope of the exercised powers of the courts is allowed since the Review contains the words 'We think that our analysis as to when orders can be made against third parties flows from the current wording of section 44.'[257]

Accordingly, the relevant uncertainty is not pertaining to the general application of the power of the courts to make orders that may be exercised against third parties. It, in fact, pertains to the lucidity of the section concerning its application in situations involving third parties. The Review highlights the need for clarity concerning 'the availability and extent of the court's powers to make the various orders set out above (including with respect to binding third parties) is determined by reference to the court's equivalent powers in civil litigation.'[258] Correspondingly, the Commission's consideration is about the clarification of the wording of the legislation. The Review poses the question of whether a minor change in the language is needed to confirm the application of courts using their powers.[259] Accordingly, as of October 2022, the Commission is seeking comments on the proposal of the Arbitration Act 1996 to expressly provide that courts have the power to make orders directly against third parties.

Another point of consideration of the Law Commission concerning third parties is on the issue of appeal. The Review highlights an 'anomaly' that the application of Section 44 produces concerning the legal position of third parties.[260] Pursuant to Rule 52 of the Civil Procedure Rules, 'a party who wishes to appeal can seek permission from the court from which it is appealing, or, if permission is not given by that court, they can seek permission from the court to which they are appealing.'[261] However, Section 44 of the Arbitration Act 1996 provides, 'The leave of the court is required for any appeal from a decision of the court under this section.'[262] This means that under Section 44, third parties, too (among arbitral parties), do not have the option to seek permission from the court to which they would be appealing and instead have a restricted right to appeal. The Review of the Law Commission indicates the restriction of the right to appeal may be considered appropriate for arbitrating parties because they have agreed to arbitration and thus, it is fair to limit their access to the court.[263] However, it also highlights that where the court exercises its power to make an order against a third party, the usual right of the third party should not be impaired.[264] Consequently, the

---

255 Ibid 7.33.
256 Ibid.
257 Ibid 7.35.
258 Thomas et al. (n 249).
259 Law Commission (n 245), 7.3.
260 Ibid 7.37.
261 Ibid. Rule 52.3(3) of Civil Procedure Rules: 'Where the lower court refuses an application for permission to appeal – (a) a further application for permission may be made to the appeal court; and (b) the order refusing permission must specify – (i) the court to which any further application for permission should be made; and (ii) the level of judge who should hear the application.'
262 Section 44(7) of the Arbitration Act 1996.
263 Law Commission (n 245), 8, Summary.
264 Ibid.

Review proposes the appeal rights of third parties be fully restored and proposes an amendment to be made accordingly.[265]

6.6. Concluding Remarks

As a general rule, the doctrine of privity of contracts draws contractual borders that exclude third parties and establishes contractual remoteness concerning the position of these parties to contracts they are 'excluded from.' Arbitration agreements possibly constituting parts of such remote contracts, the evaluation of the capability of bringing these remote third parties into the scope of arbitration is an interesting issue to be addressed. It is true that incorporation is a very common method of contract drafting for bringing such parties into the scope of arbitration agreements. Nevertheless, it is not the only method for creating such a result. Common law has devices that facilitate the inclusion of third parties into the scope of 'previously remote' agreements or generally produce 'incorporation-like results.' Such production also has a statutory reflection in English law as the Contracts (Rights of Thirds Parties) Act 1999 specifically governs the position of third parties and arbitration agreements. There are also examples, especially in insurance practice, where third parties are no longer considered remote (or simply 'third parties' anymore) to a contractual relationship due to the implementation of some contract law concepts such as assignment and subrogation. Furthermore, there are some other contractual tools at the disposal of contracting parties to bring third parties into a contract that was originally 'remote' to them. These may be regarded as tools that 'bypass' the doctrine of the privity of contracts. Implied contracts and Himalaya clauses, for instance, are widely implemented in accordance with the realities of contemporary commerce. Furthermore, practical issues concerning the London Court of International Arbitration (LCIA) Rules and third parties to arbitration, as well as quasi-contractual anti-suit injunctions, also constitute points of relevance. Accordingly, among incorporation, there are other devices that facilitate the production of 'incorporation-like' results and 'bypass' the doctrine of privity of contract. Nonetheless, these are not tools of incorporation. However, their implementation usually creates results that are similar to the incorporation of arbitration clauses and third parties.

Bibliography

Ahmed, Masood, Loosening the Grip of the Contracts (Rights of Third Parties) Act 1999 on Arbitration Agreements, 2014, *Journal of International Arbitration*, 31(5).

Ambrose, Clare, Maxwell, Karen and Collett, Michael, *London Maritime Arbitration*, Informa, 2017.

Barten, Sebastiaan, *Drafting Himalaya Clauses Covering Arbitration Clauses*, Van Steenderen Mainport Lawyers, Lexology, April 21, 2015.

Berard, Marie, Shu, Robert and Barrat, Benjamin, High Court Grants "Quasi-Contractual" Anti-Suit Injunction in Support of Arbitration Agreement, *Clifford Chance*, September 15, 2022, available at www.cliffordchance.com/content/dam/cliffordchance/briefings/2022/09/high-court-grants-quasi-contractual-anti-suit-injunction-in-support-of-arbitration-agreement.pdf (last visited September 27, 2022).

265 Ibid 7.38–7.39.

Blackstone, William, *Commentaries on the Laws of England*, Clarendon Press, 1766.

Born, Gary B., *International Commercial Arbitration*, Wolters Kluwer Law International, 2020.

Brekoulakis, Stavros, *Third Parties in International Commercial Arbitration*, Oxford University Press, 2010.

Buls, Sadie and Lacey, Stephen, English Commercial Court Considers Arbitration Clause in Implied Contract in s.67 Challenge, *Linklaters*, May 9, 2018, available at www.linklaters.com/en/insights/blogs/arbitrationlinks/2018/may/english-commercial-court-considers-arbitration-clause-in-implied-contract-in-s-67-challenge (last visited September 13, 2022).

Burrows, Andrew, The Contracts (Rights of Third Parties) Act 1999 and Its Implications for Commercial Contracts, 2000, *Lloyd's Maritime and Commercial Law Quarterly*, 540.

Curle, Jamie, Jewell, Dan and Spillett, Siona, *Why Anti-Suit Injunctions May Be on the Rise After Brexit?*, DLA Piper, October 27, 2021, available at www.dlapiper.com/de/austria/insights/publications/2021/10/why-antisuit-injunctions-may-be-on-the-rise-after-brexit/ (last visited September 27, 2022).

Diamond, Anthony, The Third Man: The 1999 Act Sets Back Separability?, 2001, *Arbitration International*, 17(2).

Dicey, A. V., Morris, John Humphrey Carlile and Collins, Lawrence, *Dicey, Morris & Collins on the Conflict of Laws*, Sweet & Maxwell, 2012, 15th Edn.

Ford, Cameron S. E. and Bloch, Christopher, Joining Parties to Arbitration: CJD v CJE [2021] SGHC 61, *Squire Patton Boggs*, March 2021, available at www.squirepattonboggs.com/-/media/files/insights/publications/2021/03/joining-parties-to-arbitration/joining-parties-to-arbitration.pdf.

Fouchard, Philippe, Gaillard, Emmanel and Savage, John, *Fouchard, Gaillard, Goldman on International Commercial Arbitration*, Kluwer Law International, 1999.

Fox, David, Munday, Roderick, Soyer, Barış, Tettenborn, Andrew and Turner, Peter (eds) *Sealy & Hooley's Commercial Law*, Oxford University Press, 2020.

Garnuszek, Anita, The Law Applicable to the Contractual Assignment of an Arbitration Agreement, 2016, *Arbitration: The International Journal of Arbitration, Mediation and Dispute Management*, 82(4).

Gélinas, P. A., Arbitration Clauses: Achieving Effectiveness, in A.J. van den Berg (ed.) *Improving the Efficiency of Arbitration Agreements and Awards: 40 Years of Application of the New York Convention*, ICCA Congress Series, 1999, ICCA, Vol. 9.

Girsberger, Daniel, The Law Applicable to the Assignment of Claims Subject to an Arbitration Agreement, in Franco Ferrari and Stefan Kröll (eds.) *Conflict of Laws in International Arbitration*, Otto Schmidt, De Gruyter European Law Publishers, 2010.

Gürses, Özlem, *Marine Insurance Law*, Routledge, 2017.

Hasab, Kohe, Evagora, Kyri Evagora and Collins, Jemma A., *Joinder of Third Parties to LCIA Arbitrations: The Case of CJD v CJE and CJF [2021] SGHC 61*, April 1, 2021, Reed Smith, available at www.reedsmith.com/en/perspectives/2021/04/joinder-of-third-parties-to-lcia-arbitrations-the-case-of-cjd-v-cje-and (last visited September 9, 2022).

Hasson, Reuben, Subrogation in Insurance Law – A Critical Evaluation, Winter 1985, *Oxford Journal of Legal Studies*, 5(3).

Ipek, Mertcan, *Assignment of Contractual Rights and İts Impact on Aritration Agreements*, MUHF-HAD C.22, S.1, 521–550, 523, available at https://dergipark.org.tr/tr/download/article-file/274363. See *Butler v Capel* [1823] 107 ER 377.

Jagusch, Stephen and Sinclair, Anthony C., The Impact of Third Parties in International Arbitration: Issues of Assignment, in Mistelis, Loukas A. and Lew, Julian D.M. (eds.) *Pervasive Problems in International Arbitration*, Kluwer Law International, 2006.

Landrove, Juan Carlos, *Assignment and Arbitration – A Comparative Study*, Schulthess Verlag, 2009.

Law Commission, *Privity of Contract: Contracts for the Benefit of Third Parties*, Law Commission No. 242, July 1996, 14.18.

Law Commission, *Review of the Arbitration Act 1996 – A Consultation Paper*, Law Com No 257, September 2022.

Liew, Ying Khai, Explaining Assignments of Arbitration Agreements, March 2021, *Cambridge Law Journal*, 80(1).

Menzies, Anthony and Gozalves, Franc, Anti-Suit Injunctions in the Post-Brexit World, *DAC Beachcroft*, September 26, 2022, available at www.dacbeachcroft.com/en/gb/articles/2022/september/anti-suit-injunctions-in-the-post-brexit-world/ (last visited September 27, 2022).

Merkin, Robert and Hjalmarsson, Johanna, *Singapore Arbitration Legislation*, Informa, 2016.

Merkin, Robert and Saintier, Séverine, Privity of Contract: Statutory Developments, in Merkin, Robert and Devenny, James (eds.) *Essays in Memory of Professor Jill Poole – Coherence, Modernisation and Integration in Contract, Commercial and Corporate Laws*, Informa Law from Routledge, 2018.

Merkin, Robert and Steele, Jenny, *Insurance and the Law of Obligations*, Oxford University Press, 2013.

Morton, Peter R., Bond, Louise and Sharma, Eklavya M., *The Law Commission Review of the Arbitration Act 1996*, K&L Gates, International Arbitration Alert, October 4, 2022, available at www.klgates.com/The-Law-Commission-Review-of-the-Arbitration-Act-1996-10-4-2022 (last visited October 15, 2022).

Mukherjee, Proshanto K., Windfall in the Law of Subrogation: Marine Insurance in Motion, in Mukherjee, Proshanto K. et al. (eds.) *Maritime Law in Motion*, WMU Studies in Maritime Affairs 8, Springer, 2020.

Naón, Grigera, Choice-of-Law Problems in International Commercial Arbitration, 2001, *Recueil des Cours*, 289, 9, 147.

Nehra, Anoushka, *Recent Developments in English Law Relevant to Arbitration*, Stewarts, June 19, 2020.

Noussia, Kyriaki, *The Principle of Indemnity in Marine Insurance Contracts – A Comparative Approach*, Springer, 2007.

Özdel, Melis, *Bills of Lading Incorporating Charterparties*, Bloomsbury, 2015.

Peel, Edwin, *Treitel on the Law of Contract*, Sweet & Maxwell, 2015.

Phang, Andrew (ed.), *Cheshire, Fifoot and Furmston's Law of Contract*, Butterworths, 1998, 2nd Singapore and Malaysian Edn.

Phang, Andrew, On Justification and Method in Law Reform – The Contracts (Rights of Third Parties) Act 1999, June 2002, *Journal of Contract Law*, 18.

Tetley, William, Himalaya Clause – Heresy or Genius?, October 1997, *Journal of Maritime Law and Commerce*, 9(1).

Tetley, William, The Himalaya Clause Revisited, 2003, *Journal of International Maritime Law*, 9, 40.

Thomas, Elinor, Fletcher, Barry, Carter, James and Chong, Philip, *The Law Commission's Review of the Arbitration Act 1996 – Polishing a Gold Standard?*, DLA Piper, September 27, 2022, available at www.dlapiper.com/fr/france/insights/publications/2022/09/the-law-commissions-review-of-the-arbitration-act-1996/ (last visited October 15, 2022).

Thompson, Michael, Title to Sue on Overseas Contracts of Sea Carriage: The Need for Reform in Australia, 1994, *MLAANZ Journal*, 10.

Todd, Paul, Arbitration, Privity of Contract and Carriage of Goods by Sea, in Jason Chuah (ed.) *Research Handbook on Maritime Law and Regulation (Research Handbooks in Private and Commercial Law)*, Edward Elgar, 2019.

Tolhurst, Greg, *The Assignment of Contractual Rights*, Hart Publishing, 2016.

Treitel, Guenter, *The Battle Over Privity in Treitel, Guenter, Some Landmarks of Twentieth Century Contract Law*, Oxford University Press, 2002.

Tweeddale, Andrew, Arbitration Under the Contracts (Rights of Third Parties) Act 1999 and Enforcement of an Award, 2011, *LCIA, Arbitration International*, 27, No. 4.

Vincze, Andrea, Arbitration Clause – Is İt Transferred to the Assignee?, 2003, *Nordic Journal of Commercial Law*, 1.

Watterson, Stephen, Subrogation, in Graham Virgo; Sarah Worthington (eds.) *Commercial Remedies: Resolving Controversies*, Cambridge University Press, 2017.

Weir, Tony, Subrogation and Indemnity, March 2012, *Cambridge Law Journal*, 71, Part 1.

Yeo, Tiong Min, When Do Third Party Rights Arise Under the Contracts (Rights of Third Parties) Act 1999 (UK)?, 2001, *Singapore Academy of Law Journal: Research Collection School of Law*, 13, No. 1.

INDEX